# GENERAL EQUILIBRIUM FOUNDATIONS OF FINANCE

THEORY AND DECISION LIBRARY

General Editors: W. Leinfellner (*Vienna*) and G. Eberlein (*Munich*)

Series A: Philosophy and Methodology of the Social Sciences

Series B: Mathematical and Statistical Methods

Series C: Game Theory, Mathematical Programming and Operations Research

Series D: System Theory, Knowledge Engineering an Problem Solving

SERIES C: GAME THEORY, MATHEMATICAL PROGRAMMING AND OPERATIONS RESEARCH

VOLUME 33



*Scope:* Particular attention is paid in this series to game theory and operations research, their formal aspects and their applications to economic, political and social sciences as well as to socio-biology. It will encourage high standards in the application of game-theoretical methods to individual and social decision making.

*The titles published in this series are listed at the end of this volume.*

# GENERAL EQUILIBRIUM FOUNDATIONS OF FINANCE

## Structure of Incomplete Markets Models

*by*

THORSTEN HENS
*University of Zurich, Switzerland*
*and Norwegian Business School, Norway*

and

BEATE PILGRIM
*Reuters AG,*
*Frankfurt, Germany*

KLUWER ACADEMIC PUBLISHERS
BOSTON / DORDRECHT / LONDON

A C.I.P. Catalogue record for this book is available from the Library of Congress.

ISBN 1-4020-7337-2

---

Published by Kluwer Academic Publishers,
P.O. Box 17, 3300 AA Dordrecht, The Netherlands.

Sold and distributed in North, Central and South America
by Kluwer Academic Publishers,
101 Philip Drive, Norwell, MA 02061, U.S.A.

In all other countries, sold and distributed
by Kluwer Academic Publishers,
P.O. Box 322, 3300 AH Dordrecht, The Netherlands.

*Printed on acid-free paper*

***To Britta and Jerome***

# Contents

# List of Figures

# Preface

The purpose of this book is to give a sound economic foundation of finance. Finance is a coherent branch of applied economics that is designed to understand financial markets in order to give advice for practical financial decisions. This book argues that for a sound economic foundation of finance the famous general equilibrium model which in its modern form emphasizes the incompleteness of financial markets is well suited. The aim of the book is to demonstrate that financial markets can be meaningfully embedded into a more general system of markets including, for example, commodity markets. The interaction of these markets can be described via the well known notion of a competitive equilibrium. We argue that for a sound foundation this competitive equilibrium should be unique. In a first step we demonstrate that this essential goal cannot be achieved based only on the rationality principle, i.e. on the assumption of utility maximization of some utility function subject to the budget constraint. In particular we show that this important lack of structure is disturbing as well for the case of mean-variance utility functions which are the basis of the Capital Asset Pricing Model, one of the cornerstones of finance. The final goal of our book is to give reasonable restrictions on the agents' utility functions which lead to a well determined financial markets model. These restrictions will be phrased in terms of the agents' beliefs and their risk attitudes which are key variables in financial markets. These achievements are obtained by a combination of recent research on incomplete financial markets combined with research on the structure of excess demand functions in general equilibrium models.
The book gives a rigorous exposition of current research on the foundation of financial markets. It requires some mathematical background. To keep the book self-contained a mathematical appendix is provided. The book should be easily accessible by advanced Ph.D. students as well as by theorists of any subfield of mathematical economics. The book is written as a monograph which may as well be used as a graduate textbook. It should be interesting both for theorists who are looking for possible applications of rigorous theory as well

as for practitioners who are looking for a theoretical foundation of their fruitful applications of financial markets' models.

The research laid down in this book is to a large extent based on the authors' recent contributions in the field of incomplete markets. Some of these contributions have also been the content of Beate Pilgrim's Diploma thesis and of her Ph.D. Thesis, which were both written under the supervision of Thorsten Hens. Moreover other parts have been the basis of Thorsten Hens' Ph.D and still some other parts of his Habilitation Thesis. The contributions of the authors have been supplemented by the joint work with various co-authors , some of them having written their Ph.D. under the supervision of Thorsten Hens. In particular we are grateful to Jörg Laitenberger who allowed us to base Chapter 8 on a part of his Ph.D. Thesis. We also like to thank very much Thomas Siwik who allowed us to present one of the main results of his Ph.D. Thesis in our Chapter 7. Various other chapters are based on published joint work with Piero Gottardi, Andras Löffler, Jean-Marc Bottazzi, Karl Schmedders and Jörg Laitenberger:

Chapter 2 is based on: "The Survival Assumption and Existence of Competitive Equilibria When Asst Markets are Incomplete", co-authored by Gottardi and Hens [1996]. Chapter 3 is based on: "An Extension of Mantel (1976) to Incomplete Markets" by Hens [2001a]. Section 6.2 of Chapter 6 based on: "On Multiplicity of Competitive Equilibria when Financial Markets are Incomplete" by Hens et al. [1999]. Section 6.3 of Chapter 6 is based on: Pilgrim [2002]. Chapter 9 is based on: "Market Demand Functions in the Capital Asset Pricing Model", co-authored by Jean-Marc Bottazzi, Thorsten Hens and Andras Löffler, [Bottazzi et al., 1998]. Chapter 10 is based on "Two Remarks on the Uniqueness of Equilibria in the CAPM", co-authored by Hens et al. [2002].

The main results presented in our book can be found in those publications. However writing a book allowed us to supplement those main results with various other results which are helpful to put the main results into a broader perspective. Finally, we found it useful to bring together all these specific results scattered in the literature. This gives one grand picture of the general equilibrium foundation of finance.

The 'product' which is given in the form of this book differentiates well from already existing books on the market. This book nicely complements more pragmatic books on finance like the well-known books by Copeland and Weston [1998] and Huang and Litzenberger [1998]. Moreover, it is narrower in scope but deeper in the specific contributions as books on financial economics like LeRoy and Werner [2001] or Eichberger and Harper [1997], for example. Our book is closest to the book by Magill and Quinzii [1996] which however does not contribute to the important questions of structure and uniqueness of equilibria in incomplete markets. Given that the book by Magill and Quinzii [1996] is a very extensive survey on the theory of incomplete markets we decided to streamline our book on those topics dealt with in Magill and Quinzii [1996]

and only to display the main contributions of the theory of incomplete markets as far as they are necessary to lay down the foundations for our book. Last but not least as compared to books on the structure of market demand as for example the books by Hildenbrand and Kirman [1988] or Hildenbrand [1994] our book is narrower in methodology since we do not incorporate any empirical evidence of our assumptions. However, our book is wider in scope since our reasoning is not only performed in the standard general equilibrium model but in the more general model of incomplete financial markets.
The innovation of our book is to transfer and to extend the theoretical results on the structure of competitive equilibria into the modern context of incomplete financial markets. This allows us to provide a sound theoretical foundation of finance.

Please visit the webpage for this book:

http://www.carlo-strub.ch/oec/thens/ (Internet)

# Acknowledgments

This monograph is the result of research carried out over a period of 10 years. The research has been supported by SFB-303 at the University of Bonn. Foremost we would like to thank the director of SFB-303 Werner Hildenbrand for his guidance and his advice. Parts of the work have been supported by the financial support through a scholarship of the DFG at the Graduirtenkolleg "Mathematische Wirtschaftsforschung" at the University of Bielefeld for which we would like to thank.
The book is based on joint work with colleagues and Ph.D. students. We are grateful to Jean-Marc Bottazzi, Piero Gottardi, Jörg Laitenberger, Andras Löffler, Karl Schmedders and Thomas Siwik. Moreover we would like to thank our teachers Roger Guesnerie, Werner Hildenbrand, Michael Magill, Herakles Polemarchakis and Martine Quinzii for giving us the opportunity to achieve top level research in mathematical economics. Special thanks go to Reinhard John who had the patience and also took the time to support us when we got stuck. Finally we would like to thank Carlo Strub. Without the tremendous effort of Carlo, who assisted us at the LaTeX-front, this book on incomplete markets could not have been completed.

# Introduction

The creation of markets for credit and insurance is a major achievement of mankind. The evolution of these markets and its "financial instruments" reflects the stage of development of the economy. And it is itself an important driving force for economic development. Recently, for example, the introduction of a plethora of new securities is striking. Markets like stock option markets have expanded manifoldly and have now been joined by markets for index options, bond options, and futures options. The volume of trade in these new "derivative securities" dwarfs that of traditional stock markets. Security markets, moreover, are now tightly integrated by "arbitrage", the construction and fine tuning of security portfolios that exploit potential discrepancies in the cost of creating the same given cash flow by two different financial strategies. Arbitrage ensures that markets are well coordinated and competitive which is crucial for the efficient allocation of risks. This fascinating development has been inspired and was to a large extent caused by a corresponding development in "finance". Finance is that subfield of economics that highlights the importance of time and uncertainty for the allocation of resources. Finance has many of its foundations in general equilibrium theory. Important cornerstones of finance like the Capital Asset Pricing Model (CAPM), the Black and Scholes Option Pricing Model or the Modigliani-Miller Theorem, for example, can all be seen as special cases of the general equilibrium model. The purpose of this book is to give an account of and to push forward the frontier of research on the general equilibrium foundations of finance.

In the preface of the famous dictionary "The New Palgrave" [Eatwell et al., 1989, p. xi] the editors appreciate the development of finance by the following assertion:

> Forty years ago primarily the province of business specialists who dealt descriptively with "corporate finance" and "stock markets", today it [finance] is a coherent branch of applied economics that among its other tools makes brilliantly perceptive use of value theory in order to understand the real workings of financial markets.

And indeed, as it was summarized recently by Campbell [2000] the Arrow-Debreu model of general equilibrium provides a foundation to most of the theoretical and empirical developments in finance:

> For roughly the last twenty years, theoretical and empirical developments in asset pricing have taken place within a well established paradigm. This paradigm emphasizes the structure placed on financial asset returns by the assumption that asset markets do not permit the presence of arbitrage opportunities – loosely, opportunities to make riskless profits on an arbitrarily large scale. In absence of arbitrage opportunities, there exists a "stochastic discount factor" that relates payoffs to market prices for all assets in the economy. This can be understood as an application of the Arrow-Debreu model of general equilibrium to financial markets. A state price exists for each state of nature at each date, and the market price of any financial asset is just the sum of its possible future payoffs, weighted by the appropriate state prices. Further assumptions about the structure of the economy produce further results. For example, if markets are complete then the stochastic discount factor is unique. If the stochastic discount factor is linearly related to a set of common shocks, then asset returns can be described by a linear factor model. If the economy has a representative agent with a well-defined utility function, then the stochastic discount factor is related to the marginal utility of aggregate consumption. Even recent developments in behavioral finance, which emphasize nonstandard preferences or irrational expectations, can be understood within this paradigm.

General equilibrium theory provides a "theory of value" for the allocation of scarce resources. The general equilibrium model is based on the seminal ideas of Adam Smith [1776], who was concerned with the fundamental question (cf. Hildenbrand [1986, p. 1])

> why in a competitive economy with private ownership where a large number of economic agents make decisions which are taken independently from each other and are motivated by self-interest, why in such a situation we do not observe chaos, but a state which definitely looks more like an equilibrium then total disorder.

Adam Smith's answer to this fundamental question of economics was the "invisible hand", a metaphor for the price mechanism. While Smith [1776] laid down the general ideas, Walras [1874] was first to formalize a general equilibrium model mathematically. In his formalization the price mechanism is described as a solution to an interdependent system of equations, each equation representing one market. Walras' formalization of general equilibrium theory has been advanced in many directions. It finds its analytically most satisfactory form in the Arrow-Debreu model (cf. Arrow and Debreu [1954]) which itself finds its most elegant presentation in the "Theory of Value" of Debreu [1959]. For many reasons the general equilibrium model seems indeed well suited to provide a foundation of finance. First of all, when pricing an asset it is extremely important not to consider this asset in isolation, but to evaluate its contribution to the portfolio of assets being available on the markets. Thus one has to study an interdependent system of markets which is the main objective of a general equilibrium model. Secondly, on many financial markets there is a large number of traders so that the assumption of "price taking" that underlies the general equilibrium model can well be justified. Moreover, the trader's portfolio decisions are clearly motivated by self-interest, which is a feature of most general equilibrium models. To a large extent traders take decisions independently from each other—however, in certain circumstances like panics, manias and crashes the interdependence of agents' decisions becomes overwhelmingly important. Finally, if for any market the fiction of a "Walrasian auctioneer" is a good approximation of reality, then it is so for financial markets, where prices are set via a huge multilateral auction.

As a "foundation" of finance, general equilibrium theory itself does not deal with the day-to-day problems of finance. It does, for example, not provide more and more accurate pricing formulas for more and more sophisticated options. It is the purpose of a "foundation" to investigate the logical consistency of more pragmatic theories like finance and, moreover, to point out their intrinsic limits. More pragmatic theories usually make more specific assumptions than the general theories do which are used for their foundations.

Of course, specific assumptions are well in place if they are plausible, e.g., because they have good empirical support, or if we can derive good predictions from them. However, such assumptions are too often used even if they are not plausible. This is the case because they simplify the problem and therefore allow to "make a certain point". This is a questionable reasoning unless it can be demonstrated that the intuition found under the specific assumptions is generally relevant. One purpose of a more general model is to check this assertion.

The specific assumptions which we have in mind when comparing models of finance and the general equilibrium model are as follows: First, in finance models attention is usually restricted to the financial aspect of markets. That is to say, models of finance do usually not incorporate "real" sectors with labor markets and commodity markets. Furthermore, in these models usually only one single good is used for consumption. This good is sometimes interpreted as "money". "Expenditure" on a bundle of commodities in the sense of a Hicks-Leontief composite commodity would be a better interpretation. Moreover, specific assumptions on agents' preferences, for example, can be found in most familiar finance models, e.g., the mean-variance assumption in the Capital Asset Pricing Model. Finally, when pricing derivatives, specific stochastic processes describing the evolution of the prices of the underlying securities are postulated. A Brownian motion, for example, is often assumed in option pricing as for example in the Black and Scholes Model.

The first purpose of a general equilibrium foundation of finance is to show that all these specific assumptions are consistent with a more general model that links finance to the other important aspects of economics like consumption. At this point it is, however, important to note that the general equilibrium model of Arrow and Debreu [1954] itself cannot be used as a foundation of finance. Incorporating time and uncertainty into this model is done by postulating that markets for present and future commodities open and close before any other economic activity actually takes place (cf. Debreu [1959, chap. 7]). Hence, in the Arrow-Debreu model there is no need for reopening spot markets and consequently there is no need for financial markets either. Modern general equilibrium theory starts from the observation that financial markets are seriously incomplete. In no way can it be said that there is a complete system of contingent contracts that opens once for all times and that markets will remain closed ever after. Clearly, a more realistic setting is a model of sequential markets, i.e., a system of reopening spot markets which are linked via a system of financial markets. In this setting the role of the financial markets is to provide means to transfer income across spot markets and hence to provide savings and insurance opportunities. Arrow [1953] was first to formulate a general equilibrium model which incorporates a system of reopening spot markets being linked by a system of financial markets. Subsequently this model has been further developed, especially by Radner [1972]. In its current form (see e.g. Geanakoplos [1990], Magill and Shafer [1991] or Hens [1998] for a survey and Magill and Quinzii [1996] for a textbook) the model is called "general equilibrium model with incomplete financial markets" (abbreviated GEI-model). The phrase "incomplete" refers to the fact that there might not be sufficiently many assets so that agents cannot transfer income across spot markets without restrictions. The GEI-model provides a unifying theory in which systems of real, financial, and monetary markets interact.

The first thing to check is whether the various components of the model fit together in a meaningful way. That is to say whether equilibria exist in the GEI-model. If so, the GEI-model provides a foundation of finance since it provides a model in which financial markets can be meaningfully embedded into the rest of the economy.

Moreover, it can be shown that the "linear pricing rule" is a consequence of GEI-equilibria. This rule claims that the price of an asset whose payoff can be duplicated by a portfolio of other assets must be equal to a linear combination of the duplicating assets' prices. The weights in the linear combination are exactly the weights the assets have in the duplicating portfolio. If the linear pricing rule did not hold, then asset traders could find a portfolio strategy that delivers some positive payoff without ever requiring any payments—a situation that is not consistent with an equilibrium. For this reason determining asset prices by the linear pricing rule is as well called "arbitrage pricing".

The absence of arbitrage is the central idea in option pricing (cf. Black and Scholes [1973]). Moreover, it is the basis for theoretical insights like the "irrelevance of the financial policy of a firm" (e.g. the irrelevance of its debt-equity ratio). The latter claim, called the Modigliani-Miller-Theorem, gives conditions under which a firm's financial policy does not matter. Doing this will then focus attention on those reasons which are relevant in practice.

Besides, relating prices in an equilibrium of some economy, arbitrage pricing can be used to determine the prices of new assets which will be issued in an economy. If the new assets are "redundant", i.e., they can be duplicated, then the linear pricing rule can be used to determine their price from the prices of the already traded assets. In a general equilibrium model pricing new assets can be seen as a question of comparative statics. And in the GEI-model it is easily demonstrated that arbitrage pricing is exactly the right answer to this question. In this sense the GEI-model provides a "foundation of arbitrage pricing". Seen slightly differently, the linear pricing rule asserts that as long as the prices of a "basis" of assets are known, all asset prices are determined. A "basis" of assets is a set of assets that can be used to duplicate any other asset. A more fundamental question is what determines the prices of the assets in a "basis". This critique to asset pricing has been formulated in its most drastic form by Summers [1985] who wrote in the Journal of Finance, that

> Financial Economists are like ketchup economists who are mainly concerned about the prices of different-sizes bottles of ketchup. They seem to ignore what seems to many to be the more important question of what determines the overall level of asset prices.

An explanation of asset prices—a theory of asset values—is missing unless this question has been answered. And again this can be done in a general equilibrium model. A simple model which can be used to serve this purpose is the CAPM. It can be seen as a specific GEI-model.

Having embedded financial markets into the general equilibrium model, the following fundamental question are important. Do there exist competitive equilibria, and if so, how many equilibria exist? If equilibria did not exist, an equilibrium model would be vacuous. If on the other hand too many equilibria do exist, then the predictive power of the model is very limited and we can hardly say it "explains" the values of assets and commodities. In the CAPM, for example, the equilibrium determines the risk premiums which have to be deducted from the expected return of assets. Risk premiums, however, differ across CAPM-equilibria. Hence, without a reasonable argument from which the uniquness of CAPM-equilibria can be concluded, the important notion of risk premium is vacuous. A quotation of Schumpeter [1954, p. 969] summarizes the importance of uniqueness of the equilibrium in general equilibrium models.

> Multiple equilibria are not necessarily useless but, from the standpoint of *any* exact science, the existence of a 'uniquely determined equilibrium (set of values)' is, of course, of the utmost importance, even if proof has to be purchased at the price of very restrictive assumptions; without any possibility of proving the existence of uniquely determined equilibrium—or at all events, of a small number of possible equilibria—at however high a level of abstraction, a field of phenomena is really a chaos that is not under analytic control.

Note that the need of a sound theoretical foundation of finance providing a unique equilibrium is not merely an intellectual satisfaction, but it is very important for many practical applications of financial markets models. Recently, the fruitful applications of computable general equilibrium models (cf. Shoven and Whalley [1992], and Kehoe [1991]) have been extended to incorporate incomplete financial markets. The flourishing literature on these computable GEI-models include, for example, Brown et al. [1996], and Schmedders [1996]. In the interesting results of this literature new insights on the welfare losses due to incomplete markets or on the famous equity premium puzzle, implicitly a unique equilibrium is assumed without ever explicitly deriving a sound foundation of their model in the sense of our book.

The aim of this book is to show that modern general equilibrium theory can indeed provide a sound foundation of finance. It does not only embed financial markets into a full fledged market system, but under specific and plausible assumptions it determines the existence of a unique equilibrium. To this end in the first chapter we will describe the general equilibrium model with incomplete markets for which we then define its central concept, the notion of a competitive equilibrium. Moreover, we outline its basic features like the "fundamental theorem of asset pricing". This theorem provides a general equilibrium foundation of the notion of no-arbitrage. Furthermore Chapter 1 shows that the standard general equilibrium model à la Arrow-Debreu can be incorporated into the more general GEI-model as an interesting special case. Hence, the results of our book in particular apply to the model which Kirman [1989] dubbed the "emperor of economic theory".

Competitive equilibria are solutions to a system of equations, formed by the excess demand functions. The properties of the excess demand functions are therefore the essential features of any general equilibrium model. In Chapter 2 we derive the important properties Walras Law, homogeneity, continuity and boundary behavior for the incomplete markets excess demand function. Walras Law is the well known accounting identity that total expenditure on commodities must always be equal to total revenue from sales of commodities, which means that the model is "closed"; i.e., no outside party receives or delivers any income from the closed economy. Homogeneity describes the "absence of money illusion", which means, for example, that on doubling all prices (and therefore doubling all incomes) no agent will change his market trades. Moreover, small changes in prices will not result in large changes in trades, i.e., under standard assumptions excess demand functions are continuous. Finally, the boundary behavior holds if for very small prices demand exceeds supply and for very high prices the reverse is true. Deriving these fundamental properties, we emphasize the additional assumptions needed over and above the complete markets model. In Chapter 5 we define and motivate the two properties being essential for a sound foundation of finance: monotonicity and gross substitution. Monotonicity holds if on a change of the price system into some direction excess demand moves into the opposite direction. Hence, "on average" falling excess demand is associated with increased prices. According to gross substitution the excess demand of a commodity decreases on an increase in its own price while it increases on an increase in the price of any other commodity. Monotonicity as well as gross substitution give a very useful structure to an interdependent system of markets. In analysing these two properties of excess demand functions, two points of view can be taken. According to the "global" point of view, we would desire to have these properties on the entire space where the excess demand functions are defined. The local point of view requires them to hold only in neighborhoods of competitive equilibria.

A fundamental insight in equilibrium analysis is the "index theorem". It demonstrates how the local and global point of view can nicely be integrated into one picture. The local structure of excess demand around equilibria determines global properties like uniqueness of equilibria. Moreover, the index theorem provides a proof of existence of competitive equilibria since it shows that the parity of the number of equilibria is odd. The index theorem is the subject of Chapter 4.

Chapter 3 further analyzes the excess demand functions. In contrast to Chapter 2, now we turn the question upside down. Whereas in Chapter 2 we asked "given any economy what are the properties of its market excess demand function" now we ask "given any candidate excess demand function, can an economy be found from which the preassigned function can indeed be derived as the economy's market excess demand function"? Hence, Chapter 3 clarifies what the minimal properties of excess demand are. It will be shown that besides Walras Law, homogeneity, continuity and boundary behavior no further properties can in general be expected. Whereas these minimal properties are definitely sufficient to obtain the existence of competitive equilibria, they are however not sufficient for a sound foundation of finance since uniqueness does not need to hold without restrictions like monotonicity or gross substitution being satisfied. The question underlying Chapter 3 was first posed by Sonnenschein [1972], Sonnenschein [1973] in the framework of the Arrow-Debreu model. In Chapter 3 we demonstrate to what extend the results of Sonnenschein [1972], Sonnenschein [1973], Mantel [1974] and Debreu [1974] which subsequently evolved out of Sonnenschein's question can be extended to the incomplete markets model. We show that—as in the complete markets model—uniqueness, stability and comparative statics can only be achieved by imposing assumptions on the agent's characteristics which go clearly beyond the standard continuity, monotonicity and convexity assumptions on agents' preferences. As we demonstrate in Chapter 9, this is even true for the special case of the CAPM, which is analyzed in the second part of this book. Hence, even the assumption of mean variance preferences does not, for example, exclude an arbitrary number of CAPM-equilibria. To prepare for this point of view on the CAPM, Chapter 7 embeds the CAPM into the GEI-Model. In particular the problem of absence of arbitrage and of the positivity of state prices is addressed. Thereafter Chapter 8 gives a general proof of existence in the CAPM. This result does not follow from the analogous results for the GEI-Model because in the CAPM satiation of utilty is possible and the consumption space is not necessarily bounded from below.

In Chapter 6 we analyze special classes of economies in which the goals for a sound foundation of finance are actually met. Following the standard approach used in the Arrow-Debreu-Model, and surveyed in Chapter 5, further restrictions on the individuals' preferences or endowments are introduced. In a financial markets context well known examples include the assumption of expected utility, homogeneous beliefs, absence of aggregate risk, small risk aversion or special functional forms of risk aversion like hyperbolic absolute risk aversion. These restrictions have been introduced into financial markets models in order to derive simple formulas determining asset prices by the characteristics of the economy. In Chapter 6 we analyze how far these well known restrictions help to determine uniqueness and stability in the complete as well as in the incomplete markets model.

To finish this introduction it is important to also point at the limitations of our book. We are not concerned with strategic interaction of agents. On some financial markets these interactions are very important. Many financial markets do, however, have a large number of potential participants, which suggests that strategic interactions should be limited here.

We limit attention to exchange economies since we have in mind a situation where a large number of traders endowed with certain assets meet in order to exchange these among each other.

Moreover, we assume that traders meet on asset markets just once, i.e., repeated trading of assets and trading of various commodities within one spot market are neglected. The latter simplification can be justified by the observation that within spot markets agents can trade on a complete system of markets. Hence, the earlier results known for the complete markets model apply within each spot market and our results demonstrate how these results can be integrated via a system of incomplete financial markets. The restriction to a two periods model which allows for just one asset trading period is a more severe restriction since many important applications of finance develop their full power only in multiple periods or even continuous time trading models. To a large extent however the two period model summarizes the basic insights of a more general discrete time model with finite horizon (cf. Magill and Quinzii [1996] and Hens [1998]).

We do not consider asymmetric information. We strongly believe that asymmetric information is important especially to explain incompleteness of financial markets. However, in a general equilibrium framework this would require to study feedback effects from commonly observed outcomes like prices and trading volume to private information (cf. Radner [1979] and Prescott and Townsend [1984]). And this is very difficult to model. To quote an authority in finance [Ross, 1989, p. 8]:

> The theory with asymmetric information is not well understood at all. In short, the exact mechanism by which prices incorporate information is still a mystery and an attendant theory of volume is simply missing.

In a few very recent contributions there has been made an attempt at integrating the GEI-model with the analysis of asymmetric information economies (see Dubey et al. [1996] and Bisin and Gottardi [1999]). See Bisin and Gottardi [1996] for a recent survey. In particular, the conditions (in terms of trading restrictions and nature of prices) under which (competitive) markets for contracts may work—equilibria exist—have to be substantially reconsidered when there is asymmetric information. Such an analysis allows possible explanations of market incompleteness and the presence of imperfections in financial markets, resulting now form incentive-compatibility constraints. Moreover, it can offer a useful theoretical construct to complement the extensive literature on contract theory.

A different approach would be to restrict attention to partial equilibrium analysis emphasizing strategic interaction. The game theoretic foundation of finance develops interesting results in this direction. We believe that a general equilibrium perspective focusing on the interdependence of markets is, however, very important. Of course, there is no single best way for understanding financial markets. The hope is that these two complementary approaches will eventually converge into a unified theory.

Finally, we should mention that in this book we are not deeply concerned with normative aspects of the general equilibrium foundation of finance. Many new normative results can be demonstrated when financial markets are incomplete. We had to limit the scope of our analysis and decided to concentrate attention on positive general equilibrium theory. A good book providing results complementary to ours is the one of Magill and Quinzii [1996].

Our book is the first systematic account of results on existence, uniqueness and structure of equilibria in incomplete financial markets. These are results which are important both from a theoretical perspective providing a sound foundation of an important and flourishing subfield of economics as well as results relevant for any successful application of financial markets models.

We hope that our book will therefore be appreciated both by theorists and practitioners interested in understanding financial markets.

# I

# THE GENERAL EQUILIBRIUM MODEL WITH INCOMPLETE MARKETS

# Chapter 1

# THE MODEL AND SOME FUNDAMENTALS

## 1. Information Structure And Commodity Space

Following Debreu [1959] commodities are distinguished by their physical characteristics and their location, as well as by the time and the event in which they are available. The GEI-model highlights these latter aspects of commodities: time and uncertainty.

In the standard GEI-model uncertainty is resolved in a finite number of steps. To model the resolution of uncertainty one considers a finite number of 'states of the world' à la Savage [1954]. Information is then modelled by partitions of the states of the world. The finer the partition, the more information one has. At the outset no agent knows which state will finally prevail; i.e., the partition consists of one set including all states. At the end of all time periods every agent knows which state has materialized; i.e., in the partition every single state forms a set on its own.

We do not give a formal modelling of this information structure because we will restrict attention to the most simple such case in which there are just two time periods, $t = 0$ and $t = 1$.

On numbering the states by $s = 1, \ldots, S$, denoting by $s = 0$ the set $\{1, \ldots, S\}$ and by $s = 1$ the set $\{1\}$, by $s = 2$ the set $\{2\}$, etc., the information structure can be represented by the simple decision tree shown in the Figure 1.1.

The restriction to two time periods is simplifying and especially helpful as we will see later on. However, many applications of finance show their full richness only in a multi-period or continuous trading context. Still the two period model enables us to gain basic knowledge for understanding discrete time models with finite horizon as it is demonstrated at full length by Magill and Quinzii [1996].

Furthermore, we assume that there is only one commodity which is available in each future state $s = 1, \ldots, S$ of the world, but not in the state $s = 0$.

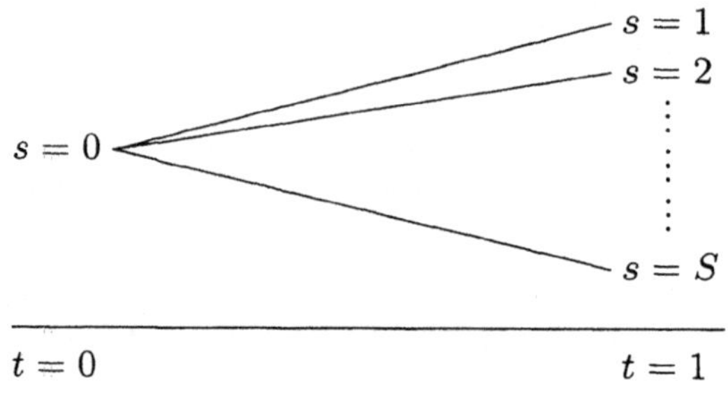


*Figure 1.1.* The information structure

This assumption does not exclude first period consumption since, as we will show below, consumption in the first period can be modelled by an appropriate restriction on the asset structure. Thus our model is more general than a model with explicit consumption in the first period. We can also cope with situations in which asset trade takes place in the first period independently from consumption. From a general equilibrium perspective the single commodity should be thought of as the aggregate commodity 'expenditure'. The underlying assumption is that relative prices of various commodities within each state play a minor role in the financial decisions of the agents. This simplification can be justified by assuming that relative prices are fixed (Hicks-Leontief aggregation) or by assuming separability of utility functions (Green-Nataf aggregation). The simplification allows us to focus on the financial aspects of the model, i.e., on the allocation of income over time and uncertainty.

Assuming that agents are only interested by state contingent consumption at the end of the model, the commodity space is the finite-dimensional Euclidean space $\mathbb{R}^S$. Note that we have assumed that the composite commodity expenditure is infinitely divisible.

## 2. Consumer Characteristics

We restrict the economy to be an exchange economy. The only units of economic activity are the consumers, also called households or agents. Having in mind a situation where a large number of traders endowed with certain incomes meet in order to insure among each other by trading assets, this limitation seems reasonable. If we allowed firms to exist, there would arise many additional difficulties which would divert from the main purposes of this book. For example it is not even clear what the firms' objective function should be when markets are incomplete since shareholder value cannot be unanimously defined. For GEI with production see Magill and Quinzii [1996, Chapter 6].

There is a discrete number $I \in \mathbb{N}$ of consumers $i = 1, \ldots, I$. For simplicity we denote the number of agents and the set of agents by the same capital letter. We do the following convention: if there is a variable which takes values $1, \ldots, N \in \mathbb{N}$, then we define $N = \{1, \ldots N\}$.
The consumers are described by their consumption sets $X^i \subset \mathbb{R}^S$, their possibly uncertain endowments $\omega^i \in \mathbb{R}^S$ of commodities, and their tastes and risk attitudes represented by utility functions $U^i : X^i \longrightarrow \mathbb{R}$.[1]
We impose some standard assumptions on the characteristics of the economy. These are not the most general assumptions under which the model works. However, these assumptions are strong enough to facilitate the exposition and thus to focus on the new aspects arising from the incompleteness of markets. The following continuity assumptions are made for the whole exposition.

ASSUMPTION 1.1 (CONTINUITY ASSUMPTIONS)
*The agents' characteristics fulfill the following properties:*

*(i)* $X^i = \mathbb{R}^S_+$ *for all* $i \in I$*;*

*(ii)* $\omega^i \in \mathbb{R}^S_+$ *for all* $i \in I$*;*

*(iii)* $U^i : \mathbb{R}^S_+ \longrightarrow \mathbb{R}$ *is continuous for all* $i \in I$*;*

*(iv)* $U^i : \mathbb{R}^S_+ \longrightarrow \mathbb{R}$ *is strictly monotonic for all* $i \in I$*;*

*(v)* $U^i : \mathbb{R}^S_+ \longrightarrow \mathbb{R}$ *is strictly quasi-concave for all* $i \in I$*.*

We call this set of assumptions Continuity Assumptions since—as we demonstrate in Chapter 2—they are essential for agents' demand to be a continuous function of prices.
Let us explain and comment on these assumptions:
Choosing $X^i$ as the set of all non-negative commodity bundles is an easy, but standard way to guarantee closedness, convexity and boundedness from below[2], which are typical requirements in the general equilibrium model according to Arrow and Debreu. Since we do not want to complicate the exposition, we take this common restriction. Note that $\omega^i_s = 0$ means that in state $s$ agent $i$ can only guarantee his subsistence level but he cannot engage in any security trading that would require him to deliver wealth in state $s$ even though such trades may be very rewarding in states different from state $s$.

[1]Note the following fact: upper indices are used for labelling the consumer while lower indices give the state of the world. For example, $\omega^i_s$ gives the endowment of consumer $i$ if state $s$ occurs tomorrow. $\omega^i$ is equal to the vector $\left(\omega^i_1, \ldots, \omega^i_S\right)^T$.

[2]Do not mind if you do not know the exact definitions of these mathematical expressions. Then, only accept $X^i$ to be the positive orthant.

We assume that every consumer should be able to find a feasible consumption bundle without trading, choosing $\omega^i$ as an element of the consumption set. With endowments outside the consumption sets serious discontinuities of demand arise that cannot be easily resolved in an economy with a finite number of agents.[3] Allowing for endowments in the boundary of the consumption set still leads to discontinuities in agents' demand functions which hinder equilibria to exist. Using appropriate restrictions on the distribution of endowments and the structure of asset markets, in Chapter 2 we demonstrate how to overcome these difficulties in proving existence of competitive equilibria with a finite number of consumers.

Continuity should be a familiar expression to the reader. Focusing on the uncertainty aspect of commodities, this assumption does not seem too restrictive. The limitation on strictly monotonic utility functions is also common.

DEFINITION 1.1 (STRICT MONOTONICITY)
*A utility function $U^i : \mathbb{R}^S_+ \to \mathbb{R}$ is strictly monotonic if $x, y \in \mathbb{R}^S_+$ with $y > x$ implies $U^i(y) > U^i(x)$.*

Note that $y > x$ is defined as $y_s \geq x_s$ for all $s \in \{1, \ldots, S\}$, and $y_s > x_s$ for some $s \in \{1, \ldots, S\}$. Hence, the level of utility of a consumer with a strictly monotonic utility function increases as soon as the consumer gets some more consumption in one of the states without getting less consumption in any other state.

The quasi-concavity has to be interpreted as risk-aversion of the consumer: he prefers any mixture of two feasible consumption bundles $x$ and $y$ to the bundle giving the minimum utility.

DEFINITION 1.2 (STRICT QUASI-CONCAVITY)
*A utility function $U^i : \mathbb{R}^S_+ \to \mathbb{R}$ is strictly quasi-concave if for every pair of vectors $x, y \in \mathbb{R}^S_+$ and all $\lambda \in (0, 1)$ it is*

$$U^i(\lambda x + (1 - \lambda) y) > \min\left\{U^i(x), U^i(y)\right\} \quad .$$

Figure 1.2 which is taken from Debreu [1959] illustrates this notion of risk aversion.

In Figure 1.2 consumption in two states is considered. $\tilde{x} = (\tilde{x}_1, \tilde{x}_2)$ and $\hat{x} = (\hat{x}_1, \hat{x}_2)$ are two risky consumption bundles yielding the same level of utility. Since the utility function is strictly quasi-concave or equivalently the 'no worse than' sets are strictly convex, any strict convex combination of $\tilde{x}$ and $\hat{x}$ improves the consumer. In particular, the risk free consumption bundle $\bar{x}$ for which $\bar{x}_1 = \bar{x}_2$ gives a strictly higher level of utility than the risk free

[3] [Lengwiler, 1998]

bundle $\overset{*}{x}$ which by construction delivers the same utility as the risky bundles $\tilde{x}, \hat{x}$. For obvious reasons $\overset{*}{x}$ is called the certainty equivalent. Finally, note that the amount $\bar{x}_1 - \overset{*}{x}_1$ gives a measure for the risk aversion of the agent.
Moreover, sometimes we would like to obtain a differentiable system of equilibrium allocations. For that purpose Debreu [1972] initiated the following set of differentiability assumptions that have to be assumed in addition to the Continuity Assumptions 1.1.

ASSUMPTION 1.2 (DIFFERENTIABILITY ASSUMPTIONS)
*The agents' characteristics fulfill the Continuity Assumptions 1.1 and additionally they satisfy:*

*(i)* $U^i : \mathbb{R}^S_+ \to \mathbb{R}$ *is infinitely often differentiable on* $\mathbb{R}^S_+$ *for all* $i \in I$;

*(ii)* $\nabla U^i(x) \in \mathbb{R}^S_{++}$ *for all* $x \in \mathbb{R}^S_+$ *and all* $i \in I$;

*(iii) for all* $i \in I$ *it is* $h\, D^2 U^i(x)\, h < 0$ *for all* $x \in \mathbb{R}^S_+$ *and all* $h \in \mathbb{R}^S \setminus \{0\}$ *with* $\nabla U^i(x)\, h = 0$;

*(iv)* $\left\{ x \in \mathbb{R}^S_+ \;\middle|\; U^i(x) \geq U^i(\bar{x}) \right\} \subset \mathbb{R}^S_{++}$ *for all* $\bar{x} \in \mathbb{R}^S_{++}$ *and all* $i \in I$.

*(v)* $\omega^i \in \mathbb{R}^S_{++}$

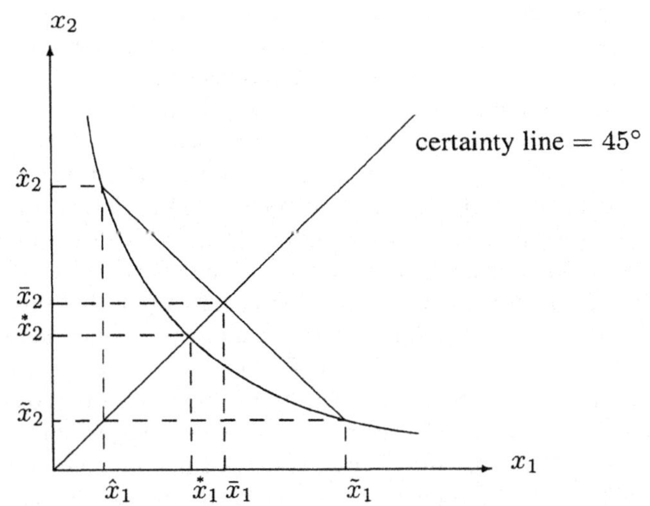


*Figure 1.2.* Risk aversion

The differentiability of a function should also be familiar to the reader. It is a technical assumption. (ii) implies strict monotonicity of the utility function. (iii) guarantees strict quasi-concavity. (iv) assures that the indifference curves of the consumer through interior consumption bundles do not intersect the boundary of the consumption sets. Together with the strict positivity of the endowments it implies that consumers who maximize their utility choose strictly positive consumption bundles, i.e., consumption bundles in the interior of their consumption sets.

## 2.1 Expected Utility Hypothesis

To illustrate Assumption 1.1 and 1.2 a little further we consider the case of an expected utility function.

DEFINITION 1.3 (EXPECTED UTILITY HYPOTHESIS)
*A utility function $U^i : \mathbb{R}^S_+ \to \mathbb{R}$ satisfies the expected utility hypothesis if there exists a probability measure $\rho^i \in \mathbb{R}^S_+$ with $\sum_{s=1}^S \rho^i_s = 1$ and a von Neumann-Morgenstern utility function $u^i : \mathbb{R}_+ \to \mathbb{R}$ such that for all $x \in \mathbb{R}^S_+$*

$$U^i(x) = \sum_{s=1}^{S} \rho^i_s u^i(x_s) \quad .$$

According to the expected utility assumption an agent's preferences over risky consumption bundles can be conceptually separated into the agent's beliefs over the likelihood of occurrence of the various states and a 'utility out of consumption within the states'. The expected utility hypothesis can be given an axiomatic foundation in terms of fundamental axioms of choice, like the 'sure thing principle' or the 'state independence axiom', first introduced by Savage [1954] for the case of a continuous state space. For an axiomatization well suited for the framework of the standard GEI-model as displayed here see, for example, Hens [1992] or Wakker [1989]. In this framework the sure thing principle requires that the choice between two consumption bundles $x$ and $y$ should not depend on the consumption in those subset of states in which $x$ and $y$ are identical. It can be demonstrated that this property holds true if and only if the utility function $U^i$ is additively separable, i.e., if for some $u^i_s : \mathbb{R}_+ \to \mathbb{R}, s = 1, \ldots, S$, it is $U^i(x) = \sum_{s=1}^S u^i_s(x_s)$ for all $x \in \mathbb{R}^S_+$. The state independence axiom requires the preferences for consumption within the states to be identical across the states, i.e., the 'in-state utility function' $u^i_s, s = 1, \ldots, S$, only differ up to some positive monotonic transformations. To complete the characterization of expected utility, note that for an expected utility function the slope of the indifference curves is constant along the certainty line, and it is actually equal to the negative ratio of the likelihood of occurrence of the states according to the agent's beliefs $\rho^i_s$. Hens [1992] has demonstrated that this property which he calls 'weak homotheticity' together with the 'sure thing principle' and the 'state independence axiom' indeed characterize expected utility in a model with a continuum of consequences and a finite number of states as for example in the standard GEI-model. An alternative representation of expected utility functions is used when for a given set of states $s = 1, \ldots, S$ with associated fixed consequences $\bar{x}_s$, $s = 1, \ldots, S$ the probability of the states $\rho_s$, $s = 1, \ldots, S$ are the object of choice. In this so called 'lottery approach' indifference curves are represented are represented in the space of probability distributions $\triangle = \left\{\rho \in \mathbb{R}^S \middle| \sum_{s=1}^S \rho_s = 1\right\}$. For example let $S = 3$ then the triangle depicted in Figure 1.3 shows all possible lotteries over the three consequences $\bar{x}_1, \bar{x}_2, \bar{x}_3$. In this representation expected utility functions have indifference curves that are straight parallel lines: Given $\bar{x}_s$ and hence given the utility levels $\bar{u}_s^i := u^i(x_s)$ an expected utility function is a mapping from $\triangle$ to $\mathbb{R}$ defined by $E_{u^i} = \sum_{s=1}^S \rho_s \bar{u}_s^i$.

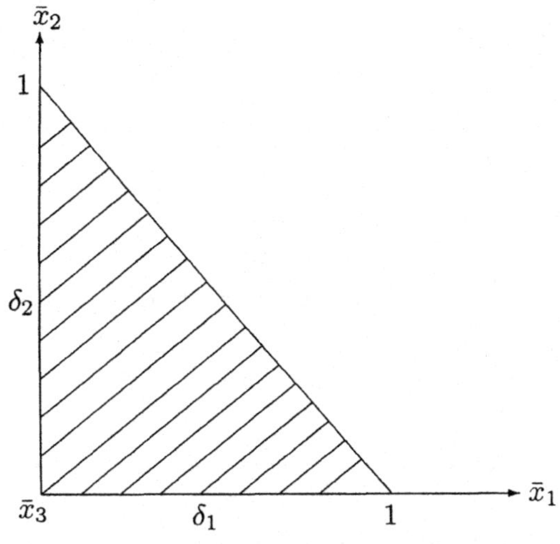


*Figure 1.3.* Probability Triangle

The Assumption 1.1 and 1.2 require the following properties of an expected utility function. Continuity and differentiability require $u^i : \mathbb{R}_+ \to \mathbb{R}$ to be continuous respectively differentiable. Strict monotonicity requires $u^i$ to be strictly increasing as well as to hold the belief that no state $s$ is impossible, i.e., that $\rho_s^i > 0, s = 1, \ldots, S$. Strict quasi-concavity requires $u^i$ to be a strictly concave function. To be precise, we give the definition:

ASSUMPTION 1.3 (DIFFERENTIABLE STRICTLY CONCAVE EXP. UTILITY)

*$U^i : \mathbb{R}^S_+ \to \mathbb{R}$ is a differentiable, strictly concave expected utility function if it has the representation $U^i(x) = \sum_{s=1}^{S} \rho^i_s u^i(x_s)$, where the beliefs satisfy: $\rho^i \in \mathbb{R}^S_{++}$ with $\sum_{s=1}^{S} \rho^i_s = 1$ and where the von Neumann Morgenstern utility function $u^i : \mathbb{R}_+ \to \mathbb{R}$ satisfies:*

*(i) $u^i$ is continuous on $\mathbb{R}_+$ and twice continuously differentiable on $\mathbb{R}_{++}$.*

*(ii) For all $x \in \mathbb{R}_{++}$ we have $u^{i\prime}(x) \in \mathbb{R}_{++}$.*

*(iii) For all $x \in \mathbb{R}_{++}$ we have $u^{i\prime\prime}(x) \in \mathbb{R}_{--}$.*

*(iv) For all sequences $(x_n)_{n\in\mathbb{N}} \in \mathbb{R}_{++}$ with $\lim_{n\to\infty} x_n = 0$ it holds that $\lim_{n\to\infty} u^{i\prime}(x_n) = \infty$.*

In particular, in the differentiability case the following measures for an agent's risk aversion can be defined.

DEFINITION 1.4 (RISK AVERSION)
*For an expected utility function*
$U^i(x) = \sum_{s=1}^{S} \rho^i_s u^i(x_s)$

- *the absolute risk aversion is defined as*

$$ARA^i(x_s) = -\frac{u^{i\,\prime\prime}(x_s)}{u^{i\,\prime}(x_s)} \text{ for all } x_s \in \mathbb{R}_{++} \tag{1.1}$$

- *and the relative risk aversion is defined as*

$$RRA^i(x_s) = -\frac{x_s u^{i\,\prime\prime}(x_s)}{u^{i\,\prime}(x_s)} \text{ for all } x_s \in \mathbb{R}_{+} \quad . \tag{1.2}$$

As shown by Arrow [1970] and Pratt [1964], the risk aversion measures determine how an investor faced with a risky and a riskless asset changes his asset allocation with increasing income. If $ARA^i$ is negative (positive) then the absolute amount of money spent on the risky asset increases (decreases) with income while if $RRA^i$ is negative (positive) then the proportion of the investor's income spent on the risky asset increases (decreases) with income. Referring back to Figure 1.2 it is obvious that both notions of risk aversion determine the curvature of the agent's indifference curves.
Utility functions which exhibit so-called 'hyperbolic absolute risk aversion', abbreviated $HARA$, are of particular importance for the structure of asset demand.

DEFINITION 1.5 (HYPERBOLIC ABSOLUTE RISK AVERSION)
*An expected utility function $U^i(x) = \sum_{s=1}^{S} \rho_s^i u^i(x_s)$ satisfies hyperbolic absolute risk aversion, $HARA$, if for all $x_s \in \mathbb{R}_+$*

$$-\frac{u^{i\,\prime\prime}(x_s)}{u^{i\,\prime}(x_s)} = \frac{1}{\alpha^i + \beta^i x_s} \quad \textit{for some} \quad \alpha^i \in \mathbb{R}_+,\, \beta^i \in \mathbb{R} \quad .$$

Hyperbolic absolute risk aversion is defined via a differential equation of the von Neumann-Morgenstern utility function $u^i$. Integration shows that $u^i$ is then of the form

$$u^i(x_s) = \begin{cases} \frac{\left(\alpha^i + \beta^i x_s\right)^{1-1/\beta^i}}{1/\beta^i(1-1/\beta^i)} & \text{if } \beta^i \neq 0, v\beta^i \neq 1 \\ -\alpha^i e^{-x_s/\alpha^i} & \text{if } \beta^i = 0 \\ \log\left(\alpha^i + x_s\right) & \text{if } \beta^i = 1 \end{cases}$$

which is defined on the domain $\alpha^i + \beta^i x_s > 0$.
Since $HARA$ utility functions give a nice structure for financial markets models, we would like to include them in our analysis. However, not all the utility functions in the $HARA$ class satisfy our Assumptions 1.1 and 1.2 without further qualifications.
For $\beta^i = -1$, for example, $u^i(x_s)$ is quadratic, which leads to the mean-variance-criterion for investment underlying the CAPM. The problem is that quadratic utility functions have satiation points; hence, (strict) monotonicity does not hold on the entire non-negative reals. Assuming that aggregate endowments are not sufficient to push any single agent over his satiation point cures this problem. Moreover, with quadratic preferences indifference curves may intersect with the boundary of the consumption sets. Hence, differentiability of demand can only be guaranteed if the optimal consumption allocation is interior to the consumption set.
A different example is the case of the Cobb-Douglas utility functions which results for $\alpha^i = 0$ and $\beta^i = 1$. In this case the Differentiability Assumptions 1.2 are satisfied except for the problem that the utility function is not defined on the boundary. Note, however, that with interior endowments for Cobb-Douglas utility functions the set of consumption bundles being at least as good as the initial endowments is strictly included in the interior of the consumption set. Hence, since trade is voluntary, again the problem is innocuous for demand.
Besides the assumption of expected utility functions the assumption of homothetic preferences is also quite common to get structure for individual demand:

ASSUMPTION 1.4 (HOMOTHETIC PREFERENCES)
*A utility function $U(x)$ represents homothetic preferences if it is homogenuous of some degree $k > 0$. I.e.:*

$$U(\lambda x) = \lambda^k U(x)$$

*for all x in X and all $\lambda > 0$.*

In particular if this assumption is combined with the expected utility assumption, as for example in the case of Cobb-Douglas utility functions, demand has a very useful structure.

# 3. Market Structure

## 3.1 Payoff Matrix

The market structure in our model is a more general, more realistic one than in the standard Arrow-Debreu model: in each future state of the world there is a market for the consumption good, whereas in the Arrow-Debreu model markets open only once, namely today.
It seems reasonable to assume that the agents can insure themselves against some states of the world. Without any insurance there would not be any trade since the agents have to fulfill their budget constraints

$$p_s x_s^i \leq p_s \omega_s^i \quad \text{for all} \quad s \in S \quad .$$

Because of the strict monotonicity of the utility functions spot prices $p_s$ have to be positive and consumers choose $x_s^i = \omega_s^i$ for maximizing their utility within their budget constraints, i.e., they always choose the no-trade solution.
But, for example, if a consumer expects a very high endowment in state $\bar{s} \in S$ and a very low endowment in state $\tilde{s} \in S$, it should be able for him to give up something of the commodity in state $\bar{s}$ to receive more in state $\tilde{s}$. To make this possible, we introduce $J$ financial contracts $j = 1, \ldots, J$ which can be traded today and pay off tomorrow. The asset payoffs are described by the matrix[4]

$$A = \left(A_s^j\right)_{\substack{s=1,\ldots,S \\ j=1,\ldots,J}} \quad .$$

$A^j = \left(A_1^j, \ldots, A_S^j\right)^T$ describes asset $j$, whereas $A_s = \left(A_s^1, \ldots, A_s^J\right)$ gives the payoffs of all assets in state $s$. We assume *real assets*, i.e. assets pay off in units of the consumption good. An alternative specification would be to assume *nominal assets* in which case the amount of consumption goods one can by per unit of asset pay off depends on the post market prices $p_s$. As an effect equilibrium allocations become indeterminate: there exists a continuum of equilibria of dimension $S - J$. See Balasko and Cass [1989] and Geanakoplos and Mas-Colell [1989]. This lack of determinancy of equilibria has been attributed to a lack of monetary policy determinating the price levels $p_s$. See for example Magill and Quinzii [1996]. We do not want to go into this discussion

[4]Upper indices mark the asset and lower ones the state such that $A_s^j$ is the units of account asset $j$ pays off in state $s$.

and hence assume that assets are real. As an effect then sport prices do not matter. They cancel from the budget restrictions and can hence be normalized to 1.
Look at the following examples of assets.

EXAMPLE 1.1 (BOND)
*Asset $j$ is a bond. Then, $A^j_s = 1$ for all $s \in S$, i.e., the asset gives a sure payoff.*

EXAMPLE 1.2 (ARROW SECURITY)
*An asset is called Arrow security if there is exactly one state of the world in which it pays off one unit of account whereas in the other states there is no payoff.*

EXAMPLE 1.3 (STOCKS)
*If asset $j$ is a share in a company that plans to realize the state contingent production plan, $y \in \mathbb{R}^S$ then $A^j_s = y_s$ for all $s \in S$.*

EXAMPLE 1.4 (CALL OPTION)
*Consider a security $j$ with payoff $A^j \in \mathbb{R}^S$. A call option, $A^c$, with exercise price $K$, written on this security delivers the non-negative payoff $A^c_s = \max\{0, A^j_s - K\}$ for all $s \in S$.*

## 3.2 Budget Set

Let $q_j \in \mathbb{R}$ be the price one has to pay or that one receives today for one unit of asset $j$. $\theta^i_j \in \mathbb{R}$ is the amount of the same asset bought or sold by agent $i$.
If $q = (q_1, \ldots, q_J)^T \in \mathbb{R}^J$ is the asset price vector and $\theta^i = (\theta^i_1, \ldots, \theta^i_J)^T \in \mathbb{R}^J$ is the portfolio bought by consumer $i$, then he has to save $q\,\theta^i$ units of account today to get $A_s\,\theta^i$ tomorrow if state $s$ occurs.
Considering trade in financial markets, the agents' budget restrictions accordingly become

$$q\,\theta^i \leq 0$$

and

$$x^i_s \leq \omega^i_s + A_s\theta^i \quad \text{for all} \quad s \in S$$

Therefore, portfolios have to be self-financing and expenditures within some state cannot exceed the income of that state altered by the asset payoff. The role of asset trade is to transfer income across the states of period one.
Denote the budget sets by $\mathbb{B}\,(q, \omega^i, A)$, i.e.

$$\mathbb{B}\left(q, \omega^i, A\right) = \Big\{ x \in \mathbb{R}^S_+ \Big| \, \exists \theta \in \mathbb{R}^J \quad \text{with} \quad q\,\theta \leq 0 \\ \wedge\, x_s \leq \omega^i_s + A_s\theta \quad \text{for all} \quad s \in S \Big\}$$

REMARK 1.1 (FIRST PERIOD CONSUMPTION)
*Note that in particular it is possible to incorporate the case of first period consumption into this model. In the case of first period consumption the budget constraints are given in the following way:*

$$x_0^i + q\,\theta^i \leq \omega_0^i$$

*(the worth of today's consumption plus savings is less than the worth of today's endowment)*
*and*

$$x_s^i \leq \omega_s^i + A_s\,\theta^i \quad \textit{for all} \quad s \in S$$

*(the worth of tomorrow's consumption is less than the worth of tomorrow's endowment plus the portfolio payoff).*
*Now choose* $\tilde{A} = \begin{pmatrix} 1 & 0 \\ 0 & A \end{pmatrix}$ *and* $\tilde{\theta}^i = \begin{pmatrix} x_0^i - \omega_0^i \\ \theta^i \end{pmatrix}$.
*Then the budget constraints change to*

$$\begin{pmatrix} 1 \\ q \end{pmatrix} \tilde{\theta}^i \leq 0$$

*and*

$$x_s^i \leq \omega_s^i + \tilde{A}_s\,\tilde{\theta}^i \quad \textit{for all} \quad s = 0, \ldots, S$$

*and relabelling states shows the equivalence to a GEI-economy without first period-consumption.*

Summarizing the description of the fundamentals, the GEI-economy is given by the commodity space $\mathbb{R}^S$, the agents' characteristics $(U^i, \omega^i)$ and the asset structure $A$:

$$GEI = \left\{\mathbb{R}^S, \left(U^i, \omega^i\right)_{i \in I}, A\right\} \tag{1.3}$$

## 4. Competitive Equilibria and No-Arbitage

### 4.1 Financial Markets Equilibrium Concept

The market structure defines the agents' choice sets. We have already given the agents their objective functions. That is to say, we assume consumers choose demand and portfolios "as if" they were maximizing utility. Now we are in a position to define an equilibrium for the general equilibrium model with incomplete markets.

DEFINITION 1.6 (FINANCIAL MARKETS EQUILIBRIUM)
*An allocation* $\left(\overset{*}{x}, \overset{*}{\theta}\right) \in \mathbb{R}_{+}^{S\times I} \times \mathbb{R}^{J\times I}$ *and a price system* $\overset{*}{q} \in \mathbb{R}^{J}$ *constitute a financial markets equilibrium (abbreviated FM-equilibrium) if*

*(i)* $\left(\overset{*}{x}^{i}, \overset{*}{\theta}^{i}\right)$ *maximizes* $U^{i}(x)$ *on* $\mathbb{B}(\overset{*}{q}, \omega^{i}, A)$ *for all* $i = 1, \ldots, I$;

*(ii)* $\sum_{i=1}^{I} \overset{*}{x}^{i} = \sum_{i=1}^{I} \omega^{i}$;

*(iii)* $\sum_{i=1}^{I} \overset{*}{\theta}^{i} = 0$.

$\mathbb{B}(q, \omega^{i}, A)$ is defined as a set of consumption plans. For ease of notation, we sometimes use it also as a set of consumption and portfolio plans where the portfolios finance the consumption plans.
(i) requires all agents to be utility maximizers accepting the prices $\overset{*}{q}$. (ii) and (iii) are the conditions for commodity respectively asset market clearing.

REMARK 1.2 (WALRAS LAW)
*Note that with strictly monotone utility functions the market clearing condition (iii) implies the market clearing condition (ii): By strict monotonicity every trader* $i$ *will exhaust his budget restriction in every state* $s$. *Adding up the budget restriction over all traders then gives* $\sum_{i=1}^{I} x^{i} = A\sum_{i=1}^{I} \theta^{i} \sum_{i=1}^{I} \omega^{i}$, *which proves our claim. One might say that due to the* $S+1$ *budget restrictions in the model there are* $S+1$ *Walras Laws. I.e. if all but* $J \leq S+1$ *markets are in equilibrium then all markets are in equilibrium. There is also a converse of this claim. If all commodity markets are in equilibrium so are all asset markets. This second claim is proved in part (ii) of the Theorem* **??** *below.*

Continuing on the fact shown in the Remark 1.2, we can then reduce the definition of a financial market equilibrium by suppressing all real variables and by focussing only on asset prices and asset trade:

DEFINITION 1.7 (FINANCIAL MARKETS EQUILIBRIUM)
*An asset allocation* $\overset{*}{\theta} \in \mathbb{R}^{J\times I}$ *and an asset price system* $\overset{*}{q} \in \mathbb{R}^{J}$ *constitute a FM-equilibrium if*

- $\overset{*}{\theta}^{i} \max U^{i}(\omega^{i} + A\theta^{i})$ *s.t.* $\omega^{i} + A\theta^{i} \geq 0 \wedge \overset{*}{q}\,\theta^{i} \leq 0$ *for all* $i = 1, \ldots, I$;
- $\sum_{i=1}^{I} \overset{*}{\theta}^{i} = 0$.

On passing this section we note that there is yet a different way of writing a financial market equilibrium. A way that does look more familiar to the notion of equilibrium found in pure finance text books:
Decompose the agents endowments into the component spanned by the asset structure, $\omega^{i}_{\langle A\rangle}$ and its orthogonal complement $\omega^{i}_{\langle A\rangle^{\perp}}$. Let $\bar{\theta}^{i}$ denote the portfolio

such that $\omega^i_{\langle A \rangle} = A\,\bar{\theta}^i$. Then we can equivalently define a financial market equilibrium as:

DEFINITION 1.8 (FINANCIAL MARKETS EQUILIBRIUM)
*An asset allocation $\overset{*}{\theta} \in \mathbb{R}^{J \times I}$ and an asset price system $\overset{*}{q} \in \mathbb{R}^J$ constitute a FM-equilibrium if*

- $\overset{*}{\theta}{}^i \max U^i \left(\omega^i_{\langle A \rangle} + A\,\theta^i\right) \quad s.t. \quad \omega^i_{\langle A \rangle} + A\,\theta^i \geq 0 \wedge \overset{*}{q}\,\theta^i \leq q\,\bar{\theta}^i$
  *for all $i = 1, \ldots, I$;*
- $\sum_{i=1}^I \overset{*}{\theta}{}^i = \sum_{i=1}^I \bar{\theta}^i$.

## 4.2 No-Arbitrage Condition

A trading strategy that delivers a positive payoff in some state without ever requiring any payments is called an "arbitrage" strategy. In equilibrium asset prices must be such that there are no arbitrage opportunities. Formally:

**NAC** There is no $\theta \in \mathbb{R}^J$ such that $q\,\theta \leq 0$ and $A\,\theta > 0$.

Sometimes it is helpful to use a stronger no-arbitrage condition than this one:

**SNAC** There is no $\theta \in \mathbb{R}^J$ such that $\begin{pmatrix} -q^T \\ A \end{pmatrix} > 0$.

This condition is stronger than (NAC) since it excludes not only arbitrage in the sense of "gaining tomorrow without paying today", but also "getting money today without any paying tomorrow".
There is a common assumption guaranteeing the equivalence of (NAC) and (SNAC). It assures that the consumer does always find a portfolio which is desirable in each future state. A consumer would demand infinitely much of such a portfolio if he were not restricted by his budget.

ASSUMPTION 1.5 (EXISTENCE OF A DESIRABLE PORTFOLIO)
*There is a $\bar{\theta} \in \mathbb{R}^J$ such that $A\,\bar{\theta} > 0$.*

Note that this condition is in particular satisfied in the case of first period consumption. If $\bar{\theta}$ did not cost anything, then—caused by the strict monotonicity of $U^i$—the consumer $i$ would like to have infinitely much of this portfolio.

LEMMA 1.1 (EQUIVALENCE OF NO-ARBITRAGE CONDITIONS)
*Under Assumption 1.5 SNAC and NAC are equivalent.*

PROOF 1.1

- *[SNAC $\rightarrow$ NAC] Assume that NAC is violated. Then, there is $\tilde{\theta} \in \mathbb{R}^J$ such that $q\,\tilde{\theta} \leq 0$ and $A\,\tilde{\theta} > 0$, i.e. especially $\begin{pmatrix} -q^T \\ A \end{pmatrix} \tilde{\theta} > 0$, which contradicts SNAC.*

- *[NAC $\rightarrow$ SNAC] Assume that SNAC is violated. Then, either there is a $\tilde{\theta} \in \mathbb{R}^J$ with $A\,\tilde{\theta} > 0$ and $q\,\tilde{\theta} \leq 0$ which contradicts NAC, or there is $\hat{\theta} \in \mathbb{R}^J$ with $A\,\hat{\theta} = 0$ and $q\,\hat{\theta} < 0$. Since $\bar{\theta} \in \mathbb{R}^J$ exists such that $A\,\bar{\theta} > 0$, there must be an $\varepsilon > 0$ such that for $\tilde{\theta} = \hat{\theta} + \varepsilon\,\bar{\theta}$ the inequalities*

$$A\,\tilde{\theta} = \underbrace{A\,\hat{\theta}}_{=0} + \varepsilon \underbrace{A\,\bar{\theta}}_{>0} > 0$$

*and*

$$q\,\tilde{\theta} = \underbrace{q\,\hat{\theta}}_{<0} + \varepsilon\, q\,\bar{\theta} \leq 0$$

*are fulfilled, again contradicting NAC.*

*q. e. d.*

## 4.3 Walras Law in the First Period

A nice consequence of Assumption 1.5 lies in the fact that all consumers with strictly monotonic preferences exploit today's budget.

LEMMA 1.2

*Under Assumption 1.1 and Assumption 1.5 a consumer exhausts today's budget, i.e. $q\,\theta = 0$.*

PROOF 1.2

*Assume the contrary: there is a consumer $i \in I$ who chooses a utility maximizing consumption plan $x^i \in \mathbb{B}\left(q, \omega^i, A\right)$, financed by the portfolio $\theta^i$, such that today's budget constraint is not fulfilled with equality, i.e.*

$$x^i = \arg\max_{x \in \mathbb{R}^S_+} U^i\left(x\right) \quad \textit{s.t.} \quad \exists\,\theta \in \mathbb{R}^J \quad \textit{with} \quad q\,\theta \leq 0 \quad \textit{and}$$
$$x_s = \omega^i_s + A_s\,\theta \quad \textit{for all} \quad s = 1, \ldots, S$$

*Suppose the solution to this maximization problem satisfies*

$$x^i = \omega^i + A\,\theta^i \quad \textit{with} \quad q\,\theta^i < 0$$

*Let $\bar{\theta}$ be such that $A\,\bar{\theta} > 0$. Because of Assumption 1.5 such a portfolio exists. Then $\hat{x}^i$, defined by*

$$\hat{x}^i = \omega^i + A\left(\theta^i + \varepsilon\,\bar{\theta}\right)$$

*is larger than $x^i$ $\left(\hat{x}^i > x^i\right)$, but also element of the budget set for $\varepsilon > 0$ small enough. Since $U^i$ is strictly monotonic, this is a contradiction to the maximizing property of $x^i$.*

*q. e. d.*

## 4.4 Fundamental Theorem of Asset Pricing

A fundamental theorem of linear algebra says that (NAC) is equivalent to the requirement that the asset price vector $q$ lies in the interior of the cone spanned by the rows of $A$, i.e.

$$\text{There is } \pi \in \mathbb{R}^S_{++} \text{ such that } q = A^T\,\pi. \quad \text{(cone)}$$

In Figure 4.4

$$A = \begin{pmatrix} 2 & 4 \\ 3 & 2 \end{pmatrix}$$

and hence for $q = (+1, -5)$ there are arbitrage opportunities. Take for example $\theta = (+5, -1)$. The set of arbitrage opportunities, denoted by the gray shaded area in the lower-right quadrant of Figure 4.4 is empty iff $q$ lies in the interior of the convex cone spanned by the rows of $A$. This fact and its relation to the agent's utility maximization problem are summarized in the following theorem.

THEOREM 1.1 (FUNDAMENTAL THEOREM OF ASSET PRICING. [MAGILL AND QUINZII, 1996]

*For a GEI-economy $\left\{\mathbb{R}^S, \left(U^i, \omega^i\right)_{i\in I}, A\right\}$, satisfying Assumption 1.1 and 1.5, the following conditions are equivalent:*

*(i) The consumer's decision problem*

$$\max U^i(x) \quad \textit{s.t.} \quad x \in \mathbb{B}\left(q, \omega^i, A\right)$$

*has a solution.*

*(ii) There are no arbitrage opportunities, i.e. NAC holds.*

*(iii) There is vector of state prices $\pi$ satisfying (Cone).*

*(iv) The consumer's budget set $\mathbb{B}\left(q, \omega^i, A\right)$ is compact.*

PROOF 1.3

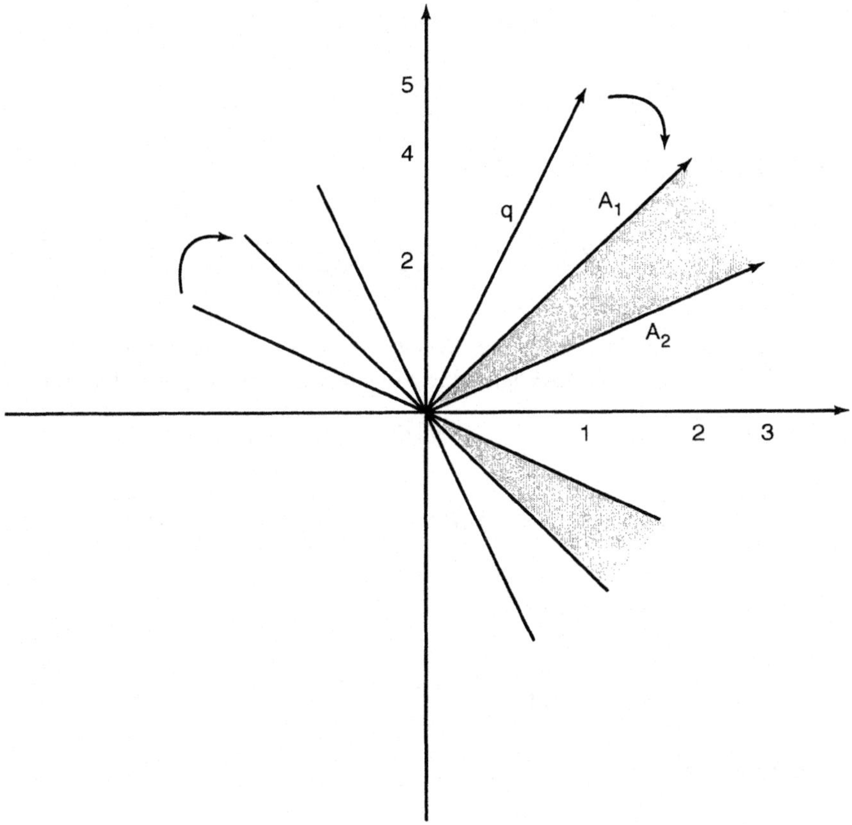


*Figure 1.4.* No-Arbitrage Condition

**(i) → (ii)** *Assume, there are arbitrage opportunities such that NAC does not hold, i.e., there is* $\tilde{\theta} \in \mathbb{R}^J$ *with* $q\,\tilde{\theta} \leq 0$ *and* $A\,\tilde{\theta} > 0$. *Let* $x^i$ *be the solution of the consumer's maximization problem:*

$$x^i = \arg\max_{x \in \mathbb{R}^S_+} U^i(x) \quad \textit{s.t.} \quad \exists\, \theta \in \mathbb{R}^J \quad \textit{with} \quad q \ldots \theta \leq 0 \quad \textit{and}$$

$$x_s = \omega^i_s + A_s\,\theta \quad \textit{for all} \quad s = 1, \ldots, S.$$

*Let* $\theta^i$ *be one financing portfolio, i.e.*

$$x^i_s = \omega^i_s + A_s\,\theta^i \quad \textit{for all} \quad s = 1, \ldots, S \quad .$$

*Since $A\tilde{\theta} > 0$, the consumption vector $\hat{x}^i$, defined by*

$$\hat{x}_s^i = \omega_s^i + A_s \left(\theta^i + \tilde{\theta}\right) \quad \text{for all} \quad s = 1, \ldots, S$$

*is larger than $x^i$ $(\hat{x}^i > x^i)$. Since*

$$q\left(\theta^i + \tilde{\theta}\right) = \underbrace{q\,\theta^i}_{\leq 0} + \underbrace{q\,\tilde{\theta}}_{\leq 0} \leq 0 \quad ,$$

*$\hat{x}^i$ is element of the budget set. But the strict monotonicity of $U^i$ implies $U^i(\hat{x}^i) > U^i(x^i)$, contradicting $x^i$ to be maximizer on the budget set.*

**(ii) → (iii)** *According to Lemma 1.1 NAC is equivalent to SNAC:*

$$\text{There is no } \theta \in \mathbb{R}^J \text{ such that } \begin{pmatrix} -q^T \\ A \end{pmatrix} \theta > 0. \qquad \text{(SNAC)}$$

*This condition is equivalent to*

$$\left\langle \begin{pmatrix} -q^T \\ A \end{pmatrix} \right\rangle \cap \mathbb{R}_+^{S+1} = \{0\}$$

*which implies*

$$\left\langle \begin{pmatrix} -q^T \\ A \end{pmatrix} \right\rangle \cap \Delta_+^{S+1} = \emptyset$$

*where*

$$\Delta_+^{S+1} = \left\{ y \in \mathbb{R}_+^{S+1} \middle| \quad y \cdot y = 1 \right\}$$

*is the non-negative simplex.*

$\left\langle \begin{pmatrix} -q^T \\ A \end{pmatrix} \right\rangle$ *is a closed, convex, non-empty set. $\Delta_+^{S+1}$ has the same properties and is even compact. Therefore, we can apply the following separation theorem.*

Lemma 1.3 (Minkowski-Farkas Separation Theorem) *Let $M_1, M_2$ be two convex, non-empty subsets of $\mathbb{R}^N$ such that $M_1 \cap M_2 = \emptyset$. If $M_1$ is closed and $M_2$ compact, then there is a $\hat{\pi} \in \mathbb{R}^N$ such that*

$$\sup_{v \in M_1} \hat{\pi}\, v < \inf_{v \in M_2} \hat{\pi}\, v$$

*With* $M_1 = \left\langle \begin{pmatrix} -q^T \\ A \end{pmatrix} \right\rangle$ *and* $M_2 = \Delta_+^{S+1}$, *there exists a* $\hat{\pi} \in \mathbb{R}^{S+1} \setminus \{0\}$ *such that*

$$\sup_{v \in \left\langle \begin{pmatrix} -q^T \\ A \end{pmatrix} \right\rangle} \hat{\pi}\, v < \inf_{v \in \Delta_+^{S+1}} \hat{\pi}\, v$$

$\hat{\pi}$ *is strictly positive, i.e.* $\hat{\pi} > 0$ . *Assume there is some* $\bar{s} \in \{0, \ldots, S\}$ *with* $\hat{\pi}_{\bar{s}} \leq 0$.[5] *The unit vector* $e_{\bar{s}}$ *is element of* $\Delta_+^{S+1}$. *Therefore*

$$\inf_{v \in \Delta_+^{S+1}} \hat{\pi}\, v \leq 0 \quad .$$

*But as* $0 \in \left\langle \begin{pmatrix} -q^T \\ A \end{pmatrix} \right\rangle$, *it follows on the other hand that*

$$\sup_{v \in \left\langle \begin{pmatrix} -q^T \\ A \end{pmatrix} \right\rangle} \hat{\pi} \geq 0 \quad ,$$

*which is a contradiction to the Separation Theorem.*

*It remains to show that for all* $v \in \left\langle \begin{pmatrix} -q^T \\ A \end{pmatrix} \right\rangle$ *it is* $\hat{\pi}\, v = 0$. *Assume there is a* $\bar{v} \in \left\langle \begin{pmatrix} -q^T \\ A \end{pmatrix} \right\rangle$ *such that* $\hat{\pi}\, \bar{v} \neq 0$, *i.e., without loss of generality* $\hat{\pi}\, \bar{v} > 0$. *Then,* $r\, \bar{v} \in \left\langle \begin{pmatrix} -q^T \\ A \end{pmatrix} \right\rangle$ *for all* $r \in \mathbb{R}_+$ *which implies*

$$sup_{v \in \left\langle \begin{pmatrix} -q^T \\ A \end{pmatrix} \right\rangle} \hat{\pi} v = \infty \quad ,$$

*contradicting the Separation Theorem because*

$$\inf_{v \in \Delta_+^{S+1}} \hat{\pi} v < \infty$$

[5]For notational convenience we label the components of $\hat{\pi}$ in this way.

*as $\Delta_+^{S+1}$ is compact. Therefore, $\hat{\pi}^T \begin{pmatrix} -q^T \\ A \end{pmatrix} = 0$, which is equivalent to*

$$q^T = \pi^T A$$

*where $\pi_s = \frac{1}{\hat{\pi}_0}\hat{\pi} \in \mathbb{R}^S_{++}$ for $s = 1, \ldots, S$.*

**(iii) → (iv)** *Let $\pi \in \mathbb{R}^S_{++}$ such that $q^T = \pi A$. Consider the budget set $\mathbb{B}(q, \omega^i, A)$:*

$$\begin{aligned}
\mathbb{B}(q,\omega^i,A) &= \Big\{x \in \mathbb{R}^S_+ \;\Big|\; \exists \theta \in \mathbb{R}^J \text{ with } q\theta \le 0 \\
&\qquad \wedge x_s \le \omega^i_s + A_s\theta \text{ for all } s = 1,\ldots,S\Big\} \\
&= \Big\{x \in \mathbb{R}^S_+ \;\Big|\; \exists \theta \in \mathbb{R}^J \text{ with } \pi A\theta \le 0 \\
&\qquad \wedge (x_s - \omega^i_s) = A_s\theta \text{ for all } s = 1,\ldots,S\Big\} \\
&= \Big\{x \in \mathbb{R}^S_+ \;\Big|\; \pi\,(x - \omega^i) \le 0 \\
&\qquad (x - \omega^i) \in \langle A \rangle \Big\}
\end{aligned}$$

*Obviously, the set $\mathbb{B}(q, \omega^i, A)$ is closed. If it is also a subset of a compact set, then we have finished since each closed subset of a compact set is compact. Look again at $\mathbb{B}(q, \omega^i, A)$:*

$$\begin{aligned}
\mathbb{B}\left(q,\omega^i,A\right) &= \left\{x \in \mathbb{R}^S_+ \middle| \pi\left(x - \omega^i\right) \le 0 \right. \\
&\qquad \left. \wedge \left(x - \omega^i\right) \in \langle A \rangle\right\} \\
&\subseteq \left\{x \in \mathbb{R}^S_+ \middle| \pi\left(x - \omega^i\right) \le 0\right\} .
\end{aligned}$$

*The last set is obviously an Arrow-Debreu budget set according to the price vector $\pi$. But the compactness of such a set is a well-known result.*

**(iv) → (i)** *According to Assumption C, $U^i$ is a continuous function on $\mathbb{R}^S_+$, i.e., especially on $\mathbb{B}^i(q, \omega^i, A)$. But a continuous function on a compact set is always taking its maximum.*

*q. e. d.*

This proof is adapted from the proof of the corresponding Magill and Quinzii [1996, Theorem 9.3] who do the proof for the special case of first period consumption.

## 4.5 Asset Pricing Theories

For an interpretation of the state prices it is useful to look at the case of first period consumption. Renumbering states we denote today's consumption by $s = 0$ and tomorrow's consumption by $s = 1, \ldots, S$. Therefore, the price of any asset $j$, $q^j$, is equal to the discounted sum of its future payoffs, where discount factors are given by $\hat{\pi}_s/\hat{\pi}_0$, $s = 1, \ldots, S$; i.e.

$$q^j = \sum_{s=1}^{S} \frac{\hat{\pi}_s}{\hat{\pi}_0} A_s^j \qquad \text{(LPR)}$$

Note that $\pi$ can be normalized such that $\sum_{s=1}^{S} \pi_s = 1$. Moreover, in the case of first period consumption if one of the assets $j = 2, \ldots, J$ is riskless, then $\pi_0$ can be interpreted as the reciprocal of that asset's price, i.e., as one plus the interest rate. With this in mind, asset prices satisfy the "martingale property", i.e., they are equal to the time-discounted expected future payoff, where expectations are taken with respect to the martingale measure $\pi_1, \ldots, \pi_S$. On the interpretation of this measure note that it depends on the equilibrium prices $\overset{*}{q}$, which in turn depend on all the characteristics of the economy. In particular, this measure does not need to have any link to objective probabilities of occurrence of the various states. Indeed, no such objective probabilities need to exist!

The correct interpretation of the martingale measure $\pi \in \mathbb{R}_{++}^{S+1}$ is that $\pi_s/\pi_0$ reflects the current-period price of one unit of account deliverable if state $s$ occurs. According to (LPR), it is the asset price of an elementary security called Arrow security[6] delivering one unit of account if state $s$ occurs; i.e., $\pi_s/\pi_0$ is the "state price" of state $s$.

The existence of an objective probability measure, say $\rho \in \mathbb{R}_{++}^{S}$ with $\sum_{s=1}^{S} \rho_s = 1$, allows a further interpretation of the linear pricing rule (LPR). On the definition of the covariance of two vectors in $\mathbb{R}^S$,

$$cov_\rho(x, y) = \mu_\rho(x \,\square\, y) - \mu_\rho(x)\,\mu_\rho(y)$$

where $\mu_\rho(z) = \sum_{s=1}^{S} \rho_s z_s$ for all $z \in \mathbb{R}^S$[7], Equation LPR can be rewritten in a risk-return style. Let $l$ be the $S$-vector $(\pi_1/\rho_1, \ldots, \pi_S/\rho_S)^T$. This vector is called the "likelihood ratio process", the "ideal security", or the "pricing portfolio". Then

[6] Compare Example 1.2.

[7] See the Glossary for a definition of $\square$.

$$\begin{aligned} q_j &= \frac{1}{\pi_0}\sum_{s=1}^{S} l_s\,\rho_s\,A_s^j \\ &= \frac{1}{\pi_0}\mu_\rho\left(l \,\square\, A^j\right) \\ &= \frac{1}{\pi_0}\left(cov_\rho\left(l, A^j\right) + \mu_\rho\left(l\right)\mu_\rho\left(A^j\right)\right) \\ &= \frac{1}{\pi_0}\left(cov_\rho(l, A^j) + \mu_\rho\left(A^j\right)\right) \end{aligned}$$

Hence, the price of an asset is equal to its discounted $\rho$-expected payoff adjusted by some risk premium. The risk premium is measured by the covariance of the asset's payoff with the pricing portfolio. Moreover, one can continue rewriting the no-arbitrage condition in an excess returns style. For this purpose let $\pi_0 = 1 + r$ where $r$ is the risk free rate. Then

$$q_j = \frac{1}{1+r}\left(cov_\rho(l, A^j) + \mu_\rho\left(A^j\right)\right)$$

which is equivalent to

$$1 + r = cov_\rho\left(l, \frac{A^j}{q^j}\right) + \mu_\rho\left(\frac{A^j}{q^j}\right)$$

which using the definition of returns $\gamma^j = \frac{A^j - q^j}{q^j}$ is equivalent to

$$\mu_\rho\left(\gamma^j\right) = r - cov_\rho\left(l, \gamma^j\right) \quad .$$

One way of reconciling the CAPM in the GEI-model is to show that in the CAPM the likelihood ratio process can be identified with the market portfolio. This follows trivially from the Tobin separation property and Mutual-Fund-Theorem (cf. Proposition 7.2 and 7.3 in Chapter 7). The first proposition shows that individual demand is in the span of $l$ and the riskless asset. The second proposition then shows that in equilibrium $l$ has to be the market portfolio.

## 4.6 No-Arbitrage Equilibrium Concept

Using Theorem 1.1 we can rewrite the agents decision problem to the following adjoint problem by which the model can equivalently be described[8].

[8] $\langle A \rangle$ denotes the column span of the matrix $A$.

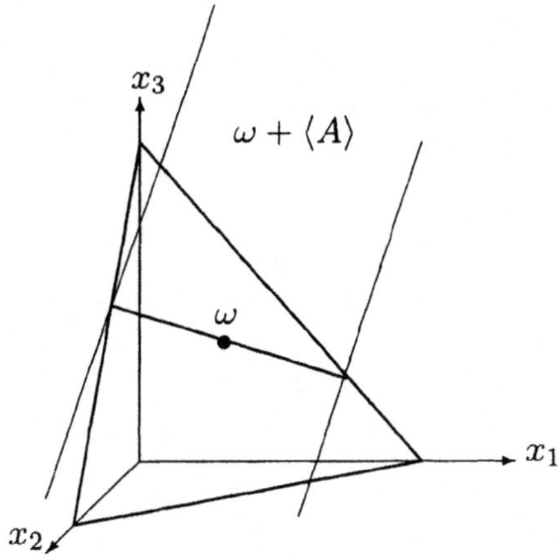


*Figure 1.5.* Budget set in Incomplete Markets

$$\max_{x \in \mathbb{R}^S_+} U^i(x)$$
$$\pi\, x \leq \pi\, \omega^i$$
$$\left(x - \omega^i\right) \in \langle A \rangle$$

Let $\mathbb{B}(\pi, \omega^i, A) := \left\{ x \in \mathbb{R}^S_+ \middle|\, \pi\, x \leq \pi\, \omega^i, (x - \omega^i) \in \langle A \rangle \right\}$ be the budget set restricted to $\langle A \rangle$. See Figure 4.6 for an illustration.
Then we can give

DEFINITION 1.9
*A No-arbitrage GEI* equilibrium is a vector of state prices $\bar{\pi} \in \mathbb{R}^S_{++}$, and an allocation of income $\bar{x} \in \mathbb{R}^{SI}_+$ such that*

*(i*)* $\bar{x}^i \in \mathbb{B}(\bar{\pi}, \omega^i, A) \quad i = 1, \ldots, I$

*(ii*)* $U^i(\tilde{x}^i) > U^i(\bar{x}^i)$ *then* $\tilde{x}^i \notin \mathbb{B}(\bar{\pi}, \omega^i, A) \quad i = 1, \ldots, I$

*(iv)* $\sum_i \bar{x}^i = \sum_i \omega^i$

Observe that $\mathbb{B}(\pi, \omega^i, A) = \mathbb{B}(\pi', \omega^i, A)$ if $A^T \pi = A^T \pi'$. This property is known as state price redundancy. The next proposition shows that the two descriptions are equivalent in a way made precise below. Look at the presentation of $\mathbb{B}(\pi, \omega^i, A)$. If $\langle A \rangle = \mathbb{R}^S$, then obviously the incomplete markets model is equivalent to the Arrow-Debreu model. Therefore, the following distinction is very decisive.

DEFINITION 1.10 (COMPLETE AND INCOMPLETE MARKETS)
*If the market subspace $\langle A \rangle$ has full dimension, i.e. $rank\ A = S$, then asset markets are said to be complete. If the transfer possibilities are limited, i.e. $rank A < S$, then financial markets are incomplete.*

The importance of the no-arbitrage equilibrium concept is the coincidence of its allocations with those of the financial markets equilibrium. This is implied by the following theorem.

PROPOSITION 1.1 (ALLOCATIONAL EQUIVALENCE)
*Let the GEI-economy $\left\{\mathbb{R}^S \left(U^i, \omega^i\right)_{i=1}^I, A\right\}$ satisfy the Assumptions 1.1 and 1.5. Then, the following equivalence holds:*

*(i) If $\left(\overset{*}{x}, \overset{*}{\theta}, \overset{*}{q}\right) \in \mathbb{R}_+^{S\times I} \times \mathbb{R}^{J\times I} \times \mathbb{R}^J$ is FM-equilibrium, then $(\overset{*}{x}, \overset{*}{\pi})$ is NA-equilibrium for some $\overset{*}{\pi} \in \mathbb{R}_{++}^S$. In particular, $\overset{*}{\pi}$ is such that $\overset{*}{q}^T = \overset{*}{\pi}^T \cdot A$.*

*(ii) If $(\overset{*}{x}, \overset{*}{\pi}) \in \mathbb{R}_+^{S\times I} \times \mathbb{R}_{++}^S$ is a NA-equilibrium, then there is a $\overset{*}{\theta} \in \mathbb{R}^{J\times I}$ and $\overset{*}{q} \in \mathbb{R}^J$ such that $\left(\overset{*}{x}, \overset{*}{\theta}, \overset{*}{q}\right)$ is a FM-equilibrium. Moreover, $\overset{*}{q}^T = \overset{*}{\pi}^T A$ for some $\overset{*}{\pi} \in \mathbb{R}_{++}^S$.*

PROOF 1.4

*(i) If $\left(\overset{*}{x}, \overset{*}{\theta}, \overset{*}{q}\right)$ is a FM-equilibrium, then $\overset{*}{x}^i$ maximizes $U^i$ on $\mathbb{B}\left(\overset{*}{q}, \omega^i, A\right)$ for all $i \in I$. According to Theorem 1.1 there exists $\overset{*}{\pi} \in \mathbb{R}_{++}^S$ such that $\overset{*}{q}^T = \overset{*}{\pi} A$ and $\mathbb{B}\left(\overset{*}{\pi}, \omega^i, A\right) = \mathbb{B}\left(\overset{*}{q}, \omega^i, A\right)$. Therefore, $\overset{*}{x}^i$ maximizes $U^i$ on $\mathbb{B}\left(\overset{*}{\pi}, \omega^i, A\right)$ for all $i = 1, \ldots, I$. The market clearing condition is obvious.*

*(ii) Take $\overset{*}{\pi} \in \mathbb{R}_{++}^S$. According to Theorem 1.1 one knows that for $\overset{*}{q}$ defined by $\overset{*}{q}^T := \overset{*}{\pi} \cdot A$ we have $\mathbb{B}^i\left(\overset{*}{\pi}, \omega^i, A\right) = \mathbb{B}^i\left(\overset{*}{q}, \omega^i, A\right)$. Since $\overset{*}{x}^i$ maximizes $U^i$ on $\mathbb{B}^i\left(\overset{*}{\pi}, \omega^i, A\right)$ for all $i \in I$, the same is true for $\mathbb{B}^i\left(\overset{*}{q}, \omega^i, A\right)$. As $\overset{*}{x}^i - \omega^i \in \langle A \rangle$, there is a $\overset{*}{\theta}^i \in \mathbb{R}^J$ such that $\overset{*}{x}^i - \omega^i = A\,\theta^i$ for $i = 2, \ldots, I$. Define $\overset{*}{\theta}^1 = -\sum_{i=2}^I \overset{*}{\theta}^i$. Then, the asset markets are cleared. For $i = 2, \ldots, I$ $\overset{*}{\theta}^i$ finances $\overset{*}{x}^i$.*

*But $\overset{*}{\theta}^1$ also finances $\overset{*}{x}^1$, since—because of goods market clearing—*

$$\begin{aligned}\overset{*}{x}^1 - \omega^1 &= -\sum_{i=2}^{I}\left(\overset{*}{x}^i - \omega^i\right) \\ &= -\sum_{i=2}^{I} A\overset{*}{\theta}^i \\ &= A\left(-\sum_{i=2}^{I}\overset{*}{\theta}^i\right) \\ &= A\overset{*}{\theta}^1\end{aligned}$$

*q. e. d.*

An *Arrow-Debreu economy* is a collection of agent characteristics $(U^i, \omega^i)$ defined on $\mathbb{R}^S_+$ together with a market structure consisting of contingent contracts for all commodities. Thus a Arrow-Debreu consumer solves

$$\max_{x \in \mathbb{R}^S_+} U^i(x) \quad \text{subject to} \quad px \leq p\omega^i$$

Let $B(p, \omega^i) := \left\{x \in \mathbb{R}^S_+ \middle| px \leq p\omega^i\right\}$ denote agent $i$'s Arrow-Debreu budget set.

DEFINITION 1.11
*An Arrow-Debreu equilibrium is a price vector $\bar{p} \in \mathbb{R}^S_{++}$ and an allocation $\bar{x} \in \mathbb{R}^{SI}_+$ such that*

- $\bar{x}^i$ *maximizes* $U^i(x^i) \in B(\bar{p}, \omega^i) \quad i = 1, \ldots, I$
- $\sum_i \bar{x}^i = \sum_i \omega^i.$

Obviously from Proposition 1.2 we get the important

COROLLARY 1.1
*If markets are complete, i.e. if rank $A = S$ then the Arrow-Debreu and the GEI model have the same equilibrium allocations. In the case of complete markets we summarize the characteristics of the economy as:*

$$GE = \left\{\left(\mathbb{R}^S, U^i, \omega^i\right)_{i \in I}\right\}$$

REMARK 1.3 (CASS TRICK)
*Even when markets are incomplete one can advance the notion of a No-arbitrage equilibrium one step further into the direction of an Arrow-Debreu Equilibrium.*

*Note that without loss of generality in the No-Arbitrage definition of a competitive equilibrium we can let one agent, say $i = 1$, be unconstrained by the asset structure. Obviously, when all other agents' excess demand are in the span of the market subspace, then in equilibrium also agent one has an excess demand that satisfies the spanning constraint. However the excess demand of agent 1 is a standard Arrow-Debreu excess demand that satisfies e.g. the standard boundary behaviour which for may cases is quite useful to know because it is inherited by market excess demand.*

## 5. Dual concepts of excess demand

[9] In this section we will briefly describe the linear algebra of the no-arbitrage condition.[10] This abstract approach drastically simplifies the exposition of the other sections.

Every portfolio $\theta \in \mathbb{R}^J$ generates a vector of income transfers $z := A\,\theta \in \mathbb{R}^S$. That is to say, the $S \times J$ Matrix $A$ defines a linear mapping $\mathcal{A}$ from $\mathbb{R}^J$ to $\mathbb{R}^S$. It will often be of interest to have the inverse relationship $z \mapsto \theta$ available. If $rank\, A = J$, $\mathcal{A}$ is injective, but as long as $J < S$ , $\mathcal{A}$ is not surjective. To $\mathcal{A}$ we can assign a bijective mapping $\tilde{\mathcal{A}} : \mathbb{R}^J \rightarrow \langle A \rangle$ given by $\tilde{\mathcal{A}}(\theta) := A\,\theta$. Thus $\mathcal{A}$ can be thought of as the composition of $\tilde{\mathcal{A}}$ and the embedding $\tau$ of $\langle A \rangle$ in $\mathbb{R}^S$. On the other hand to the quantity spaces just defined correspond the dual price spaces, i.e. the set of linear functionals $\mathbb{R}^{J^*}, \mathbb{R}^{S^*}$ on $\mathbb{R}^J$ and $\mathbb{R}^S$ respectively. Thus the matrix $A^T$ defines a linear mapping $\mathcal{A}^*$ from the space of state prices $\mathbb{R}^{S^*}$ to the space of asset prices $\mathbb{R}^{J^*}$ by $q := A^T\pi$. And again to this surjective but not injective mapping we can assign a bijective mapping $\tilde{\mathcal{A}}^*$ from a subspace of $\mathbb{R}^{S^*}$ to $\mathbb{R}^{J^*}$. To get this bijective mapping one has to define a space of state prices consisting of selections out of the equivalence classes formed by the preimage of q under $A^T$. One way to do this, is to project $\mathbb{R}^S$ onto the orthogonal complement of the nullspace of $A^T$ , $N\left(A^T\right)^{\perp}$. Thus $\mathcal{A}^*$ can be seen as the composition of the projection $\rho$ of $\mathbb{R}^{S^*}$ onto $N\left(A^T\right)^{\perp}$ and the bijective mapping $\tilde{\mathcal{A}}^* : N\left(A^T\right)^{\perp} \rightarrow \mathbb{R}^{J^*}$. Let $\tilde{\mathcal{A}}^{-1}, \tilde{\mathcal{A}}^{*^{-1}}$ denote the inverse of $\tilde{\mathcal{A}}$ respectively $\tilde{\mathcal{A}}^*$. The inverse mappings are given by the generalized inverse (or pseudoinverse) of the matrix $A$ respectively $A^T$, which will be denoted by $A^+$ resp. $\left(A^T\right)^+$.

The following properties of a generalized inverse will be very useful[11].

[9] For similar exposition see section 13 of Chapter 2 in Magill and Quinzii [1996].

[10] For a more detailed discussion see e.g. Murata [1977, Chapter 6] or Magill and Quinzii [1996].

[11] For a proof and discussions of this Lemma see e.g. Murata [1977].

LEMMA 1.4
*Let $A \in \mathbb{R}^{S\times J}$ with rank $A = J$ then $\tilde{A}^{-1} : \langle A\rangle \to \mathbb{R}^J$, $\tilde{A}^{-1}(z) := A^+z$ is a linear bijective mapping, furthermore $A^+ = \left(A^TA\right)^{-1} A^T$ and $(A^+)^T = \left(A^T\right)^+$.*

Let us now apply these linear algebra properties to our model. To do so, define for all $q \in Q$ the asset excess demand correspondence of agent $i$, $g^i : Q \to \mathbb{R}^J$, where $Q := \left\{q \in \mathbb{R}^J\right\}$ such that $q = A^T\pi$ for some $\pi \in \mathbb{R}^S_{++}$ by:

$$g^i(q) := \arg\max_{\theta\in\mathbb{R}^J} U^i\left(\omega^i + A\,\theta\right) \quad q\,\theta \leq 0 \quad \omega^i + A\,\theta \geq 0$$

Analogously for all $\pi \in \mathbb{R}^S_{++}$ define agent i's income excess demand correspondence $z^i : \mathbb{R}^S_{++} \to \mathbb{R}^S$ by

$$z^i(\pi) = \arg\max_{z\in\langle A\rangle} \quad U^i\left(\omega^i + z\right)$$
$$\pi\,z \leq 0$$
$$\omega^i + z \geq 0 \quad .$$

In the proof of Proposition 1.1 we in particular have shown

COROLLARY 1.2
*If rank $A = J$ then $z^i(\pi) = A\,g^i\left(A^T\pi\right)$ for all $\pi \in \mathbb{R}^S_{++}$ and $g^i(q) = A^+z^i\left({A^+}^T q\right)$ for all $q \in Q, i = 1,\ldots,I$ where $(A^+)$ is the generalized inverse of A [Murata, 1977].*

Corollary 1.2 shows that the following Diagram (figure 1.6) commutes.
In the diagram we used the fact that $\mathbb{R}^{J^*} = \mathbb{R}^J, \mathbb{R}^{S^*} = \mathbb{R}^S$ and $N\left(A^T\right)^\perp = \langle A\rangle$. In the next section, we will derive the properties of $g^i$ and thus those of $z^i$. In doing this, we will always use the excess demand approach that makes the particular property most transparent.

## 6. Pricing of Derivatives

One of the most important application of the GEI-model is to use it as a foundation for the pricing of derivatives. Derivative like options, warrants, structured product are assets with a pay off depending on the pay off of some underlying asset. In the case of a call option for example the pay off is the maximum of 0 and the difference of the pay off of the underlying to the exercise price of the option. Ever since Black and Scholes [1972] a whole industry has emerged that is concerned with the financial engineering and the pricing of derivatives. As we will see now, in the light of the GEI-model pricing of *redundant* derivatives is an easy exercise of comparative statics. The linear pricing rule outlined give the price at which the additional asset fits into the existing market equilibrium without changing the equilibrium allocation. This result is neat but also a bit disturbing. As Hakansson [1979] has emphasized, since the redundant asset does not change the existing equilibrium, from an allocational point of view the additional asset is clearly superfluous. In the other case however, when the additional asset is not redundant then in general it changes the equilibrium allocation and the equilibrium prices of the already existing assets so that as a consequence the price of the new asset cannot be determined by a simple linear relation from the prices of the existing assets that we observe before the innovation of the non-redundant asset. This dichotomy of asset pricing for into the case of redundant and non-redundant assets is one of the major puzzles of finance.

Consider first the introduction of redundant assets. In doing this it is especially helpful that $\pi$ allows to evaluate any payoff stream that is a linear combination of the payoffs of the given assets $j = 1, \ldots, J$. In particular, the price of a payoff stream in the market subspace must be a linear combination of the prices of the duplicating assets' prices, where the weights in the linear combination must be identical to the weights of the assets in the duplicating portfolio. That is to say, (Cone) is a linear pricing rule. Hence, knowing the prices of assets and shares which form a basis of the market subspace, then the price of any

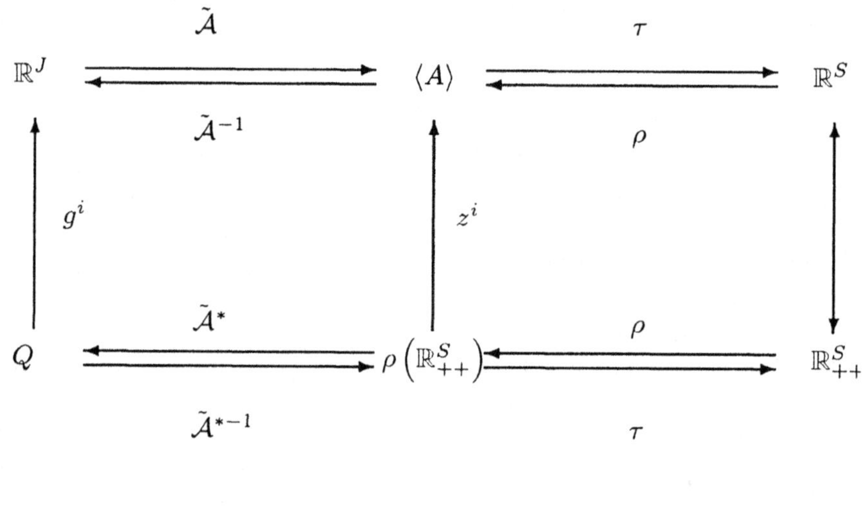


*Figure 1.6.* Duality of Excess Demand

payoff vector in the market subspace can be deduced, i.e., of any duplicable (redundant) asset. Thus knowledge of the prices of a basis of assets is sufficient for 'asset pricing', i.e., pricing redundant assets.

COROLLARY 1.3 *[Pricing of Redundant Assets]*
*Let $\left\{\mathbb{R}^S, (U^i,\omega^i)_{i=1}^I, A\right\}$ be a GEI-economy which satisfies Assumptions 1.1 and 1.5. If one of the assets is redundant, i.e. $A^k = \sum_{j\in J\setminus\{k\}} \alpha_j A^j$ for some $\alpha_j \in \mathbb{R}$, $j \in J\setminus\{k\}$, then in each FM-equilibrium asset prices $\overset{*}{q}$ fulfill*

$$\overset{*}{q}_k = \sum_{j\in J\setminus\{k\}} \alpha_j \overset{*}{q}_j \quad .$$

Assume $\left(\overset{*}{x},\overset{*}{\theta},\overset{*}{q}\right) \in \mathbb{R}_+^{S\times I} \times \mathbb{R}^{J\times I} \times \mathbb{R}^J$ is a FM-equilibrium for the GEI-economy where $A^1 = \sum_{j=2}^J \alpha_j A^j$ since without loss of generality it is $k = 1$. According to Theorem 1.1 equilibrium prices fulfill (Cone), i.e., there is $\pi \in \mathbb{R}_{++}^S$ such that $\overset{*}{q}^T = \overset{*}{\pi}\cdot A$ which implies $\overset{*}{q}_1 = \sum_{j=2}^J \alpha_j\, \overset{*}{\pi}\cdot A^j = \sum_{j=2}^J \alpha_j\, \overset{*}{q}_j$.

EXAMPLE 1.5 (PRICING OF A CALL OPTION)
*Let there be two states $s = 1, 2$ and three assets. The first asset, the underlying has a period 0 price $q$ which may either increase to $u\,q$ or decrease to $d\,q$. The second asset is a riskless bond whose period 0 price has been normalized to 1. Its payoff in the second period is thus $R = 1 + r$. It is assumed that $u > R > d > 0$. The task is to price a call option with exercise price $K$ written on the underlying. Suppose the call option is in the money only if state $s = 1$ occurs, i.e. $q\,u > K < q\,d$. Then it is easy to calculate that the portfolio $\alpha_1 = \frac{uq-K}{uq-dq}, \alpha_2 = \frac{(K-u\,q)d\,q}{(u\,q-d\,q)R}$ hedges the call option. Thus the price of the call option must be $q^c = \alpha_1 q + \alpha_2 = \frac{(u\,q-K)(R-d)}{(u-d)R}$. Equivalently one could have computed the state prices $\pi_1 = \frac{(R-d)}{(u-d)}, \pi_2 = \frac{(d-R)}{(u-d)}$. Which using $q^c = \frac{1}{R}\left(\pi_1\,(u\,q-K) + \pi_2\,0\right)$ gives the same value for the call option.*

The Corollary 1.3 is a consequence of the fact that introducing a redundant asset leaves the no-arbitrage equilibrium unaffected. Trading the new asset is unnecessary, and its price can be determined by the linear pricing rule. Corollary 1.3 has shown how easy redundant assets can be added to any GEI-economy. That is the reason why for the rest of this book we will assume that there are no redundant assets.

ASSUMPTION 1.6 *[Non-redundant Assets]*
*There are no redundant assets, i.e. $rank\, A = J$.*

Recently the pricing of non-redundant assets has achieved a lot of attention in the literature. See Elsinger and Summer [2000] for a nice survey in terms of the two periods GEI-model with finitely many states. In this literature one builds on the assumption that the underlying equilibrium prices do not change on the introduction of the new asset and then discusses various measures to price the additional asset. One point of view starts from the fact that the non-redundant asset cannot be perfectly hedged by the existing assets. Thus one may want to minimize the non-hedge able risk measured by some notions of risk. We will not go into this technically and conceptually quite difficult problem. We just present a simple example which shows that assuming the underlying price measure does not change may lead to serious miscalculations of the new assets' price. The following example demonstrates that the introduction of non-redundant assets leads to drastic changes of the equilibrium. The characteristics of the underlying economy are chosen in a way such that introducing a new asset completes the asset markets.

EXAMPLE 1.6 (PRICING OF NON-REDUNDANT ASSETS 2)
*Consider an economy which is described by the following characteristics. There are $I = 2$ consumers who can trade $J = 2$ assets paying off in $S = 3$ future states of the world. Their utility functions $U^i$ are of the Cobb-Douglas type:*

$$U^1(x) = \ln x_1 + \ln x_2$$

$$U^2(x) = \ln x_2 + \ln x_3$$

*Consumers' endowments are given by:*

$$\omega^1 = \begin{pmatrix} 0 \\ 1 \\ 2 \end{pmatrix}, \quad \omega^2 = \begin{pmatrix} 2 \\ 1 \\ 0 \end{pmatrix}$$

*The asset structure is described by the matrix*

$$A = \begin{pmatrix} 1 & 0 \\ 0 & 1 \\ 0 & 1 \end{pmatrix}$$

*i.e. there are two assets: an Arrow security for the first state and an asset which pays off the same amount in states $s = 2$ and $s = 3$.*[12]
*For incomplete markets the equilibrium allocations and the asset price vector are given by*

[12] Obviously, this economy does neither satisfy the strict monotonicity nor the strict quasi-concavity assumption. But this is only to simplify the computation of the equilibria. The example is robust in the sense that perturbing the utility function slightly in order to satisfy these assumptions would not change the qualitative features of the example.

$$\overset{*}{x}^1 = \begin{pmatrix} 2 \\ 1/2 \\ 3/2 \end{pmatrix}, \qquad \overset{*}{x}^2 = \begin{pmatrix} 0 \\ 3/2 \\ 1/2 \end{pmatrix},$$
$$\overset{*}{\theta}^1 = \begin{pmatrix} 2 \\ -1/2 \end{pmatrix}, \qquad \overset{*}{\theta}^2 = \begin{pmatrix} -2 \\ 1/2 \end{pmatrix},$$
$$\overset{*}{q} = \begin{pmatrix} 1 \\ 4 \end{pmatrix}$$

*Therefore, the relative price of asset* $1$ *to asset* $2$ *is* $\frac{1}{4}$.
*Now introduce an Arrow security for the third state so that markets are complete. Then the equilibrium allocation is given by the following vectors:*

$$\overset{*}{x}^1 = \begin{pmatrix} 2 \\ 1 \\ 0 \end{pmatrix}, \overset{*}{x}^2 = \begin{pmatrix} 0 \\ 1 \\ 2 \end{pmatrix}, \overset{*}{\pi} = \begin{pmatrix} 1 \\ 2 \\ 1 \end{pmatrix}$$

*Therefore, the relative price of asset* $1$ *to asset* $2$ *is*

$$\frac{\overset{*}{q}_1}{\overset{*}{q}_2} = \frac{\pi_1}{\pi_2 + \pi_3} = \frac{1}{3}$$

*Obviously, the relative prices for complete and incomplete markets differ. Incomplete markets guarantee a higher payoff for consumer* $1$ *than complete markets do, where both consumers receive the same utility. Moreover, note that the new equilibrium price vector is* $\overset{*}{q} = (1, 3, 1)$
*According to Föllmer and Sondermann [1986] non-redundant assets should be priced in the following way: project the new asset on the subspace* $\langle A \rangle$. *The projection vector is a linear combination of the 'old' assets. Combine the prices in the same way and you get a good idea for the new asset price.*
*The projection on the span of the matrix A is given by the linear mapping*

$$proj_A : a \mapsto \underbrace{A \left(A^T A\right)^{-1} A^T}_{=: A_{proj}} a$$

*In the example economy one gets*

$$A_{proj} = \frac{1}{2} \begin{pmatrix} 2 & 0 & 0 \\ 0 & 1 & 1 \\ 0 & 1 & 1 \end{pmatrix}$$

*If* $A^3 = \begin{pmatrix} 0 \\ 0 \\ 1 \end{pmatrix}$ *is the introduced asset, consider the projection*

$$proj_A\left(A^3\right) = A_{proj}\, A^3 = \frac{1}{2}\begin{pmatrix}0\\1\\1\end{pmatrix}$$

*Thus*

$$proj_A\left(A^3\right) = \frac{1}{2}A^2$$

*such that according to Föllmer and Sondermann [1986] the new asset price is*

$$q_3^{FS} = \frac{1}{2}\mathring{q}_2 = 2$$

*Hence the price vector according to the Föllmer-Sondermann calculation would be $q^{FS} = (1, 4, 2)$. The new asset would be priced at the double price of the first asset while in the new equilibrium it would actually have the same value as the first asset.*

The situation depicted in the preceding examples is the typical problem when a non-redundant asset is introduced. We finish this discussion with mentioning that in the very particular case of quadratic utilities however the innovation of any assets leaves the price of the existing assets unaffected.

PROPOSITION 1.2 ([OH, 1994])
*Suppose all agents have quadratic utilities $U^i(x) = \sum_s \rho_s x_s - \frac{\gamma^i}{2}\sum_s \rho_s (x_s)^2$ then in an interior financial market equilibrium the relative price of any asset $j$ to that of any asset $k$ is independent of the other assets pay offs.*

PROOF 1.5
*Consider the utility maximization problem of any agent $i$:*

$$\max_{\theta^i \in \mathbb{R}^J} \sum_{s=1}^{S} \rho_s \left(\omega_s^i + A_s\,\theta^i\right) - \frac{\gamma^i}{2}\sum_s^S \rho_s \left(\omega_s^i + A_s\,\theta^i\right)^2 \quad s.t. \quad q\,\theta^i \le 0 \quad .$$

*The first order condition for an interior maximum is:*

$$\frac{\sum_s \rho_s A_s^j - \gamma^i \sum_s^S \rho_s \left(\omega_s^i + A_s\,\theta^i\right) A_s^j}{\sum_s \rho_s A_s^k - \gamma^i \sum_s^S \rho_s \left(\omega_s^i + A_s\,\theta^i\right) A_s^k} = \frac{q^j}{q^k} \quad .$$

*which is equivalent to:*

$$\sum_s \rho_s A_s^j - \gamma^i \sum_s^S \rho_s \left(\omega_s^i + A_s\,\theta^i\right) A_s^j$$

$$= \frac{q^j}{q^k}\sum_s \rho_s A_s^k - \gamma^i \sum_s^S \rho_s \left(\omega_s^i + A_s\,\theta^i\right) A_s^k \quad .$$

*dividing both sides of this equation by $\gamma^i$ and adding over all agents leads to:*

$$\sum_i \left( \frac{1}{\gamma^i} \sum_s \rho_s A_s^j - \sum_s^S \rho_s \left( \omega_s^i + A_s \theta^i \right) A_s^j \right)$$
$$= \frac{q^j}{q^k} \left( \sum_i \frac{1}{\gamma^i} \sum_s \rho_s A_s^k - \sum_s^S \rho_s \left( \omega_s^i + A_s \theta^i \right) A_s^k \right) .$$

*which using the equilibrium definition $\sum_i \theta^i = 0$ and the definitions $\sum_i \frac{1}{\gamma^i} = \gamma^{-1}$ for the harmonic mean of the agents risk aversion parameters and $\omega = \sum_i \omega^i$ for the market portfolio yields:*

$$\frac{q^j}{q^k} = \frac{\sum_s \left(\gamma^{-1} - \omega_s\right) \rho_s A_s^j}{\sum_s \left(\gamma^{-1} - \omega_s\right) \rho_s A_s^k} .$$

*Hence the relative asset price of any two assets does not depend on the pay off of any other asset.*

## 7. Efficiency of GEI-equilibria

Even though the main focus of this book is on the positive aspects of the GEI-model, before finishing the description of the economic fundamentals we would like to mention the normative properties. It will be shown that GEI-equilibria are not Pareto-efficient unless the set of alternative allocations is restricted to the incomplete asset markets. That is to say GEI-equilibria are constrained Pareto-efficient. This fact will then be used in Chapter 6 to derive new results on the uniqueness of GEI-equiliria. We begin with some standard definitions:

DEFINITION 1.12 (ATTAINABLE ALLOCATION)
*An allocation $x \in \mathbb{R}^{SI}$ is attainable, if $x \geq 0$ and $\sum_{i=1}^I x^i \leq \sum_{i=1}^I \omega^i$.*

DEFINITION 1.13 (PARETO-EFFICIENCY)
*An attainable allocation x is Pareto-efficient, if there is no other attainable allocation $\hat{x}$ with $U^i\left(\hat{x}^i\right) \geq U^i\left(x^i\right)$, i=1,...,I, and $\exists\, j \in \{1, \ldots, I\}$ with $U^j\left(\hat{x}^j\right) > U^j\left(x^j\right)$.*

It is not surprising that when markets are incomplete Pareto-efficiency can in general not be achieved. Intuitively this is because an incomplete set of markets does not suffice to equalize all marginal rates of consumption among agents. Indeed, one can show that generically the agents utility functions have gradients that are pairwise non parallel to each other. For a derivation of this result see Magill and Quinzii [1996][Chapter 2]. Yet, with an appropriate restriction of the set of attainable allocations a weaker form of Pareto-efficiency can be obtained.

DEFINITION 1.14 (CONSTRAINED ATTAINABILITY)
*An allocation $x \in \mathbb{R}^{SI}$ is constrained attainable if*

- $x \geq 0$
- $\sum_{i=1}^{I} x^i \leq \sum_{i=1}^{I} \omega^i$
- $(x^i - \omega^i) \in \langle A \rangle\,, \quad i=1,\ldots,I$

DEFINITION 1.15 (CONSTRAINED PARETO-EFFICIENCY)
*An allocation x is constrained Pareto-efficient, if is constrained attainable and there is no other constrained attainable allocation $\hat{x}$ such that $U^i\left(\hat{x}^i\right) \geq U^i\left(x^i\right) \forall i = 1,\ldots,I$ and $\exists\, j \in \{1,\ldots,I\}$ mit $U^j\left(\hat{x}^j\right) > U^j\left(x^j\right)$.*

Now we are in a position to prove a version of the first welfare theorem adapted to incomplete markets:

THEOREM 1.2 (FIRST WELFARE THEOREM)
*Let GEI = $\left(\mathbb{R}^S, \left(U^i, \omega^i\right)_{i=1}^I, A\right)$ with $A\,\theta > 0$ some $\theta$ and $U^i$ strictly monotone, $i = 1,\ldots,I$, and such that there exist a portfolio $\bar{\theta}$ with $A\bar{\theta} > 0$. If $\left(\overset{*}{q}, \overset{*}{x}, \overset{*}{\theta}\right)$ is a financial market equilibrium then its allocation $\overset{*}{x}$ is constrained Pareto-efficient.*

PROOF 1.6
*Let $\overset{*}{x}$ be a financial market equilibrium allocation. Suppose there is an alternative constrained attainable allocation $\hat{x} \in \mathbb{R}_+^{SI}$ such that $\sum_{i=1}^I \hat{x}^i \leq \sum_{i=1}^I \omega^i$, $\left(\hat{x}^i - \omega^i\right) \in \langle A \rangle\ \forall\, i$ and $U^i\left(\hat{x}^i\right) \geq U^i\left(\overset{*}{x}{}^i\right)\ \forall\, i$ and $U^j\left(\hat{x}^j\right) > U^j\left(\overset{*}{x}{}^j\right)$ for some $j$.*
*Let $\hat{\theta}^i$ be such that $\hat{x}^i - \omega^i = A\,\hat{\theta}^i$ (this is well defined because $\hat{x}^i - \omega^i \in \langle A \rangle$). Then summing over agents we get*

$$A \sum_{i=1}^{I} \hat{\theta}^i = \sum_{i=1}^{I} \left(\hat{x}^i - \omega^i\right) \leq 0$$

$$\underset{\substack{No\\Arbitrage}}{\Rightarrow} \quad \overset{*}{q} \sum_{i=1}^{I} \hat{\theta}^i \leq 0$$

*From*

$$U^j\left(\hat{x}^j\right) > U^j\left(\overset{*}{x}{}^j\right) \quad \Rightarrow \quad \hat{x}^j \notin \mathcal{B}^i\left(\overset{*}{q}, \omega^i, A\right)$$
$$= \left\{x \in \mathbb{R}_+^S \,\middle|\, \exists \theta \in \mathbb{R}^J \quad \textit{with} \quad \overset{*}{q}\theta \leq 0 \textit{ and } x \leq \omega^i + A\theta \right\} \quad .$$

*Recall that $\hat{\theta}$ was defined such that $\hat{x}^i - \omega^i = A\hat{\theta}$. Hence the budget restriction in $t = 0$ must be violated:*

$$\overset{*}{q}\hat{\theta}^j > 0.$$

*Moreover,*

$$\overset{*}{q}\hat{\theta}^i \geq 0 \quad \forall i.$$

*Otherwise, for some $i$, $\overset{*}{q}\left(\hat{\theta}^i + \varepsilon\,\bar{\theta}\right) \leq 0$ for $\varepsilon > 0$ small enough and $\omega^i + A(\hat{\theta}^i + \varepsilon\bar{\theta}) >> \hat{x}^i$ which by strict monotonicity of $U^i$ is a contradiction to the optimality of $\hat{x}^i$. This implies that*

$$\underbrace{\overset{*}{q}\sum_{i=1}^{I}\hat{\theta}^i}_{\leq 0} > 0,$$

*which is a contradiction!*

*q. e. d.*

# Chapter 2

# EXISTENCE OF EQUILIBRIA

Demonstrating the existence of competitive equilibria is the first and most fundamental check whether a model based on the notion of a competitive equilibrium is well defined. One would like to be able to do this for the most general assumptions. There are various ways how to proceed in proving the existence of competitive equilibria. In this book we follow the so called *excess demand approach*. See Debreu [1982] for a survey of approaches to prove existence of competitive equilibria. The excess demand approach is interesting in itself since it is based on deriving properties of excess demand that are useful also for more elaborate questions like uniqueness of equilibria. To get the idea of the existence theorem consider the graph of an excess demand as depicted in Figure 2.1. Suppose there are just two commodities so that a zero excess demand of the commodity considered in this graph is by Walras Law already a competitive euqilibrium. Now suppose that the graph is continuous and that it satisfies the boundary behavior. Then from the intermediate value theorem there exists an equilibrium. In this chapter we show how this idea can be made more general and more precise also. The discussion begins with a series of examples which show that, if markets are incomplete, the standard Walrasian assumptions on the agents' characteristics are no longer sufficient to guarantee Walras Law, Continuity or Boundary behavior of excess demand. That is to say, even if we assume that utility functions are continuous and strictly monotone and that individual endowment vectors are non-negative and non-zero (while aggregate endowments are strictly positive), even then competitive equilibria need not exist when markets are incomplete. In particular the lack of existence of equilibria arises from the fact that agents' endowments lie in the boundary of their consumption set. As long as markets are complete boundary endowments do not raise any serious problems because if an agent has positive income in some state then this is already sufficient to guarantee that his demand is contin-

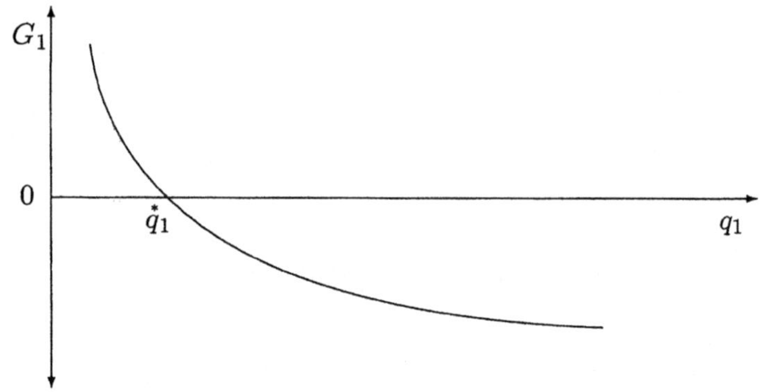


*Figure 2.1.* Asset Excess Demand

uous. At any arbitrage free prices he will be able to offer some Arrow security. However when markets are incomplete the agent might not be able to transfer wealth out of the states with positive income because this may require him to deliver wealth in states where his endowment is zero. Imagine for example some agent endowed with a claim to some plot of land where with some chance oil could be found. If this agent is pretty poor otherwise and if there is no Arrow security for the state in which the oil is found on the plot of land then for some prices this agent may not be able to trade while for other prices his trading opportunities suddenly increase. Hence the agents' demand is discontinuous.

## 1. Assumptions to obtain Existence

We will work under the strict monotonicity, continuity and strict quasi-concavity assumptions taken from the Arrow-Debreu Model as they have been given in the previous chapter: Assumption 1.1. Under these assumption the existence of Walrasian equilibria follows provided that total endowments are strictly positive. See for example Hildenbrand and Kirman [1988]. In order to be able to refer to the Arrow-Debreu assumption on endowments we give:

ASSUMPTION 2.1 (ENDOWMENTS)
*The collection of individual endwoments $(\omega^i)_{i \in I}$ satisfies: $\omega^i \geq 0$ for all $i \in I$ and $\sum_{i \in I} \omega^i >> 0$.*

As we will argue now the assumptions of the Arrow-Debreu-Model are however not sufficient to prove existence when markets are incomplete.
Assuming monotonicity ensures that one is able to work in the reduced form given by the second definition of the financial market equilibrium, Definition 1.7, outlined in the previous chapter. Yet the first example shows that nevertheless the budget identity $(q\, g^i\,(q) = 0 \quad \text{for all} \quad q \in Q)$ does not necessarily hold.

EXAMPLE 2.1
*Let* $S = 2, A = \begin{pmatrix} 1 \\ -1 \end{pmatrix}$. *Consider the budget set for* $q = 1, \mathbb{B}(1, w^1, A) = \{\theta \in \mathbb{R} | \theta \leq 0 \wedge w_1^1 + \theta \geq 0 \wedge w_2^1 - \theta \geq 0\}$. *Now for* $U^1(x) = \sqrt{x_1} + \sqrt{x_2}$ *and* $w^1 = (3, 1), \theta = -1$ *is the agent's best choice. Thus* $g^1$ *does not satisfy the budget identity.*

The problem with the asset structure of Example 2.1 is that even with zero asset prices, there are no arbitrage opportunities. Furthermore, including zero asset prices into the domain of $g^i$, we cannot avoid that asset demand changes discontinuously, if asset prices cross zero. This is because at $q = 0$ the budget correspondence $\mathbb{B}(q, \omega^i, A)$ is not necessarily lower hemi-continuous (abbreviated: l.h.c.). See Appendix A for a definition of l.h.c..

EXAMPLE 2.1 (CONTINUED)
*Let* $q^n < 0$ *converge to zero. Then* $\mathbb{B}(q^n, w, A) = [0, w_2]$. *But* $\mathbb{B}(0, w, A) = [-w_1, w_2]$. *Hence* $\mathbb{B}(q, w, A)$ *is not l.h.c. at* $q = 0$.
Given the experience with Example 2.1 it should not be surprising that for asset structures which do not even potentially allow for arbitrage, one can construct robust economies without equilibria. A similar example, however with two assets and four states can be found in Polemarchakis and Siconolfi [1991]. Moreover, in their example there do not exist equilibria, even if one forces agents to satisfy their budget restrictions with equality.

EXAMPLE 2.1 (CONTINUED)
*The asset excess demand of agent 1 is*

$$g^1(q) = \begin{cases} 0 & q < 0 \\ -1 & q \geq 0 \end{cases} .$$

*Now introduce a second agent with the same utility function but with endowments* $w^2 = (1, 5)$. *This agent's excess demand is*

$$g^2(q) = \begin{cases} 2 & q \leq 0 \\ 0 & q > 0 \end{cases} .$$

*Thus for no* $q \in \mathbb{R}^J$ *asset markets clear.*
To restore the budget identity we therefore recall from Chapter 1 the Assumption 1.5 which states that with zero asset prices there exist arbitrage opportunities, i.e. $\exists \theta : A\theta > 0$. Imposing this assumption rules out discontinuities of the budget correspondence caused by zero asset prices are out of our concern.

The next problem that arises with incomplete markets is that even with strictly positive asset prices, the budget correspondence is not necessarily l.h.c., as Example 2.2 shows:

EXAMPLE 2.2
*There are three states $S = 3$, two consumers, $I = 2$ and two assets, $J = 2$. Asset payoffs are*

$$A = \begin{pmatrix} 1 & 0 \\ 1 & 1 \\ 0 & 1 \end{pmatrix} .$$

*There are two agents with endowments,*

$$\omega^{1^T} = (1 \quad 1 \quad 1) \quad \text{and} \quad \omega^{2^T} = (1 \quad 0 \quad a) \quad (\text{where} \quad a < 1)$$

*respectively. The agents have the same utility function $u(x) = \sqrt{x_1} + \sqrt{x_2} + \sqrt{x_3}$. Clearly, Assumptions 1.1 and 1.5 are satisfied and $\omega^1 \gg 0$ ensures that the Condition 2.3 stated below holds which will be essential in the next example. However, it cannot be ensured in this example that demand is continuous for all interior asset prices because the second agents' endowments are in the boundary of his consumption set and hence with incomplete markets for $q = 1/2$ his budget set has an empty interior.*

In this case too an equilibrium does not exist. It is convenient here to normalize prices on the simplex and to write agents' demand, $g^i(0)$ as a function of one of the two prices, say $q_1$. For $q_1 = \frac{1}{2}$, $g_1^1(q_1) = 0$ whereas $g_1^2(q_1) < 0$. Thus $q_1 = \frac{1}{2}$ cannot be an equilibrium. From the non negativity constraint $\omega^2 + A\,g^2 \geq 0$ we see that $g_1^2(q_1) \geq 0$ for $q_1 < \frac{1}{2}$ and $g_1^2(q_1) \leq 0$ for $q_1 > \frac{1}{2}$. Consider the first order condition for an interior optimum of agent 1's maximization problem. Since $\omega^1 \gg 0$ and marginal utility at the boundary is infinite, (2.1) is indeed necessary for a solution.

$$\frac{1 - q_1}{\sqrt{(1 - q_1)(1 + \theta_1^1)}} + \frac{1 - 2\,q_1}{\sqrt{(1 - q_1) + (1 - 2\,q_1)\,\theta_1^1}} = \frac{q_1}{\sqrt{1 - q_1 - q_1\,\theta_1^1}} \tag{2.1}$$

From (2.1) we see that $\left.\frac{dg_1^1}{dq_1}\right|_{q_1 = \frac{1}{2}} < 0$. Hence for $q_1 < \frac{1}{2}$, in a neighborhood of $q_1 = \frac{1}{2}$ we have $g_1^1(q_1) > 0$. But for an equilibrium to exist for $q_1 < \frac{1}{2}$ we need $g_1^1(q_1) \leq 0$ (since $\forall\, q_1 \leq \frac{1}{2} g_1^2(q_1) \geq 0$). Thus by continuity of demand we must be able to find a price $q_1^* < \frac{1}{2}$ such that $g_1^1(q_1^*) = 0$ . However, from (2.1) we see that $g_1^1(q_1) = 0$ only for $q_1 = \frac{1}{2}$. A perfectly symmetric argument applies for $q_1 > \frac{1}{2}$, completing then the argument.

q. e. d.

We learn from this example that with incomplete markets it is harder to guarantee that in the agents' budget sets there are points that are cheaper than the value of their endowments. This is the so called cheaper point assumption which we need to impose in the following form:

ASSUMPTION 2.2 (CHEAPER POINT ASSUMPTION (C.P.A.))

$$\forall i \in I, \forall q \in Q, \mathring{\mathbb{B}}_0 \left(q, \omega^i, A\right) \neq \emptyset$$
$$\textit{where} \quad \mathring{\mathbb{B}}_0 \left(q, \omega^i, A\right) = \left\{\theta \in \mathbb{R}^J \middle| \, q\,\theta < 0 \quad \textit{and} \quad \omega^i + A\,\theta \geq 0\right\}.$$

In the Section 3 we show that this assumption does indeed guarantee continuity of excess demand. Moreover, in the next section we discuss which restrictions on the distribution of endowments and the asset structure are sufficient to obtain this assumption. Yet one more problem arises:

EXAMPLE 2.3
*There are three states of the world, one commodity, two consumers and two assets. The assets' payoffs are given by*

$$A = \begin{pmatrix} 1 & 1 \\ 1 & 2 \\ 1 & 1 \end{pmatrix} \quad .$$

*The two consumers have endowments*

$$\omega^{1^T} = (1 \quad 1 \quad 0) \quad \textit{and} \quad \omega^{2^T} = (0 \quad 1 \quad 1) \quad .$$

*They have the same utility function* $u^i(x) = \sqrt{x_1} + \sqrt{x_2} + \sqrt{x_3}, \quad i = 1, 2.$

Let $g^i : Q \to \mathbb{R}^2$ be agent $i$'s asset demand function. From the symmetry of the example we see that $g^1(q) = g^2(q)$ for all $q \in Q$.
Note that Assumptions 1.1, 2.2 and 1.5 hold. But still this economy has no equilibrium (as it lacks the needed boundary behavior). To see this observe that for all $q \in Q$ there is $\theta \in \mathbb{B}_0(q, \omega^2, A)$ such that the resulting consumption plan $\omega^2 + A\theta$ is strictly positive and this is strictly preferred to $\omega^2$. Hence aggregate excess demand $\sum_i g^i(q) = 2g^2(q) \neq 0$ for all $q \in Q$
The problem that arises in this example is that for prices in the boundary of the no-arbitrage price set both agents' budget sets may have an empty interior: Note that at $\bar{q} = (1, 1) \in \partial Q, \mathring{\mathbb{B}}_0(\bar{q}, \omega^i, A) = \emptyset \quad i = 1, 2$. Having strictly positive aggregate endowments is definitely not sufficient for this. We need to impose the so called boundary behavior assumption:

ASSUMPTION 2.3 (BOUNDARY BEHAVIOR ASSUMPTION (B.B.A.))

$$\forall q \in \bar{Q} \setminus \{0\} \, \exists i : \mathring{\mathbb{B}}_0 \left(q, \omega^i, A\right) \neq \emptyset$$
$$\textit{where} \quad \mathring{\mathbb{B}}_0 \left(q, \omega^i, A\right) = \left\{ \theta \in \mathbb{R}^J \middle| \, q\,\theta < 0 \quad \textit{and} \quad \omega^i + A\,\theta \geq 0 \right\}.$$

In Section 3 we show that this assumption does indeed guarantee that excess demand has a proper boundary behavior, i.e. that as prices tend to the boundary the norm of excess demand tends to infinity. Moreover, in the next section we discuss which restrictions on the distribution of endowments and the asset structure are sufficient to obtain this assumption.

## 2. Discussion of the Assumptions

As the examples in the previous section have shown, boundary endowments, giving rise to zero income in some states, may generate an empty interior of the agents' budget set when markets are incomplete and thus may cause a lack of existence of competitive equilibria. To prevent this from happening, we imposed two additional Assumptions, 2.2 and 2.3, whose implications are discussed in this section.

### 2.1 Cheaper Point Assumption

In discussing the Cheaper Point Assumption 2.2, it is interesting to compare it with a standard assumption often used in proving existence of competitive equilibria, the resource relatedness assumption, r.r.a. which goes back to McKenzie [1959]. The usefulness of this assumptions is in proving existence of competitive equilibria via the existence of quasi-equilibria. A quasi-equilibrium is aa equilibrium in which instead of utility maximzation the agents only satisfy expenditure minimization, i.e. for the chosen allocation there is no other allocation with the same utility that needs less expenditure. As a final step one then needs to ensure that at the obtained prices all agents have positive wealth. Since aggregate endwoments are strictly positive and since the price vector is non-negative and non-zero, at least on agent has positive wealth. If then all other agents are resource related to this agent, i.e. if they do have resources that the agent with positive wealth would like, then at those prices all agents must have positive wealth. In an incomplete market framework this assumption can be phrased as follows:

ASSUMPTION 2.4 (RESSOURCE RELATEDNESS ASSUMPTION (R.R.A.)) $\forall \, \{I_1, I_2\}, I_1 \cap I_2 = \emptyset, I_1 \cup I_2 = I, \forall \, (x^i)_{i \in I} \in \mathbb{R}_+^{SI}$, *such that:*

$$\sum_{i \in I} x^i = \sum_{i \in I} \omega^i \quad \textit{and} \quad \left(x^i_s - \omega^i_s\right)_{s=1,\ldots,S} \in \langle A \rangle \quad \forall \, i \in I\,,$$

*$\exists\, y \in \mathbb{R}^{SI}$ such that:*

$$\sum_{i \in I} y^i = 0 \quad \text{and} \quad y^i_s, s = 1, \ldots, S \in \langle A \rangle, \omega^i + y^i \geq 0 \quad \forall i \in I_1$$

*and*

$$U^i\left(x^i + y^i\right) \geq U^i\left(x^i\right) \quad \forall i \in I_2 \quad ,$$

*the inequality being strict for some $i \in I_2$.*

To compare the c.p.a. with the resource relatedness assumption it is useful to recall from Chapter 1 that the agents' maximization problem, can be equivalently written (using the no arbitrage condition), as follows:

$$\left(M^i_z\right) \max_z U^i\left(\omega^i + z\right)$$
$$s.t. \quad z \in \hat{\mathbb{B}}_0\left(\pi, \omega^i, A\right) := \left\{ z \in \mathbb{R}^S \middle| \, \pi\, z \leq 0 \wedge z \in \langle A \rangle \wedge \omega^i + z \geq 0 \right\}$$

The portfolios in

$$\mathring{\mathbb{B}}_0\left(\pi, \omega^i, A\right) := \left\{ z \in \mathbb{R}^S \middle| \, \pi\, z \leq 0 \wedge z \in \langle A \rangle \wedge \omega^i + z \geq 0 \right\}$$

are in a one to one correspondence with the non-negative demand vectors $x$ that are attainable using the asset structure and cheaper than the endowments (i.e. such that $x - \omega^i$ is $\in \mathring{\mathbb{B}}_0\left(\pi, \omega^i, A\right)$). Therefore we can call either of those the "set of cheaper points".

Consider then the following pair of linear programs:

$$\begin{array}{cc} (P^i) & (D^i) \\ \min_\theta \, q\,\theta & \max_{\pi \geq 0} \, -\pi\,\omega^i \\ \omega^i + A\,\theta \geq 0 & A^T \pi = q \end{array}$$

Given $\left((\omega^i)_{i \in I}, A\right)$ the cheaper point assumption is satisfied iff $\left(v^{i^*}\right)$, the value of the objective function of the primal program $(P^i)$ or equivalently of the dual program $(D^i)$ at the optimum, is negative for all $q \in Q$ and for all $i$.

We will need a further piece of notation. The endowment $\omega^i$ of each agent $i$ defines a partition of the rows of $A$ into the two submatrices $A^{i0}$ and $A^{i+}$, where $A^{i0}$ $(A^{i+})$ is composed of the rows of $A$ corresponding to states $s$ in which $\omega^i_s = 0 \quad (\omega^i_s > 0)$. Any S-dimensional vector $x \in \mathbb{R}^S$ can also be decomposed in the same way (up to a permutation of its elements): $x = \left[x_{[i0]}, x_{[i+]}\right]$.

PROPOSITION 2.1
*The cheaper point assumption holds iff:*

$$\forall i, \exists \theta : \quad A^{i+}\theta < 0 \; \wedge A^{i0}\,\theta = 0 \quad . \tag{2.2}$$

PROOF 2.1 ((2.2) $\Rightarrow$ C.P.A.)
*We show first that c.p.a. can be rewritten as follows:*

$$\forall i, \forall \pi \gg 0 \exists \theta : \pi\, A\,\theta < 0 \wedge \; A^{i0}\,\theta \geq 0 \quad . \tag{2.3}$$

*It is obvious that c.p.a. implies* (2.3). *On the other hand, if in* (2.3) $\theta$ *is replaced with* $\epsilon\,\theta$, *for any* $\epsilon > 0$, *the inequalities in* (2.3) *still hold. Since we can always find* $\epsilon > 0$ *such that* $\omega^i_{[i+]} + A^{i+}\,\theta\,\epsilon \geq 0$, *c.p.a. also holds.*
*The remaining part of the argument is immediate:*
*by* (2.2) *there is* $\theta$ *such that* $A^{i+}\,\theta < 0$ *and* $A^{i0}\,\theta = 0$, *so that* $\pi\, A\,\theta < 0 \quad \forall \pi \gg 0$. *This implies that* (2.3) *holds, and so does c.p.a.*
(2.2) $\Leftarrow$ *c.p.a. :*
*Here we will proceed by contradiction. Suppose* (2.2) *does not hold, i.e.:*

$$\exists i : \forall \theta\, A^{i+}\,\theta < 0 \Rightarrow A^{i0}\,\theta \neq 0$$

*From this follows:* $A\,\theta < 0 \Rightarrow A^{i0}\,\theta < 0$.
*Thus* $\hat{q} = \pi_{[i0]}A^{i0}$, *with* $\pi_{[i0]} \gg 0$, *is a no arbitrage asset price* ($\hat{q} \in Q$), *and for* $q = \hat{q}\, v^{i^*} = 0$, *i.e. c.p.a. does not hold, a contradiction.*

*q. e. d.*

The above result has a neat geometric interpretation. As is well known, the closure $\bar{Q}$ of the set of no arbitrage prices is a polyhedral cone, of dimension $J$, and under Assumption 1.5 $\bar{Q} \subset \mathbb{R}^J$. Let $H$ be a supporting hyperplane of the closed and convex set $\bar{Q}$; $H \cap \bar{Q}$ defines a face of $\bar{Q}$ (see McMullen and Shepherd [1971]). Condition (2.2) in Proposition 2.1 says that all the rows of $A$ associated with the states in which agent $i$ has zero income must lie on a single face (itself a polyhedral cone of dimension at most $J - 1$) of $\bar{Q}$.

REMARK 2.1
*An alternative, equivalent formulation of* (2.2) *is:*

$$K\left[A^{i0}\right] \cap Q = \emptyset \quad \forall i$$

*i.e. the cone generated by the rows of* $A^{i0}$ *must have an empty intersection with the domain of asset prices (recall that* $\bar{Q} = K\,[A]$*). If we would find an admissible vector of asset prices* $q \in K\,[A^{i0}]$, *in view of the equivalence between* $(P^i)$ *and* $(D^i)$ *it is evident that at* $q$ *agent* $i$*'s income would be zero, thus c.p.a. would be violated.*

REMARK 2.2
*The cheaper point assumption requires that for all asset prices $q \in Q$ there is an admissible portfolio choice $\theta$ for every agent $i$ which has negative value at $q$. Hence the specification of $\theta$ may well depend on $q$. Proposition 2.1 shows that this possibility is inessential: c.p.a. in fact implies the existence of an admissible portfolio which has negative value for any possible value of the asset prices $q \in Q$.*

The maximal number of zero elements in the endowment vector $\omega^i$ of any agent $i$ compatible with the validity of c.p.a. is given by the maximal number of row vectors lying on a single face of $K[A]$. This is equal to $J-1$ if $A$ is in general position[1], but otherwise could be as big as $S-1$.
An interesting result obtains when $A$ is completely decomposable, i.e. can be transformed by elementary operations into a matrix of the form $\begin{pmatrix} A^1 & 0 \\ 0 & A^2 \end{pmatrix}$.

COROLLARY 2.1
*If $A$ is completely decomposable, c.p.a. holds iff*

$$\forall i \quad \exists \theta = \left(\theta^1, \theta^2\right) :$$
$$\left\{A^{1,i+}\,\theta^1 < 0 \wedge A^{1,i0}\,\theta^1 = 0\right\} \quad \textit{or} \quad \left\{A^{2,i+}\,\theta^2 < 0 \wedge A^{2,i0}\,\theta^2 = 0\right\}$$

The proof is immediate.
If $A$ is decomposable it is then sufficient to check the validity of the property stated in Proposition 2.1 for a single block of $A$: $A^1$ or $A^2$. A special case of this obtains when there is first period consumption (i.e. $A = \begin{pmatrix} 1 & 0^T \\ 0 & A^1 \end{pmatrix}$); this was indeed the situation considered by Werner [1985]. Note that the above result could be easily extended to the case in which A decomposes into more than two blocks.
Now we are in a position to compare c.p.a. and the r.r.a.. The latter is a joint restriction on $\left[(U^i, \omega^i)_{i \in I}, A\right]$ whereas c.p.a. is a joint restriction on $\left[(\omega^i)_{i \in I}, A\right]$ only. Clearly c.p.a. implies r.r.a. (this follows from Proposition 2.1). Furthermore, if markets are complete under Assumptions 2.1 and 1.1 both c.p.a. and r.r.a. hold. Thus there can only be a distinction between c.p.a. and r.r.a. when markets are incomplete. To show that indeed resource relatedness is weaker than c.p.a. consider the following slight modification of Example 2.2:

[1] A matrix $A \in \mathbb{R}^{S \times J}$ with $J \leq S$ is in general position if every $J \times J$ submatrix has $rank\ J$.

EXAMPLE 2.2 (CONTINUED)

*In the economy of this Example we can ensure the validity of r.r.a. and hence the existence of an equilibrium if the first agent's preferences are slightly modified. Let* $U^1(x) = b\sqrt{x_1} + \sqrt{x_2} + \sqrt{x_3}$. *We will show that for some appropriately chosen value of* $b > 0$ *agent 2 can always offer something valuable to agent 1. Recall that agent 2 can only offer agent 1 to exchange* $y$ *units of income in state 1 against* $y$ *units of income in state 3 (for* $-1 \leq y \leq a$*).*
*Thus agent 2 can always improve agent 1's welfare if b is such that at any feasible allocation agent* $i$*'s marginal rate of substitution between states 1 and 3 is different from one. A sufficient condition for this is* $b^2 < \frac{1-a}{1+a}$. *Note that in this case an equilibrium exists (even though c.p.a. fails).*

PROPOSITION 2.2

*Under Assumptions 2.1 and 1.5, the validity of r.r.a. for all preference distributions* $(U^i)_{i \in I}$ *satisfying 1.1 is equivalent to c.p.a.*

PROOF 2.2

*Since as we already argued c.p.a. always implies r.r.a., it remains to show that r.r.a. for all* $(U^i)_{i \in I}$ *requires c.p.a. Suppose c.p.a. does not hold, i.e. there exists* $i \in I$, *say* $i = 1$, *such that* $\omega^1 - A\theta \geq 0$ *implies* $\bar{\pi} A\theta \leq 0$ *for some* $\bar{\pi} \gg 0$. *Now let* $U^j \quad j \neq 1$ *be such that at some feasible allocation the gradient* $\nabla U^j(x^j)$ *is collinear to* $\bar{\pi}$. *Since* $U^j(x^j + A\theta) > U^j(x^j)$ *requires* $\nabla U^j(x^j) A\theta > 0$ *we get a contradiction to r.r.a.*

*q. e. d.*

The above results illustrate the close relationship between r.r.a. and c.p.a.. Therefore in characterizing the economies satisfying the required conditions for r.r.a. we can conveniently focus on c.p.a.
Proposition 2.3 characterizes the class of endowments such that the cheaper point assumption holds irrespectively of the asset structure.

PROPOSITION 2.3

*The cheaper point assumption holds for all asset structures if and only if endowments are strictly positive, i.e.*

$$\mathring{\mathbb{B}}_0\left(q, \omega^i, A\right) \neq \emptyset \quad \forall q \in Q \quad \forall A \in \mathbb{R}^{S \times J} \Leftrightarrow \omega^i \gg 0 \quad .$$

PROOF 2.3

$\Leftarrow$: *Assume* $\omega^i \gg 0$. *Since by Assumption 1.5* $q \in Q \Rightarrow q \neq 0, A^T\pi = q$ *and* $\pi \geq 0$ *implies* $\pi > 0$. *Hence, from the dual program* $(D^i)$ *we immediately see that* $v^{i^*} < 0$.

$\Rightarrow$: *Suppose* $\omega_s^i = 0$ *for some* $s \in \{1, \ldots, S\}$*; say without loss of generality,* $\omega_1^i = 0$. *Consider A such that* $A_1 \in$ *int conv cone* $\{A_2, \ldots, A_s\}$ *where* $A_s$, *for* $s \in \{1, \ldots, S\}$, *denotes the s-th row of matrix A. Thus* $A_1 \in Q$, *and* $A^T \pi = A_1$, *for* $\pi = e_1$.[2] *Since* $-e_1 \omega^i = 0$ *we have* $v^{i^*} = 0$.

*q. e. d.*

The next proposition takes the opposite point of view. It characterizes the asset structures such that the cheaper point assumption holds for all endowments.

PROPOSITION 2.4
*The cheaper point assumption holds for all endowments satisfying 2.1 if and only if asset markets are complete, i.e.*

$$\mathring{\mathbb{B}}_0\left(q, \omega^i, A\right) \neq \emptyset \quad \forall q \in Q \quad \forall \omega^i \in \mathbb{R}_+^S \setminus \{0\} \Leftrightarrow rank\, A = S \quad .$$

PROOF 2.4

$\Leftarrow$: *If markets are complete there exists* $\bar{\theta}^i : A\,\bar{\theta}^i = \omega^i$. *Since* $\omega^i > 0, \bar{\theta}^i$ *must have a positive value for all no arbitrage prices* $q \in Q$.

$\Rightarrow$: *Suppose* $rank\, A < S$ *and consider any* $\bar{q} \in Q$. *From state price redundancy there exists a representation of* $\bar{q}$, $A^T \bar{\pi} = \bar{q}, \bar{\pi} \geq 0$, *such that* $\bar{\pi}_z = 0$ *for some* $z \in \{1, \ldots, S\}$. *Then for* $\omega^i = e_z$ *c.p.a. does not hold.*

*q. e. d.*

This completes the discussion of c.p.a. and r.r.a.

## 2.2 Boundary Behavior Assumption

Next we turn our attention to the boundary behavior Assumption 2.3. This is also a joint restriction on $\left[(\omega^i)_{\in I}, A\right]$. Using the above notation 2.3 can be rewritten as follows:

$$\forall q \in \bar{Q} \setminus \{0\} \, \exists i : \mathring{\mathbb{B}}_0\left(q, \omega^i, A\right) \neq \emptyset \quad .$$

First we give an equivalent condition for 2.3 to hold.

PROPOSITION 2.5
*Assumption 2.3 holds iff:*

[2] $e_i$ denotes the i-th unit vector in $\mathbb{R}_+^S$.

$$\forall q \in \bar{Q} \setminus \{0\}, \exists i, \theta : q\theta < 0 \wedge A^{i0}\theta \geq 0 \tag{2.4}$$

The proof is immediate (given the earlier results in this section) and is thus omitted.

REMARK 2.3
*Again we can give an equivalent formulation of* (2.4) *in terms of the properties of the cone defined by the rows associated with the states in which agent i has zero income:*

$$\bar{Q} \setminus \{0\} \cap \left( \bigcap_{i=1}^{I} K\left[A^{i0}\right] \right) = \emptyset \quad .$$

To be able to better see the implications of assumption b.b.a. it is convenient to rewrite it as the combination of the two following assumptions:

ASSUMPTION 2.5 (BOUNDARY BEHAVIOR ASSUMPTION)

$$\forall q \in Q \, \exists i : \mathring{\mathbb{B}}_0 \left(q, \omega^i, A\right) \neq \emptyset \tag{i}$$

$$\forall q \in \partial Q \setminus \{0\} \, \exists i : \mathring{\mathbb{B}}_0 \left(q, \omega^i, A\right) \neq \emptyset \tag{ii}$$

It is in fact immediate to see that c.p.a. implies the validity of 2.5 (i). On the other hand as shown in the next section, under Assumptions 1.1, 2.1 and 1.5, 2.5 (ii) ensures the validity of the property that market excess demand explodes near the boundary of the price domain:

$$q^n \in Q, q^n \to \partial Q \setminus \{0\} \Rightarrow \|G(q^n)\| \to \infty \quad .$$

Hence in a sense 2.5 (ii) as the core of the boundary behavior assumption (b.b.a.). As Example 2.3 has shown, a lack of boundary behavior may cause the failure of an equilibrium to exist.

PROPOSITION 2.6
*Assumption 2.5 (i) holds for all endowment distributions satisfying 2.1 only if markets are complete.*

PROOF 2.5
*Suppose rank $A < S$. Then there exists an asset price vector $\bar{q} \in Q$ such that $\bar{q} \in K\left[A^1\right] \cap K\left[A^2\right]$ where $A^1, A^2$ is an appropriately chosen partition of the rows of A. Now consider $\left(\omega^i\right)_{i \in I}$ such that for all $i$ $\omega^i_s > 0$ for exactly one of the two subsets of $S$ induced by the partition of A. Hence at $\bar{q}\, v^{i^*} = 0 \quad \forall i$.*

*q. e. d.*

An immediate extension of Proposition 2.6 then shows that Assumption 2.5 (i) holds for all asset structures only if some agent has interior endowments. Consider $A = \begin{pmatrix} 1 \\ \vdots \\ 1 \end{pmatrix}$; then every row of $A$ can be dispensed with in representing $q = 1$. Thus unless $\omega^i \gg 0$ for some $i, v^{i*} = 0$ for all $i = 1, \ldots, I$.
Considering next 2.5 (ii), a geometric argument can help us in the understanding of this condition. Given the polyhedral structure of the no arbitrage price domain, its boundary $\partial Q$ is the set of the faces of $\bar{Q}$. These are in finite number (say $\kappa$) and each face $k, k = 1, \ldots, \kappa$, can be described as the cone $K\left[\bar{A}^k\right]$ generated by the collection of rows $\bar{A}^k$ lying on a given supporting hyperplane.

COROLLARY 2.2
*Assumption 2.3 (ii) holds if:*

$$\forall \bar{A}^k, k = 1, \ldots, \kappa, \exists i, \theta : \bar{A}^{k,i0}\,\theta = 0 \wedge \bar{A}^{k,i+}\,\theta < 0 \quad . \tag{2.5}$$

PROOF 2.6
*Consider any* $q \in \partial Q \setminus \{0\}$. *Then there exist* $\bar{A}^k$ *such that* $q \in int\, K\left[A^k\right]$ *(i.e* $\bar{A}^k$ *identifies the minimal face where q lies). From* (2.5) *we get that* $\exists\, i, \theta$ : $q\,\theta < 0, \bar{A}^{k,i0}\,\theta = 0$. *Moreover, since the rows of* $\bar{A}^k$ *lie all on the same face of* A, $\exists\, \bar{\theta} : \bar{A}^k\,\bar{\theta} = 0 \wedge A_s\,\bar{\theta} > 0 \quad \forall A_s \notin \bar{A}^k$.
*Consider then* $\theta_\lambda = \lambda_1\,\theta + \lambda_2\,\bar{\theta}$, *for* $\lambda_1, \lambda_2 \in \mathbb{R}$. *From the above it follows that* $q\,\theta_\lambda < 0 \quad \forall \lambda_1, \lambda_2 > 0$ *and that we can always find* $\lambda_2$ *big enough so that* $A^{i0}\theta_\lambda \geq 0$. *This shows that* (2.4) *holds (and hence 2.5 (ii), by Proposition 2.5).*

*q. e. d.*

Condition (2.5) requires that for each face $K\left[\bar{A}^k\right]$ of $\bar{Q}$ there is at least one agent such that the rows of $\bar{A}^k$ associated with the states in which the agent has zero income must lie on the boundary (i.e. on a lower-dimensional face) of the given face of $\bar{Q}$. This is then the analogue of condition (2.2), which we showed to be equivalent to c.p.a. On the other hand, (2.5) is only sufficient but not necessary for 2.5 (ii). It may well be in fact that $K\left[\bar{A}^{k,i0}\right] \cap intK\left[\bar{A}^k\right] \neq \emptyset \quad \forall i$, but $\bigcap_i K\left[\bar{A}^{k,i0}\right] = \emptyset$ so that 2.5 (ii) still holds.
Similarly, we can find sufficient conditions on $A$ such that (ii) holds for all $(\omega_i)_{i \in I}$.

PROPOSITION 2.7
*The boundary behavior Assumption 2.5 (ii) holds for all collections of endowments satisfying 2.1 if the matrix of asset returns is in general position.*

PROOF 2.7

*When $A$ is in general position, the matrix formed by the rows lying on the k-th face of $\bar{Q}$, $\bar{A}^k$, is of full row rank, and this for all $k = 1, \ldots, \kappa$. From 2.1 and the general position of $A$ it follows that for at least some agent $i$, $\bar{A}^{k,i0}$ will be of lower rank than $\bar{A}^k$. Hence $\exists \theta : \bar{A}^{k,i0}\,\theta = 0$ and $\bar{A}^{k,i+}\,\theta < 0$, i.e. (2.5) holds.*

*q. e. d.*

From the proof of the above proposition it is clear that the condition that $A$ is in general position can be considerably relaxed. All that is needed is that the boundary of the closed convex polyhedral cone $\bar{Q}$ has no redundancies, i.e. no row $A_s$ lying on the boundary of $\bar{Q}$ could be dropped from $A$ without affecting $K[A]$.

On the other hand, if we require the boundary behavior Assumption 2.5 (ii) to hold for all asset structures $A \in \mathbb{R}^{S \times J}$, this holds if some agent's endowments are strictly positive. Again this is now only a sufficient condition.

PROPOSITION 2.8

*The boundary behavior Assumption 2.5 (ii) holds for all asset structures if some agent has strictly positive endowments.*

PROOF 2.8

*For any $q \neq 0$, $A^T\,\pi = q$ for $\pi \geq 0$ implies $\pi > 0$. Hence, it is immediate that $v^{i^*} < 0$ for agent $i$ if $\omega^i \gg 0$.*

*q. e. d.*

The converse of Proposition 2.8 does not hold, i.e. there exist endowment vectors not strictly positive for any agent, satisfying 2.1, such that the boundary behavior assumption holds for all asset structures. For example, let $S = I = 3$ and let $\omega = \begin{pmatrix} 1 & 0 & 1 \\ 1 & 1 & 0 \\ 0 & 1 & 1 \end{pmatrix}$ be the endowment matrix, where columns correspond to agents and rows to states. If $rank\ A = 1$, then under 1.5 $\partial\,Q = \{0\}$; thus, $\partial\,Q \setminus \{0\} = \emptyset$ and b.b.a., trivially, holds. If $rank\ A = 3$, markets are complete and again b.b.a. holds. It remains to consider the case: $rank\ A = 2$. Suppose b.b.a. does not hold for some $\bar{q} \in \partial\,Q \setminus \{0\}$. Then $v^{i^*} = 0$ for $q = \bar{q}$ for all $i = 1, 2, 3$, but from $(D^i)$, $i = 1, 2, 3$ we see that this implies $A^T\,e_i = \bar{q}$ for the three unit vectors $e_i \in \mathbb{R}^3_+$. Thus $rank\ A = 1$; a contradiction.

Note that in this example the endowment matrix $\omega := \left(\omega^i\right)_{i \in I} \in \mathbb{R}_+^{S \times I}$ is non decomposable. However, non decomposability of $\omega$ is not itself sufficient to guarantee the boundary behavior assumption irrespectively of the asset structure. To see this consider an economy with four agents and four states where the endowment matrix and the asset structure are

$$\omega = \begin{pmatrix} 1 & 0 & 0 & 1 \\ 1 & 1 & 0 & 0 \\ 0 & 1 & 1 & 0 \\ 0 & 0 & 1 & 1 \end{pmatrix} \quad \text{and} \quad A = \begin{pmatrix} 1 & 0 \\ 1 & 1 \\ 1 & 0 \\ 1 & 1 \end{pmatrix} .$$

$\omega$ is indecomposable and from $(D^i)$ we see that, when the assets' price is $(1,0)$, $v^{i^*} = 0 \quad \forall i, i = 1,2,3,4$. Thus there exist $\bar{q} \in \partial Q \setminus \{0\}$ such that $\mathring{\mathbb{B}}_0 (\bar{q}, \omega^i, A) = \emptyset \quad \forall i.$

The above discussion shows that to generalize the condition of strictly positive endowments for all agents still ensuring the validity of 2.1 we have to look for joint restrictions on endowments and asset payoffs, on $\left( (\omega^i)_{i=1}^{I}, A \right)$. An instance of this is the case of spanned endowments. Under this condition, not surprisingly, both c.p.a. and b.b.a. hold. Some other, more interesting and not known condition, however also obtain from the previous discussion.

COROLLARY 2.3
*Suppose $A$ is completely decomposable into $F$ (diagonal) blocks, with the submatrices $A^f, f = 1, \ldots, F$, along the diagonal.*
*The cheaper point and the boundary behavior assumptions then hold if:*

*(i)* $\forall i \quad \exists f, \theta^f : \left\{ A^{f,i+} \theta^f < 0 \wedge A^{f,io} \theta^f = 0 \right\}$

*(ii) one of the two following conditions is satisfied:*

*(iia)* $\forall f$, $A^f$ *is in general position*

*(iib)* $\forall f \quad \exists i : \omega^i_s > 0$ *for all states s associated to the rows in* $A^f$.

Therefore, when conditions (i) and either (iia) or (iib) hold, an equilibrium exists with boundary endowments. Werner [1985] has shown existence in an incomplete market model with first period consumption, i.e. with $A = \begin{pmatrix} 1 & 0^T \\ 0 & \bar{A} \end{pmatrix}$, when for all $i = 1, \ldots, I$, one of the two following conditions is satisfied: $\omega^i_1 > 0$ or $\omega^i_s > 0 \quad \forall s > 1$. Evidently, this is a special case of conditions (i), (iib) in the above Corollary 2.3.

## 2.3 A Final Remark

In 1.1 we required the agents' utility functions to be strictly monotone and strictly quasi-concave over all the nonnegative orthant of the S-dimensional Euclidean space. However we can show that the results we derived extend to the case in which these monotonicity and concavity properties only hold in the interior of the consumption space, $\mathbb{R}^S_{++}$. This is important as utility functions leading to smooth demand functions fall into this class. Moreover, the behavior of preferences on the boundary of the consumption space is particularly relevant

here where we let endowments lie on the boundary and market incompleteness constrains reallocation of resources.
Let us consider then the "farthest possible" case from 1.1: suppose $U^i$ is continuous, strictly monotone and strictly concave on $\mathbb{R}^S_{++}\ \forall i$, and that on the boundary, $\mathbb{R}^S_+ \backslash \mathbb{R}^S_{++}$, agents are indifferent. In this situation a solution to agent $i$'s problem $(M^i)$ exists if $\nexists\theta : q\theta \leq 0, A\theta > 0, A^{i0}\theta \gg 0$. It follows that the set $Q^i$ of no arbitrage prices for agent $i$ (i.e. for which the above condition is satisfied) is now given by $Q^i = intK\,[A] \cup K\,[A^{i0}]$. Thus the price domain for the economy, $\bigcap_i Q^i$, coincides with Q, the price domain considered in the earlier sections, if $\bigcap_i K\,[A^{i0}] \cap \partial K\,[A] = \emptyset$. This last condition, it was shown before (see Remark 2.3), is equivalent to the boundary behavior Assumption 2.5 (ii). Since the validity of c.p.a. and b.b.a. on a (possibly) larger price domain ($\bigcap_i Q^i$) clearly implies the validity of those properties on Q, it follows that under b.b.a. $\bigcap_i Q^i = Q$. Thus the analysis of the previous sections extends to the case in which agents are indifferent on the boundary (and a fortiori to all other intermediate cases).

## 3. Properties of Excess Demand and Existence of Equilibria

In this section we want to show that if c.p.a. and b.b.a. are added to the standard assumptions known from the complete markets case we can prove existence of competitive equilibria when asset markets are incomplete. In doing so we will follow the so-called excess demand approach. See Debreu [1982] for a survey of various approaches to prove existence of competitive equilibria. Even though , as we have shown in the first section of this chapter, the excess demand for assets and that for income transfers are closely related, the latter is not appropriate to prove existence via the excess demand approach. Because of state price redundancy the excess demand for assets does not satisfy an appropriate boundary behavior and the Cass trick to cure this deficiency will only work if some agent has strictly positive endowments which is an unnecessary strong assumption. Moreover the asset excess demand approach is in itself interesting. It is the basis for extensions of the GEI-model to transaction costs [Judd et al., 1999] and also to asymmetric information [Zigrand, 2002].
We begin proving the existence of equilibria by showing which properties for the market excess demand can be derived from the assumptions that we discussed above:

PROPOSITION 2.9 (PROPERTIES OF INDIVIDUAL EXCESS DEMAND) *Let rankA $= J$ and $U^i : \mathbb{R}^S_+ \to \mathbb{R}$ be a continuous, strictly monotone and strictly quasi-concave utility function then* [3]

[3] $\mathbb{1}$ denotes the vector in which all components are 1.

*(i)* $|g^i(q)| = 1$ *for all* $q \in Q$.

*(ii)* $A\, g^i(Q) \geq k\, \mathbb{1}$ *for some* $k \in \mathbb{R}$.

*(iii)* $g^i(\lambda\, q) = g^i(q)$ *for all* $q \in Q$, *all* $\lambda > 0$.

*(iv)* *If* $A\,\theta > 0$ *for some* $\theta \in \mathbb{R}^J$ *then* $(q \cdot g^i(q) = 0)$ *for all* $q \in Q$.

*(v)* *If* $(\omega^i, A)$ *satisfies the cheaper point assumption then* $g^i(\cdot)$ *is a continuous function on* $Q \backslash \{0\}$.

Proposition 2.9 is the GEI analogue of Proposition 3.1 in Hildenbrand and Kirman [1988]. The standard arguments for the Walrasian model are taken from them. However, some important modifications are in order if markets are incomplete.
To prepare this proof we will first show that the cheaper point assumption guarantees that the budget correspondence is continuous.

LEMMA 2.1
*The incomplete markets budget correspondence* $\mathbb{B}(.,\omega^i, A) := \left\{\theta \in \mathbb{R}^J \middle|\, q\,\theta \leq 0 \wedge \omega^i + A\,\theta \geq 0\right\}$ *is continuous at* $\bar{q} \in Q$ *if the set* $\mathring{\mathbb{B}}(\bar{q}, \omega^i, A) := \left\{\theta \in \mathbb{R}^J \middle|\, q\,\theta < 0 \wedge \omega^i + A\,\theta \geq 0\right\}$ *is nonempty.*

PROOF 2.9

**Lower hemi continuity** *The proof follows a standard argument used for the complete markets case (see e.g. Takayama [1985]). Let* $q^n \to \bar{q}, \bar{\theta} \in \mathbb{B}(\bar{q}, \omega^i, A)$ *and* $\hat{\theta} \in \mathring{\mathbb{B}}(\bar{q}, \omega^i, A)$. *For n large enough define* $\theta^n := \lambda^n\,\bar{\theta} + (1-\lambda^n)\,\hat{\theta}$ *where* $\lambda^n$ *is maximal in* $[0,1]$ *such that* $q^n\,\theta^n \leq 0$. *Observe that* $\omega^i + A\,\theta^n = \lambda^n\,(\omega^i + A\,\bar{\theta}) + (1-\lambda^n)\left(\omega^i + A\,\hat{\theta}\right) \geq 0$. *To prove lower hemi continuity, we simply have to show that* $\lambda^n$ *tends to* $1$ *as* $n$ *tends to infinity.*

*Suppose* $\lambda^n$ *is bounded away from* $1$. *Hence there is a subsequence* $\lambda^r$ *such that* $\lambda^r \to \bar{\lambda} < 1$. *Note that* $\lambda^r < 1$ *implies* $q^r\,\theta^r = 0$.

*Hence,* $q^n\,\theta^n \to \bar{\lambda}\,\bar{q}\,\bar{\theta} + (1-\bar{\lambda})\,\bar{q}\,\hat{\theta} = 0$, *which implies* $\bar{q}\,\bar{\theta} > 0$ *contradicting* $\bar{\theta} \in \mathbb{B}(\bar{q}, \omega^i, A)$.

**Upper hemi continuity** *At* $\bar{q} \in Q$, *the graph correspondence* $\mathbb{B}(.,\omega^i, A)$ *is obviously closed. For the upper hemi continuity it remains to show compactness. From the "dual" representation of the model we know that the set of the admissible consumption choices for the individual problem* $\left(\hat{M}^i\right)$, $\mathbb{B}(\pi, \omega^i, A)$ *is a subset of the Arrow-Debreu budget set* $B(\pi, \omega^i) :=$

$\left\{x \in \mathbb{R}^S_+ \middle| \ \pi x \le \pi \omega^i\right\}$. *From the standard arguments in the Arrow-Debreu model we know that for any sequence of strictly positive prices, $\pi^n \gg 0$ converging to some strictly positive price vector, $\bar{\pi} \gg 0$, the union of the budget sets $\bigcup_n B(\pi^n, \omega^i)$, is contained in a compact set. The set of admissible portfolios $\mathbb{B}(q, \omega^i, A)$ is the preimage of the admissible consumption choices under the linear mapping $A : \mathbb{R}^J \to \mathbb{R}^S$. Hence, since rank $A = J$, for any sequence of asset prices $q^n \in Q, q^n \to \bar{q} \in Q$, the set $\bigcup_n \mathbb{B}(q^n, \omega^i, A)$ is compact and consequently $\mathbb{B}(., \omega^i, A)$ is upper hemi continuous at $\bar{q} \in Q$.*

*q. e. d.*

Now we are in a position to give the proof of Proposition 2.9.

PROOF 2.10 (OF PROPOSITION 2.9)

(i) *In view of Corollary 2.2, we start by showing that $z^i(\pi) \neq \emptyset$, compact for $\pi \in \mathbb{R}^S_{++}$. But this is obvious since $z^i(\pi) + \omega^i$ is the maximand of a continuous function on the compact set*

$$B\left(\pi, \omega^i\right) \cap \left\{x \in \mathbb{R}^S \middle| \left(x - \omega^i\right) \in \langle A \rangle\right\} \quad ,$$

*where the first set in the intersection is the Walrasian budget set which is compact for strictly positive prices, since $0 \le x_s \le \frac{\pi \cdot \omega^i}{\pi_s}$ for all $s \in S$. Since $U^i$ is strictly quasi-concave there is then a unique maximand.*

(ii) *Property (ii) is true, since income transfers are bounded below by $-\omega^i$.*

(iii) *Follows immediately from the homogeneity of degree zero of the budget set $\mathbb{B}(q, \omega^i, A)$.*

(iv) *Has already been proved in Section 4.3 of Chapter 1.*

(v) *Given Lemma 2.1 from the maximum theorem[4] it follows that the asset excess demand function, $g^i$, is continuous on $Q$.*

*This completes the proof of Proposition 2.9.*

*q. e. d.*

Now we derive the corresponding properties for market excess demand $G(q) := \sum_{i=1}^I g^i(q)$:

[4] See Appendix A.

PROPOSITION 2.10
*Let rank* $A = J$, $A\theta > 0$ *for some* $\theta \in \mathbb{R}^J$ , *let* $(\omega^i, A)$ $i = 1, \ldots, I$ *satisfy the cheaper point assumption and the boundary behavior assumption, and let* $U^i$ $i = 1, \ldots, I$ *be* $I$ *strictly monotone, continuous, strictly quasi concave utility functions, then*

*(i)* $G : Q \longrightarrow \mathbb{R}^J$ *is a continuous function* *(Continuity)*

*(ii)* $G(\lambda q) = G(q)$ *for all* $q \in Q$, $\lambda > 0$ *(Homogeneity)*

*(iii)* $q \cdot G(q) = 0$ *for all* $q \in Q$ *(Walras Law)*

*(iv)* $A\, G(Q) \geq k\, 1\!\!1$ *for some* $k \in \mathbb{R}$ *(Boundedness below)*

*(v)* $q^n \in Q$, $q^n \longrightarrow q \in \partial Q$, $q \neq 0$ *then* $\|G(q^n)\| \longrightarrow \infty$ *(Boundary Behavior)*

Let $Z(\pi) := \sum_i z^i(\pi)$ be the income transfer market excess demand, then the properties of Proposition 2.9 carry over to $Z$ using the adjoint operations.

PROOF 2.11
*The properties (i)–(iv) are inherited from the corresponding properties of individual excess demand. Thus it remains to prove the boundary behavior assumption:*
*We show first the following:*
*Let* $q^n \in Q, q^n \to \bar{q} \in \bar{Q} \setminus \{0\}$ *for some* $\bar{q}$ *with* $\mathring{\mathbb{B}}(\bar{q}, \omega^i, A) \neq \emptyset$. *Furthermore, let* $\theta^n = g^i(q^n)$ *and* $\theta^n \to \bar{\theta}$. *Then* $\bar{\theta} = g^i(\bar{q})$ *if* $u^i$ *is continuous.*
*The proof is standard (see e.g. Hildenbrand and Kirman [1988, Proposition 3.1.(3)]). Since* $\theta^n = g^i(q^n)$, *we know* $\theta^n \in \mathbb{B}(q^n, \omega^i, A)$. *By closedness of* $\mathbb{B}(., \omega^i, A)$ , $\bar{\theta} \in \mathbb{B}(\bar{q}, \omega^i, A)$. *Thus it remains to show that* $\bar{\theta}$ *is maximal in* $\mathbb{B}(\bar{q}, \omega^i, A)$.

**Case 1** *consider* $y \in \mathbb{B}(\bar{q}, \omega^i, A)$ *with* $\bar{q}\, y < \bar{q}\, \bar{\theta}$. *Then for n large enough,* $q^n y < q^n \bar{\theta}$. *By maximality of* $g^i(q^n)$ *it follows that* $u^i(\omega^i + A\, g^i(q^n)) \geq u^i(\omega^i + A\, y)$. *Since* $u^i$ *is continuous and the sequence* $g^i(q^n)$ *converges to* $\bar{\theta}$ *it follows that* $u^i(\omega^i + A\, \bar{\theta}) \geq u^i(\omega^i + A\, y)$.

**Case 2** *consider* $y \in \mathbb{B}(\bar{q}, \omega^i, A)$ *with* $\bar{q}\, y = \bar{q}\, \bar{\theta}$. *Since* $\mathring{\mathbb{B}}(\bar{q}, \omega^i, A) \neq \emptyset$ *there exists a sequence* $y^n \in \mathring{\mathbb{B}}(\bar{q}, \omega^i, A)$ *such that* $y^n \to y$. *Thus* $\bar{q}\, y^n < \bar{q}\, \bar{\theta}$ *and from the above* $u^i(\omega^i + A\, \bar{\theta}) \geq u^i(\omega^i + A\, y^n)$ *so that by continuity of* $u^i$, $u^i(\omega^i + A\, \bar{\theta}) \geq u^i(\omega^i + A\, y)$.

*We can now complete the proof of (v):*
*Suppose* $q^n \in Q$, $q^n \to \bar{q} \in \partial Q \setminus \{0\}$ *but* $\left\|\sum_i g^i(q^n)\right\|$ *remains bounded. Since* $A\, g^i(q)$, $i = 1, \ldots, I$ *is bounded below for all* $i$ *there exists a converging sequence* $\theta^i_n = g^i(q^n)$ *with* $\theta^i_n \to \bar{\theta}^i$. *By assumption, for some*

*$i$ $\mathring{\mathbb{B}}(q,\omega^i,A) \neq \emptyset$. This implies that $\bar{\theta}^i = g^i(\bar{q})$ which cannot be true since $g^i(\bar{q})$ is not defined for $q \in \partial Q$.*

*q. e. d.*

The following theorem will be shown to be true.

THEOREM 2.1 (EXISTENCE OF EQUILIBRIA. [GOTTARDI AND HENS, 1996]

*Let $((U^i,\omega^i)_{i\in I}, A)$ be a GEI model with*

*(i) $rank\, A = J$ and $A\theta > 0$ for some $\theta \in \mathbb{R}^J$,*

*(ii) $(\omega^i, A)_{i\in I}$ satisfies the cheaper point and the boundary behavior assumption,*

*(iii) $(U^i)_{i\in I}$ are strictly monotone, continuous and strictly quasi-concave,*

*Then there exists a GEI-equilibrium.*

To prove Theorem 2.1 we apply the following lemma, which is a generalization of Grandmont's[5] Market Equilibrium Lemma to closed convex cones.

LEMMA 2.2
*Let $\bar{C} \subset \mathbb{R}^J$ be a closed convex cone which is not a linear space. Denote by $C$ the (relative) interior of $\bar{C}$ and by $\hat{C} := \{q \in C \mid \|q\| = 1\}$. Let $G : \hat{C} \to \mathbb{R}^J$ be a continuous function satisfying $q \cdot G(q) = 0$ for all $q \in C$ and let $g$ satisfy the boundary behavior $(*)$:*

*$(*)$ $q^n \in \hat{C}, q^n \to q \in \partial\bar{C}$ implies $\exists N$ such that $\hat{q} \cdot G(q^n) > 0$ for all $n \geq N$, for some $\hat{q} \in \hat{C}$.*

*Then there exists a $q^* \in C$ such that $G(q^*) = 0$.*

The proof of Lemma 2.2 can be deduced from Grandmont's Market Equilibrium Lemma using Debreu's[6] Equilibrium Existence Lemma for closed convex cones which are not a linear space. Using these results, the proof of Lemma 5 is an obvious extension of proof 18.14. in Border [1985].
The usefulness of Lemma 2.2 is the very weak criterion $(*)$ which is still sufficient to get existence of a fixed point. Given Lemma 2.2 the proof of Theorem 2.1 is obvious:

PROOF 2.12 (OF THEOREM 2.1)
*By Proposition 2.9 the asset market excess demand function $G : Q \to \mathbb{R}^J$*

[5] [Grandmont, 1977]
[6] [Debreu, 1956]

*satisfies properties (i)–(v) of that proposition. And* $\bar{Q}$ *is a closed convex cone which is not a linear space because by assumption there exists* $\theta$ *with* $A\,\theta > 0$. *Thus Lemma 2.2 is applicable to* $G$. *Because of Homogeneity the equilibrium set remains basically unchanged if we consider* $G$ *restricted to normalized prices* $\hat{Q}$. *Therefore it remains to check whether condition (*) of Lemma 2.2 holds. To see this, consider a sequence* $q^n \in \hat{Q}$ *converging to* $q \in \partial Q$ *and compute* $\hat{q} \cdot G(q^n)$ *for some* $\hat{q} \in \hat{Q}$. *Since* $\hat{q} \in Q$ *the latter scalar product is equivalent to* $\hat{\pi}^T A\,G(q^n)$ *with* $\hat{\pi} \gg 0$. *Now, since* $\|A\,G\,(q^n)\| \to \infty$ *but* $A\,G\,(q^n)$ *is bounded below there must exist some* $N$ *such that for all* $n \geq N$, $\hat{q}^T\,G\,(q^n) > 0$.

*q. e. d.*

# Chapter 3

# STRUCTURE OF GEI-EXCESS DEMAND

## 1. The Intrinsic Limits of the Rationality Hypothesis

Finance is built on the assumption of complete rationality. The absence of arbitrage based on the utility maximization principle is then the most fundamental insight of this theory. Therefore it is important to know that, as we have shown in Chapter 2, the model is logically consistent, i.e. that under some mild assumptions on the characteristics of the model competitive equilibria exist. In this section we show that without any further assumptions than those made in Chapter 1 the no-arbitrage condition is actually all we can conclude from the model. That is to say, any arbitrage free vector of asset prices is the equilibrium price vector of some economy. Following the argument of Harrison and Kreps [1978] one can show that this result is trivial when the state space is finite and no restrictions on the trading volume are required. A single agent economy in which the agent has a risk neutral expected utility function with beliefs equal to the martingale measure generates the given asset prices. However in a single agent economy there is no trade—an obvious contradiction to what we observe. In this chapter we show that even with an arbitrary preassigned trading volume the no-arbitrage condition is all we can expect. Even worse we will show that in some economies there may be arbitrarily many ways of having a no-arbitrage condition that is compatible with the economic fundamentals because the number of equilibria is not restricted by the rationality hypothesis. In particular this shows that without knowledge of the characteristics of the economy finance has no empirical implications! Only if auxiliary assumptions like small or constant absolute risk aversion are made we get definite conclusions from the rationality hypothesis. If as it is nowadays put forward by many empirical studies (see for example Campbell [2000], Hirshleifer [2001] and De Bondt [1999] for surveys) there are serious asset price "anomalies" then it is unclear whether those refute

the fundamental assumption of rationality or rather the auxiliary assumptions made to make the model well determined.
In passing we should note that this critique on the rationality hypothesis has long ago been recognized in the Sonnenschein-Mantel-Debreu Model. Sonnenschein [1972] and Sonnenschein [1973] has put the question into public domain whether Continuity, Homogeneity and the Walras Law may exhaust the properties of market excess demand. Debreu [1974] and Mantel [1974] and Mantel [1976] were the first rigorous affirmative answers to Sonnenschein's question. And recently this literature has found its ultimate stage in Chiappori and Ekeland [2002]. Our contribution to this point of view is to show that with incomplete markets the picture does not change much. Still Continuity, Homogeneity and the Walras Law do exhaust the properties of GEI-market excess demand.

## 2. Mantel's Theorem in Complete Markets

The theorem which we generalize to incomplete markets is due to Mantel [1976]. It shows that not even the assumption of homothetic preferences is enough to get well determined equilibria. In order to put our result into the correct perspective we will briefly recall Mantel's Theorem.
Let $\mathbb{R}^n$ be the commodity space and let $H := \{p \in \mathbb{R}^n | \sum_{l=1}^n p_l = 1\}$ be the set of normalized prices. For every compact convex subset $P \subset H$ Mantel defines $P^* := \{x \in \mathbb{R}^n | p\,x \geq 0 \quad \text{for all} \quad p \in P\}$ the positive polar of the set $P$. Given these definitions we can state

THEOREM 3.1 ([MANTEL, 1976])
*Let $P \subset H$ be compact, convex. Let $Z : P \to \mathbb{R}^n$ be $C^2$ on $P$ and satisfy $p\,Z(p) = 0$ for all $p \in P$. Let $\omega^i \in P^*$, $i = 1, \ldots, n$ be independent vectors. Then there exists a real $k > 0$, a convex cone $X \subset P^*$, and $n$ unsatiated consumers with strictly concave, homogeneous utility functions $U^i : X \to \mathbb{R}$ and initial endowments $k\,\omega^i$, whose excess demand functions add up to $Z$ on $P$.*

If one wants to apply Mantel's Theorem to the standard Arrow-Debreu model (see e.g. Shafer and Sonnenschein [1982, Theorem 7]) one could set

$$P = \left\{ p \in \mathbb{R}^n \,\middle|\, p_l \geq \epsilon, l = 1, \ldots, n \sum_{l=1}^n p_l = 1 \right\}$$

and gets that $P^*$ comes close to the nonnegative orthant for small $\epsilon > 0$.

## 3. Some Preliminaries

Recall the consumer's decision problem from Chapter 1:

$$\bar{g}^i(q) := \underset{\theta \in \mathbb{R}^J}{\arg\max}\, U^i\left(\omega^i + A\,\theta\right) \text{ s.t. } \quad \omega^i + A\,\theta \geq 0 \quad \text{and} \quad q\,\theta \leq 0.$$

The market excess demand for assets is correspondingly defined as $G(q) := \sum_i \bar{g}^i(q)$. Recall also that excess demand is only well defined if asset prices do not allow for arbitrage, i.e. if $q$ is in the set

$$Q := \left\{ q \in R^J \,\middle|\, \text{ there is no } \quad \theta \quad \text{with} \quad \begin{pmatrix} -q^T \\ A \end{pmatrix} \theta > 0 \right\}$$
$$= \left\{ q \in \mathbb{R}^J \,\middle|\, q = A^T \pi \quad \text{for some} \quad \pi \in \mathbb{R}^S_{++} \right\}$$

Furthermore, note that in this model, it may happen that all asset prices are negative, so that the price normalization chosen by Mantel is not appropriate. Since asset prices must be no-arbitrage prices, using the existence of strictly positive state prices, we will normalize the set of asset prices indirectly by a normalization on state prices $\pi$ in the standard Walrasian way, i.e. $Q_\epsilon := \left\{ q \in \mathbb{R}^J \,\middle|\, q = A^T \pi \quad \text{for some} \quad \pi \in S_\epsilon \right\}$, where

$$S_\epsilon := \left\{ \pi \in \mathbb{R}^S_{++} \,\middle|\, \pi_s \geq \epsilon, s = 1, \ldots, S \|\pi\| = 1 \right\} \quad .$$

In our main result the set $X := \left\{ x \in \mathbb{R}^S_{++} \,\middle|\, x = A\,\theta \quad \text{for some} \quad \theta \in \mathbb{R}^J \right\}$ and the preimage of $X$ under the linear mapping $A$, the set $\Theta := \left\{ \theta \in \mathbb{R}^J \,\middle|\, A\,\theta \gg 0 \right\}$, will be of considerable interest. We will choose $\omega^i \in X$ so that the GEI economy, which we construct to generate the asset market excess demand, will in particular satisfy the spanning condition $\omega^i \in \langle A \rangle, i = 1, \ldots, I$. Moreover by an application of a result by Chipman, Hurwicz and Uzawa (see Lemma 3.1 below) we get the stronger conclusion that the utility functions (defined on subsets of $X$) are not only unsatiated but monotone.

## 4. Anything Goes

The following proposition will be shown to be true.

THEOREM 3.2 (GEI-MANTEL. [HENS, 2001A])
*Let $A \in \mathbb{R}^{S \times J}$ be any asset structure with rank $A = J$ and $A\,\theta > 0$ for some $\theta \in \mathbb{R}^J$. Furthermore, let $G : Q \to \mathbb{R}^J$ be $C^1$ and $C^2$ on $Q_\epsilon$ and let $G$ satisfy $G(\lambda\, q) = G(q)$ for all $q \in Q, \lambda > 0$ ,and $q \ldots G(q) = 0$ for all $q \in Q$. Then for every $\epsilon > 0$ the following is true: Let $\omega^i \in X, i = 1, \ldots, J$ be linearly independent vectors, then there exists a real $k > 0$, and $J$ consumers with continuous strictly quasi-concave, monotone, linearly homogeneous utility*

*functions $U^i : X \to \mathbb{R}$ and initial endowments $k\,\omega^i$, whose asset excess demand functions add up to $G$ on $Q_\epsilon$.*

To prove this theorem we do not directly use duality theory but follow a hint given by Richter (which was made public in Shafer and Sonnenschein [1982]) and write down the demand functions directly in order to apply the Integrability Theorem for demand functions which are linear in income.

Let $\Omega_\epsilon := \left\{\pi \in \mathbb{R}^S_{++} \middle| \pi_s > \epsilon, s = 1, \ldots, S\right\} \times \mathbb{R}_+$ for all $\epsilon \geq 0$ and let $X_f$ be the image of a function $f$ defined on $\Omega_\epsilon$, i.e. $X_f = f(\Omega_\epsilon)$. Endowed with this notation we recall from Chipman [1974] and Hurwicz and Uzawa [1971]:

LEMMA 3.1 ([CHIPMAN, 1974] AND [HURWICZ AND UZAWA, 1971])
*Let f satisfy the following properties:*

| | | | |
|---|---|---|---|
| $(A)$ | $f : \Omega_\epsilon \to \mathbb{R}^S_+$, | | |
| $(B)$ | $\pi\, f(\pi, b) = b$ | for all | $(\pi, b) \in \Omega_\epsilon$, |
| $(D)$ | $f$ | is differentiable on | $\Omega_\epsilon$, |
| $(L)$ | $f(\pi, \lambda\, b) = \lambda\, f(\pi, b)$ | for all | $(\pi, b) \in \Omega_\epsilon$ all $\lambda \geq 0$, |
| $(S)$ | $\partial_\pi\, f(\pi, b)$ | is symmetric for all | $(\pi, b) \in \Omega_\epsilon$, |
| $(N)$ | $\partial_\pi\, f(\pi, b)$ | is negative semi-definite for all | $(\pi, b) \in \Omega_\epsilon$. |

*Then there exists a continuous, strictly quasi-concave, monotone, linearly homogeneous function $U : X_f \to \mathbb{R}$ such that*
$f(\pi, b) = \arg\max_{x \in X_f} U(x)$, *subject to* $\pi\, x \leq b$.

REMARK 3.1
*The lemma stated above cannot be found in exactly the way we stated it. One difference is that Chipman, Hurwicz and Uzawa let the function $f$ be defined on $\Omega_\epsilon$ for $\epsilon = 0$. But for any other $\epsilon \geq 0$ the theorem is still true, it only will become progressively weaker if $\epsilon$ is larger. This can be seen from a careful reading of the proof given in Hurwicz and Uzawa [1971]. The key mathematical step is to solve a system of partial differential equations, which can be done for every $\epsilon \geq 0$, as long as the Frobenius integrability conditions are satisfied. These conditions applied to the function $f$ require the Slutzky matrix of $f$, $S_f(\pi, b) := \partial_\pi\, f(\pi, b) + \partial_b\, f(\pi, b)\, f^T(\pi, b)$ to be negative semi-definite and symmetric. Another difference is that instead of requiring these properties of the Slutzky matrix, we assure these properties by the analogous ones of the Jacobian matrix; conditions (S) and (N). This is correct, because it is well known that negative semi-definiteness of the Jacobian $\partial_\pi\, f(\pi, b)$ implies negative semi-definiteness of the Slutzky matrix $S_f(\pi, b)$ see e.g. Hildenbrand and Jerison [1989]. Finally, with linear Engelcurves (i.e. assumption (L)) we get $\partial_b\, f(\pi, b)\, f^T(\pi, b) = \frac{1}{b}\, f(\pi, b)\, f^T(\pi, b)$ so that symmetry carries over as well.*

In the proof of our main result we will use the definition of excess demand as excess demand for assets and that as excess demand for income transfers. The first description is easier when one wants to guarantee that excess demand stays in $\langle A \rangle$. The second definition is more convenient when one wants to apply results (like the theorem of Chipman, Hurwicz and Uzawa) that have been proved in the Arrow-Debreu model. In Section 5 of Chapter 1 we have shown how to transfer one excess demand approach into the other we will go back and forth between the two approaches whenever this allows to shorten the proof. We have stated our main result in terms of asset excess demand. However, as will be seen from our proof, which uses both formulations of excess demand, we have then also shown the corresponding result for the income excess demand.

PROOF 3.1 (OF MAIN RESULT)
*We first follow the decomposition given by Mantel [1976]. Let $\bar{\theta}^i \in \Theta$ be the unique $\theta \in \mathbb{R}^J$ such that $\omega^i = A\,\bar{\theta}^i$, $i = 1, \ldots, J$. Take any $J$ independent vectors $c^i \in H := \left\{ y \in \mathbb{R}^J_{++} \middle| \sum_{j=1}^J y_j = 1 \right\}$. Define the $J \times J$ matrices $W = \left(\bar{\theta}^1, \ldots, \bar{\theta}^J\right)$; $C = \left(c^1, \ldots, c^J\right)$; $B = CW^T$; and $M = \left(W^T\right)^{-1}$.*
*Before we proceed, note that $\forall\, q \in Q$, $B\,q = C\,W^T\,q \gg 0$ since $q^T \bar{\theta}^i = \pi^T A\,\bar{\theta}^i = \pi^T\,\omega^i \geq 0$ and $W^T\,q \neq 0$.*

$$\text{Let} \quad g^i\left(q, b^i\right) := \underbrace{\left[-\left(\frac{1}{k}\right)\partial_q\,G^T\,(q)\,m^i + B^T\widehat{B\,q}^{-1}c^i\right]}_{\tilde{g}^i(q)} b^i$$

*where $(\widehat{\;\;})$ transforms an $J$ vector into a $J \times J$ diagonal matrix with coordinates of the vector along its main diagonal and where $m^i$ is the ith column of $M$.*
*Define by $\mathbb{1}$ the column vector $(1, \ldots, 1)^{\mathrm{T}}$ and consider the aggregate asset demand:*

$$\begin{aligned}
\sum_i g^i\left(q, q \ldots k\,\bar{\theta}^i\right) &= -\partial_q\,G^T\,(q)\,MW^Tq + k\,B^T\widehat{B\,q}^{-1}CW^Tq \\
&= -\partial_q\,G^T\,(q)\,q + k\,B^T\widehat{B\,q}^{-1}B\,q \\
&= G\,(q) + k\,B^T\mathbb{1} \perp \quad \textit{(from Walras Law)} \\
&= G\,(q) + k\,WC^T\mathbb{1} \perp \\
&= G\,(q) + k\sum_i \bar{\theta}^i
\end{aligned}$$

*Thus the $g^i\,(q, q\,k\,\bar{\theta}^i) - k\,\bar{\theta}^i$ add up to $G\,(q)$.*

*So far we are in line with Mantel's proof. But now we deviate from it and show that for every $\epsilon > 0$ there exists some $k > 0$ such that the asset demand functions $g^i(q, b^i)$, $i = 1, \ldots, I$ satisfy the following six properties:*

| | | | |
|---|---|---|---|
| $(\hat{N})$ | $\partial_q g^i(q, b^i)$ | negative semi-definite for all | $(q, b^i) \in \hat{Q}_\epsilon$ |
| $(\tilde{A})$ | $A\, g^i(q, b^i) \in \mathbb{R}^S_+$ | | $(q, b^i) \in \tilde{Q}_\epsilon$ |
| $(\tilde{B})$ | $q\, g^i(q, b^i) = b^i$ | for all | $(q, b^i) \in \tilde{Q}$ |
| $(\tilde{D})$ | $g^i$ | is differentiable on | $\tilde{Q}_\epsilon$ |
| $(\tilde{L})$ | $g^i(q, \lambda b^i) = \lambda g^i(q, b^i)$ | for all | $(q, b^i) \in \tilde{Q}$ |
| $(\tilde{S})$ | $\partial_q g^i(q, b^i)$ | symmetric for all | $(q, b^i) \in \tilde{Q}$ |
| $(\tilde{N})$ | $\partial_q g^i(q, b^i)$ | negative semi-definite for all | $(q, b^i) \in \tilde{Q}_\epsilon$ |

*where $\tilde{Q}_\epsilon := Q_\epsilon \times \mathbb{R}_+$ and $\tilde{Q} := Q \times \mathbb{R}_+$.*
*The arguments are as follows:*

- $(\tilde{D})$ $(\tilde{L})$ *are given by assumption.*
- $(\tilde{A})$ : *It is sufficient to show that $A\, B^T y \gg 0$ for all $y \in \mathbb{R}^J_{++}$, because for $k > 0$ large enough the second term in (1) dominates the first and because $Q_\epsilon$ is compact. But $A\, B^T y = A\, W\, C^T y \gg 0$ since $\bar{\theta}^i \in \Theta$.*
- $(\tilde{B})$:

$$q\, g^i(q, b^i) = q\left[-\left(\frac{1}{k}\right)\partial_q G(q)^T m^i + B^T \widehat{B\,q}^{-1} c^i\right] b^i$$

$$= \left[-\left(\frac{1}{k}\right) q\, \partial_q G^T(q)\, m^i + q\, B^T \widehat{B\,q}^{-1} c^i\right] b^i = \left[1 \perp c^i\right] b^i = b^i$$

*In the last equation $q^T \partial_q G^T(q) = 0$ follows from differentiating $G(\lambda q) = G(q)$ with respect to $\lambda$.*

*To verify $(\tilde{N})$ and $(\tilde{S})$ we note that $\tilde{g}^i(q)$ is the gradient of*

$$v^i(q) := -\left(\frac{1}{k}\right) m^i\, G(q) + c^i \log B\, q \quad .$$

*Thus the second derivative of $v^i$ is symmetric and since $G$ is $C^2$, there exists $k > 0$ large enough so that $v^i(q)$ is concave on the compact set $Q_\epsilon$.*
*In order to apply Lemma 3.1 we transfer the asset demand problem to its dual, the income transfer problem. I.e. we consider $f^i : \Omega \to X$ defined by*

$$f^i(\pi, b^i) := A\, g^i(A^T \pi, b^i) \tag{3.1}$$

*and verify that $f^i$ satisfies $(A), (B), (D), (L), (S)$ and $(N)$.*

*$(A), (B), (L)$ and $(D)$ follow directly from $(\tilde{A}), (\tilde{B}), (\tilde{D}), (\tilde{L})$ respectively. To verify $(S)(N)$ we fix $b^i$ and differentiate* (3.1) *with respect to* $\pi$

$$\partial_\pi f^i\left(\pi, b^i\right) = A\, \partial_q\, g^i\left(q, b^i\right) A^T.$$

*From this equation we see that the Jacobian of income excess demand inherits the negative semi-definiteness and symmetry from the Jacobian of asset excess demand.*
*Thus we are in a position to apply the lemma and get that*

$$f^i\left(\pi, b^i\right) = \arg\max_{x \in X_{fi}} U^i\left(x\right) \quad \pi\, x \leq b^i,$$

*where $X_{fi} \subset \langle A \rangle \cap \mathbb{R}^S_+$ and $U^i$ is continuous, monotone, strictly quasi-concave and linearly homogeneous.*
*Resubstitution of $A\,\theta$ for $x$ and $q$ for $A^T\,\pi$ leads to*

$$g^i\left(q, q\, k\, \bar{\theta^i}\right) = \arg\max_{\theta \in \Theta} U^i\left(A\, \theta\right) \quad q\,\theta \leq q\, k\, \bar{\theta^i} \quad ,$$

*i.e. $g^i$ is the asset demand function derived from a continuous, monotone and strictly quasi concave utility function, which is linearly homogeneous.*

*q. e. d.*

## 5. Debreu's Theorem

The theorem we have proved above is the first global decomposition result of excess demand when markets are incomplete. Moreover it is the first decomposition result in incomplete markets that holds even with homothetic preferences. Our result was obtained from a careful application of the seminal result of Mantel [1976]. The degree to which we could borrow arguments from Mantel [1976] was surprising to us because, as we show now, without further restrictions the competing decomposition result of Debreu [1974] is not applicable to obtain a global decomposition result when markets are incomplete[1].
To this end let $p \in \mathbb{R}^n \setminus \{0\}$ be some non-zero price vector and let $z\left(p\right) \in L\left(p\right) \subset p^\perp$ be the excess demand at $p$ which lies in some linear subspace being a subset of the space orthogonal to $p$.
In this abstract formulation Debreu's[2] decomposition goes as follows:

[1]While in our result the number of agents is, as usual in those results, equal to the dimension of the budget set, recently, Momi [2002] was able to generalize the result of Debreu to incomplete markets by allowing for an arbitrary finite number of agents.
[2][Debreu, 1974]

Add to $z(p)$ some positive multiple, say $\lambda$, of the price vector $p$ and decompose the resulting vector $z(p)+\lambda\, p$ into the weighted sum of the $n$ unit vectors in $\mathbb{R}^n$, where the weights are the $n$ coordinates of the vector $z(p)+\lambda\, p$. Finally apply the orthogonal projection onto $L(p)$, say $proj_{L(p)}$, to the resulting equation to obtain the decomposition:

$$z(p) = \sum_{i=1}^{n} \beta_i(p)\; proj_{L(p)}\, e_i \quad .$$

where $e_i$ denotes the i-th unit vector in $\mathbb{R}^n$.
In the rationalization step of Debreu's proof the residual vectors

$$\nabla_i = e_i - proj_{L(p)}\, e_i$$

are of considerable importance because by construction of the preferences they will become the gradient vectors of the utility functions.
This general procedure can be applied to the asset excess demand and to the income excess demand of the incomplete markets model. In both cases, as we show next, the monotonicity of preferences cannot be guaranteed.

**Asset excess demand** In this case the linear subspace $L(p)$ is the space of vectors orthogonal to the asset price vector, i.e. the space $q^{\perp}$. Hence applying Debreu's decomposition, the gradient of the indirect utility of assets, $V^i(\theta^i) = U^i(\omega^i + A\,\theta^i)$, which we denote by $\nabla^i$, is collinear to the asset price vector $q$, say $\nabla^i = \alpha^i\, q$. Monotonicity of the direct utility function $U^i(x^i)$ requires that $A\,\nabla^i \in \mathbb{R}^S_{++}$. By the no-arbitrage relation this is equivalent to $\alpha^i\, A\, A^{\top} \pi \in \mathbb{R}^S_{++}$. This need however not be the case. For example choose an asset matrix with two assets and two states such that the scalar product of the two different rows of $A$ is negative. Then $A\,A^{\top}$ is a two dimensional square matrix with negative off diagonal. Thus some $\pi \in \mathbb{R}^2_{++}$ can be found for which $\alpha^i\, A\, A^{\top}\, \pi$ has a positive and a negative component. Hence the income utility function is not monotone.

**Income excess demand** Let $n = 3, p = c\,\mathbb{1}, A = (1,1,-2)^{\top}$ and let $L(p) = p^{\perp} \cap \langle A \rangle$, where $c = 1/\sqrt{3}$. Then

$$proj_{L(p)}\, e_1 = A\left(A^{\top} A\right)^{-1} A^{\top}\, e_1 = (1/6)\,(1,1,-2)^{\top}$$

and

$$\nabla_1 = e_1 - proj_{L(p)}\, e_1 = (1/6)\,(5,-1,2)^{\top} \notin \mathbb{R}^3_{++}$$

is the gradient vector of the direct utility function $U^1(\omega^1 + z^1)$, which is not monotone either.

Because of the monotonicity problem that arises in applying Debreu's[4]proof to incomplete markets Bottazzi and Hens [1996] have chosen a different decomposition which is however not able to generate excess demand globally.

# Chapter 4

# THE INDEX-THEOREM

## 1. The Idea of the Index Theorem

The index theorem, introduced to economics by Dierker [1972], allows to answer the question of uniqueness, which is a property of the excess demand considered globally, from the local structure of the excess demand around its potential equilibria. To get the idea of the index theorem consider the following graph of an excess demand for some commodity. Suppose there are just two commodities so that a zero excess demand of the commodity considered in the graph is by Walras Law already a competitive equilibrium. Now suppose furthermore that the graph is continuous and that it satisfies the boundary behaviour. Then, as has been proved in the previous section an equilibrium needs to exist. Note that in this case this conclusion can already be drawn from the intermediate value theorem. The astonishing feature of the Figure 4.1 is that we also get some idea on the number of equilibria. First of all, as Figure 4.1 shows, there may be a continuum of equilibria when the graph of the excess demand is flat at zero. This however is not a generic situation. On perturbing the characteristics of the economy one finds that the graph is transversal to the zero line. Hence generically equilibria are locally unique and since the set of equilibria is compact generically there is a finite number of those. Moreover suppose you do not know the graph globally but you only know how the graph cuts through the zero line. Then knowing that it will always cut from above shows that there is a unique equilibrium. Or to put it the other way round, knowing that at some equilibrium the graph cuts from below we can conclude that there must be multiple equilibria. When the graph cuts from above, respectively from below, the "index" is $+1$, respectively $-1$. The index is equal to the sign of the determinant of the derivative of excess supply. Of course cutting rom above and from below is no longer well defined if the graph is of higher

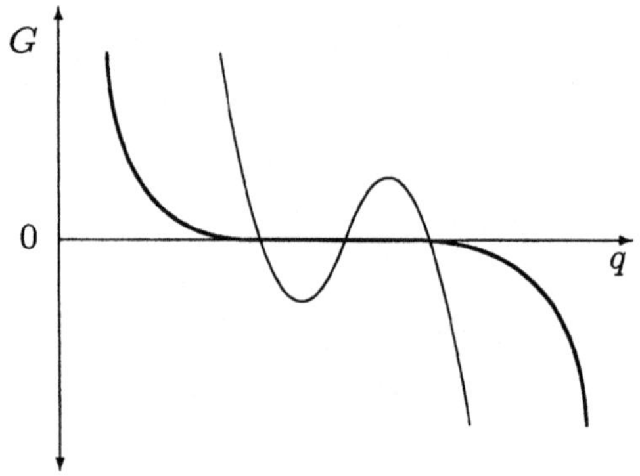


*Figure 4.1.* Asset Excess Demand

dimension. In this case it is more convenient to look at the vector field generated by market excess demand. The "index " is then a way of measuring in how many directions the vector field is changing its orientation in the neighborhood of an equilibrium. This interesting topological properties of excess demand will be made precise in this chapter.
We will first show that asset market excess demand is equivalent to a continuous vector field on some compact set of normalized asset prices which "points inwards" on the boundary. A fortiori by the inward pointing vector field theorem we then have shown that GEI equilibria exist. However in order to get the right inward pointing boundary property we will show that asset excess demand satisfies a stronger condition than condition (4.3) of Lemma 2.2. We continue by showing that for a generic set of GEI economies in equilibrium the rank of the Jacobian of asset market excess demand is maximal. Then we are in a position to apply Poincaré-Hopf's Theorem to get the "index formula". The index theorem has been successfully applied for example in GEI sunspot models. For a reference on this technique to detect sunspot equilibria see e.g. Chiappori and Guesnerie [1991]. We begin with proving the differentiability of excess demand.

## 2. Differentiability of Excess Demand

PROPOSITION 4.1 (DIFFERENTIABILITY OF EXCESS DEMAND)
*Let rank $A = J$ and $A\,\theta > 0$ for some $\theta \in \mathbb{R}^J$, $w^i \gg 0$. If $U^i$ is $r$-differentiable strictly concave then $g^i(\cdot)$ is a $C^{r-1}$ function on $Q$.*

This Proposition is the GEI analogue of Proposition 3.1 in Mas-Colell [1985]. The standard Walrasian arguments for the proof are taken from there. However, some important modifications are in order if markets are incomplete.

PROOF 4.1 (OF PROPOSITION 4.1)
*Since $U^i$ is differentiable strictly concave and $w^i \gg 0$ , $g^i$ is the solution to the first order conditions for an interior solution to the agents asset demand problem:*

$$\underset{\theta \in \mathbb{R}^J}{\arg\max} \quad U^i\left(\omega^i + A\,\theta\right)$$

$$q\,\theta \leq 0 \qquad \omega^i + A\,\theta \geq 0$$

$$\nabla U^i\left(\omega^i + A\,\theta^i\right)A - \lambda^i\,q^T = 0, \tag{4.1}$$

$$q \cdot \theta^i = 0 \tag{4.2}$$

*where $x = \omega^i + A\,\theta$ and $\lambda \neq 0$ is the Lagrangeian multiplier. To study how this solution changes with price changes, we have to consider the system of equations*

$$\begin{bmatrix} A^T\,D^2\,U^i\,(x)\,A & -q \\ -q^T & 0 \end{bmatrix} \cdot \begin{pmatrix} d\,\theta \\ d\,\lambda \end{pmatrix} = \begin{bmatrix} \lambda\,I \\ \theta^T \end{bmatrix} d\,q \quad .$$

*By the implicit function theorem, outlined in the appendix, it suffices to show that*

$$D := \begin{bmatrix} A^T\,D^2\,U^i\,(x)\,A & -q \\ -q^T & 0 \end{bmatrix}$$

*is invertible. Suppose it is not invertible, i.e. suppose there exist $(\nu, \mu) \neq 0$ $\nu \in \mathbb{R}^J$, $\mu \in \mathbb{R}$ such that $D\begin{pmatrix}\nu \\ \mu\end{pmatrix} = 0$. This implies $A^T\,D^2\,U^i\,(x)\,A\,\nu = \mu\,q$ and $\nu^\top q = 0$, so that $\nu \neq 0$ and $\nu^\top\,A^T\,\partial\,x\,U^i\,(x)\,A\,\nu = 0$. Since rank $A = J$, $h := A\,\nu \neq 0$, i. e. there exists $h \in \mathbb{R}^S$, $h \neq 0$, $\partial_x\,U^i\,(x) \cdot h = 0$ such that $h^\top\,D^2\,U^i\,(x)\,h = 0$, a contradiction. This completes the proof of Proposition 4.1.*

*q. e. d.*

Let $G\,(q) := \sum\limits_i g^i\,(q)$ be the asset market excess demand function, from Proposition 4.1 we then immediately get

PROPOSITION 4.2
*Let rank $A = J$, $A\,\theta > 0$ for some $\theta \in \mathbb{R}^J$. If for all $i = 1, ..., I$, $U^i$ is $r$-differentiable strictly concave and $w^i \gg 0$ then $G(q)$ is $C^{r-1}$.*

Let $Z(\pi) := \sum\limits_i z^i\,(\pi)$ be the income transfer market excess demand, then the properties of Proposition 4.1 carry over to $Z$ using the adjoint operations.

## 3. Equivalent Inward Pointing Vector Field

We begin our arguments with the following mathematical lemma, which shows how to construct an "equivalent inward pointing vector field" for some function that satisfies a certain boundary behaviour. Note, that the boundary behaviour used in the Lemma on which we based our existence theorem, Lemma 2.2 is slightly weaker than that of the following Lemma since, in contrast to Lemma 2.2, in Lemma 4.1 the interior point $\hat{q}$ may depend on the particular sequence for which the value condition $\hat{q}\, G\,(q^n) > 0,\ n \geq N$ is checked[1].

LEMMA 4.1
*Let $Q$ be an open subset of the $J-1$ dimensional unit sphere $S^{J-1}$ and $Q_\epsilon := \{q \in Q |\, dist\,(q, \partial\, Q) \geq \epsilon\}$. Moreover, let*

*(i) $\hat{q} \in Q$ such that $q\,\hat{q} > 0$ for all $q \in Q$*

*(ii) $G : Q \to \mathbb{R}^J$ satisfy:*
*If $q^n \in Q, q^n \to q \in \partial\, Q$ then $\exists\, N$ such that $\hat{q}\, G\,(q^n) > 0$ for all $n \geq N$*

*Then there exists an $\epsilon > 0$ and a function $\tilde{G} : Q_\epsilon \to \mathbb{R}^J$ with*

*(iii) $\tilde{G}$ points inwards on $\partial\, Q_\epsilon$, i.e. $q + \tilde{G}\,(q)$ is collinear to $\hat{q}$,*

*(iv) $\tilde{G}\,(q) = 0$ if and only if $G\,(q) = 0$.*

PROOF 4.2
*Define the following auxiliary function*

$$\hat{G} : Q \to \mathbb{R}^J \quad by \quad \hat{G}\,(q) := \frac{\hat{q}}{\hat{q}\, q} - q \quad .$$

*$\hat{G}$ is a continuous vector field (i.e. $q\,\hat{G}\,(q) = 0$) which points inwards (i.e. condition (iii)). Now consider the set*

$$K := \left\{ q \in Q \,\middle|\, \exists\, \lambda \in [0,1] : \lambda\, G\,(q) + (1-\lambda)\, \hat{G}\,(q) = 0 \right\} \quad .$$

*Then there exists a $\delta > 0$ with $K \subseteq Q_\delta$: Suppose such a $\delta$ would not exist. Then for all $n \in \mathbb{N}$ there would exist $q^n \in K$ with $dist\,(q^n, \partial\, Q) < \frac{1}{n}$. Thus there would exist a convergent subsequence $q^{n'}$ of $q^n$ with $q^{n'} \to q \in \partial\, Q$. Because of (ii) we then would have that $\hat{q}\, G\left(q^{n'}\right) > 0$ for $n'$ large enough and per definition of $\hat{G}, \hat{q}\,\hat{G}\left(q^{n'}\right) = \frac{1}{\hat{q}\, q^{n'}} - \hat{q}\, q^{n'} > 0$, since $\hat{q}, q^{n'} \in S^{J-1}, \hat{q} \neq q^{n'}$ for $n'$ large. Hence this would imply that $\lambda^{n'}\,\hat{q}\, G\left(q^{n'}\right) + \left(1 - \lambda^{n'}\right) \hat{q}\,\hat{G}\left(q^{n'}\right) > 0$ for $n'$ sufficiently large, which contradicts $q^{n'} \in K$.*

[1] For an example which makes exactly this point see Neuefeind [1980].

*For $\delta > \epsilon > 0$ there exists a continuous Urysohn function $\alpha : Q_\epsilon \longrightarrow [0,1]$ such that $\alpha(\partial Q_\epsilon) = 0$ and $\alpha(Q_\delta) = 1$, because $\partial Q_\epsilon \cap Q_\delta = \emptyset$. Now define $\tilde{G} : Q_\epsilon \longrightarrow \mathbb{R}^J$ by $\tilde{G}(q) := \alpha(q) G(q) + (1 - \alpha(q)) \hat{G}(q)$. Thus it remains to check that $\tilde{G}$ satisfies properties (iii) and (iv).*

*(iii)* *If $q \in \partial Q_\epsilon$ then $\tilde{G}$ inherits the inward pointing property from $\hat{G}$.*

*(iv)* *$\tilde{G}(q) = 0$ implies $q \in K$; thus $\alpha(q) = 1$ and $G(q) = 0$. Finally, $G(q) = 0$ implies $q \in K$ thus $\tilde{G}(q) = 0$.*

*q. e. d.*

REMARK 4.1
*Note that for the proof we did neither use that G is continuous nor that it satisfies Walras Law. However, if G has these properties, so does $\tilde{G}$.*

## 4. Local Uniqueness and the Index Theorem

To show that generically GEI equilibria are locally unique, we will first apply the

LEMMA 4.2 (PARAMETRIC TRANSVERSALITY THEOREM)
*Consider two open subsets of full dimension $U \subseteq \mathbb{R}^n$, $V \subseteq \mathbb{R}^k$ and let $f : U \times V \longrightarrow \mathbb{R}^m$ be a continuously differentiable function such that*

$$f(x,a) = 0 \Rightarrow rank\, \partial_a f(x,a) = m \quad . \tag{4.3}$$

*Then for all $a \in V$, except for a critical set $C$ of k-dimensional measure zero, $f(x,a) = 0$, implies $rank\, \partial_x f(x,a) = m$. Moreover, if the equilibrium correspondence $E : V \longrightarrow U$ defined by $E(a) := \{x \in U \,|\, f(x,a) = 0\}$ is u.h.c., then $C$ can be taken to be closed.*

The idea of this theorem is that knowing in how many directions some exogenous variable can change the excess demand will be sufficient to conclude in how many directions the endogenous price variable will be able to change the excess demand. For a discussion and a sketch of a proof of Lemma 4.2 see e.g. Magill and Quinzii [1996].
As the exogenous parameters we choose the endowments of some agent, say agent 1. It will not be necessary to perturb the first agent's endowment vector $\omega^1$ in all possible directions of $\mathbb{R}^S$. A perturbation in $\langle A \rangle$ is sufficiently rich. To see this let $\omega^1 \equiv e^1 + \bar{\omega}^1$ where $e^1$ is the rest left after projecting $\omega^1$ onto $\langle A \rangle$ . Now fix $e^1$ and consider $\Theta := \left\{ \bar{\theta}^1 \in \mathbb{R}^J \middle| e^1 + A\,\bar{\theta}^1 \gg 0 \right\}$. Obviously $\Theta$ is open and $dim\, \Theta = J$. Define

$$\hat{g}^1\left(q,\bar{\theta}^1\right) := \arg\max_{\theta\in\mathbb{R}^J} U^1\left(e^1 + A\,\theta\right)$$

$$\text{s.t.}\quad q\,\theta \leq q\,\bar{\theta}^1, e^1 + A\,\theta \geq 0 \quad .$$

$$g^1\left(q,\bar{\theta}^1\right) := \hat{g}^1\left(q,\bar{\theta}^1\right) - \bar{\theta}^1 \quad \text{and} \quad G\left(q,\bar{\theta}^1\right) := g^1\left(q,\bar{\theta}^1\right) + \sum_{i=2}^{I} g^i\,(q) \quad .$$

The first step of our arguments is to prove

LEMMA 4.3 (CONTROLLABILITY OF $G\,(q,\bar{\theta}^1)$) *Let $rank\,A = J$ and $A\,\theta > 0$ for some $\theta \in \mathbb{R}^J$. Furthermore let $U^i$ be monotone, continuous and strictly quasi concave $i = 2,\ldots,I$, and $U^1$ differentiable, strictly concave and $\omega^1 \gg 0$. Then $rank\,\partial_{\bar{\theta}^1}\,G\,(q,\bar{\theta}^1) = J - 1$ for all $q \in Q$.*

PROOF 4.3 *Take $y^1 \in \Theta$ such that $q\,y^1 = 0$. Then $g^1\,(q,\bar{\theta}^1 + \epsilon\,y^1) = g^1\,(q,\bar{\theta}^1) - \epsilon\,y^1$.*
*For $\epsilon \to 0$ by the definition of the directional derivative we get*

$$\partial_{\bar{\theta}^1}\,g^1\left(q,\bar{\theta}^1\right)y^1 = -y^1 \quad .$$

*Thus $\partial_{\bar{\theta}^1}\,G\,(q,\bar{\theta}^1) = \partial_{\bar{\theta}^1}\,g^1\,(q,\bar{\theta}^1)$ is an isomorphism on $\{\theta \in \Theta|\,q\,\theta = 0\}$, hence $rank\,\partial_{\bar{\theta}^1}\,G\,(q,\bar{\theta}^1) = J - 1$.*

*q. e. d.*

Now, in addition we would like to have that the equilibrium correspondence $E\,(\bar{\theta}^1) := \{q \in Q\;|G\,(q,\bar{\theta}^1) = 0\}$ is u.h.c., which is the content of Lemma 4.4:

LEMMA 4.4
*Let $G : Q \times \Theta \to \mathbb{R}^J$ be a continuous function on some open subsets $Q,\Theta$ of some Euclidian spaces, where the first set $Q$ is assumed to be bounded. Let $E\,(\theta) := \{q \in Q\,|G\,(q,\theta) = 0\}$ assume $E\,(\theta) \neq \emptyset$ for all $\theta \in \Theta$. Then $E : \Theta \to Q$ is u.h.c. if $G$ satisfies the following boundary behaviour:*

$$q^n \in Q, q^n \to q, q \notin Q \quad \textit{implies} \quad \|G\,(q^n)\| \to \infty \quad .$$

PROOF 4.4
*Let $\theta^n \in \Theta$ be a sequence converging to $\theta \in \Theta$. Consider $q^n \in E\,(\theta^n)\,n \in \mathbb{N}$. Then, since $q^n \in Q$ and $Q$ is bounded, there exists a convergent subsequence $q^{n'} \to q$. Because of the boundary behaviour $q \in Q$, hence by continuity of $G, q \in E\,(\theta)$.*

*q. e. d.*

Combining these results we get

PROPOSITION 4.3 (GENERIC LOCAL UNIQUENESS)
*Let rank $A = J$ and $A\,\theta > 0$ for some $\theta \in \mathbb{R}^J$, $w^i \gg 0, i = 1, \ldots, I$ and let $U^i$ be differentiable, strictly concave $i = 1, \ldots, I$, then except for a closed set $C$ of measure zero in the parameter space $\Theta := \left\{\bar\theta \in \mathbb{R}^J \middle| e^1 + A\,\bar\theta \gg 0\right\}$ we have rank $\partial_q\, G\,(q) = J - 1$ for all $q \in \{q \in Q\,|G\,(q) = 0\}$.*

Local uniqueness follows from Proposition 4.3 by application of the implicit function theorem. And since the equilibrium set is compact, local uniqueness implies the finiteness of equilibria.
Furthermore, note that by the same argument as in the proof of Proposition 2.10 we know that $G$ satisfies assumption (ii) of Lemma 4.1. Finally, note that because of $A\,\theta > 0$ for some $\theta \in \mathbb{R}^J$, there exists a $\hat{q} \in Q$ which satisfies property (i) of that Lemma.
Therefore, we are in a position to apply

LEMMA 4.5 (POINCARÉ AND HOPF)
*Let $\mathcal{N}$ be a compact n dimensional $C^1$ manifold with boundary and $f$ a continuous vector field on $\mathcal{N}$. Suppose that:*

*(i) $f$ points outward at $\partial\,\mathcal{N}$,*

*(ii) $f$ has a finite number of zeros.*

*Then the sum of the indices of $f$ at the different zeros equals the Euler characteristic of $\mathcal{N}$.*

For a discussion of Lemma 4.5 see e.g. Mas-Colell [1985, J.3.2]. There we can also find that the index of $f$ at $x$ can be computed by $sign\ |\partial\, f\,(x)|$. Evidently, if $G$ points inwards then $-G$ points outwards. To apply the lemmata from above, note that because of Walras-Law or Homogeneity $|\partial\, G\,(q^*)| = 0$ where $q^*$ is a zero of $G$. Thus one has to work on a normalized price space e.g. on $\hat{Q}_\epsilon := \{q \in Q\,|\|q\| = 1 \quad \text{and} \quad dist\,(q, \partial\, Q) > \epsilon\}$. Finally note, that the Euler characteristic of $\hat{Q}_\epsilon$ is 1. All these arguments are fairly standard and can be found e.g. in Mas-Colell [1985]. Summing up, we have shown:

THEOREM 4.1 (INDEX THEOREM. [HENS, 1991])
*Let $\left((U^i, \omega^i)_{i \in I}, A\right)$ be a GEI model with*

*(i) rank $A = J$ and $A\,\theta > 0$ for some $\theta \in \mathbb{R}^J$,*

*(ii) $U^i$ differentiable, strictly concave $i = 1, \ldots, I$,*

*(iii)* $\omega^i \gg 0, \quad i = 1, \ldots, I$

*then for all* $\bar{\theta}^1 \in \left\{\theta \in \mathbb{R}^J \middle| e^1 + A\,\theta \gg 0\right\}$, *except for a closed set of measure zero, the set* $E(\bar{\theta}^1) := \{q \in Q \,|G\,(q, \bar{\theta}^1) = 0\}$ *is finite and* $\sum_{q^* \in E} index\,(q^*) = +1$, *where* $index\,(q^*) := sign\left|-\partial\,\hat{G}\,(q^*)\right|$; $\partial\,\hat{G}\,(q^*)$ *is obtained from* $\partial\,G\,(q^*)$ *by deleting the last row and column.*

Chapter 5

# UNIQUENESS OF COMPETITIVE EQUILIBRIA IN THE ARROW-DEBREU MODEL

## 1. Introduction

The purpose of this chapter is to give an overview of various conditions on consumers' characteristics in an Arrow-Debreu economy which imply uniqueness of the equilibrium. Understanding these conditions in the complete markets case of the GEI-model lays the foundations of the results for incomplete markets presented in the next chapter.

The framework of this chapter is the no-arbitrage approach of the Finance GEI-model because as mentioned before this is totally equivalent to the Arrow-Debreu model when markets are complete.

The focus is on a summary of assumptions on the individual utility functions and endowments which are strong enough to guarantee a unique equilibrium and not on formulating all properties of market demand functions which assure uniqueness. Therefore, we only present those of these properties used later on to prove results in the first sense. Besides, we do not give detailed proofs, but only relevant references and sketches of proofs.

After defining uniqueness of the equilibrium in its different forms, we shortly present some well-known results on local uniqueness. Starting from some special properties of market excess demand functions, we give a complete overview of conditions at the individual level of economies which assure a unique equilibrium. At this point, the reader should have his eye on the last section of this chapter where a figure gives a summary.

As one special aspect we consider the fact that assuming the satisfaction of the expected utility hypothesis for some objective probability measure is not sufficient to obtain a unique equilibrium whenever one allows for aggregate risk. This gains some interest because it refers to the aspect of complete risk sharing which is of growing importance.

## 2. Defining Uniqueness of Arrow-Debreu Equilibria

Consider a GEI-economy with complete markets, i.e.

$$\langle A \rangle = \mathbb{R}^S \quad .$$

For simplification we name an NA-equilibrium under the assumption of complete markets an Arrow-Debreu equilibrium which is legitimate since $B(\pi)$ describes the standard Arrow-Debreu budget set.

DEFINITION 5.1 (ARROW-DEBREU EQUILIBRIUM)
*A tuple $x^* \in \mathbb{R}_+^{S \times I}$ and a (state) price vector $\pi^* \in \mathbb{R}_{++}^S$ constitute an Arrow-Debreu equilibrium if the following conditions hold:*

- $x^{*i} = arg \max U^i(x)$ *s.t.* $\pi^* \cdot (x - \omega^i) \leq 0$ *for all* $i = 1, \ldots, I$;
- $\sum_{i=1}^I x^{*i} = \sum_{i=1}^I \omega^i$.

To express this definition in terms of excess demand: an equilibrium price system $\pi^*$ is defined as a zero of market excess demand, i.e.

$$z(\pi^*) = 0 \quad .$$

Considering consumers' maximization problems, one observes homogeneity of degree zero of excess demand in prices, i.e. $z^i(\pi) = z^i(\lambda \pi)$ for all $\lambda > 0$. Hence, if $\pi^*$ is an equilibrium price system, this is the same for $\lambda \pi^*$ with $\lambda > 0$. Without any price normalization there is always a continuum of equilibrium price systems! Therefore, a price normalization has to be defined, i.e. the restriction to a set

$$\hat{\mathcal{P}}_{c,n} := \left\{ \pi \in R_{++}^S \middle| \pi \cdot n = c \right\}$$

for some $n \in \mathbb{R}_+^S \setminus \{0\}$ and $c > 0$.

DEFINITION 5.2 (LOCAL UNIQUENESS OF ARROW-DEBREU EQUILIBRIA)

*Given $GE = \left\{ \mathbb{R}^S, (U^i, \omega^i)_{i \in I} \right\}$, an Arrow-Debreu equilibrium $(x^*, \pi^*) \in \mathbb{R}_+^{S \times I} \times \hat{\mathcal{P}}_{c,n}$ is locally unique if there is some $\epsilon > 0$ such that $\|\pi - \pi^*\| < \epsilon$ and $\pi \in \hat{\mathcal{P}}_{c,n}$ imply $z(\pi) \neq 0$.*

In this context $\|\ldots\|$ is an arbitrary vector norm on $\mathbb{R}^S$.
Local uniqueness is a very helpful property, but nevertheless it is much more convenient if equilibria are globally unique.

DEFINITION 5.3 (GLOBAL UNIQUENESS OF ARROW-DEBREU EQUILIBRIA)

*Given* $GE = \left\{\mathbb{R}^S \left(U^i, \omega^i\right)_{i\in I}\right\}$, *an Arrow-Debreu equilibrium* $(x^*, \pi^*) \in \mathbb{R}_+^{S\times I} \times \hat{\mathcal{P}}_{c,n}$ *is globally unique if there is no other* $\pi \in \hat{\mathcal{P}}_{c,n}$ *with* $z(\pi) = 0$.

Throughout this section we will assume that agents characteristics satisfy the Differentiability Assumptions 1.2. Hence a unique equilibrium price vector also implies a unique equilibrium allocation. Since the main focus of this book is on global uniqueness, the term "uniqueness" always refers to the global aspect.

# 3. Useful Properties of Market Excess Demand

At least since Sonnenschein [1973], Debreu [1974], and Mantel [1974] it is known that in addition to continuity, Walras' Law, and Homogeneity no additional properties are always satisfied by the market excess demand function. Nevertheless, some excess demand functions exhibit special structures assuring, for example, uniqueness. The most basic property is the Weak Axiom of Revealed Preferences.

DEFINITION 5.4 (WEAK AXIOM OF REVEALED PREFERENCES)
*The excess demand function* $z : \mathbb{R}_{++}^S \to \mathbb{R}^S$ *satisfies the Weak Axiom of Revealed Preferences (WARP) if*

$$\pi \cdot z(\tilde{\pi}) \leq 0 \Rightarrow \tilde{\pi} \cdot z(\pi) > 0$$

*for all* $\pi, \tilde{\pi} \in \mathbb{R}_{++}^S$ *with* $z(\pi) \neq z(\tilde{\pi})$.

A sufficient condition for this is given by

$$[\pi \cdot v = 0, z(\pi) \cdot v = 0] \Rightarrow v \cdot D_\pi z(\pi) v < 0$$

for all $v \in \mathbb{R}^S \setminus \{0\}$ and $\pi \in \mathbb{R}_{++}^S$. Allowing that the inequality is weak, the condition is also necessary, i.e.

$$\text{WARP} \Rightarrow v \cdot D_\pi z(\pi) v \leq 0$$

for all $v \in \mathbb{R}^S, \pi \in \mathbb{R}_{++}^S$ with $z(\pi) \cdot v = 0$. For a proof compare Mas-Colell [1985, Proposition 5.7.3].

The definition of the Weak Axiom of Revealed Preferences was chosen under the consideration of the Differentiability Assumptions 1.2.

The idea underlying this property comes from individual excess demand functions which always satisfy this axiom. As soon as a consumer chooses a consumption bundle $x(\pi)$ even though he can afford also $x(\tilde{\pi})$, $x(\pi)$ has to be better for him than $x(\tilde{\pi})$. Since he chooses $x(\tilde{\pi})$ at prices $\tilde{\pi}$, consistency of decisions is only given when he cannot afford $x(\pi)$ at prices $\tilde{\pi}$.

Regrettably, WARP is not an additive property: even though individual excess demand functions satisfy the axiom, this need not to be true for market excess demand (compare Hicks [1956]).

A stronger property for excess demand functions is monotonicity.

DEFINITION 5.5 (MONOTONICITY WITH NORMALIZING VECTOR) *Let $n \in \mathbb{R}_{+}^{S} \backslash \{0\}$. The excess demand function $z : \mathbb{R}_{+}^{S} \longrightarrow \mathbb{R}^{S}$ is monotone with respect to $n$ if*

$$(\pi - \tilde{\pi}) \cdot [z(\pi) - z(\tilde{\pi})] < 0$$

*for all $\pi, \tilde{\pi} \in \mathbb{R}_{++}^{S}$ with $(\pi - \tilde{\pi}) \cdot n = 0$ and $z(\pi) \neq z(\tilde{\pi})$.*

Note that for distinction we use the term "monotone" in contrast to the term "monotonic" in the sense of Definition 1.1.
A sufficient condition for monotonicity with respect to $n$ is given by the strict form

$$v \cdot n = 0 \Rightarrow v \cdot D_{\pi} z(\pi) v < 0$$

for all $v \in \mathbb{R}^{S} \backslash \{0\}$ and $\pi \in \mathbb{R}_{++}^{S}$. Again a necessary condition is given by

$$v \cdot n = 0 \Rightarrow v \cdot D_{\pi} z(\pi) v \leq 0$$

for all $v \in \mathbb{R}^{S}$ and $\pi \in \mathbb{R}_{++}^{S}$. These statements can also be found in Mas-Colell [1985, Proposition 5.7.3].
In addition, Mas-Colell [1985, p. 216] demonstrates that it is really necessary to restrict price systems $\pi$ by normalization since otherwise monotonicity would never be fulfilled. In contrast to WARP, monotonicity passes from individual to market excess demand, but only if the underlying normalizing vector is the same for all individuals. The economic interpretation for WARP and monotonicity is that these properties assure demands to move in opposite directions of prices. For WARP this only has to be true for compensated price changes in the sense that $v \cdot z(\pi) = 0$ (compare Mas-Colell [1985, p. 217]).

PROPOSITION 5.1 (UNIQUENESS FOR MONOTONICITY AND WARP) *Suppose $GE = \left\{\mathbb{R}^{S}, (U^{i}, \omega^{i})_{i \in I}\right\}$ such that market excess demand satisfies monotonicity or WARP. If the economy is regular, it has a unique Arrow-Debreu equilibrium.*

Given the strong differentiable versions of monotonicity and WARP, Mas-Colell [1985, p. 216] proves a chain of implications:

Monotonicity $\Rightarrow$ WARP $\Rightarrow$ positive index for all equilibria

which proves uniqueness because of the Index Theorem 4.1.
Given monotonicity and WARP in their weak forms, Mas-Colell [1985, Proposition 5.7.2] proves monotonicity to imply WARP. WARP, however, assures

convexity of the normalized equilibrium price set (compare Mas-Colell et al. [1995, p. 609]) which under local uniqueness implies global uniqueness.
A last property helpful when considering uniqueness of the equilibrium is the strict gross substitution property which requires demand for a commodity to be strictly increasing in other commodities' prices and strictly decreasing in its own price.

DEFINITION 5.6 (STRICT GROSS SUBSTITUTION)
*The excess demand function $z : \mathbb{R}^S_{++} \to \mathbb{R}^S$ satisfies the property of strict gross substitution whenever the Jacobian matrix has strictly positive off-diagonal elements and strictly negative diagonal elements.*

The definition of the weak gross substitution property is nearly the same, but allows that elements of the matrix are zero.
Arrow and Hahn [1971] give different proofs for strict gross substitution to imply uniqueness. One idea (compare Arrow and Hahn [1971, Chapter 9, Corollary 7]) is to do an indirect proof: assuming the existence of two equilibrium price systems $\pi^*$ and $\pi^{**}$, they can be normalized such that $\pi^* \leq \pi^{**}$ and they are equal in (at least) one state. This leads to a contradiction with market clearing when applying strict gross substitution for this state.

PROPOSITION 5.2 (UNIQUENESS FOR STRICT GROSS SUBSTITUTION)

*Suppose $GE = \left\{\mathbb{R}^S, (U^i, \omega^i)_{i \in I}\right\}$ such that market excess demand satisfies the property of strict gross substitution. Then the economy has a unique Arrow-Debreu equilibrium.*

Monotonicity and gross substitution are equivalent if there are only two states, i.e. $S = 2$. For relations between gross substitution and the Weak Axiom of Revealed Preferences compare Kehoe and Mas-Colell [1982] and Kehoe [1985].

## 4. How to Obtain Uniqueness

When searching for conditions on the consumers' characteristics guaranteeing a unique equilibrium we apply four different approaches. The reader will observe that these overlap in the sense that some proofs can be done in different manners.
The first approach is to derive an explicit pricing formula from equilibrium conditions. There are only quite a few economies which allow to proceed in this way, but they are extremely nice to handle.
The second approach is to prove the existence of a representative consumer, i.e. it is possible to prove the existence of a utility function and endowments such that an Arrow-Debreu economy with a single consumer defined hereby has the same market excess demand function as the original economy. If the characteristics of the representative consumer can be explicitly given, one also

obtains an explicit pricing formula, namely the (normalized) gradient of his utility in his endowments.

Since individual excess demand functions satisfy WARP, existence of a representative consumer implies WARP for market excess demand. This is also true if market excess demand is monotone with respect to some normalizing vector. Therefore, the third approach proving uniqueness via monotonicity is linked to the second one.

The last approach is to work with the gross substitution property.

Figure 5.4 at the end of this chapter demonstrates among other things the links between the different approaches.

## 4.1 Explicit Pricing Formulas

### 4.1.1 No-Trade Equilibrium

Clearly, the simplest pricing formula is obtainable whenever a priori any trade is excluded. Imagine the situation where all consumers are identical in utility $\bar{U}$ as well as in endowments $\bar{\omega}$. Then, it is no question to state the pricing vector to be collinear to $\nabla \bar{U}(\bar{\omega})$. If the chosen normalization is $\hat{\mathcal{P}}$, the normalized equilibrium price system is

$$\pi^{*T} = \frac{1}{\partial_{x_1} \bar{U}(\bar{\omega})} \nabla \bar{U}(\bar{\omega}) \quad .$$

However, this constitutes only a special case of the situation where the endowment distribution is Pareto-efficient.

PROPOSITION 5.3 (UNIQUENESS FOR PARETO-EFFICIENT ENDOWMENTS)

*Given* $GE = \left\{\mathbb{R}^S, (U^i, \omega^i)_{i \in I}\right\}$ *with* $(\omega^i)_{i \in I}$ *a Pareto-efficient allocation, the no-trade equilibrium is the unique equilibrium with equilibrium price system* $\pi^* \in \hat{\mathcal{P}}$ *collinear to* $\nabla U^i(\omega^i)$ *for all* $i \in I$.

The proof is very simple. Mas-Colell et al. [1995, Proposition 17.F.5] show that as soon as $(\omega^i)_{i \in I}$ constitutes an Arrow-Debreu equilibrium allocation, it has to be unique because otherwise the convex combination of this equilibrium with an alternative one would be an improvement. However, if $(\omega^i)_{i \in I}$ is Pareto-efficient it has to be an equilibrium because in an equilibrium each individual $i$ behaves individually rational and no one would choose an alternative plan which worsens his situation in comparison to $\omega^i$. The pricing formula follows from first order conditions for the maximization problem.

### 4.1.2 Complete Risk Sharing

Risk sharing is a fascinating idea which found many powerful applications in insurance markets. It finds its microeconomic foundation in different economic models. Most of them are based on the expected utility hypothesis (compare, for example, Borch [1962]).

A foundation of phenomena like risk sharing is only sound for a unique competitive equilibrium by which the allocation in the markets is explained. As it is well-known, uniqueness is satisfied for the case of no aggregate risk and complete markets.

A large part of the literature in risk sharing excludes aggregate risk (compare Malinvaud [1972], Malinvaud [1973] and Levine and Zame [1999]) where aggregate risk is defined in different ways. The definition applied here is the most common one (compare, for example, Magill and Quinzii [1996]) which defines aggregate risk as fluctuations of aggregate endowments.

PROPOSITION 5.4 (UNIQUENESS WITH COMPLETE RISK SHARING)
*Assume* $GE = \left\{\mathbb{R}^S, \left(U^i, \omega^i\right)_{i \in I}\right\}$ *such that all consumers satisfy the expected utility hypothesis with respect to an objective probability measure* $\bar{p} \in \hat{\mathcal{P}}_{1,\mathbb{1}}$[1], *i.e.*

$$U^i(x) = \sum_{s=1}^{S} \bar{p}_s \, u^i(x_s)$$

*for some* $u^i : \mathbb{R}_+ \rightarrow \mathbb{R}$ *infinitely often differentiable, strictly monotonic, and strictly concave with* $\lim_{x_s \rightarrow 0} \left(u^i\right)'(x_s) = \infty$. *If there is no aggregate risk, i.e.*

$$\omega = \bar{\omega} \, \mathbb{1}$$

*for some* $\bar{\omega} \in \mathbb{R}_{++}$, *the economy is characterized by a unique Arrow-Debreu equilibrium and normalizing price systems to the unit simplex leads to* $\pi^* = \bar{p}$.

Economists, Cass and Shell [1983, p. 209] for example, ascribe this result to Malinvaud [1972], Malinvaud [1973] who—among other things—considers Pareto-efficient allocations in a similar framework. As soon as an allocation is risky, it could not be Pareto-efficient since averaging over states with weighting by the objective probability measure improves consumers because of strict concavity: each Pareto-efficient allocation has to be totally riskless. $\pi^* = \bar{p}$ follows directly from first order conditions for the maximization problems.

Recently the consequences of aggregate risk have become a central question in (financial) economics (compare Tesar [1993], Townsend [1995], Heaton and Lucas [1996], and Crès and Rossi [2000]). Therefore, it is interesting to know whether Proposition 5.4 also holds without the assumption of a riskless aggregate endowment, i.e. without $\omega = \bar{\omega} \, \mathbb{1}$ for some $\bar{\omega} \in \mathbb{R}_{++}$. In the

[1] $\hat{\mathcal{P}}_{1,\mathbb{1}}$ is the interior of the unit simplex.

following it is shown by means of an example that deviating to aggregate risk might lead to multiple equilibria. This is the same for giving up the assumption of complete markets, but this topic is placed in Chapter 6.
Consider an Arrow-Debreu economy with $I = 2$ consumers and $S = 2$ states. The consumers are characterized by endowments

$$\omega^1 = \frac{4}{3}\begin{pmatrix}1\\1\end{pmatrix} \quad \text{and} \quad \omega^2 = \frac{2}{3}\begin{pmatrix}1\\4\end{pmatrix} \quad . \tag{5.1}$$

Obviously, *only* the second consumer is directly confronted with uncertainty, whereas uncertainty happens to the first consumer only indirectly via the other's endowment.
Both consumers profit in the *same* way by consumption of the good, i.e. there is a common utility function

$$u : \mathbb{R}_+ \longrightarrow \mathbb{R}$$

with $u^i = u$ for $i = 1, 2$. Additionally to the standard assumptions, we restrict $u$ via some values of its first derivative, namely (see Figure 5.1)

$$\begin{aligned} u'\left(\tfrac{5}{6}\right) &= 24\,, \quad u'(1) = 5\,, \quad u'\left(1\tfrac{1}{6}\right) = 4\,, \\ u'\left(1\tfrac{1}{3}\right) &= 3\,, \quad u'(2) = 2\tfrac{1}{2}\,, \quad u'\left(2\tfrac{2}{3}\right) = \tfrac{1}{2}\,. \end{aligned} \tag{5.2}$$

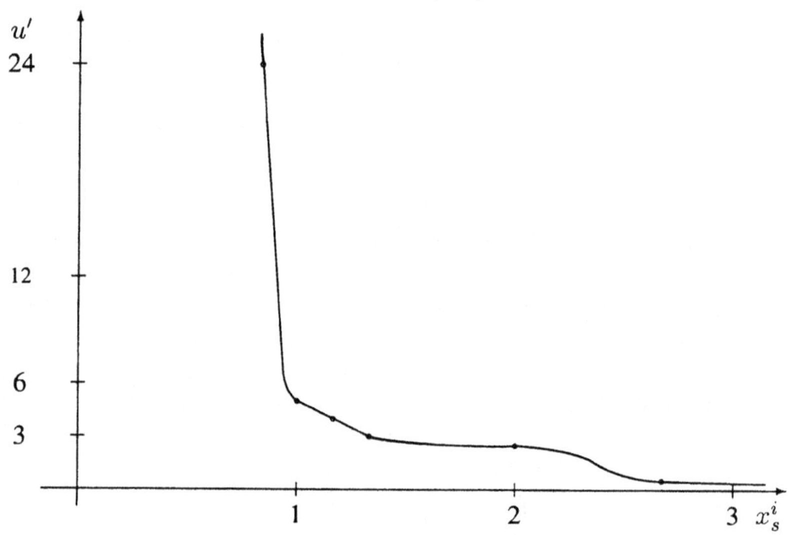


*Figure 5.1.* A possible form of $u'$.

Obviously, these values of the derivative are compatible with the Assumption 1.2 on $U^i, i = 1, 2$, and the implied requirements on $u$.
Both consumers take the two states of the world for equally likely to occur, i.e. both states have the same objective probability $\bar{\rho}_1 = \bar{\rho}_2 = 1/2$.
We claim that the economy defined in this way has at least the following two equilibria:

$$\begin{aligned} x^{*1} = x^{*2} &= \begin{pmatrix} 1 \\ 2 \end{pmatrix}, \\ \pi^* &= \begin{pmatrix} 2 \\ 1 \end{pmatrix}, \\ \hat{x}^1 &= \tfrac{1}{6}\begin{pmatrix} 7 \\ 16 \end{pmatrix}, \\ \hat{x}^{*2} &= \tfrac{1}{6}\begin{pmatrix} 5 \\ 8 \end{pmatrix}, \\ \hat{\pi} &= \begin{pmatrix} 8 \\ 1 \end{pmatrix}. \end{aligned} \tag{5.3}$$

Market clearing is obvious. To verify the maximization condition, remember first order conditions for $i \in I$:

$$\bar{\rho}_1 u'\left(x_1^i\right) - \lambda^i \pi_1 = 0, \tag{5.4}$$

$$\bar{\rho}_2 u'\left(x_2^i\right) - \lambda^i \pi_2 = 0, \tag{5.5}$$

$$\pi \cdot \left(x^i - \omega^i\right) = 0 \tag{5.6}$$

where $\lambda^i > 0$ is the Lagrangian multiplier. Substitute the values of (5.1)–(5.3) into (5.4)–(5.6) to obtain the following system of equations:

$$\begin{aligned} \tfrac{1}{2} \cdot 5 - \lambda^{*1} \cdot 2 &= 0, & \tfrac{1}{2} \cdot 5 - \lambda^{*2} \cdot 2 &= 0, \\ \tfrac{1}{2} \cdot 2\tfrac{1}{2} - \lambda^{*1} \cdot 1 &= 0, & \tfrac{1}{2} \cdot 2\tfrac{1}{2} - \lambda^{*2} \cdot 1 &= 0, \\ 2 \cdot \left(-\tfrac{1}{3}\right) + 1 \cdot \tfrac{2}{3} &= 0, & 2 \cdot \tfrac{1}{3} + 1 \cdot \left(-\tfrac{2}{3}\right) &= 0, \end{aligned}$$

$$\begin{aligned} \tfrac{1}{2} \cdot 4 - \hat{\lambda}^1 \cdot 8 &= 0, & \tfrac{1}{2} \cdot 24 - \hat{\lambda}^2 \cdot 8 &= 0, \\ \tfrac{1}{2} \cdot \tfrac{1}{2} - \hat{\lambda}^1 \cdot 1 &= 0, & \tfrac{1}{2} \cdot 3 - \hat{\lambda}^2 \cdot 1 &= 0, \\ 8 \cdot \left(-\tfrac{1}{6}\right) + 1 \cdot 1\tfrac{1}{3} &= 0, & 8 \cdot \tfrac{1}{6} + 1 \cdot \left(-1\tfrac{1}{3}\right) &= 0. \end{aligned}$$

This system is solved for $\lambda^{*1} = \lambda^{*2} = 1\,\frac{1}{4}$ and $\hat{\lambda}^1 = \frac{1}{4}$, $\hat{\lambda}^2 = 1\,\frac{1}{2}$. Therefore, the equilibrium properties are proved.
Note that the example is constructed in a way such that there has to be a change in the sign of the third derivative of $u$. The sign of the third derivative can be interpreted with respect to precautionary saving and prudence (cf. Kimball

[1990]). The importance of these concepts in the context of non-insurable idiosyncratic risk was pointed out by Franke et al. [1992] and Weil [1992]. Nevertheless, by deviating from the assumption of identical preferences the example can be modified such that the third derivatives are strictly positive. All the data of the example remain the same, but (5.2) is substituted by (compare Figures 5.2 and 5.3)

$$(u^1)'\left(1\,\tfrac{1}{6}\right) = 4, \quad (u^1)'\left(1\tfrac{1}{5}\right) = 3\,\tfrac{1}{2}, \quad (u^1)'\left(2\,\tfrac{2}{3}\right) = \tfrac{1}{2}, \quad (u^1)'(3) = \tfrac{14}{50},$$

$$(u^2)'\left(\tfrac{4}{5}\right) = 62\,\tfrac{1}{2}, \quad (u^2)'\left(\tfrac{5}{6}\right) = 24, \quad (u^2)'(1) = 5, \quad (u^2)'\left(1\,\tfrac{1}{3}\right) = 3.$$

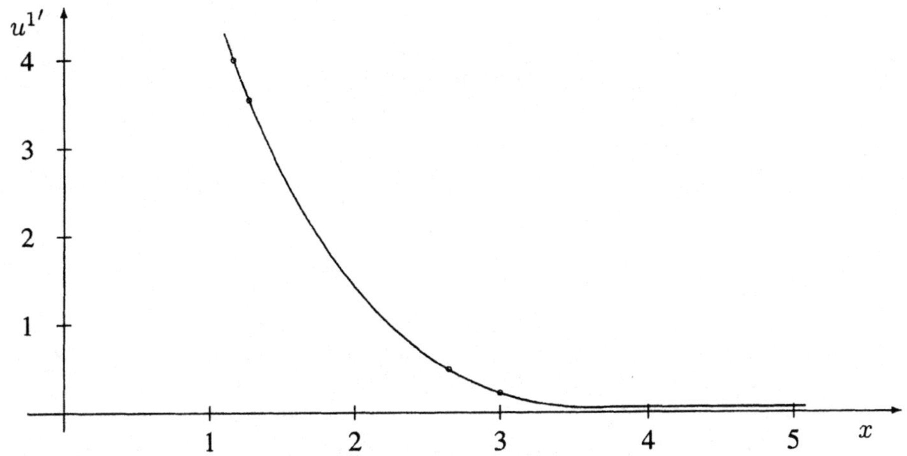


*Figure 5.2.* A possible form of $(u^1)'$.

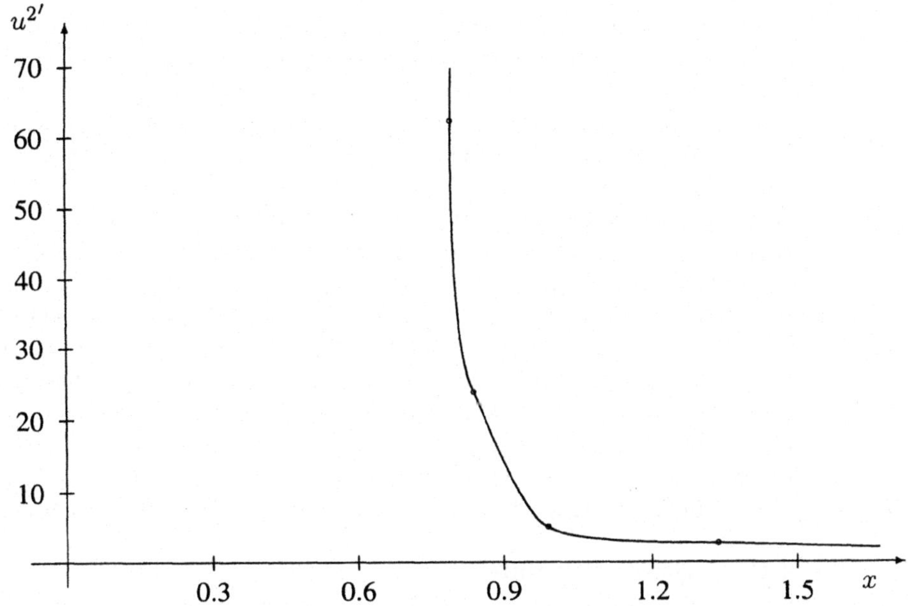


*Figure 5.3.* A possible form of $(u^2)'$.

The values are compatible with $u^1, u^2$ satisfying the standard assumptions and having a strictly positive third derivative, presumably even showing decreasing absolute risk aversion in the sense of Arrow [1970] and Pratt [1964].
The equilibrium $(\hat{x}^1, \hat{x}^2, \hat{\pi})$ with the Lagrangian multipliers $\hat{\lambda}^1, \hat{\lambda}^2$ is preserved. A second equilibrium is given by

$$\bar{x}^1 = \frac{1}{5}\begin{pmatrix} 6 \\ 15 \end{pmatrix}, \bar{x}^2 = \frac{1}{5}\begin{pmatrix} 4 \\ 5 \end{pmatrix}, \bar{\pi} = \frac{1}{2}\begin{pmatrix} 25 \\ 2 \end{pmatrix}$$

where $\bar{\lambda}^1 = \frac{7}{50}$ and $\bar{\lambda}^2 = 2\,\frac{1}{2}$.
Multiplicity of competitive equilibria when there is aggregate risk has recently also been demonstrated by Crès and Rossi [2000]. Their model is directly based on Malinvaud [1973]. Therefore, they allow that different states are realized for different consumers. Consumers do not differ in their characteristics (utility functions are not of the expected utility type), but only in the state realized for them. Besides, multiple commodities exist. Within this context according to Malinvaud [1972], Malinvaud [1973] no aggregate risk means that the proportion of consumers in each state is a priori fixed and endowments for each consumer only depend on his "own" state. Crès and Rossi [2000] however allow that endowments in one special commodity depend also on other consumers' state realizations, nevertheless they assume that this "collective component of risk" vanishes at the aggregate level. Within their framework they implicitly show the multiplicity of equilibria because they demonstrate the possible existence of asymmetric equilibria (in addition to a symmetric equilibrium).
Our example can also be given an intertemporal interpretation. Imagine $s = 1$ respectively 2 realizes in the first respectively second period. Then, multiplicity of competitive equilibria can be interpreted as multiplicity of competitive interest rates—a result which can be traced back at least to Fisher [1907].[2]
It would be interesting to know which kind of assumptions may be sufficient to obtain a unique Arrow-Debreu equilibrium even for aggregate risk. One example, as Hens and Löffler [1995] point out, is the assumption of a relative risk aversion less than one (Proposition 5.10). Similarly, new results might be found using the notion of "risk vulnerability" (compare Gollier and Pratt [1996]) or Ross' [Ross, 1981] conditions on decreasing risk aversion.

### 4.1.3 Quadratic Utility

If utility functions do not only satisfy the expected utility hypothesis with respect to an objective probability measure, but even are quadratic, then there is a unique Arrow-Debreu equilibrium despite aggregate risk.

[2] We are grateful to John Geanakoplos for pointing out this historical result.

PROPOSITION 5.5 (UNIQUENESS WITH QUADRATIC UTILITY)
*Assume* $GE = \left\{\mathbb{R}^S, (U^i, \omega^i)_{i \in I}\right\}$ *such that all consumers satisfy the expected utility hypothesis with respect to an objective probability measure* $\bar{\rho} \in \hat{\mathcal{P}}_{1,1}$ *and state utility is quadratic, i.e.*

$$U^i(x) = \sum_{s=1}^{S} \bar{\rho}_s \left(x_s - \frac{1}{2} \gamma^i x_s^2\right) \quad . \tag{5.7}$$

*If* $\gamma^i \in \left(0, \min_{s \in S} \frac{1}{\omega_s}\right)$, *then the economy is characterized by a unique interior Arrow-Debreu equilibrium and normalizing the first state price to one leads to*

$$\pi^{*T} = \left(1, \frac{\bar{\rho}_2 \left(\sum_{i=1}^{I} \frac{1}{\gamma^i} - \omega_2\right)}{\bar{\rho}_1 \left(\sum_{i=1}^{I} \frac{1}{\gamma^i} - \omega_1\right)}, \ldots, \frac{\bar{\rho}_S \left(\sum_{i=1}^{I} \frac{1}{\gamma^i} - \omega_S\right)}{\bar{\rho}_1 \left(\sum_{i=1}^{I} \frac{1}{\gamma^i} - \omega_1\right)}\right) \quad .$$

Note that $x_s - \frac{1}{2} \gamma^i x_s^2$ in (5.7) is a HARA-function which can be easily transferred to the form of equation (1.5) given in Definition 1.5.
The assumptions on $(\gamma^i)_{i \in I}$ and $\omega$ together with the form of $(U^i)_{i \in I}$ assure strict monotonicity of utility. Strict concavity therefore guarantees the first order conditions to be necessary for utility maximization whenever consumption plans are in the interior of the consumption set. The idea of the proof is to apply individual first order conditions. Normalizing $\pi_1^* = 1$ allows to eliminate the Lagrangian multipliers from these equations. Division by $\gamma^i$ and summing up over all individuals leads to the pricing formula given in the proposition because one can apply market clearing.
Note that equilibrium prices are totally independent of the distribution of income and risk aversion among consumers. Besides without aggregate risk the equilibrium pricing formula is the same as in the last Proposition 5.4 (except for normalization).

### 4.1.4 On Cobb-Douglas Utility

Another class of utility functions satisfying the expected utility hypothesis (and even exhibiting hyperbolic absolute risk aversion) is the class of Cobb-Douglas utility functions. In the framework of the Arrow-Debreu model they are widely used because they enable explicit computation of demand functions and equilibrium prices without any further restrictions on probability measures and endowments.

PROPOSITION 5.6 (UNIQUENESS WITH COBB-DOUGLAS UTILITY)
*Assume* $GE = \left\{\mathbb{R}^S, (U^i, \omega^i)_{i \in I}\right\}$ *such that all consumers satisfy the expected utility hypothesis and state utility is logarithmic, i.e.*

$$U^i(x) = \sum_{s=1}^{S} \rho_s^i \ln x_s. \tag{5.8}$$

*Then the economy is characterized by a unique Arrow-Debreu equilibrium and normalizing the first state price to one leads to*

$$\pi_{-1}^* = -\left[\begin{pmatrix} \sum_{i=1}^{I} \rho_2^i \, \omega_{-1}^{iT} \\ \vdots \\ \sum_{i=1}^{I} \rho_S^i \, \omega_{-1}^{iT} \end{pmatrix} - \begin{pmatrix} \omega_2 & & \\ & \ddots & \\ & & \omega_S \end{pmatrix}\right]^{-1} \begin{pmatrix} \sum_{i=1}^{I} \rho_2^i \, \omega_1^i \\ \vdots \\ \sum_{i=1}^{I} \rho_S^i \, \omega_1^i \end{pmatrix} .$$

PROOF 5.1

*The properties of* $(U^i)_{i \in I}$ *assure first order conditions to be necessary and sufficient for utility maximization under budget constraints. Simple calculations lead to demand functions*

$$x_s^i(\pi) = \rho_s^i \, \frac{\pi \cdot \omega^i}{\pi_s} \quad \textit{for all} \quad i \in I,\ s \in S \quad .$$

*From market clearing one therefore obtains the system of linear equations*

$$\sum_{i=1}^{I} \rho_s^i \left(\pi \cdot \omega^i\right) - \sum_{i=1}^{I} \pi_s \, \omega_s^i = 0 \quad \textit{for all} \quad s \in S \quad ,$$

*which can be rewritten as*

$$\left[\begin{pmatrix} \sum_{i=1}^{I} \rho_1^i \, \omega^{iT} \\ \vdots \\ \sum_{i=1}^{I} \rho_S^i \, \omega^{iT} \end{pmatrix} - \begin{pmatrix} \omega_1 & & 0 \\ & \ddots & \\ 0 & & \omega_S \end{pmatrix}\right] \pi = 0 \quad . \tag{5.9}$$

*From Theorem 2.1 there has to be some strictly positive solution* $\pi^*$. *Since the entries of the first matrix in* (5.9) *are strictly positive and the second matrix is a diagonal one with strictly positive diagonal entries,* $[\ldots]$ *is a strict gross substitute matrix, i.e. has strictly positive off-diagonal and strictly negative diagonal entries. Therefore, eliminating the first column and the first row from* $[\ldots]$ *results in a matrix which has a row dominant diagonal*[3] *because* (5.9) *implies*

[3] A matrix $D \in \mathbb{R}^{n \times n}$ is row diagonal dominant if there exists some $\Pi \in \mathbb{R}^n_{++}$ such that

$$\Pi_i \, |D_{ii}| > \sum_{j=i} \Pi_j \, |D_{ij}| \quad \text{for all} \quad i = 1, \ldots, n \quad .$$

$$
\begin{pmatrix} \sum_{i=1}^{I} \rho_2^i \left(0, \omega_3^i, \ldots, \omega_S^i\right) \\ \vdots \\ \sum_{i=1}^{I} \rho_S^i \left(\omega_2^i, \ldots, \omega_{S-1}^i, 0\right) \end{pmatrix} \pi_{-1}^*
$$

$$
= \begin{pmatrix} \pi_2^* \left(\omega_2 - \sum_{i=1}^{I} \rho_2^i \omega_2^i\right) \\ \vdots \\ \pi_S^* \left(\omega_S - \sum_{i=1}^{I} \rho_S^i \omega_S^i\right) \end{pmatrix} - \pi_1^* \begin{pmatrix} \sum_{i=1}^{I} \rho_2^i \omega_1^i \\ \vdots \\ \sum_{i=1}^{I} \rho_S^i \omega_1^i \end{pmatrix}
$$

$$
< \begin{pmatrix} \pi_2^* \left(\omega_2 - \sum_{i=1}^{I} \rho_2^i \omega_2^i\right) \\ \vdots \\ \pi_S^* \left(\omega_S - \sum_{i=1}^{I} \rho_S^i \omega_S^i\right) \end{pmatrix} = \begin{pmatrix} \pi_2^* \left|\omega_2 - \sum_{i=1}^{I} \rho_2^i \omega_2^i\right| \\ \vdots \\ \pi_S^* \left|\omega_S - \sum_{i=1}^{I} \rho_S^i \omega_S^i\right| \end{pmatrix} .
$$

*A matrix with a row dominant diagonal is invertible because obviously its transposed has a column dominant diagonal. Following Murata [1977, Theorem 21 and Theorem 24] this transposed is invertible and therefore also the original matrix. Because of Walras' Law the first line of* (5.9) *is redundant. Therefore, normalizing* $\pi_1^* = 1$, *it is equivalent to*

$$
\left[ \begin{pmatrix} \sum_{i=1}^{I} \rho_2^i \omega_{-1}^{iT} \\ \vdots \\ \sum_{i=1}^{I} \rho_S^i \omega_{-1}^{iT} \end{pmatrix} - \begin{pmatrix} \omega_2 & & \\ & \ddots & \\ & & \omega_S \end{pmatrix} \right] \pi_{-1}^* = - \begin{pmatrix} \sum_{i=1}^{I} \rho_2^i \omega_1^i \\ \vdots \\ \sum_{i=1}^{I} \rho_S^i \omega_1^i \end{pmatrix}
$$

*or*

$$
\pi_{-1}^* = - \left[ \begin{pmatrix} \sum_{i=1}^{I} \rho_2^i \omega_{-1}^{iT} \\ \vdots \\ \sum_{i=1}^{I} \rho_S^i \omega_{-1}^{iT} \end{pmatrix} - \begin{pmatrix} \omega_2 & & \\ & \ddots & \\ & & \omega_S \end{pmatrix} \right]^{-1} \begin{pmatrix} \sum_{i=1}^{I} \rho_2^i \omega_1^i \\ \vdots \\ \sum_{i=1}^{I} \rho_S^i \omega_1^i \end{pmatrix} .
$$

*q. e. d.*

If one wants to obtain uniqueness and is not interested in an explicit pricing formula, one can stop with equation (5.9): from Theorem 2.1 one knows the existence of a solution for this equation; from Theorem 4.3 one knows generic local uniqueness of equilibria after normalization. Therefore, because the set of solutions of (5.9) is a linear subspace of $\mathbb{R}^S$ and corresponds to the non-normalized equilibrium price set, generically it has to be of dimension one which is equivalent to a unique (normalized) equilibrium price system.
Note that Cobb-Douglas utility functions evoke the gross substitution property of individual and therefore market demand such that also Proposition 5.2

can be applied. Besides the functions are homothetic such that under further restrictions uniqueness can be obtained with the Proposition 5.7 in the next section.

## 4.2 Existence of a Representative Consumer

The existence of a representative consumer is extremely comfortable because it allows to use his preferences as a measure of social welfare (compare Mas-Colell et al. [1995]). A thorough discussion of the question when market demand is a consumer demand can be found in Shafer and Sonnenschein [1982] who refer for this topic to their predecessors Antonelli [1886], Gorman [1953], Nataf [1953], Eisenberg [1961], Chipman [1974], and Chipman and Moore [1976]. To summarize those results important for my interest on uniqueness of Arrow-Debreu equilibria: as soon as consumers preferences are either identical homothetic or homothetic and endowments are collinear[4], there exists a representative consumer.

The main idea is to use homogeneity of demand in income to obtain the Strong Axiom of Revealed Preferences (SARP), i.e. symmetry and negative semi-definiteness of the Slutzky matrix of market demand.

Therefore, since demand of a single (here the representative) consumer satisfies WARP, uniqueness of the Arrow-Debreu equilibrium is obtained.

PROPOSITION 5.7 (UNIQUENESS FOR HOMOTHETICITY)
*Suppose* $GE = \left\{\mathbb{R}^S \left(U^i, \omega^i\right)_{i\in I}\right\}$ *such that all* $U^i, i = 1, \ldots, I$, *are homothetic, then there is a unique Arrow-Debreu equilibrium whenever either all* $U^i$ *are identical or the endowments* $\left(\omega^i\right)_{i\in I}$ *are collinear, i.e. there is some vector* $\delta \in \hat{\mathcal{P}}_{1,1}$ *with* $\omega^i = \delta_i\, \omega$ *for all* $i \in I$.

The idea of the proofs for the existence of a representative consumer are simple (compare Shafer and Sonnenschein [1982, Theorem 2 and Theorem 4]). For identical homothetic utility functions one applies that all consumers are characterized by the same demand function which is linear in income such that a representative consumer is described by the given utility function and his endowment is the aggregate endowment, i.e. his characteristics are independent of the income distribution. For homothetic preferences and collinear endowments one can prove that a representative consumer is given by utility

$$U(x) = \max_{x\in\mathbb{R}^S_+} \prod_{i\in I} \left(U^i\left(x^i\right)\right)^{\delta^i} \quad \text{s.t.} \quad \sum_{i\in I} x^i = x$$

and his endowments are the aggregate endowments. The main point of the proof is to show that a consumer with these characteristics chooses the $x^i, i =$

[4]Collinear endowments imply a price independent distribution of relative wealth in an economy.

$1, \ldots, I$, in a way such that they not only satisfy his own budget restrictions, but also those of the single consumers.

Regrettably, it is not clear which are necessary or sufficient conditions for the existence of a representative consumer. From the results of Sonnenschein [1973], Debreu [1974], and Mantel [1974] it is known for a long time that in general market excess demand cannot be represented by a single consumer's excess demand. Mantel [1976] proves that even restricting market excess demand to come from individuals with homothetic preferences (which are not identical) is not sufficient. Kirman and Koch [1986] on the other hand show that also for an economy in which consumers are characterized by identical utility functions and collinear endowments there does not necessarily exist a representative consumer. In other words: neither identical preferences combined with collinear endowments nor homotheticity alone are sufficient to obtain the Weak Axiom of Revealed Preferences to be satisfied by market excess demand.

However, Shafer [1977, p. 1178] points out that homotheticity is not necessary under the assumption of two states where WARP and the so-called Strong Axiom of Revealed Preferences (SARP) are equivalent. For $S \geq 3$ compare Shafer and Sonnenschein [1982, Example 5].

Non-sufficiency of collinear endowments for the existence of a representative consumer without any further restrictions on utility follows from results in Wold [1953, p. 119]. Shafer and Sonnenschein [1982, Example 3] point out that also homotheticity alone is not sufficient. Their example, however, is quite strange what concerns utility functions ($U^1(x) = x_1$ and $U^2(x) = x_2$).

## 4.3 How to Obtain Monotonicity

### 4.3.1 Quasi-Linear Utility

There is a further class of utility functions which assures a unique Arrow-Debreu equilibrium, namely the class of quasi-linear utility functions. Let me emphasize that we defined quasi-linearity with respect to the first state. As soon as one deviates from this such that linearity is given with respect to different states for different consumers, the uniqueness property might fail as follows from Mas-Colell et al. [1995, Example 15.B.2].

PROPOSITION 5.8 (UNIQUENESS FOR QUASI-LINEARITY)
*Assume $GE = \left\{\mathbb{R}^S \left(U^i, \omega^i\right)_{i \in I}\right\}$ such that $U^i$ is quasi-linear for all $i \in I$, i.e. there exist some strictly concave functions $\tilde{U}^i : \mathbb{R}_+^{S-1} \to \mathbb{R}, i = 1, \ldots, I$, such that*

$$U^i(x) = x_1 + \tilde{U}^i(x_{-1})$$

*and all* $\tilde{U}^i$ *satisfy Assumption 1.2 on* $\mathbb{R}_+^{S-1}$. *Then, the economy displays a unique Arrow-Debreu equilibrium if endowments in state one are sufficiently large for all consumers.*

The idea of the proof is to show monotonicity of individual demand functions with respect to the normalizing vector $e^1$. Because the normalizing vector is the same for all consumers, monotonicity is additive and Proposition 5.1 can be applied.
Monotonicity for individual demand can be deferred in the following way: solving budget constraints to state 1 consumption $x_1^i$, it is possible to eliminate $x_1^i$ from the maximization problem. By application of the Implicit Function Theorem on the corresponding first order conditions one obtains the Jacobian $D_\pi z_{-1}(\pi)$. One observes negative definiteness of $\partial_{\pi_{-1}} z_{-1}(\pi)$ because of strict concavity of $\tilde{U}^i$. First order conditions however are necessary and sufficient: when maximizing without any restrictions on state 1 consumption, the assumptions on $\tilde{U}^i$ and $\omega^i$ imply necessity and sufficiency. It can be shown that given large $\omega_1^i$ state 1 consumption is always chosen strictly positive such that it does not matter if it is restricted from below by zero.
Quasi-linear utility functions gain special interest for partial equilibrium analysis (compare, for example, Mas-Colell et al. [1995, Chapter 10]). In this context it may be reasonable not to restrict consumption in the state of linearity.

### 4.3.2 The Mitjushin-Polterovich Coefficient

Given a strictly concave utility function $U^i$, the Mitjushin-Polterovich coefficient is a measure for the curvature of the indifference curves:

$$MP_{U^i}(x) := -\frac{x^T D^2 U^i(x)\, x}{\nabla U^i(x)\, x} \quad \text{for all} \quad x \in \mathbb{R}_{++}^S \setminus \{0\} \quad .$$

If $U^i$ in addition satisfies the expected utility hypothesis, an upper bound for the Mitjushin-Polterovich coefficient is equivalent to an upper bound for the relative risk aversion (compare Mas-Colell [1991, p. 283]). If $U^i$ is homogeneous of degree $k$ with $k \in (0, 1)$, its corresponding Mitjushin-Polterovich coefficient is $1 - k$.
Given a strictly concave utility function with a Mitjushin-Polterovich coefficient less than 4, individual demand is monotone with respect to the endowment vector. The original proof is given by Mitjushin and Polterovich [1978], but can be also found in Mas-Colell [1991, Theorem 1] and Hildenbrand [1994, Appendix 4]. The main idea is to prove monotonicity of the inverse demand function and not of demand itself. Note that the original proof considers consumers with a fixed income and not with income depending on prices.

PROPOSITION 5.9 (UNIQUENESS VIA MITJUSHIN-POLTEROVICH)
*Given* $GE = \left\{\mathbb{R}^S \left(U^i, \omega^i\right)_{i \in I}\right\}$ *such that all* $U^i$ *are strictly concave and*

$$MP_{U^i}(x) < 4 \quad \textit{for all} \quad x \in \mathbb{R}^S_+ \setminus \{0\}, i \in I \quad ,$$

*the economy has a unique Arrow-Debreu equilibrium if endowments are collinear, i.e. there is some* $\delta \in \hat{\mathcal{P}}_{1,1}$ *with* $\omega^i = \delta_i \, \omega$ *for all* $i \in I$.

The monotonicity property is additive since the normalizing vectors $(\omega^i)_{i \in I}$ are collinear. Uniqueness follows from Proposition 5.1.
Mas-Colell [1991, Example 1] proves 4 to be the "magic" number in the proposition.

REMARK 5.1
*Going back to the notion of a preference relation, the MP-criterion looks a bit ambigious because any utility representation of the preference relations is only specified up to a monotonic transformation. However, different such representations have different MP-coefficients. Recently Quah [2002] has found a criterion to check the MP-coefficient of a preference relation by analyzing an arbitrary representation of it: If for all* $x, x' \in \mathbb{R}^S_+$ $MP_u(x) - MP_{\bar{u}}(x') < 4$ *then the preference relation that* $u$ *represents leads to a monotone demand function.*

## 4.4 How to Obtain the Property of Gross Substitution

Another class of Arrow-Debreu economies allows to obtain uniqueness of the equilibrium via gross substitution of market demand. Once again, utility functions which fulfill the expected utility hypothesis are considered.
Hens and Löffler [1995] prove that market demand satisfies the property of strict gross substitution whenever consumers have a constant absolute risk aversion, complete risk sharing in the equilibrium is given (compare p. 85), or the relative risk aversion is less or equal to one. In the first two situations the property of strict gross substitution is directly shown for market demand whereas in the latter case it is demonstrated via individual demand to satisfy this property. Both proofs strongly refer to the Jacobian of the Lagrangian multipliers as functions of prices. The second one even applies strict gross substitution for $\lambda^i(\pi), i \in I$.

PROPOSITION 5.10 (UNIQUENESS FROM GROSS SUBSTITUTION) [5]
*Given* $GE = \left\{\mathbb{R}^S \left(U^i, \omega^i\right)_{i \in I}\right\}$ *such that utility functions* $\left(U^i\right)_{i \in I}$ *satisfy the expected utility hypothesis, there is a unique Arrow-Debreu equilibrium if one of the following conditions is satisfied:*

[5] [Hens and Löffler, 1995]

- *consumers have constant absolute risk aversion, i.e. for all $i \in I$ it is*

$$ARA^i(x_s) = c^i \quad \textit{for all} \quad x_s \in \mathbb{R}_{++}$$

  *where $c^i > 0$;*

- *complete risk sharing holds in the equilibrium;*

- *consumers have a relative risk aversion less or equal to one, i.e. for all $i \in I$ it is*

$$RRA^i(x_s) \leq 1 \quad \textit{for all} \quad x_s \in \mathbb{R}_{++} \quad .$$

Hens and Löffler [1995] show that the last condition can be relaxed to

$$\left(x_s - \omega_s^i\right) ARA^i(x_s) < 1 \quad \text{for all} \quad i \in I,\ x_s \in \mathbb{R}_{++} \tag{5.10}$$

such that the size of endowments contributes to the determinacy of the equilibrium. Besides, it is sufficient if utility functions are additively separable and condition (5.10) is satisfied for each state utility function.

Note that when complete risk sharing is given in the equilibrium, Hens and Löffler [1995] only prove the property of strict gross substitution to hold in equilibrium. Even though gross substitution does not hold in general, this is sufficient for a unique equilibrium (compare Mas-Colell [1985, Example 5.7.9]).

## 5. Overview of Conditions for Uniqueness in the Arrow-Debreu Model

Figure 5.4 at the end of this section provides an overview of well-known conditions which guarantee a unique equilibrium in an Arrow-Debreu economy or equivalently in a GEI-economy with complete markets. It has to be read as described below:

Following a broken arrow starting at the top, one crosses different conditions which all together guarantee either a special property for market demand (demand can be interpreted as the demand of a representative consumer, monotonicity with respect to a normalizing vector, gross substitution) or an explicit equilibrium pricing formula (which depends on the parameters of the economy) such that the equilibrium is unique.

EXAMPLE 5.1

*Looking on the right broken arrow one recognizes that as soon as all consumers are characterized by identical utility functions* ***and*** *endowments there exists a representative consumer* ***and*** *an explicit pricing formula. For such an economy the equilibrium price system is unique.*

Non-broken arrows indicate implications which hold in general. They allow to obtain additional conclusions. Some of these arrows are labeled with supplementary information, meaning that the implication holds only under this additional restriction.

EXAMPLE 5.2
*Cobb-Douglas utility functions are homothetic. Besides for these functions relative risk aversion is defined and (less or) equal to one. This in addition implies strict concavity and a Mitjushin-Polterovich coefficient less than four. Since Cobb-Douglas utility functions are homothetic supplementary to the existence of a pricing formula one knows that a representative consumer exists as soon as the utility functions are identical across all consumers or endowments are collinear. Under collinear endowments monotonicity can also be derived from the size of the Mitjushin-Polterovich coefficient.*

Naturally, Figure 5.4 cannot contain *each* implication and conclusion and we do not claim completeness. For example, grouping all $U^i$ to be identical with all $\omega^i$ to be identical would imply Pareto-efficiency of the endowment distribution. Besides, utility classes overlap, for example, some homothetic utility functions satisfy the expected utility hypothesis. Including all these details would divert from the essential.
Nevertheless, Figure 5.4 visualizes a great part of the content of this chapter and might be helpful when examining uniqueness of equilibria. Note that we did not include negative results like the fact that with aggregate risk utility functions which satisfy the expected utility hypothesis with respect to an objective probability measure do *not* guarantee a unique equilibrium. There would not even be a chance of partial completeness!

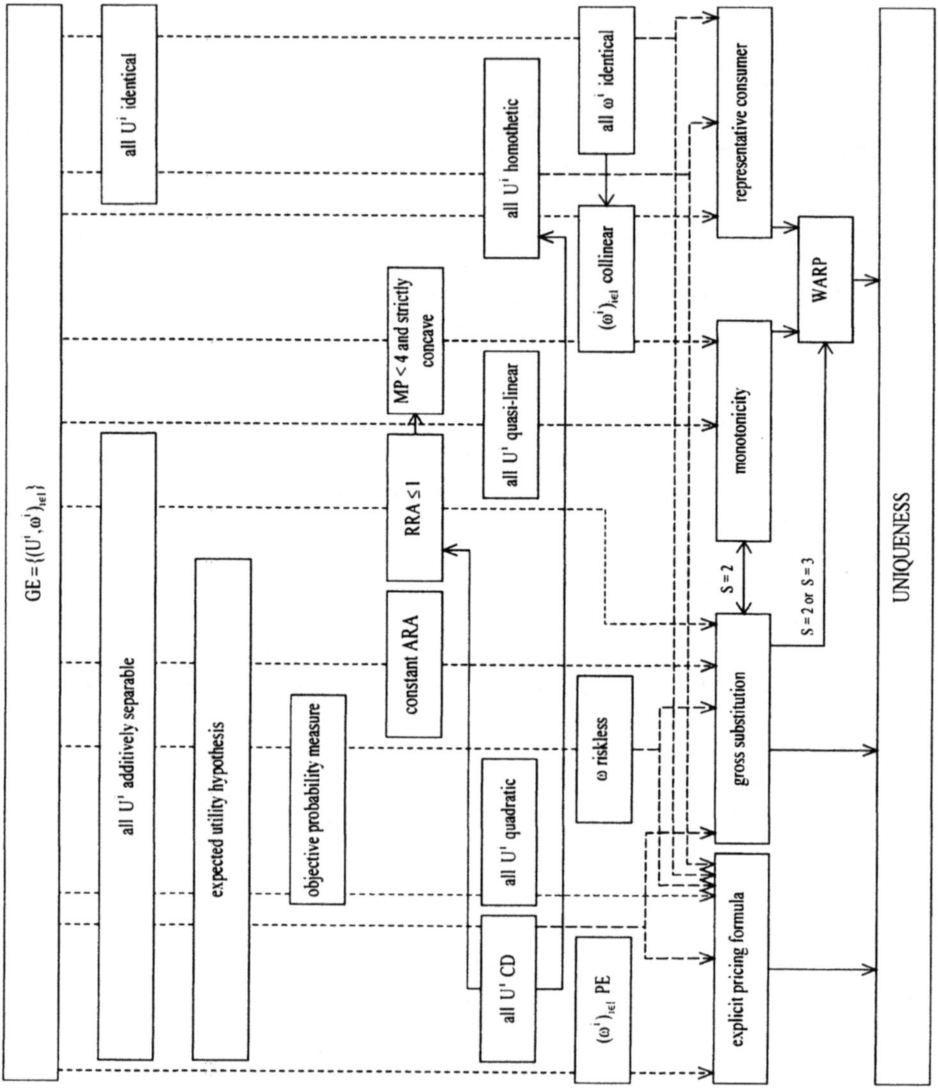


*Figure 5.4.* Conditions for uniqueness in the Arrow-Debreu model.

# Chapter 6

# UNIQUENESS OF COMPETITIVE EQUILIBRIA IN THE FINANCE GEI-MODEL

## 1. Introduction

The study of uniqueness in the Finance GEI-model done in this chapter can be divided into several parts.

The first aim of this chapter is to describe the latest developments in studies on certain conditions guaranteeing a unique equilibrium. Therefore, we start with a thorough definition of local and global uniqueness for the different equilibrium concepts in the GEI-model. We also give basic results. In correspondence to Chapter 5, we recall some properties of market demand which lead to a unique equilibrium. A new result here is the fact that monotonicity is satisfied independently of the chosen representation of the asset span. Only the considered vector of normalization changes. The presented properties of demand functions have been applied to find conditions on the individual characteristics and asset structures for which equilibria are unique. The presentation of the properties of demand functions and their application on uniqueness results in GEI-models is close to the presentation in Hens et al. [1999], even though we choose a classification of the uniqueness results which in some parts is different from theirs and we add some points. In the end we give a diagram visualizing all these results which is helpful when checking for a GEI-economy whether it has a unique equilibrium. During this whole section we stay in analogy to the previous chapter.

In Section 5 we clarify in how far—when the dimension of the asset span remains fixed—it is possible to perturb the asset structure without changing the number of equilibria. This observation is important with regard to the second section because it implies that conditions given there are too restrictive. It also lays the foundations for Sections 6 and 7. On the one hand we consider the limits of transferability from the Arrow-Debreu model to incomplete markets models:

switching from complete to incomplete markets might lead from a unique to multiple equilibria. On the other hand the reverse is also true: incompleteness of markets might create uniqueness of the equilibrium. In the light of Section 5, most of the examples used for proofs in Sections 6 and 7 are known to be not exceptional. These observations on non-equivalence of uniqueness of competitive equilibria in complete and in incomplete markets models give some insight in the consequences of different asset structures on the equilibria which might motivate the reader to think of further extensions of Section 4.

## 2. Defining Uniqueness of Financial Markets Equilibria

The first point is to start with a definition of a unique competitive equilibrium for GEI-economies. It is possible to work with the financial markets or no-arbitrage equilibrium concept. It will become clear that it is more convenient to refer to the first one since the definition there can be done with respect to the price systems.

As it is obvious from the consumers' maximization problem, individual and market demand functions are homogeneous of degree zero in asset prices (cf. Chapter 2). This means—in correspondence to the Arrow-Debreu model—that as soon as $q^* \in Q(A)$ constitutes an equilibrium price system, this is also true for $\lambda q^*$ whenever $\lambda > 0$. An appropriate price normalization has to be defined. This was simple for the Arrow-Debreu model since prices there are always strictly positive. For incomplete markets one has to assure that a normalizing vector $n \in \mathbb{R}^J$ satisfies

$$q \cdot n > 0 \quad \text{for all} \quad q \in Q(A) \quad , \tag{6.1}$$

i.e. the normalizing vector has to include an acute angle with each arbitrage-free asset price system $q$. Define

$$\hat{\mathcal{Q}}_{c,n}(A) = \{q \in Q(A) | \, q \cdot n = c\}$$

where $c > 0$ and $\hat{\mathcal{Q}}(A) := \hat{\mathcal{Q}}_{1,e^1}(A)$ whenever $A_{\cdot 1} > 0$.

In correspondence to the Arrow-Debreu model local and global uniqueness have to be distinguished.

DEFINITION 6.1 (LOCAL UNIQUENESS OF FM-EQUILIBRIA)
*Given* $GEI = \left\{\mathbb{R}^S, (U^i, \omega^i)_{i \in I}, A\right\}$, *an FM-equilibrium* $(\theta^*, q^*) \in \mathbb{R}^{J \times I} \times \hat{\mathcal{Q}}_{c,n}(A)$ *is locally unique if there is some* $\epsilon > 0$ *such that* $\|q - q^*\| < \epsilon$ *and* $q \in \hat{\mathcal{Q}}_{c,n}(A)$ *imply* $G(q) \neq 0$.

$\|\ldots\|$ is an arbitrary vector norm on $\mathbb{R}^J$.

DEFINITION 6.2 (GLOBAL UNIQUENESS OF FM-EQUILIBRIA)
*Given* $GEI = \left\{\mathbb{R}^S, (U^i, \omega^i)_{i \in I}, A\right\}$, *an FM-equilibrium* $(\theta^*, q^*) \in \mathbb{R}^{J \times I} \times \hat{\mathcal{Q}}_{c,n}(A)$ *is globally unique if there is no other* $q \in \hat{\mathcal{Q}}_{c,n}(A)$ *with* $G(q) = 0$.

Throughout this section we will assume that agents characteristics satisfy the Differentiability Assumptions 1.2. Hence a unique equilibrium price vector also implies a unique equilibrium allocation. Again, the term "uniqueness" alone refers to the global aspect.
The number of FM-equilibria can be defined via normalized equilibrium price systems, i.e. for given $c \in \mathbb{R}_{++}$ and $n \in \mathbb{R}^J$ satisfying condition (6.1) the number of FM-equilibria is

$$\sharp\left\{q \in \hat{\mathcal{Q}}_{c,n}(A) \middle| G(q) = 0\right\} \quad .$$

Because of the allocational equivalence given in Proposition 1.1 the careful reader becomes aware of two further aspects.

PROPOSITION 6.1 (INDEPENDENCE OF THE REPRESENTATION)
*Consider two economies* $GEI = \left\{\mathbb{R}^S, (U^i, \omega^i)_{i \in I}, A\right\}$ *and* $GEI = \left\{\mathbb{R}^S, (U^i, \omega^i)_{i \in I}, \tilde{A}\right\}$ *with* $\langle A \rangle = \langle \tilde{A} \rangle$. *Then, both economies are characterized by the same number of equilibria.*

The importance of the proposition comes from the fact that it allows to choose always that representation of the asset span which is most suitable. For example, under Assumption 1.5 it is possible to use a representation $\tilde{A} \in \mathbb{R}^{S \times J}$ with $\langle A \rangle = \langle \tilde{A} \rangle$ and $\tilde{A}_{\cdot 1} > 0$ which allows application of the normalizing vector $e^1$ (compare condition (6.1)). Proposition 6.1 follows directly from the equivalence of uniqueness between FM- and NA-equilibria such that not only the number of equilibria is the same, but even the consumption allocations at the equilibria.

PROPOSITION 6.2 (SAME EQUILIBRIUM NUMBER)
$GEI = \left\{\mathbb{R}^S, (U^i, \omega^i)_{i \in I}, A\right\}$ *has the same number of FM-equilibria as of NA-equilibria.*

The number of NA-equilibria has to be defined in terms of consumption allocations, i.e. it is the number of feasible allocations which together with some state price system $\pi \in \mathbb{R}^S_{++}$ form an NA-equilibrium. If this number is equal to one, there is a unique NA-equilibrium. We omit a formal definition because it would be notationally costly, but not more informative. It is not possible to define uniqueness of NA-equilibrium in terms of equilibrium price systems normalized in the standard way, because for the same commodity allocation there may exist multiple state price vectors because $x^i(\pi^*) = x^i(\tilde{\pi})$ for some

$\pi^*, \tilde{\pi} \in \mathbb{R}^S_{++}$ which satisfy $A^T \pi^* = A^T \tilde{\pi}$, i.e. which generate the same asset price system.
The last proposition can be directly derived from the allocational equivalence in Proposition 1.1.
Let us finish with the remark that—as will become clear later on—uniqueness sometimes can be proven only with respect to some special normalization, but as soon as it holds for this special one it holds for all.

# 3. Properties of Market Demand for Assets

## 3.1 Decomposition of the Jacobian-Matrix

### 3.1.1 Individual Demand for Assets

Recall that the individual demand for assets, $g^i(q)$, is derived from

$$\max_{\theta \in \mathbb{R}^J} U^i\left(\omega^i + A\,\theta\right) \quad \text{s.t.} \quad q^T \theta \leq 0 \quad \wedge \quad \omega^i + A\,\theta \geq 0$$

The Kuhn-Tucker-Conditions[1] for this optimization problem are satisfied if $x^i = \omega^i + A\,g^i(q)$ is a strictly positive consumption plan, i.e. $x^i$ is an interior optimum. For this to be satisfied we need the following condition:

ASSUMPTION 6.1 (STRONG CHEAPER POINT ASSUMPTION)
*For all $i \in I$ and for all $q \in Q$ there is some $\theta \in \mathbb{R}^J$ with $q^T \theta \leq 0$ and $\omega^i + A\,\theta \gg 0$.*

If $(\omega^i, A)$ satisfies this assumption then for $i$ there exists a strictly positive feasible consumption plan: $\hat{x}^i = \omega^i + A\,\theta \gg 0$. Because of the Differentiability Assumption 1.2 we then know that solutions on the boundary of the consumption space will have lower utility than interior points so that any solution $x^i = \omega^i + A\,g^i(q)$ has to be strictly interior. Strict quasi-concavity then ensures that the Kuhn-Tucker-Conditions are also sufficient. Note that strict quasi-concavity is inherited by the indirect utility function $V^i(\theta) := U^i(\omega^i + A\,\theta)$ from the strictly concave direct utility $U^i$ if there are no redundant assets, i.e. if $rank\,A = J$.
The strong cheaper point assumption is evidently satisfied if $\omega^i \gg 0$ for all $i \in I$.
The following example demonstrates that the stong cheaper point assumption is indeed stronger than the Cheaper Point Assumption 2.2.

EXAMPLE 6.1
*Consider an economy with one consumer in which*

[1] Cf. Mas-Colell/Whinston/Green [Mas-Colell et al., 1995, Theorem M.K.2].

$$A = \begin{pmatrix} 1 & 0 \\ -1 & 0 \\ 0 & 1 \end{pmatrix} \quad \text{and} \quad \omega^i = \begin{pmatrix} 0 \\ 0 \\ \omega_3^i \end{pmatrix} \quad \text{with} \quad \omega_3^i > 0 \quad .$$

*Assumption 6.1 is not satisfied, because from $\omega^i + A\,\theta \gg 0$ follows from $\theta_1 > 0$ and $-\theta_1 > 0$. Which is a contradiction.*
*However, Assumption 2.2 is satisfied: let $\theta_1 = 0$ and $\theta_2 = -\omega_3^i$. Then $q^T\theta = -q_2\omega_3^i < 0$ ($q \in Q \Rightarrow q_2 > 0$) and $\omega^i + A\,\theta = (0 \quad 0 \quad 0)^T \geq 0$.*

The Assumption 2.2 and 6.1 are related in the following way:

PROPOSITION 6.3 (CHEAPER POINT ASSUMPTIONS)

*(i) Under the Assumption 1.5 we get:*

*Assumption 6.1 $\Rightarrow$ Assumption 2.2.*

*(ii) If there is some $\theta \in \mathbb{R}^J$ with $A\,\theta \gg 0$[2], then:*

*Assumption 2.2 $\Rightarrow$ Assumption 6.1.*

PROOF 6.1
*Without loss of generality we can prove the proposition for any agent $i$, that is to say we can just skip the index $i$ here.*
*Ad 6.3: Let $q \in Q$. By assumption there is some $\tilde{\theta} \in \mathbb{R}^J$ with*

$$q^T\,\tilde{\theta} \leq 0 \quad \text{and} \quad \omega^i + A\,\tilde{\theta} \gg 0 \quad .$$

*If $q^T\,\tilde{\theta} < 0$, then Assumption 2.2 is satisfied. Hence, suppose $q^T\,\tilde{\theta} = 0$. By Assumption 1.5 there is some $\theta \in \mathbb{R}^J$ with $A\,\theta > 0$, and due to the No-Arbitrage-Condition $q^T\,\theta > 0$. Define $\bar{\theta} := \lambda\,(-\theta) + (1-\lambda)\,\tilde{\theta}$ with $\lambda \in (0,1)$. Then*

$$q^T\,\bar{\theta} = -\lambda \underbrace{q^T\,\theta}_{>0} + (1-\lambda) \underbrace{q^T\,\tilde{\theta}}_{=0} < 0$$

*for all $\lambda \in (0,1)$ and*

$$\omega^i + A\,\bar{\theta} = \omega^i - \lambda\,A\,\theta + (1-\lambda)\,A\,\tilde{\theta} = \lambda \underbrace{\omega^i}_{\geq 0} - \lambda \underbrace{A\,\theta}_{>0} + (1-\lambda) \underbrace{\left(\omega^i + A\,\tilde{\theta}\right)}_{\gg 0} > 0$$

[2]This condition is for example satisfied if there is a riskless asset, i.e. if $\mathbb{1} \in \langle A \rangle$.

*for $\lambda$ close enough to 0.*
*Ad 6.3: Let $q \in Q$. By assumption there is some $\bar{\theta} \in \mathbb{R}^J$ with*

$$q^T \bar{\theta} < 0 \quad \textit{and} \quad \omega^i + A\bar{\theta} \geq 0$$

*and there is also an $\hat{\theta} \in \mathbb{R}^J$ whit*

$$A\hat{\theta} \gg 0 \quad .$$

*Then for $\theta := r\,\hat{\theta}$ with $r \in \mathbb{R}_{++}$ sufficiently large we get that*

$$A\,\theta = r\,A\,\hat{\theta} \gg A\,\bar{\theta} \quad .$$

*Define $\tilde{\theta} := \lambda\,\theta + (1-\lambda)\,\bar{\theta}$ with $\lambda \in (0,1)$. Then we obtain*

$$q^T\tilde{\theta} = \lambda q^T\theta + (1-\lambda)\underbrace{q^T\bar{\theta}}_{<0} < 0$$

*for $\lambda$ close enough to 0 and*

$$\begin{array}{rcl} \omega^i + A\,\tilde{\theta} & = & \omega^i + \lambda\,A\,\theta + (1-\lambda)\,A\,\bar{\theta} \\ & \gg & \omega^i + \lambda\,A\,\bar{\theta} + (1-\lambda)\,A\,\bar{\theta} \\ & = & \omega^i + A\,\bar{\theta} \\ & \geq & 0 \end{array}$$

*for all $\lambda \in (0,1)$.*

*q. e. d.*

Now we are in a position to consider the first-order conditions explicitly:

$$\begin{array}{rcl} D_x\,U^i\,(\omega^i + A\,\theta^i)\,A - \lambda^i\,q^T & = & 0 \\ -q^T\,\theta^i & = & 0 \quad , \end{array} \tag{6.2}$$

where $\lambda^i \neq 0$ is the Lagrangian-Multiplier.
Differentiating (6.2) leads to:

$$\begin{pmatrix} A^T\,D^2_{xx}\,U^i\,(\omega^i + A\,\theta^i)\,A & -q \\ -q^T & 0 \end{pmatrix} \begin{pmatrix} d\,\theta^i \\ d\,\lambda^i \end{pmatrix} = \begin{pmatrix} \lambda^i\,I_J \\ \theta^{iT} \end{pmatrix} d\,q$$

Let

$$H^i := A^T\,D^2_{xx}\,U^i\left(\omega^i + A\,\theta^i\right)A$$

be the Hessian-Matrix of the consumers' indirect utility for assets, $V^i\,(\theta) := U^i\,(\omega^i + A\,\theta)$, and let

$$H_g^i := \begin{pmatrix} A^T D_{xx}^2 U^i(\omega^i + A\theta^i) A & -q \\ -q^T & 0 \end{pmatrix}$$

be the corresponding bordered Hessian-Matrix. Because of strict quasi-concavity, imposed by Assumption 1.2, $H_g^i$ is invertible, so that by the application of the implicit function theorem the Jacobian-Matrix is obtained as:

$$\begin{pmatrix} D_q \theta^i \\ D_q \lambda^i \end{pmatrix} = \begin{pmatrix} A^T D_{xx}^2 U^i(\omega^i + A\theta^i) A & -q \\ -q^T & 0 \end{pmatrix}^{-1} \begin{pmatrix} \lambda^i I_J \\ \theta^{iT} \end{pmatrix} \tag{6.3}$$

$H_g^i$ is a partitioned Matrix, with inverse:[3]

$$\begin{aligned} H_g^{i^{-1}} &= \begin{pmatrix} H^i & -q \\ -q^T & 0 \end{pmatrix}^{-1} \\ &= \begin{pmatrix} H^{i^{-1}} + \mu^i H^{i^{-1}} q q^T H^{i^{-1}} & \mu^i H^{i^{-1}} q \\ \mu^i q^T H^{i^{-1}} & \mu^i \end{pmatrix} \end{aligned}$$

where $\mu^i = -1/\left(q^T H^{i^{-1}} q\right)$. The Jacobian matrix can then be written as:

$$D_q g^i = \lambda^i H^{i^{-1}} + \lambda^i \mu^i H^{i^{-1}} q q^T H^{i^{-1}} + \mu^i H^{i^{-1}} q \theta^{iT} \tag{6.4}$$

The decompositions (6.3) resp. (6.4) are of considerable use in the search of assumptions leading to uniqueness.

### 3.1.2 Market Demand for Assets

Recall that the market demand for assets $G(q)$ is defined as:

$$G(q) = \sum_{i=1}^{I} g^i(q)$$

Differentiability of market demand is inherited from individual demand. And we get the analogous decomposition of the Jacobian for market demand:

$$D_q G = \sum_{i=1}^{I} \left[\lambda^i H^{i^{-1}} + \lambda^i \mu^i H^{i^{-1}} q q^T H^{i^{-1}} + \mu^i H^{i^{-1}} q \theta^{iT}\right]$$

In view of the index theorem as outlined in Chapter 4 any condition that implies that the index at every equilibrium is positive implies uniqueness of equilibria. In particular the index is positive if the normalized Jacobian is negative definite or gross substitutes at equilibrium. These are the conditions that we consider in the following subsection.

[3] Cf. Murata [1977, Theorem 1.3].

## 3.2 WARP and Monotonicity

Not only for the Arrow-Debreu model, but also for the GEI-model it has been shown in Chapter 3 that in general market demand (for assets) does not satisfy any other properties than continuity, homogeneity, and Walras' Law. However, in line with the Arrow-Debreu model it is still useful to define strong structural properties like WARP, monotonicity, and the property of gross substitution for asset market demand $G : Q(A) \to R^J$. These properties are the goals for formulating specific assumptions on the characteristics of the economy. When defining these structural properties at some points caution is advisable.
A property satisfied by all individual demand functions for assets is the Weak Axiom of Revealed Preferences.

DEFINITION 6.3 (WEAK AXIOM OF REVEALED PREFERENCES) *The demand function $G : Q(A) \to \mathbb{R}^J$ satisfies the Weak Axiom of Revealed Preferences (WARP) if*

$$q \cdot G(\tilde{q}) \leq 0 \Rightarrow \tilde{q} G(q) > 0$$

*for all $q, \tilde{q} \in Q(A)$ with $G(q) \neq G(\tilde{q})$.*

This property implies negative semi-definiteness of the Jacobian matrix of $\theta$ on the orthogonal space with respect to $\theta$, i.e.

$$v \cdot D_q G(q) v \leq 0$$

for all $v \in \mathbb{R}^J$ and $q \in Q(A)$ such that $G(q) \cdot v = 0$. Requiring the inequality to be strict on the orthogonal space with respect to $q$ and $G(q)$ it is a sufficient condition, i.e.

$$([q \cdot v = 0,\ G(q) \cdot v = 0,\ v \neq 0] \Rightarrow v \cdot D_q G(q) v < 0) \Rightarrow WARP.$$

The proof is analogue to Mas-Colell et al. [1995, Sections 2.F and 17.F]. Since it is known that this property not necessarily transfers from individual to market demand, consider the stronger property of monotonicity.

DEFINITION 6.4 (MONOTONICITY WITH NORMALIZING VECTOR) *Let $n \in \mathbb{R}^J$ such that $q \cdot n > 0$ for all $q \in Q(A)$. The asset demand function $G : Q(A) \to \mathbb{R}^J$ is monotone with respect to $n$ if*

$$(q - \tilde{q}) \cdot [G(q) - G(\tilde{q})] < 0$$

*for all $q, \tilde{q} \in Q(A)$ with $(q - \tilde{q}) \cdot n = 0$ and $G(q) \neq G(\tilde{q})$.*

Considering the differential version of monotonicity, a necessary condition is given by

$$v \cdot n = 0 \Rightarrow v \cdot D_q G(q) v \leq 0$$

for all $v \in \mathbb{R}^J$ and $q \in Q(A)$ which is also sufficient in its strong version, i.e.

$$v \cdot n = 0 \Rightarrow v \cdot D_q G(q) v < 0$$

for all $v \in \mathbb{R}^J \setminus \{0\}$ and $q \in Q(A)$.
To be precise we summarize the various monotonicity properties in the following definition. Note that negative definiteness with respect to some normalizing vector is also called negative quasi-definiteness:

DEFINITION 6.5 (NEG. QUASI-DEFINITENESS AND MONOTONICITY)

*(i)* $D_q G(q)$ *is negative quasi-definite on* $T_q \cap T_{G(q)}$, *that is, for all* $v \in \mathbb{R}^J \setminus \{0\}$ *with* $q^T v = 0$ *and* $G^T(q) v = 0$

$$v^T D_q G(q) v < 0 \quad .$$

*(ii)* *There exists an* $n \in \mathbb{R}^J$ *with* $q^T n > 0$ *for all* $q \in Q$ *such that* $D_q G(q)$ *is negative quasi-definite on* $T_n$, *that is, for all* $v \in \mathbb{R}^J \setminus \{0\}$ *with* $n^T v = 0$

$$v^T D_q G(q) v < 0 \quad .$$

*(iii)* *There exists an* $n \in \mathbb{R}^J$ *with* $q^T n > 0$ *for all* $q \in Q$ *such that* $G(q)$ *is strictly monotone with regard to* $n$, *that is, for all* $q, \tilde{q} \in Q$ *with* $(q - \tilde{q})^T n = 0$ *and* $G(q) \neq G(\tilde{q})$

$$(q - \tilde{q})^T (G(q) - G(\tilde{q})) < 0 \quad .$$

In Properties (ii) and (iii) the normalizing vector $n$ has to be such that the angle between the normalizing vector and any NA price vector is smaller than $90°$. By consequence of Assumption 1.5, it is always possible to find an admissible normalizing vector [4] because there exists a $\bar{\theta} \in \mathbb{R}^J$ with $A\bar{\theta} > 0$. Therefore, for all $q \in Q$

$$q^T \bar{\theta} = \underbrace{\pi^T}_{\gg 0} \underbrace{A \bar{\theta}}_{> 0} > 0 \quad .$$

As in the case of complete markets, the following also applies here:

[4]This assumption even ensures the existence of such normalizing vector in $Q$. However, if this were made a general requirement, the normalizing vectors in the condition of restricted monotonicity, for instance, would no longer be necessarily admissible.

(ii) $\Rightarrow$ (i)
(ii) $\Rightarrow$ (iii)
(iii) $\Rightarrow$ (ii) with weak inequality

These proofs are analogous to the proofs given for complete markets. Regarding uniqueness, the following holds

THEOREM 6.1 (UNIQUENESS)
*Let an economy* $GEI = \left\{\mathbb{R}^S, (U^i, \omega^i)_{i \in I}, A\right\}$ *satisfy Assumptions 1.2,* $rank A = J$*, 1.5 and 2.1. Then:*

*(i) If market demand* $G(q)$ *satisfies Property (i) (or even (ii)), the economy has a unique FM equilibrium.*

*(ii) If the economy is regular and market demand* $G(q)$ *satisfies Property (iii), the economy has a unique FM equilibrium.*

PROOF 6.2
*By way of direct application of the proofs for the Arrow-Debreu model.*[5]

Given the existence of a representative agent, any FM equilibrium would also be unique in the case of incomplete markets.

DEFINITION 6.6 (REPRESENTATIVE AGENT II)
*In an economy* $GEI = \left\{\mathbb{R}^S, (U^i, \omega^i)_{i \in I}, A\right\}$ *there exists a representative agent if there exists a utility function* $U: \mathbb{R}^S_+ \to \mathbb{R}$ *and an initial endowment* $\omega \in \mathbb{R}^S_+$ *such that the demand for securities of an agent defined by* $U$ *and* $\omega$ *corresponds to market demand.*

This is obviously tantamount to assuming the existence of an agent whose individual demand for goods corresponds to the market demand for goods. Provided a representative agent with utility function $U$ and an initial endowment $\omega$ exists, the Jacobian matrix for market demand $G(q)$ can be written as follows by reason of $(J^{ii})$.

$$D_q G = \lambda H^{-1} + \lambda \mu H^{-1} q q^T H^{-1} + \mu H^{-1} q \theta^T \quad , \tag{6.5}$$

where $H = A^T D^2_{xx} U(\omega + A\theta) A$ denotes the Hessian-Matrix of the representative agent, $\lambda$ the Lagrange multiplier and $\mu = -1/\left(q^T H^{-1} q\right)$.
If $D_q \theta$ satisfies the condition for negative quasi-definiteness on $T_q \cap T_{G(q)}$, uniqueness of the FM equilibrium follows by application of Theorem 6.1.(i).

[5]Cf. Mas-Colell [1985, Chapter 5].

For this to be true it suffices that $\lambda H^{-1} + \lambda \mu H^{-1} q q^T H^{-1}$ is negative definite on $T_q$. This follows by analogy with the complete case. By the above considerations the next theorem is proved.

THEOREM 6.2 (UNIQUENESS)
*If there exists a representative agent for an economy* $GEI = \left\{\mathbb{R}^S, (U^i, \omega^i)_{i \in I}, A\right\}$, *with differentiable utilities (Assumption 1.2)in which if* $rank\ A = J$ *and there are desirable portfolios (Assumption 1.5) then economy has a unique FM equilibrium.*

The findings concerning negative quasi-definiteness and monotonicity regarding $G(q)$ are obviously not restricted to "truly incomplete" markets ($J < S$), but remain valid for $J = S$. For the sake of brevity, any definitions and propositions for incomplete markets shall from now on automatically also apply to complete markets. Where this is not the case, it is made clear by explicitly requiring $J < S$.
For a proof transfer Mas-Colell [1985, Proposition 5.7.3 (iii)] to the GEI-model. The interpretation of these properties is the same as with complete markets, i.e. they assure demands to move in opposite directions of prices, for WARP with the restriction to compensated price changes. Note that monotonicity behaves nice in the sense that it is an additive property whenever the normalizing vector is the same for all individuals.
An interesting observation is given by the fact that if monotonicity is satisfied by market demand for some asset matrix, it is satisfied independently of the chosen representation of the asset span. Only the normalizing vector changes.

PROPOSITION 6.4 (MONOTONICITY AND REPRESENTATION)
*Consider two economies* $GEI = \left\{\mathbb{R}^S, (U^i, \omega^i)_{i \in I}, A\right\}$ *and* $GEI = \left\{\mathbb{R}^S, (U^i, \omega^i)_{i \in I}, \hat{A}\right\}$ *where* $\langle A \rangle = \left\langle \hat{A} \right\rangle$ *with corresponding market demand functions* $G : Q(A) \to \mathbb{R}^J$ *and* $\hat{G} : \mathcal{Q}\left(\hat{A}\right) \to \mathbb{R}^J$. *Then, G is monotone with respect to* $n \in \mathbb{R}^J$ *if and only if* $\hat{G}$ *is monotone with respect to* $\hat{n} = M^{-1} n$ *with* $M \in \mathbb{R}^{J \times J}$ *being the invertible matrix such that* $A\, M = \hat{A}$.

PROOF 6.3
*The dependence between individual demand functions for the two economies is given by*

$$
\begin{aligned}
g^i(q) &= \arg\max_{\theta \in \mathbb{R}^J} U^i\left(\omega^i + A\,\theta\right) \quad s.t. \quad q \cdot \theta = 0 \quad \wedge\, \omega^i + A\,\theta \geq 0 \\
&= \arg\max_{\theta \in \mathbb{R}^J} U^i\left(\omega^i + A\,M\,M^{-1}\theta\right) \quad s.t. \quad q \cdot M\,M^{-1}\theta = 0 \\
&\quad \wedge\, \omega^i + A\,M\,M^{-1}\theta \geq 0 \\
&= M\left[\arg\max_{\hat{\theta} \in \mathbb{R}^J} U^i\left(\omega^i + \hat{A}\,\hat{\theta}\right) \quad s.t. \quad (q \cdot M)\,\hat{\theta} = 0 \right. \\
&\quad \left. \wedge\, \omega^i + \hat{A}\,\hat{\theta} \geq 0\right] \\
&= M\,\hat{g}^i\left(M^T q\right)
\end{aligned}
$$

*which transfers to market demand. Besides*

$$
\begin{aligned}
M^T Q(A) &= M^T\left\{q \in \mathbb{R}^J \middle|\, q = A^T \pi \quad \text{for some} \quad \pi \in \mathbb{R}^S_{++}\right\} \\
&= M^T\left\{q \in \mathbb{R}^J \middle|\, M^T q = M^T A^T \pi \quad \text{for some} \quad \pi \in \mathbb{R}^S_{++}\right\} \\
&= M^T\left\{\left(M^T\right)^{-1} \hat{q} \in \mathbb{R}^J \middle|\, \hat{q} = \hat{A}^T \pi \quad \text{for some} \quad \pi \in \mathbb{R}^S_{++}\right\} \\
&= \mathcal{Q}\left(\hat{A}\right)
\end{aligned}
$$

*where the product of a matrix and a set is defined as the set consisting of all elements equal to an element of the original set multiplied with the matrix. Now observe*

$$
\begin{aligned}
&(q-\tilde{q})\cdot[G(q)-G(\tilde{q})]<0 \quad \forall q,\tilde{q}\in Q(A)\\
&\text{s.t.}\quad (q-\tilde{q})\cdot n=0 \quad \wedge G(q)\neq G(\tilde{q})
\end{aligned}
$$

$$
\begin{aligned}
\Leftrightarrow\quad &(q-\tilde{q})\cdot M\left[M^{-1}G(q)-M^{-1}G(\tilde{q})\right]<0\\
&\forall M^T q, M^T\tilde{q}\in M^T Q(A)\\
&\text{s.t.}\quad (q-\tilde{q})\cdot M\,M^{-1}n=0 \quad \wedge M^{-1}G(q)\neq M^{-1}G(\tilde{q})
\end{aligned}
$$

$$
\begin{aligned}
\Leftrightarrow\quad &\left(M^T q-M^T\tilde{q}\right)\cdot\left[\hat{G}\left(M^T q\right)-\hat{G}\left(M^T\tilde{q}\right)\right]<0\\
&\forall M^T q,\, M^T\tilde{q}\in \mathcal{Q}\left(\hat{A}\right)\\
&\text{s.t.}\quad \left(M^T q-M^T\tilde{q}\right)\cdot\hat{n}=0 \quad \wedge \hat{G}\left(M^T q\right)\neq\hat{G}\left(M^T\tilde{q}\right)
\end{aligned}
$$

$$
\begin{aligned}
\Leftrightarrow\quad &\left(\hat{q}-\hat{\tilde{q}}\right)\cdot\left[\hat{G}(\hat{q})-\hat{G}\left(\hat{\tilde{q}}\right)\right]<0 \quad \forall\hat{q},\hat{\tilde{q}}\in\mathcal{Q}\left(\hat{A}\right)\\
&\text{s.t.}\quad \left(\hat{q}-\hat{\tilde{q}}\right)\cdot\hat{n}=0 \quad \wedge \hat{G}(\hat{q})\neq\hat{G}\left(\hat{\tilde{q}}\right) \quad .
\end{aligned}
$$

*q. e. d.*

## 3.3 Gross Substitution

The last property to consider is the property of strict gross substitution. Regrettably, for incomplete markets models it looses much of its power with respect to uniqueness of FM-equilibria. If the financial markets are incomplete ($J < S$) and an equilibrium exists, market excess demand for goods $Z(\pi)$ never satisfies the requirements for ordinary gross substitution, that is, the Jacobian-Matrix never has just negative diagonal and positive off-diagonal elements for all state price vectors. Let us nevertheless assume this property was satisfied. In that case it would be possible to normalize two equilibrium price vectors $\pi, \tilde{\pi}$ by reason of the homogeneity of $Z$ such that $\pi_t = \tilde{\pi}_t$ for some $t \in S$ and $\pi_s \lneq \tilde{\pi}_s$ for all $s \in S$ otherwise. As in the general equilibrium model it then follows that $\pi$ and $\tilde{\pi}$ are equal. However, this is in contradiction to the well-known fact that even after normalization the indeterminiteness of equilibrium price vectors still has the dimension $S - J > 0$.
Instead, it is possible to examine gross substitution in a weaker form:

DEFINITION 6.7 (RESTRICTED GROSS SUBSTITUTION)
*An excess demand function for goods $Z: \mathbb{R}^S_{++} \to \mathbb{R}^S$ satisfies the restricted form of gross substitution if there exists a subset $R \subseteq S$ with $\#R = J$ such that for all $\pi \in \mathbb{R}^S_{++}$*

$$\partial_{\pi_s} Z_s(\pi) < 0 \quad \textit{for all} \quad s \in R$$

*and*

$$\partial_{\pi_t} Z_s(\pi) > 0 \quad \textit{for all} \quad (s,t) \in R \times R \quad \textit{with} \quad s \neq t \quad .$$

In other words: By deleting $S-J$ rows as well as their corresponding columns, a sub-matrix of the Jacobian-Matrix can be found whose elements are negative on the diagonal and positive otherwise.
It is obvious that the definition of restricted gross substitution in the case of complete securities markets corresponds to the initial definition of strict gross substitution in the previous chapter.
The following example of incomplete securities markets shows that agents exist whose individual excess demand satisfies the requirements for restricted gross substitution. It therefore makes sense to examine this property.

EXAMPLE 6.2 (RESTRICTED GROSS SUBSTITUTION)
*Let*

$$A = \begin{pmatrix} 1 & 0 \\ -1 & 1 \\ -1 & 1 \end{pmatrix}, \omega^i = \begin{pmatrix} 1 \\ 1 \\ 1 \end{pmatrix} \quad \textit{and} \quad U^i(x) = \sum_{s=1}^{3} \frac{1}{3} \ln x_s \quad .$$

*Using the NA approach, it is possible to express the agent's maximization problem as:*

$$\max_{x^i \in \mathbb{R}^3_+} \tfrac{1}{3} \ln x_1^i + \tfrac{1}{3} \ln x_2^i + \tfrac{1}{3} \ln x_3^i \quad \textit{s.t.} \quad \pi^T x^i = \pi_1 + \pi_2 + \pi_3$$
$$\wedge \exists \theta^i \in \mathbb{R}^2$$
$$\textit{with} \quad x_1^i = 1 + \theta_1^i$$
$$\wedge \quad x_2^i = x_3^i = 1 - \theta_1^i + \theta_2^i$$

*By inserting the second constraint into the first, we get:*

$$\begin{array}{rrcl} & \pi_1 \theta_1^i + (\pi_2 + \pi_3)(-\theta_1^i + \theta_2^i) & = & 0 \\ \Leftrightarrow & -\theta_1^i + \theta_2^i & = & -\frac{\pi_1}{\pi_2 + \pi_3} \theta_1^i \end{array}$$

*Therefore the maximization problem is equivalent to:*

$$\max_{\theta_1^i \in \mathbb{R}} \frac{1}{3} \ln\left(1 + \theta_1^i\right) + \frac{2}{3} \ln\left(1 - \frac{\pi_1}{\pi_2 + \pi_3} \theta_1^i\right)$$

*The corresponding first-order condition is:*

$$\frac{1}{1 + \theta_1^i} - \frac{2\pi_1}{\pi_2 + \pi_3 - \pi_1 \theta_1^i} = 0$$

*Thus:*

$$\theta_1^i = \frac{\pi_2 + \pi_3 - 2\,\pi_1}{3\pi_1} = \frac{\pi_2 + \pi_3}{3\,\pi_1} - \frac{2}{3}$$
$$\wedge \quad -\theta_1^i + \theta_2^i = -\frac{1}{3} + \frac{2\,\pi_1}{3\,(\pi_2 + \pi_3)}$$

*It follows that:*

$$z_1^i(\pi) = \theta_1^i = \frac{\pi_2 + \pi_3}{3\,\pi_1} - \frac{2}{3}$$
$$\wedge \quad z_2^i(\pi) = z_3^i(\pi) = -\theta_1^i + \theta_2^i = -\frac{1}{3} + \frac{2\pi_1}{3\,(\pi_2 + \pi_3)}$$

*We therefore obtain the following Jacobian-Matrix:*

$$D_\pi\, z^i(\pi) = \begin{pmatrix} -\frac{\pi_2+\pi_3}{3\pi_1^2} & \frac{1}{3\pi_1} & \frac{1}{3\pi_1} \\ \frac{2}{3(\pi_2+\pi_3)} & -\frac{2}{3}\frac{\pi_1}{(\pi_2+\pi_3)^2} & -\frac{2}{3}\frac{\pi_1}{(\pi_2+\pi_3)^2} \\ \frac{2}{3(\pi_2+\pi_3)} & -\frac{2}{3}\frac{\pi_1}{(\pi_2+\pi_3)^2} & -\frac{2}{3}\frac{\pi_1}{(\pi_2+\pi_3)^2} \end{pmatrix} = \begin{pmatrix} - & + & + \\ + & - & - \\ + & - & - \end{pmatrix}$$

*restricted gross substitution is therefore satisfied for* $R = \{1, 2\}$.

This example reveals why the strict gross substitution property of the demand for goods is missing in the case of truly incomplete markets ($J < S$). This is because in states 2 and 3 the same payment is always made. As a consequence both states are complements in the securities matrix. Yet in the utility function they are substitutes. (Restricted) gross substitution is not given because the complementarity is stronger than the substitutivity.

Note that restricted gross substitution carries over from the individual excess demands to market excess demand only if the underlying sets $R^i$ are equal for all $i \in I$.

Regarding uniqueness the following can be shown:

THEOREM 6.3 (UNIQUENESS)

*Let the market excess demand for goods* $z : \mathbb{R}^S_{++} \to \mathbb{R}^S$ *of an economy* $GEI = \left\{\mathbb{R}^S, (U^i, \omega^i)_{i \in I}, A\right\}$ *satisfy restricted gross substitution 6.7 with respect to a set* $R \subseteq S$ *with* $\#R = J$. *Then: If the rows* $A_s$ *of* $A$ *for* $s \in R$ *are linear independent*[6] *any NA equilibrium, if it exists, is unique.*

[6]Note that this is satisfied in Example 6.2.

PROOF 6.4 [7]

*Without loss of generality let $R = \{1, \ldots, J\}$. Let $\pi, \tilde{\pi} \in \mathbb{R}^S_{++}$ be two equilibrium price vectors with $\pi^T A \neq \lambda \tilde{\pi}^T A$ for all $\lambda \in \mathbb{R}_{++}$. Due to homogeneity on the one side and the linear independence of rows $A_s$ from $A$ for $s \in R$ on the other side [8] it is assumed without loss of generality that*

$$\pi_s = \tilde{\pi}_s \quad \textit{for all} \quad s \in S \backslash R \quad \textit{and at least one} \quad \bar{s} \in R \quad ,$$

$$\pi_s \leq \tilde{\pi}_s \quad \textit{for all} \quad s \in S \quad ,$$

*with at least one strict inequality by reason of the conditions on $\pi$ and $\tilde{\pi}$. We then get a finite sequence [9] of prices $(\pi^n)_{n=1,\ldots,J-1}$, starting in $\pi$, ending in $\tilde{\pi}$ and for which*

$$\pi^n_s = \pi_s \quad \textit{for all} \quad s \in \{\bar{s}\} \cup S \backslash R \quad \textit{and all} \quad n \in \{1, \ldots, J-1\} \quad ,$$

$$\pi^n \leq \pi^{n+1} \quad \textit{for all} \quad n \in \{1, \ldots, J-2\} \quad ,$$

$$\pi^{\bar{n}} < \pi^{\bar{n}+1} \quad \textit{for at least one} \quad \bar{n} \in \{1, \ldots, J-2\} \ .$$

*However, as a result of restricted gross substitution it follows that*

$$0 = z_{\bar{s}}(\pi) \leq z_{\bar{s}}\left(\pi^{\bar{n}}\right) < z_{\bar{s}}\left(\pi^{\bar{n}+1}\right) \leq z_{\bar{s}}(\tilde{\pi}) = 0 \quad .$$

*This is a contradiction!*

*q. e. d.*

Instead of the demand for goods one can examine the demand for securities with respect to the property of strict gross substitution.

DEFINITION 6.8 (STRICT GROSS SUBSTITUTION)

*A securities demand function $g: \quad Q \rightarrow \mathbb{R}^J$ satisfies strict gross substitution if for each $q \in Q$*

$$\partial_{q_j} g_j(q) < 0 \quad \textit{for all} \quad j \in J$$

[7] Cf. Arrow and Hahn [1971, Chapter 9, Corollary 7] for the general equilibrium model.

[8] Let $\bar{q} \in \mathbb{R}^J$. Then $\bar{q} = A^T \tilde{\pi}$ is a system of linear equations with $J$ equations and $S$ unknowns $\tilde{\pi}_s$. Since we require linear independence, the columns $A_1^T, \ldots, A_J^T$ of $A^T$ are linear independent so that it is possible to choose the $\pi_s$ for $s \in S \backslash R$ as parameters.

[9] The sequence is obtained by simply starting with $\pi^1 = \pi$, increasing one of the coordinates to the corresponding value of $\tilde{\pi}$ at each further step. In doing so, there are not more than $J-1$ different coordinates.

*and*

$$\partial_{q_j} g_k(q) > 0 \quad \textit{for all} \quad (j,k) \in J \times J \quad \textit{with} \quad j \neq k \quad .$$

If this property is satisfied, it is superior to the demand for goods because it is additive. In Sections 4.6 and 4.7.2 we will consider economies in which the market demand for securities satisfies strict gross substitution. However, a continuation of Example 6.2 will show that cases exist where the demand for goods satisfies restricted gross substitution, but where the demand for securities is not gross substitutive.

EXAMPLE 6.3 (EXAMPLE 6.2 CONTINUED)
*Using the financial markets approach, the agent's maximization problem is as follows:*

$$\max_{\theta^i \in \mathbb{R}^2} \frac{1}{3} \ln\left(1+\theta_1^i\right) + \frac{2}{3} \ln\left(1-\theta_1^i+\theta_2^i\right) \quad \textit{s.t.} \quad q^T \theta^i = 0$$

*By inserting the constraint* $\theta_2^i = -\frac{q_1 \theta_1^i}{q_2}$ $(q_2 > 0$ *for all* $q \in Q)$ *we get:*

$$\max_{\theta_1^i \in \mathbb{R}} \frac{1}{3} \ln\left(1+\theta_1^i\right) + \frac{2}{3} \ln\left(1+\left(-1-\frac{q_1}{q_2}\right)\theta_1^i\right)$$

*The corresponding first-order condition is:*

$$\frac{1}{1+\theta_1^i} - \frac{2(q_2+q_1)}{q_2-(q_2+q_1)\theta_1^i} = 0$$

*Thus:*

$$\theta_1^i = \frac{-q_2 - 2q_1}{3(q_2+q_1)}$$

*By differentiation:*

$$\begin{aligned}\partial_{q_2}\theta_1^i &= \frac{-3(q_2+q_1)+3(q_2+2q_1)}{9(q_2+q_1)^2} \\ &= \frac{q_1}{3(q_2+q_1)^2}\begin{cases} <0 & \textit{for} \quad q_1<0 \\ =0 & \textit{for} \quad q_1=0 \\ >0 & \textit{for} \quad q_1>0 \end{cases}\end{aligned}$$

*Therefore* $g^i(q)$ *does not satisfy strict gross substitution on* $Q$.

Nor is the reverse true. The restricted gross substitution of the demand for goods does not follow from the strict gross substitution of the demand for securities as the following example shows:

EXAMPLE 6.4 (GROSS SUBSTITUTION)
*Let*

$$A = \begin{pmatrix} 1 & 1 \\ 0 & 1 \\ 0 & 1 \end{pmatrix}, \omega^i = \begin{pmatrix} 1 \\ 0 \\ 0 \end{pmatrix} \quad \text{and} \quad U^i(x) = \sum_{s=1}^{3} \frac{1}{3} \ln x_s .$$

*Using the financial markets approach, the agent's maximization problem can be expressed as:*

$$\max_{\theta^i \in \mathbb{R}^2} \frac{1}{3} \ln\left(1 + \theta_1^i + \theta_2^i\right) + \frac{2}{3} \ln \theta_2^i \qquad s.t. \quad q^T \theta^i = 0$$

*By inserting the constraint* $\theta_1^i = -\frac{q_2 \theta_2^i}{q_1}$ $(q_1 > 0$ *for all* $q \in Q)$ *we get:*

$$\max_{\theta_2^i \in \mathbb{R}} \frac{1}{3} \ln\left(1 + \left(\frac{q_1 - q_2}{q_1}\right)\theta_2^i\right) + \frac{2}{3} \ln \theta_2^i$$

*The corresponding first-order condition is:*

$$\frac{1}{1 + \left(\frac{q_1 - q_2}{q_1}\right)\theta_2^i} \cdot \frac{q_1 - q_2}{q_1} + \frac{2}{\theta_2^i} = 0$$

*This is equivalent to:*

$$(q_1 - q_2)\,\theta_2^i + 2\left(q_1 + (q_1 - q_2)\,\theta_2^i\right) = 0$$

*Therefore:*

$$\theta_2^i = -\frac{2\,q_1}{3\,(q_1 - q_2)}$$

$$\theta_1^i = \frac{2\,q_2}{3\,(q_1 - q_2)}$$

*We obtain the following Jacobian-Matrix:*

$$D_q\, g(q) = \begin{pmatrix} -\frac{2\,q_2}{3(q_1 - q_2)^2} & \frac{2\,q_1}{3(q_1 - q_2)^2} \\ \frac{2\,q_2}{3(q_1 - q_2)^2} & -\frac{2\,q_1}{3(q_1 - q_2)^2} \end{pmatrix} = \begin{pmatrix} - & + \\ + & - \end{pmatrix}$$

*Since* $Q \subset \mathbb{R}^J_{++}$ *is satisfied,* $g^i(q)$ *satisfies strict gross substitution on* $Q$*.*
*To calculate the excess demand for goods* $z^i(\pi)$ *from* $g^i(q)$ *the relation* $q = A^T \pi$ *is used, that is:*

$$\begin{aligned} q_1 &= \pi_1 \\ q_2 &= \pi_1 + \pi_2 + \pi_3 \end{aligned}$$

*Thus:*

$$\begin{aligned} z^i(\pi) &= A\,g^i(q) = \begin{pmatrix} \theta_1^i + \theta_2^i \\ \theta_2^i \\ \theta_2^i \end{pmatrix} \\ &= \begin{pmatrix} \frac{2q_2}{3(q_1-q_2)} - \frac{2q_1}{3(q_1-q_2)} \\ -\frac{2q_1}{3(q_1-q_2)} \\ -\frac{2q_1}{3(q_1-q_2)} \end{pmatrix} = \begin{pmatrix} -\frac{2}{3} \\ \frac{2\pi_1}{3(\pi_2+\pi_3)} \\ \frac{2\pi_1}{3(\pi_2+\pi_3)} \end{pmatrix} \end{aligned}$$

*We therefore obtain the following Jacobian-Matrix:*

$$\begin{aligned} D_\pi z^i(\pi) &= \begin{pmatrix} 0 & 0 & 0 \\ \frac{2}{3(\pi_2+\pi_3)} & -\frac{2\pi_1}{3(\pi_2+\pi_3)^2} & -\frac{2\pi_1}{3(\pi_2+\pi_3)^2} \\ \frac{2}{3(\pi_2+\pi_3)} & -\frac{2\pi_1}{3(\pi_2+\pi_3)^2} & -\frac{2\pi_1}{3(\pi_2+\pi_3)^2} \end{pmatrix} \\ &= \begin{pmatrix} 0 & 0 & 0 \\ + & - & - \\ + & - & - \end{pmatrix} \end{aligned}$$

*Hence the restricted gross substitution of the demand for goods is not satisfied.*

Under certain conditions the restricted gross substitution of an agent's excess demand for goods is equivalent to the strict gross substitution of his demand for securities. The cases discussed below include all economies of Section 4.6. Chapter 4.7 discusses further economies for which $D_\pi\, z^i(\pi)$ and $D_q\, g^i(q)$ exhibit the required structure. However, Becker[10] provides two examples where neither an agent's excess demand for goods nor his demand for securities satisfy the property of (restricted) gross substitution (despite von-Neumann-Morgenstern utility functions with relative risk aversion $\leq 1$). Section 4.6.1 will deal with this issue in more detail.
We begin with the following definition:

DEFINITION 6.9 (WEAKLY SEPARATING MATRIX)
*A matrix $A \in \mathbb{R}^{S\times J}$ is weakly separating[11] if $A_s^j \neq 0$ for some $j \in J$ implies $A_s^k = 0$ for $k \in J \setminus \{j\}$.*

[10] Cf. Becker [1995, p. 38-40].
[11] For this term, see Bettzüge [1997, Example 2.5.4].

*For these matrices define*

$$S_A^j := \left\{ s \in S \;\middle|\; A_s^j \neq 0 \right\} \quad .$$

In each state only one security pays off. Therefore, the following theorem is true:

THEOREM 6.4 (EQUIVALENCE OF THE GROSS SUBSTITUTION PROPERTIES)

*Let the securities matrix $A \in \mathbb{R}^{S \times J}$ have no redundant assets, and let it be non-negative and weakly separating. Then: restricted gross substitution of $z^i(\pi)$ and strict gross substitution of $g^i(q)$ are equivalent.*

PROOF 6.5
*Since $A$ is weakly separating and non-negative and also $rank \quad A = J$, there exists a set $R \subseteq S$ with $\#R = J$ such that $A_R := (A_s)_{s \in R}$ is a diagonal matrix with positive diagonal elements. Without loss of generality let $R = \{1, \ldots, J\}$. With $q = \pi^T A$ the following relations is true*

$$z^i(\pi) = A\, g^i\left(\pi^T A\right) \quad ,$$

*also for $s \in R$*

$$z_s^i(\pi) = d_s\, g_s^i\left(\pi^T A\right) \quad ,$$

*$d_s \in \mathbb{R}_{++}$ denoting the corresponding entries of the diagonal matrix. Differentiating $z_s^i$ with respect to $\pi_t$ for $t \in R$ yields*

$$\begin{aligned} \partial_{\pi_t} z_s^i(\pi) &= d_s \sum_{j=1}^{J} \partial_{q_j}\, g_s^i\left(\pi^T A\right) A_t^j \\ &= \underbrace{d_s\, d_t}_{>0}\, \partial_{q_t}\, g_s^i\left(\pi^T A\right) \quad , \end{aligned}$$

*so that the equivalence is evident.*

*q. e. d.*

For the relationship between uniqueness and strict gross substitution of the demand for securities the following theorem applies:

THEOREM 6.5 (UNIQUENESS)
*Let the market demand $G: \quad Q \rightarrow \mathbb{R}^J$ of an economy $GEI = \left\{\mathbb{R}^S, \left(U^i, \omega^i\right)_{i \in I}, A\right\}$ satisfy strict gross substitution 6.8. Then: Provided the set of no-arbitrage prices is $Q \subseteq \mathbb{R}_{++}^J$ and the economy has an FM equilibrium, the equilibrium is unique.*

PROOF 6.6 [12]
*Let $\mathring{q}$ and $\tilde{q}$ be two equilibrium prices in $Q$. Since $\theta$ is homogeneous and $Q \subseteq \mathbb{R}^J_{++}$ one can assume, without loss of generality, that $\tilde{q} \geq \mathring{q}, \tilde{q}_j = \mathring{q}_j$ for a $j \in J$.*
*Let $\mathring{q} \neq \tilde{q}$. Then there exists a sequence of prices $\left(q^0, \ldots, q^N\right) \in Q$ with $q^0 = \mathring{q}$, $q^N = \tilde{q}, q^{n+1} > q^n$ for all $n \in \{0, \ldots, N-1\}$ and $q^n_j = \mathring{q}_j$ for all $n \in \{0, \ldots, N\}$.*[13] *Due to the strict gross substitution property:*

$$g_j\left(q^n\right) < g_j\left(q^{n+1}\right) \quad \textit{for all} \quad n \in \{0, \ldots, N-1\} \quad .$$

*Thus*

$$0 = g_j\left(\mathring{q}\right) < g_j\left(\tilde{q}\right) = 0 \quad .$$

*Because of this contradiction $\mathring{q}$ and $\tilde{q}$ must be equal.*

*q. e. d.*

Note that to deduce the uniqueness of the FM equilibrium from various strict gross substitution properties, the matrix $A$ must satisfy a number of requirements.

## 3.4 Negative Definiteness versus Gross Substitution

Strict gross substitution 6.8 does not generally imply the property of negative quasi-definiteness 6.5.(ii). For $A \geq 0$ this property follows from strict gross substitution in equilibrium as in the case of complete markets. [14] Unit vectors can be used as normalizing vectors.[15]
This leads to a further proof that FM equilibria are unique where strict gross substitution is satisfied for the demand for securities, the initial endowments are strictly positive and the payoff matrix non-negative.

[12] Cf. Arrow and Hahn [1971, Chapter 9, Corollary 7] for the general equilibrium model.
[13] In the complete markets case a sequence with this property contains not more than $S-1$ elements. In the incomplete case $N$ may need to be larger than $J-1$ because it may not be possible to adjust the coordinates at each step without leaving $Q$. Instead we proceed as follows: Since Q is open, there exists a neighborhood $U_n$ for $q^n$ in $Q$ containing an open cube. Now take any point $\bar{q}$ within the cube and on the line segment between $q^n$ and $\tilde{q}$ and construct between $q^n$ and $\bar{q}$ a sequence with the required properties containing not more than $J-1$ elements. To obtain the next part of the sequence, start again with $\bar{q}$. The goal is reached in a finite number of steps since the segment between $\mathring{q}$ and $\tilde{q}$ is bounded and closed, that is, compact in accordance with the theorem of Forster [1991, Theorem 3.5] so that each covering with open cubes contains a finite sub-covering.
[14] A proof for the general equilibrium model can be found in Mas-Colell [1985, Example 5.7.9]. It is possible to extend the proof directly to the incomplete case with a non-negative payoff matrix.
[15] For all $q \in Q$ $q^T e^j > 0$ since

$$q^T e^j = \pi^T A e^j = \underbrace{\pi^T}_{\gg 0} \underbrace{A^j}_{> 0} > 0 \quad .$$

For two securities the following equivalence relation can be shown:

THEOREM 6.6 (STRICT GROSS SUBSTITUTION AND MONOTONICITY) *Let* $GEI = \left\{\mathbb{R}^S, (U^i, \omega^i)_{i \in I}, A\right\}$ *be an economy with* $J = 2$ *securities whose payoffs are non-negative (that is,* $A \in \mathbb{R}_+^{2 \times S}$*). Furthermore, let Assumptions 1.2, the Assumption of no redundant assets and the Cheaper Point Assumption 2.2 be satisfied. Then:* $g(q)$ *satisfies strict gross substitution on* $Q$ *6.8 if and only if the Jacobian-Matrix of* $g(q)$ *is negative quasi-definite on* $T_{e^j}$ *for all unit vectors* $e^j$, $j \in J$ *(Property 6.5.(ii)).*

PROOF 6.7

$\Rightarrow$: *Let* $n = (1 \quad 0)^T$. *It then follows from* $n^T v = 0$ *for* $v \neq 0$ *that* $v = (0 \quad k)^T$ *for some* $k \in \mathbb{R} \setminus \{0\}$. *However, by strict gross substitution*

$$v^T D_q g(q) v = k^2 \partial q_2 \partial q_2 \, g(q) < 0 \quad .$$

*For* $n = (0 \quad 1)^T$ *the above applies accordingly.*

$\Leftarrow$: *Let* $n = (1 \quad 0)^T$ *and* $v = (0 \quad 1)^T$. *It then follows from the negative quasi-definiteness that*

$$v^T D_q g(q) v = \partial \, q_2 \, \partial \, q_2 \, g(q) < 0 \quad .$$

$\partial_{q_1} g_1(q) < 0$ *applies accordingly. The rest of the strict gross substitution property follows from the homogeneity of* $g(q)$ *since the no-arbitrage condition yields* $Q \subseteq \mathbb{R}^J_{++}$.

*q. e. d.*

As a final remark on the gross substitution property we point out that it depends on the chosen representation of the asset span. For an example assume there are two states $S = 2$ and two assets $J = 2$. Now consider the matrices

$$A = \begin{pmatrix} 1 & 0 \\ 0 & 1 \end{pmatrix} \quad \text{and} \quad \hat{A} = \begin{pmatrix} 1 & 0 \\ 0 & -1 \end{pmatrix}$$

which generate the same asset span. Since

$$A \cdot \begin{pmatrix} 1 & 0 \\ 0 & -1 \end{pmatrix} = \hat{A} \quad ,$$

one knows from the proof of Proposition 6.4 that

$$G_A(q) = \begin{pmatrix} 1 & 0 \\ 0 & -1 \end{pmatrix} G_{\hat{A}}\left(\begin{pmatrix} 1 & 0 \\ 0 & -1 \end{pmatrix} q\right) \tag{6.6}$$

and if $q \in Q(A)$, then $\hat{q} = \begin{pmatrix} 1 & 0 \\ 0 & -1 \end{pmatrix} q = \begin{pmatrix} q_1 \\ -q_2 \end{pmatrix} \in \mathcal{Q}\left(\hat{A}\right)$. From differentiation of (6.6) with respect to $q$ one obtains

$$DG_A(q) = \begin{pmatrix} 1 & 0 \\ 0 & -1 \end{pmatrix} DG_{\hat{A}}(\hat{q}) \begin{pmatrix} 1 & 0 \\ 0 & -1 \end{pmatrix}$$

which is equivalent to

$$\begin{pmatrix} 1 & 0 \\ 0 & -1 \end{pmatrix} DG_A(q) \begin{pmatrix} 1 & 0 \\ 0 & -1 \end{pmatrix} = DG_{\hat{A}}(\hat{q}) \quad .$$

Now assume $DG_A(q)$ has strictly negative diagonal and strictly positive off-diagonal entries. Then the last equation implies that $DG_{\hat{A}}(\hat{q})$ has only strictly negative entries which contradicts the gross substitution property for demand $G_{\hat{A}}$.

# 4. How to Obtain Uniqueness

## 4.1 Introduction

In this section we shall formulate conditions for economies under which the corresponding demand functions yield properties that will allow us to apply the theorems of the last chapter. Moreover, on the basis of the results from Chapter 5 we can extend various statements concerning uniqueness.

First we exploit the assumption of (constrained) Pareto efficiency. If an equilibrium is constrained efficient then there are no mutual gains from trade and hence the economy has a unique no-trade equilibrium. In particular then there is an explicit pricing formula relating the prices of assets to the characteristics of the economy. In the second section (Section 4.2.3) we shall examine special utility functions which lead to the uniqueness of the FM equilibrium, and where the uniqueness is largely independent of the financial contracts available, namely: quadratic, quasi-homothetic and quasi-linear utility functions. In the first two cases we formulate mainly familiar results for the general case without consumption in the first period. For quasi-linear utility functions we will show uniqueness with consumption in the first period.

In Section 4.5 we will describe the conditions under which it is possible to apply the theorem by Mitjushin-Polterovich so that the monotonicity of the securities demand function and thus, provided the initial endowments are collinear, the uniqueness of the FM equilibrium follow. After formulating this theorem for complete markets, we will examine any given utility functions with sufficiently small Mitjushin-Polterovich coefficients and spanned initial endowments. Moreover, we will also investigate agents using von-Neumann-

Morgenstern utility functions with a sufficiently low risk aversion. Under additional conditions on the initial endowments and the securities matrix, we can reduce the initial maximization problems to the maximization of other utility functions in fewer variables, so that we can apply Mitjushin-Polterovich's theorem in its familiar form.[16]

Section 4.6 examines the conditions for strict gross substitution of the individual demand for securities under which the collinearity of initial endowments no longer is a necessary requirement for global uniqueness. As in the case of complete markets, we will consider von-Neumann-Morgenstern utility functions with low relative risk aversion. Unfortunately, the conditions on the payoff matrix are very strong (in each state only one of the non-negative securities pays off, or this assumption applies in a slightly weaker form). A close examination of the conditions will show what, in the economies given by Becker [1995, p. 38-40] as counter-examples for strict gross substitution, causes a violation of this condition.

For economies with two securities (Section 4.7)—of which one is non-negative—Becker and Bettzüge have proved the uniqueness of an FM equilibrium for von-Neumann-Morgenstern utility functions with low risk aversion and strictly positive initial endowments.[17] We will show that a security need not be non-negative and the condition on initial endowments is too strong. In the case of two non-negative securities strict gross substitution even applies with respect to the demand for securities.

Section 6.2 on page 196 describes an example by Hens et al. [1999], which shows that, without certain assumptions regarding the securities structure, the uniqueness of the equilibrium does not generally follow despite presupposing von-Neumann-Morgenstern utility functions with low relative risk aversion, even if this is true in the case of complete markets.

In a final example we shall demonstrate that without the constraint of non-negativity with respect to consumption, low relative risk aversion does not suffice to guarantee uniqueness.

## 4.2 Explicit Pricing Formulas

### 4.2.1 No-Trade Equilibrium

Obviously, not only for complete markets, but also for incomplete markets the simplest pricing formula is given when each equilibrium has to be no-trade equilibrium.

[16][Bettzüge, 1997, p. 55-64]

[17][Bettzüge, 1997, Proposition 2.2].

This is clear if there does not exist any asset or only one. With no asset there cannot be any trade because there is nothing to exchange. For a single asset Assumption 1.5 assures either all consumers to demand or to supply the asset. These two cases as well as the one of identical consumers constitute economies with constrained Pareto-efficient endowments. More generally, the following proposition holds.

PROPOSITION 6.5 (UNIQUENESS FOR CONSTRAINED PARETO-EFFICIENCY)

*Given* $GEI = \left\{\mathbb{R}^S, (U^i, \omega^i)_{i \in I}, A\right\}$ *with* $(\omega^i)_{i \in I}$ *a constrained Pareto-efficient allocation, the no-trade equilibrium is the unique equilibrium with equilibrium price system* $q^* \in Q(A)$ *collinear to* $(\nabla U^i(\omega^i) A)^T$ *for all* $i \in I$.

PROOF 6.8

*Because of Assumption 1.5 and Proposition 6.1 assume without loss of generality* $A_{\cdot 1} > 0$. *Then for* $q^T = \left(1, \frac{\nabla U^1(\omega^1) A_{\cdot 2}}{\nabla U^1(\omega^1) A_{\cdot 1}}, \ldots, \frac{\nabla U^1(\omega^1) A_{\cdot J}}{\nabla U^1(\omega^1) A_{\cdot 1}}\right)$ *the equilibrium properties are obvious.*

*Assume, there is another equilibrium allocation* $\left(\tilde{\theta}^i\right)_{i=1,\ldots,I}$ *with corresponding price system* $\tilde{q}$, *then the no-trade allocation* $(\theta^i = 0)_{i=1,\ldots,I}$ *also satisfies the budget constraints. Therefore, it is*

$$U^i\left(\omega^i + A\,\tilde{\theta}^i\right) \geq U^i\left(\omega^i\right) \quad \text{for all} \quad i = 1, \ldots, I \quad .$$

*Since the no-trade allocation is constrained Pareto-efficient, this implies*

$$U^i\left(\omega^i + A\,\tilde{\theta}^i\right) = U^i\left(\omega^i\right) \quad \text{for all} \quad i = 1, \ldots, I \quad .$$

*Therefore, together with* $rank\, A = J$ *and strict quasi-concavity of* $U^i, i = 1, \ldots, I$, *one obtains a contradiction for* $\tilde{\theta}^i \neq 0$ *because each strict convex combination of* $\omega^i + A\,\tilde{\theta}^i$ *and* $\omega^i = \omega^i + A\,\theta^i$ *(or equivalently of* $\tilde{\theta}^i$ *and* $\theta^i$*) would improve the consumer.*

*q. e. d.*

A nice property with respect to constrained Pareto-efficiency for an asset structure $A$ admits conclusions on constrained Pareto-efficiency for asset structures which allow trade in a subspace of the original one.

LEMMA 6.1 (IMPLICATIONS OF CONSTRAINED PARETO-EFFICIENCY)

*If* $(\theta^i)_{i=1,\ldots,I} \in \mathbb{R}^{J \times I}$ *with* $\theta^i = 0$ *for all* $i = 1, \ldots, I$, *i.e. the no-trade allocation, is constrained Pareto-efficient in the GEI-economy* $\left\{\mathbb{R}^S, (U^i, \omega^i)_{i=1,\ldots,I}, A\right\}$

*where $A \in \mathbb{R}^{S\times J}$ and $A_{\cdot 1} > 0$, then this is also true for all $\left\{\mathbb{R}^S, (U^i, \omega^i)_{i=1,\ldots,I}, \tilde{A}\right\}$ with $\tilde{A} \in \mathbb{R}^{S\times \tilde{J}}$ where $\tilde{J} \leq J$, $\tilde{A}_{\cdot 1} > 0$*[18]*, $\langle \tilde{A}\rangle \subseteq \langle A\rangle$ and the no-trade allocation is $\left(\tilde{\theta}^i\right)_{i=1,\ldots,I} \in \mathbb{R}^{\tilde{J}\times I}$ with $\tilde{\theta}^i = 0$ for all $i = 1, \ldots, I$.*

PROOF 6.9 *Since $\langle \tilde{A}\rangle \subseteq \langle A\rangle$, for $\tilde{A}_{\cdot k}, k = 1, \ldots, \tilde{J}$, there is some $c_{\cdot k} \in \mathbb{R}^J$ with $\tilde{A}_{\cdot k} = \sum_{j=1}^J c_{j\,k} A_{\cdot j}$. Therefore, for all $k = 1, \ldots, \tilde{J}$ one gets*

$$\begin{aligned}
\frac{\nabla U^1(\omega^1)\tilde{A}_{\cdot k}}{\nabla U^1(\omega^1)\tilde{A}_{\cdot 1}} &= \frac{\sum_{j=1}^J c_{j\,k}\nabla U^1(\omega^1) A_{\cdot j}}{\sum_{j=1}^J c_{j\,1}\nabla U^1(\omega^1) A_{\cdot j}} \\
&= \frac{\sum_{j=1}^J c_{jk}\frac{\nabla U^i(\omega^i)A_{\cdot j}\cdot\nabla U^1(\omega^1)A_{\cdot 1}}{\nabla U^i(\omega^i)A_{\cdot 1}}}{\sum_{j=1}^J c_{j\,1}\frac{\nabla U^i(\omega^i)A_{\cdot j}\cdot\nabla U^1(\omega^1)A_{\cdot 1}}{\nabla U^i(\omega^i)A_{\cdot 1}}} \\
&= \frac{\sum_{j=1}^J c_{j\,k}\nabla U^i(\omega^i) A_{\cdot j}}{\sum_{j=1}^J c_{j1}\nabla U^i(\omega^i) A_{\cdot j}} \\
&= \frac{\nabla U^i(\omega^i)\tilde{A}_{\cdot k}}{\nabla U^i(\omega^i)\tilde{A}_{\cdot 1}} \quad \textit{for all} \quad i = 2, \ldots, I
\end{aligned}$$

*where the second equality follows from constrained Pareto-efficiency in the economy $\left\{\mathbb{R}^S, (U^i, \omega^i)_{i=1,\ldots,I}, A\right\}$.*

*q. e. d.*

Combining Proposition 6.5 and Lemma 6.1 leads to a further result on uniqueness of FM-equilibria.

PROPOSITION 6.6 (INCLUSION PROPERTY)
*If $GEI = \left\{\mathbb{R}^S, (U^i, \omega^i)_{i=1,\ldots,I}, A\right\}$ with $A \in \mathbb{R}^{S\times J}$ and $A_{\cdot 1} > 0$ is characterized by the unique (constrained Pareto-efficient) no-trade equilibrium, this is also true for all economies $GEI = \left\{\mathbb{R}^S, (U^i, \omega^i)_{i=1,\ldots,I}, \tilde{A}\right\}$, $\tilde{A} \in \mathbb{R}^{S\times \tilde{J}}$ with $\tilde{J} \leq J$, $\tilde{A}_{\cdot 1} > 0$ and $\langle \tilde{A}\rangle \subseteq \langle A\rangle$.*

Constrained Pareto-efficiency might induce a reduction of the number of equilibria for incomplete markets in comparison to complete markets. In Chapter 6 we give further results on uniqueness of competitive equilibria exploiting the assumption of constrained Pareto efficiency. In particular there we derive unique equilibria with small positive trading volume. That section relies on the technical section, Section 5, in which pertubations of equilibria with respect to

[18] It would be sufficient to demand $\tilde{A}\,\tilde{\theta} > 0$ for some $\tilde{\theta} \in \mathbb{R}^{\tilde{J}}$.

the asset structure are considered. Therefore we have decided to postpone the further conditions leading to uniqueness that are based on constrained Pareto efficiency to the very end of this chapter.

### 4.2.2 Complete Risk Sharing

As pointed out in Section 4.1 the idea of risk sharing in equilibrium models is recently extended from complete to various incomplete markets models. Regrettably, as soon as trading possibilities are restricted, it becomes much more difficult to obtain complete risk sharing in equilibrium. In addition to the requirements when markets are complete (satisfaction of the expected utility hypothesis and no aggregate risk) the commodity endowments have to be substituted by asset endowments, i.e. commodity endowments have to be elements of the asset span. What happens without this additional assumption is examined in Section 5.

PROPOSITION 6.7 (COMPLETE RISK SHARING)
*Let an economy* $GEI = \left\{\mathbb{R}^S, (U^i, \omega^i)_{i=1,\ldots,I}, A\right\}$ *with* $A_{\cdot 1} > 0$ *be given such that for all* $i = 1, \ldots, I$ *the expected utility hypothesis is satisfied, i.e.*

$$U^i(x) = \sum_{s=1}^{S} \bar{\rho}_s \, u^i(x_s) \quad ,$$

*where* $u^i$ *satisfies standard assumptions and* $\bar{\rho} \in \hat{\mathcal{P}}_{1,1}$ *is an objective probability measure. Endowments are spanned, i.e.*

$$\omega^i = A\,\theta^i_\omega \quad \textit{for some} \quad \theta^i_\omega \in \mathbb{R}^J \quad .$$

*If* $\omega$ *is riskless (i.e.* $\omega = \bar{\omega}\,\mathbb{1}$ *for some* $\bar{\omega} \in \mathbb{R}_{++}$*), the economy has a unique FM-equilibrium where normalizing the first asset price to one, one obtains the pricing formula*

$$q^{*T} = \left(1, \frac{\sum_{s=1}^{S} \bar{\rho}_s\, A_{s2}}{\sum_{s=1}^{S} \bar{\rho}_s\, A_{s1}}, \ldots, \frac{\sum_{s=1}^{S} \bar{\rho}_s\, A_{sJ}}{\sum_{s=1}^{S} \bar{\rho}_s\, A_{s1}}\right) \quad .$$

PROOF 6.10
*There is exactly one normalized equilibrium price system* $q^*$ *such that the corresponding allocation is riskless. This follows because then first order conditions* (6.21) *determine price-ratios to be*

$$\frac{q_j}{q_1} = \frac{\sum_{s=1}^{S} \bar{\rho}_s\, A_{sj}}{\sum_{s=1}^{S} \bar{\rho}_s\, A_{s1}}, j \in \{1, \ldots, J\} \quad .$$

*Note that the assumptions on the economy imply that all equilibrium allocations are riskless. Suppose not. Let* $(\hat{x}^i)_{i=1,\ldots,I}$ *be the corresponding allocation with*

$\hat{x}^i = A\left(\theta^i_\omega + \hat{\theta}^i\right)$ *for some* $\hat{\theta}^i \in \mathbb{R}^J, i = 1, \ldots, I$, *with* $\sum_{i=1}^I \hat{\theta}^i = 0$. *Strict concavity of* $u^i, i = 1, \ldots, I$, *assures that* $x^{*i} = \left(\sum_{s=1}^S \bar{\rho}_s\, \hat{x}^i_s\right) \mathbb{1}, i = 1, \ldots, I$, *improves all consumers and at least one of them strictly. Since*

$$\sum_{i=1}^I x^{*i} = \sum_{i=1}^I \left(\sum_{s=1}^S \bar{\rho}_s\, \hat{x}^i_s\right) \mathbb{1} = \sum_{s=1}^S \bar{\rho}_s \left(\sum_{i=1}^I \hat{x}^i_s\right) \mathbb{1} = \sum_{s=1}^S \bar{\rho}_s\, \omega_s\, \mathbb{1} = \bar{\omega}\, \mathbb{1}$$

*and*

$$x^{*i} = \sum_{s=1}^S \bar{\rho}_s\, A_{s\cdot} \left(\theta^i_\omega + \hat{\theta}^i\right) \mathbb{1} = \omega^i + A\, \theta^{*i}$$

*with* $\theta^{*i} = \frac{1}{\bar{\omega}} \sum_{s=1}^S \bar{\rho}_s\, A_{s\cdot} \left(\theta^i_\omega + \hat{\theta}^i\right) \left(\sum_{i=1}^I \theta^i_\omega\right) - \theta^i_\omega$, *this contradicts the constrained Pareto-efficiency of equilibria.*

*q. e. d.*

Note that asset prices refer to the expected asset payoffs and are independent of aggregate endowments as well as of the endowment distribution.

### 4.2.3 Quadratic Utility Functions

If the agents' utility functions $U^i$ are quadratic, it is a known fact that the interior FM equilibria of the examined economy are unique.[19] Interior FM equilibria are FM equilibria with respect to which each agent possesses a strictly positive consumption plan.

DEFINITION 6.10 (QUADRATIC UTILITY FUNCTION)
*A utility function* $U^i: \mathbb{R}^S_+ \to \mathbb{R}$ *of the form*

$$U^i(x) = \sum_{s=1}^S \rho^i_s \left(x_s - \frac{1}{2}\alpha^i x^2_s\right)$$

*with* $\rho^i \in \mathbb{R}^S_{++}$, $\sum_{s=1}^S \rho^i_s = 1$ *and* $\alpha^i \in \mathbb{R}_{++}$ *is called a quadratic utility function.*

Where all agents $i \in I$ have quadratic utility functions, the following additional assumption shall be made for the array $\left((\alpha^i)_{i \in I}, (\omega^i)_{i \in I}\right)$ and $A$:

[19] For the capital asset pricing model with quadratic utility functions and consumption in the first period see, for example, Bettzüge [1997, Proposition 2.1]. However, he overlooked the following problem: His failure to bound consumption from below (typical for CAPM) means that the condition on utility functions and initial endowments (Cf. Assumption 6.2) does not ensure monotonicity as he supposes. However, a lower bound for consumption only results in the uniqueness of interior equilibria since the proof requires a first-order condition that is not necessarily satisfied in boundary equilibria.

ASSUMPTION 6.2 (MONOTONICITY)
*Let* $\left((\alpha^i)_{i \in I}, (\omega^i)_{i \in I}, A\right) \in \mathbb{R}^I_{++} \times \mathbb{R}^{S \times I}_{++} \times \mathbb{R}^{S \times J}$ *be such that:*

*(i) with* $\omega = \sum_{i=1}^I \omega^i$ *for all* $i \in I$ *and for all* $s \in S$: $1 - \alpha^i \omega_s > 0$,

*(ii) at least one security pays off only positively, that is, there exists a* $j \in J$ *with* $A^j \geq 0$.

Assumption 6.2.(i). guarantees strict monotonicity of the utility functions in the area that is relevant for our study of equilibria. Since all consumption plans $x^i$ must be non-negative and feasible, $x^i_s \leq \omega_s$ holds for all $i \in I$ and all $s \in S$. Hence the gradient of the utility function is strictly positive for all $i \in I$:

$$\partial_{x_s} U^i(x) = \rho^i_s \left(1 - \alpha^i x^i_s\right) \geq \rho^i_s \left(1 - \alpha^i \omega_s\right) > 0$$

Moreover, since the Hessian-Matrices are negative definite it follows that the utility functions $U^i$ are strictly concave:

$$D^2_{xx} U^i(x) = \begin{pmatrix} -\rho^i_1 \alpha^i & & 0 \\ & \ddots & \\ 0 & & -\rho^i_S \alpha^i \end{pmatrix}$$

THEOREM 6.7 (UNIQUENESS)
*Let an economy* $GEI = \left\{\mathbb{R}^S, (U^i, \omega^i)_{i \in I}, A\right\}$ *satisfy the Differentiability Assumptions 1.2 and let the endowments be strictly positive. Let the utility functions be quadratic and satisfy Assumption 6.2. Let the probability distribution of all possible states be objective, that is, there exists a* $\rho \in \mathbb{R}^S_{++}$ *with* $\rho = \rho^i$ *for all* $i \in I$. *Then not more than one interior FM equilibrium of the economy exists.*

PROOF 6.11
*The maximization problem of agent* $i$ *can be written as:*

$$\max_{\theta^i \in \mathbb{R}^J} \sum_{s=1}^S \rho_s \left(\omega^i_s + A_s \theta^i - \frac{1}{2} \alpha^i \left(\omega^i_s + A_s \theta^i\right)^2\right)$$

$$\text{s.t.} \quad q^T \theta^i = 0 \quad \wedge \quad \omega^i + A \theta^i \geq 0$$

*Since our investigation extends to interior equilibria only and* $U^i$ *are concave, the following first-order condition is necessary and sufficient:*

$$\sum_{s=1}^S \rho_s \left(A^j_s - \alpha^i \left(\omega^i_s + A_s \theta^i\right) A^j_s\right) - \lambda^i q_j = 0, \quad j = 1, \ldots, J \quad , \qquad (6.7)$$

$$q^T \theta^i = 0 \quad , \tag{6.8}$$

*$\lambda^i$ being the corresponding Lagrange multiplier.*
*Without loss of generality let $j = 1$ satisfy Assumption 6.2.(ii) such that the homogeneity of $g^i(q)$ enables us to normalize $q_1 = 1$. It then follows from (i) for $j = 1$*

$$\sum_{s=1}^{S} \rho_s \left( A_s^1 - \alpha^i \left( \omega_s^i + A_s \theta^i \right) A_s^1 \right) = \lambda^i \quad .$$

*It follows from* (6.8) *that:*

$$\theta_1^i = - \sum_{k=2}^{J} q_k \, \theta_k^i$$

*Now insert $\lambda^i$ $f(tm)\, r \quad j = 2, \ldots, J$ in* (6.7) *in order to get*

$$\sum_{s=1}^{S} \rho_s \left[ A_s^j - \alpha^i \left( \omega_s^i + A_s \, \theta^i \right) A_s^j \right] - \sum_{s=1}^{S} \rho_s \left[ A_s^1 - \alpha^i \left( \omega_s^i + A_s \, \theta^i \right) A_s^1 \right] q_j = 0 \quad .$$

*On dividing the equation by $\alpha^i$ and summing over all $i$, with the equilibrium condition $\sum_{i=1}^{I} \theta^i = 0$ we obtain*

$$\sum_{i=1}^{I} \sum_{s=1}^{S} \left( \frac{\rho_s}{\alpha^i} A_s^j - \rho_s \, \omega_s^i \, A_s^j \right) - \sum_{i=1}^{I} \sum_{s=1}^{S} \left( \frac{\rho_s}{\alpha^i} A_s^1 - \rho_s \, \omega_s^i \, A_s^1 \right) q_j = 0 \quad .$$

*With $k := \sum_{i=1}^{I} \frac{1}{\alpha^i}$ this is equivalent to*

$$\sum_{s=1}^{S} \rho_s \, A_s^j \, (k - \omega_s) - \sum_{s=1}^{S} \rho_s \, A_s^1 \, (k - \omega_s) \, q_j = 0 \quad .$$

*Due to Assumption6.2.(i) $\frac{1}{\alpha^i} - \omega_s > 0$. Summing over all $i \in I$ yields $k - \omega_s \geq k - I\,\omega_s > 0$ so that, since $A^1 > 0$, the coefficient of $q_j$ is non-zero. It therefore follows that*

$$q_j = \frac{\sum_{s=1}^{S} \rho_s \, A_s^j \, (k - \omega_s)}{\sum_{s=1}^{S} \rho_s \, A_s^1 \, (k - \omega_s)}, \quad j = 2, \ldots, J.$$

*Thus $q$ is unique up to a scaling factor.*

*q. e. d.*

Remark: No assertions are made with respect to the existence of interior equilibria or the number of boundary equilibria.
In accordance with Theorem 6.1 on page 103, where two economies with the same span of the payoff matrix are shown to be equivalent in terms of the uniqueness of any FM equilibrium, Assumption 6.2.(ii) does not impose a restriction. However, in this context the goods allocation of the unique equilibria of $\varepsilon$ and $\hat{\varepsilon}$ is equal so that either both economies have strictly positive equilibrium allocations, that is, interior equilibria, or none. The rest follows under Assumption 1.3 applied to the expected utility hypothesis.

## 4.3 Quasi-homothetic Utility Functions

In the general equilibrium model the existence of a representative agent has been shown for economies with homothetic, identical utility functions and any given initial endowments, and, respectively, for economies with collinear initial endowments. [20] Together with the implications of negative quasi-definiteness this leads to the uniqueness of the NA equilibrium for complete markets.
This poses the question under which conditions a representative agent exists in the case of incomplete financial markets. It is obviously true where all agents are identical. The same holds when no or only one security can be traded because then the agents consume their initial endowments only. [21]
As in the case of complete markets, homothetic utility functions play an important role for incomplete markets.

DEFINITION 6.11 (QUASI-HOMOTHETIC UTILITY FUNCTIONS)

- *A utility function $V^i : \mathbb{R}^S_+ \to \mathbb{R}$ is called homogeneous if there is a $k \in \mathbb{R}$ such that for all $x \in \mathbb{R}^S_+$ and all $\lambda > 0$*

$$V^i(\lambda x) = \lambda^k V^i(x) \quad .$$

  *Then $V^i$ is homogeneous of order $k$.*

- *A utility function $U^i : \mathbb{R}^S_+ - \{\alpha^i\} \to \mathbb{R}$ is called quasi-homothetic if, given some constant vector $\alpha^i \in \mathbb{R}^S$, there exists a strictly monotone function $m^i : \mathbb{R} \to \mathbb{R}$ and a homogeneous function $V^i : \mathbb{R}^S_+ \to \mathbb{R}$ such that for all $x \in \mathbb{R}^S_+ - \{\alpha^i\}$*

---

[20] [Shafer and Sonnenschein, 1982, Section 3].

[21] For $J = 1$ it follows from $A\,\tilde{\theta} > 0$ for a $\tilde{\theta}$ that $q \neq 0$ and therefore $\theta = 0$ follows from $q\,\theta = 0$.

$$U^i(x) = m^i \circ V^i\left(\alpha^i + x\right) \quad .$$

REMARK 6.1
*If the utility function $V^i: \quad \mathbb{R}_+^S \to \mathbb{R}$ is homogeneous, then, given an income $w$, the maximizer $x^i(\pi, w)$ of the utility function must be*

$$x^i(\pi, w) = w\, x^i(\pi, 1) \quad .$$

The set of quasi-homothetic utility functions $U^i$ is closely related to the set of expected utility functions whose state utility functions $u^i$ belong to the so-called HARA family (Hyperbolic Absolute Risk Aversion). This family of functions underlies much of the finance literature.
The corresponding functions $U^i$ are therefore additively separable in the different states. State utility functions $u^i$ need not be defined on $\mathbb{R}_+$. It suffices when they are defined on $\mathbb{D}^i \subseteq \mathbb{R}$. $u^i: \quad \mathbb{D}^i \to \mathbb{R}$ shall be continuous on $\mathbb{D}^i$ and twice continuously differentiable, strictly monotone and strictly concave on $\mathring{\mathbb{D}}^i$. There is a vector $\rho^i \in \mathbb{R}_{++}^S$ with $\sum_{s=1}^S \rho_s^i = 1$ such that

$$U^i(x) = \sum_{s=1}^{S} \rho_s^i\, u^i(x_s)$$

for all $x \in \left(\mathbb{D}^i\right)^S$.
Recall from Chapter 1 the definition:

DEFINITION 6.12 (HARA FAMILY)
*A function $u^i: \mathbb{D}^i \to \mathbb{R}$ is an element of the HARA family if $(\bar{\alpha}^i, \beta) \in \mathbb{R}_+ \times \mathbb{R}$ exists, such that $\mathbb{D}^i = \{x \in \mathbb{R} \mid \bar{\alpha}^i + \beta\, x \geq 0\}$ and $u^i$ can be written as:*

$$u^i(x) = \begin{cases} \frac{\left(\bar{\alpha}^i + \beta\, x\right)^{1-\frac{1}{\beta}}}{\frac{1}{\beta}\left(1-\frac{1}{\beta}\right)} & \textit{for} \quad \beta \neq 0 \quad \textit{and} \quad \beta \neq 1\,, \\ -\bar{\alpha}^i \exp\left(-\frac{x}{\bar{\alpha}^i}\right) & \textit{for} \quad \beta = 0\,, \\ \ln\left(\bar{\alpha}^i + x\right) & \textit{for} \quad \beta = 1\,. \end{cases}$$

The functions $u^i$ of the HARA family exhibit all properties required above by the state utility functions.[22]
The risk tolerance $T^i(x)$ of a function $u^i$ is defined by

$$T^i(x) := -\frac{u^{i\prime}(x)}{u^{i\prime\prime}(x)} = \left[RA^i(x)\right]^{-1}$$

[22] In the literature $\mathring{\mathbb{D}}^i$ is often chosen as domain for $u^i$ in order to avoid problems with respect to the application of first-order conditions. See, for example, Magill and Quinzii [1996, p. 174].

for all $x \in \mathring{\mathbb{D}}^i$. Elements of the HARA family are characterized by linear risk tolerance or, equivalently, by hyperbolic absolute risk aversion, that is,

$$T^i(x) = \bar{\alpha}^i + \beta\, x = \left[RA^i(x)\right]^{-1}$$

for all $x \in \mathring{\mathbb{D}}^i$. In particular, this means that:[23]

- For $\beta > 0$ the absolute risk aversion is decreasing.
- For $\beta < 0$ the absolute risk aversion is increasing.
- For $\beta = 0$ absolute risk aversion is constant.
- For $\beta > 0$ and $\bar{\alpha}^i = 0$ relative risk aversion is constant.
- For $\beta = -1$ the utility function is quadratic.

For the sake of simplicity we shall from now on refer to an expected utility function $U^i$ for which $u^i$ is an element of the HARA family as HARA function. By comparison with quasi-homothetic utility functions, we find that:

- HARA functions with $\beta = 1$ are obviously quasi-homothetic.
- HARA functions with $\beta > 0$, $\beta \neq 1$ are also quasi-homothetic. To validate this, define

$$V^i(x) := \frac{\beta^{2-\frac{1}{\beta}}}{1-\frac{1}{\beta}} \sum_{s=1}^{S} \rho_s^i\, x_s^{1-\frac{1}{\beta}} \quad ,$$

which is homogeneous of order $k := 1 - \frac{1}{\beta} \in \mathbb{R}$. Let the domain be $\mathbb{R}_+^S$. Further define $\alpha^i := \frac{\bar{\alpha}^i}{\beta} e \in \mathbb{R}^S$. It then follows for all $x \in \left\{x \in \mathbb{R}^S \middle| x_s \in \mathbb{D}^i\right\} = \left(\mathbb{D}^i\right)^S$ that

$$\begin{aligned} U^i(x) &= \sum_{s=1}^{S} \rho_s^i\, u^i(x_s) \\ &= \sum_{s=1}^{S} \rho_s^i \frac{\left(\bar{\alpha}^i + \beta\, x_s\right)^{1-\frac{1}{\beta}}}{\frac{1}{\beta}\left(1-\frac{1}{\beta}\right)} \\ &= \frac{\beta^{2-\frac{1}{\beta}}}{1-\frac{1}{\beta}} \sum_{s=1}^{S} \rho_s^i \left(\frac{\bar{\alpha}^i}{\beta} + x_s\right)^{1-\frac{1}{\beta}} \\ &= V^i\left(\alpha^i + x\right) \quad . \end{aligned}$$

[23] [Magill and Quinzii, 1996, p. 174 f.].

The domain of $U^i$ is admissible for a quasi-homothetic function since

$$\begin{aligned} x \in \left(\mathbb{D}^i\right)^S &\Leftrightarrow \bar{\alpha}^i e + \beta x \geq 0 \\ &\Leftrightarrow \alpha^i + x \geq 0 \\ &\Leftrightarrow x \in \mathbb{R}_+^S - \left\{\alpha^i\right\} \end{aligned}$$

Consequently, the $\mathbb{R}_+^S$ as domain of $V^i$ is sufficiently large. Thus $U^i$ is quasi-homothetic.

- As regards $\beta < 0$, the domain of a HARA function $U^i$ does not satisfy all of the conditions required in the case of a quasi-homothetic function because

$$\begin{aligned} x \in \left(\mathbb{D}^i\right)^S &\Leftrightarrow \bar{\alpha}^i e + \beta x \geq 0 \\ &\Leftrightarrow x \leq -\frac{\bar{\alpha}^i}{\beta} e \\ &\Leftrightarrow x \in \underbrace{\mathbb{R}_-^S - \left\{\frac{\bar{\alpha}^i}{\beta} e\right\}}_{\neq \mathbb{R}_+^S - \{\alpha^i\} \text{ for all } \alpha^i \in \mathbb{R}^S} \quad . \end{aligned}$$

  Furthermore, the domain of this HARA function cannot be modified accordingly, because doing so means that the functions $u^i$ might assume complex values, or would no longer be necessarily monotone and strictly concave.[24]

  For $\beta < 0$ the HARA functions are therefore not quasi-homothetic.

- For $\beta = 0$ it can be shown that the HARA functions $U_\beta$ are limits of HARA functions $U_{\beta_n}$ for $\beta_n \in \mathbb{R}_{++}$ $(n \in \mathbb{N})$, and $\lim_{n\to\infty} \beta_n = 0$:

$$\lim_{n\to\infty} U_{\beta_n}(x) = U_\beta(x) \quad .$$

  For a detailed discussion, see Pollak [1971, p. 405]. However, while the functions $U_{\beta_n}$ are quasi-homothetic in accordance with the preceding considerations, this is not true for $U_\beta$. [25]

- Conversely, each additive quasi-homothetic function $U^i$ is also a HARA function. This follows by a theorem that can be found in Pollak [1971,

[24]Consider for example $\beta = -1$ for $\bar{\alpha}^i e - x < 0$.

[25][Detemple and Gottardi, 1998, footnote 9].

p. 405], according to which each additive function generating a demand function that is affine linear in income must be HARA. [26]

- Moreover, the non-additive, but homogeneous function $U^i(x) = x_1^{\frac{1}{2}} x_2^{\frac{1}{2}} + x_3$[27] illustrates that quasi-homothetic functions need not be HARA functions.

For a more detailed discussion of the family of HARA functions, we refer to the relevant literature, in particular to Rubinstein [1974] and Milne [1979]. The next theorem lists some conditions under which a representative agent exists:

THEOREM 6.8 (REPRESENTATIVE AGENT. [DETEMPLE AND GOTTARDI, 1998])
*Let an economy* $GEI = \left\{\mathbb{R}^S, (U^i, \omega^i)_{i \in I}, A\right\}$ *satisfy Assumptions 1.2. Furthermore, let the utility functions* $U^i$ *be quasi-homothetic, the functions* $V^i$ *continuous on* $\mathbb{R}^S_+$ *and strictly monotone and strictly quasi-concave on* $\mathbb{R}^S_{++}$*, and for the initial endowments the inequality* $\alpha^i + \omega^i \gg 0$ *holds. Then:*

[26] In the case of quasi-homothetic functions, the affine linearity of the demand function can be obtained as follows :

$$
\begin{aligned}
x^i(\pi, w) &:= \arg\max_{x \geq -\alpha^i} U^i(x) \quad \text{s.t.} \quad \pi^T x = w \\
&= \arg\max_{x \geq -\alpha^i} V^i\left(\alpha^i + x\right) \quad \text{s.t.} \quad \pi^T x = w \\
&= \arg\max_{x \geq -\alpha^i} V^i\left(w \tfrac{1}{w}\left(\alpha^i + x\right)\right) \quad \text{s.t.} \quad \pi^T \tfrac{1}{w} x = 1 \\
&= \arg\max_{x \geq -\alpha^i} w^k V^i\left(\tfrac{1}{w}\left(\alpha^i + x\right)\right) \quad \text{s.t.} \quad \pi^T \tfrac{1}{w} x = 1 \\
&= w \left[\arg\max_{y \geq 0} V^i(y) \quad \text{s.t.} \quad \pi^T y = 1 + \pi^T \tfrac{1}{w} \alpha^i\right] - \alpha^i \\
&= w(1 + \pi^T \frac{1}{w} \alpha^i \left[\arg\max_{y \geq 0} V^i(y) \quad \text{s.t.} \quad \pi^T y = 1\right] - \alpha^i \\
&= w \bar{x}^i(\pi, 1) + \left[\pi^T \alpha^i \bar{x}^i(\pi, 1) - \alpha^i\right],
\end{aligned}
$$

with

$$
\bar{x}^i(\pi, 1) := \arg\max_{y \geq 0} V^i(y) \quad \text{s.t.} \quad \pi^T y = 1 \ .
$$

[27] Obviously $U^i(\lambda x) = \lambda U^i(x)$.

*(i) A representative agent exists where the utility functions $U^i$ are such that $V^i = V$ for all $i \in I$ and for all $i \in I$ there exists a $\bar{\theta}^i \in \mathbb{R}^J$ with $\alpha^i + \omega^i = A\,\bar{\theta}^i$.*

*(ii) A representative agent exists where the utility functions $U^i$ are such that $V^i = V$ for all $i \in I$ and there exists $\delta \in \mathbb{R}^I_{++}$ with $\sum_{i=1}^I \delta^i = 1$, an $\alpha \in \mathbb{R}^S$ and an $\omega \in \mathbb{R}^S_{++} - \{\alpha\}$ with $\alpha^i + \omega^i = \delta^i\,(\alpha + \omega)$.*

*(iii) The economy has a representative agent if the $V^i$ satisfy Assumption 1.1, there exists a $\delta \in \mathbb{R}^I_{++}$ with $\sum_{i=1}^I \delta^i = 1$, an $\alpha \in \mathbb{R}^S$ and an $\omega \in \mathbb{R}^S_{++} - \{\alpha\}$ with $\alpha^i + \omega^i = \delta^i\,(\alpha + \omega)$ and for all $i \in I$ there exists a $\bar{\theta}^i$ with $\alpha^i + \omega^i = A\,\bar{\theta}^i$.*

PROOF 6.12

**Proof of (i):** *For all $i \in I$ $\alpha^i + \omega^i$ is in the span of $A$. It follows that:*

$$
\begin{aligned}
g^i(q) &= \arg\max_{\theta \in \mathbb{R}^J} U^i\left(\omega^i + A\,\theta\right) \quad s.t. \quad q^T\theta = 0 \\
&\qquad\qquad\qquad\qquad \wedge \quad \omega^i + A\,\theta \geq -\alpha^i \\
&= \arg\max_{\theta \in \mathbb{R}^J} m^i \circ V\left(\alpha^i + \omega^i + A\,\theta\right) \quad s.t. \quad q^T\,\theta = 0 \\
&\qquad\qquad\qquad\qquad \wedge \quad \alpha^i + \omega^i + A\,\theta \geq 0 \\
&= \arg\max_{\theta \in \mathbb{R}^J} V\left(A\left(\theta + \bar{\theta}^i\right)\right) \quad s.t. \quad q^T\left(\theta + \bar{\theta}^i\right) = q^T\,\bar{\theta}^i \\
&\qquad\qquad\qquad\qquad \wedge \quad A\left(\theta + \bar{\theta}^i\right) \geq 0 \\
&= \left[\begin{array}{ll} \arg\max_{\hat{\theta} \in \mathbb{R}^J} V\left(A\,\hat{\theta}\right) \quad s.t. & q^T\hat{\theta} = q^T\,\bar{\theta}^i \\ & \wedge \quad A\,\hat{\theta} \geq 0 \end{array}\right] - \bar{\theta}^i \\
&= \left[\begin{array}{ll} argmax_{\hat{\theta} \in \mathbb{R}^J} V\left(q^T\,\bar{\theta}^i\,A\frac{1}{q^T\,\bar{\theta}^i}\,\hat{\theta}\right) \quad s.t. & q^T\,\frac{1}{q^T\,\bar{\theta}^i}\,\hat{\theta} = 1 \\ & \wedge \quad A\,\frac{1}{q^T\,\bar{\theta}^i}\,\hat{\theta} \geq 0 \end{array}\right] - \bar{\theta}^i \\
&= q^T\,\bar{\theta}^i\,\tilde{g}\,(q, 1) - \bar{\theta}^i
\end{aligned}
$$

*with*
$$
\tilde{g}\,(q,1) = \arg\max_{\tilde{\theta} \in \mathbb{R}^J} V\left(A\,\tilde{\theta}\right) \quad s.t. \quad q^T\,\tilde{\theta} = 1 \quad \wedge \quad A\tilde{\theta} \geq 0 .
$$

*These transformations are possible, since for all $q \in Q$*

$$
q^T\,\bar{\theta}^i = \underbrace{\pi^T}_{\gg 0}\,\underbrace{A\,\bar{\theta}^i}_{\gg 0} > 0
$$

*and V is homogeneous.*

*It therefore follows for market demand* $g(q)$*:*

$$\begin{aligned}
g(q) &= \sum_{i=1}^{I} g^i(q) \\
&= q^T \sum_{i=1}^{I} \bar{\theta}^i \tilde{g}(q,1) - \sum_{i=1}^{I} \bar{\theta}^i \\
&= \tilde{g}\left(q, q^T \sum_{i=1}^{I} \bar{\theta}^i\right) - \sum_{i=1}^{I} \bar{\theta}^i \\
&= \left[ \begin{array}{ll} \arg\max_{\tilde{\theta} \in \mathbb{R}^J} V\left(A\tilde{\theta}\right) & s.t.\ \ q^T\tilde{\theta} = q^T \sum_{i=1}^{I} \bar{\theta}^i \\ & \wedge\ \ A\tilde{\theta} \geq 0 \end{array} \right] - \sum_{i=1}^{I} \bar{\theta}^i \\
&= \arg\max_{\theta \in \mathbb{R}^J} V\left(A\left(\theta + \textstyle\sum_{i=1}^{I} \bar{\theta}^i\right)\right) \quad s.t.\ \ q^T\theta = 0 \\
&\qquad\qquad \wedge\ \ A\left(\theta + \textstyle\sum_{i=1}^{I} \bar{\theta}^i\right) \geq 0 \\
&= \arg\max_{\theta \in \mathbb{R}^J} V(\alpha + \omega + A\theta) \quad s.t.\ \ q^T\theta = 0 \\
&\qquad\qquad \wedge\ \ \alpha + \omega + A\theta \geq 0
\end{aligned}$$

*with* $\alpha + \omega = A \sum_{i=1}^{I} \bar{\theta}^i$. *This is satisfied for* $\alpha = \sum_{i=1}^{I} \alpha^i$ *and* $\omega = \sum_{i=1}^{I} \omega^i$, *whereby a representative agent is found.* [28]

[28] For similar results, see also Detemple and Gottardi [1998, Theorem 3.1] who conduct a local analysis in a model with consumption in the first period. However, there is an inconsistency: $U^i$ and $V^i$ are both defined on $\mathbb{R}^S_+$. In the following Detemple/Gottardi then proceed as if the domain of $V^i$ were given by $\mathbb{R}^S_+ + \{\alpha^i\}$. As a result, the constraint in the proof ensuring the lower bound for consumption is dependent on the agent's $\alpha^i$ so that it is impossible to construct a demand function $\tilde{\theta}$ that is independent of $i$.

**Proof of (ii):** *The following applies:*

$$
\begin{aligned}
g^i(q) &= \arg\max_{\theta\in\mathbb{R}^J} U^i\left(\omega^i + A\,\theta\right) \quad s.t. \quad q^T\theta = 0 \\
&\qquad\qquad\qquad \wedge \quad \omega^i + A\,\theta \geq -\alpha^i \\
&= \arg\max_{\theta\in\mathbb{R}^J} m^i \circ V\left(\alpha^i + \omega^i + A\,\theta\right) \quad s.t. \quad q^T\theta = 0 \\
&\qquad\qquad\qquad \wedge \quad \alpha^i + \omega^i + A\,\theta \geq 0 \\
&= \arg\max_{\theta\in\mathbb{R}^J} V\left(\delta^i\left(\alpha+\omega\right) + \delta^i A\,\tfrac{1}{\delta^i}\,\theta\right) \quad s.\ t. \quad q^T\,\tfrac{1}{\delta^i}\,\theta = 0 \\
&\qquad\qquad\qquad \wedge \quad \delta^i\left(\alpha+\omega\right) + A\,\theta \\
&= \arg\max_{\theta\in\mathbb{R}^J} \left(\delta^i\right)^k V\left(\alpha+\omega + A\,\tfrac{1}{\delta^i}\,\theta\right) \quad s.\ t. \quad q^T\,\tfrac{1}{\delta^i}\,\theta = 0 \\
&\qquad\qquad\qquad \wedge \quad \alpha+\omega + A\,\tfrac{1}{\delta^i}\,\theta \geq \\
&= \delta^i \left[\begin{array}{lll} \arg\max_{\tilde\theta\in\mathbb{R}^J} V\left(\alpha+\omega + A\tilde\theta\right) & s.t. & q^T\tilde\theta = 0 \\ & \wedge & \alpha+\omega + A\,\tilde\theta \geq 0 \end{array}\right] \\
&= \delta^i\,\tilde g(q)
\end{aligned}
$$

*with*

$$
\begin{aligned}
\tilde g(q) = \arg\max_{\tilde\theta\in\mathbb{R}^J} V\left(\alpha+\omega + A\,\tilde\theta\right) \quad & s.t. \quad q^T\tilde\theta = 0 \\
& \wedge \quad \alpha+\omega + A\tilde\theta \geq 0
\end{aligned}
$$

*Thus, for market demand $g(q)$ the following holds:*

$$
g(q) = \sum_{i=1}^{I} g^i(q) = \sum_{i=1}^{I} \delta^i \tilde g(q) = \tilde g(q) \quad ,
$$

*that is, the agent $(V(\alpha + x), \omega)$ is a representative agent.*

**Proof of (iii):** [29] *Define $\bar\theta := \sum_{i=1}^{I} \bar\theta^i$. Then: $\alpha + \omega = A\bar\theta$ and $\bar\theta^i = \delta^i\bar\theta$.*

*The maximization problem of agent $i$ is given by:*

[29] This proof follows Detemple and Gottardi [1998, Theorem 4.1] closely. In addition to the problems already mentioned in the proof of (i), their theorem also lacks assumptions for $U^i$ that ensure the differentiability of $V^i$ and the condition on the indifference curves of $V^i$. Without these the demand function is not necessarily differentiable, which is why Chipman's results [Chipman, 1974] do not apply.

$$\max_{\theta \in \mathbb{R}^J} \quad m^i \circ V^i \left( \alpha^i + \omega^i + A\,\theta \right) \quad s.t. \quad q^T \theta = 0$$
$$\wedge \quad \alpha^i + \omega^i + A\,\theta \geq 0$$

*By virtue of the above assumptions, it can be transformed into:*

$$\max_{\tilde{\theta} \in \mathbb{R}^J} V^i \left( A\,\tilde{\theta} \right) \quad s.t. \quad q^T \tilde{\theta} = \delta^i q^T \bar{\theta} \quad \wedge \quad A\,\tilde{\theta} \geq 0$$

*Since $V^i(\cdot)$ is homogeneous and agent $i$ has a constant share of income, together with Chipman's findings the assertion is proved.* [30]

*q. e. d.*

Provided Assumption 1.1 is satisfied with respect to the functions $V^i$, the application of the Theorem 6.2 on page 111[31] to the economies considered under Theorem 6.8 will lead to the uniqueness of the FM equilibria.[32]

## 4.4 Quasi-linear Utility Functions

In the general equilibrium model and thus for complete markets it is a well-known fact that, in the case of quasi-linear utility functions, under certain conditions on initial endowments, the Jacobian-Matrix of the individual excess demand is negative quasi-definite on $T_{e^s}$, with $e^s$ being the $s - th$ unit vector and $s$ the good in which the utility function is quasi-linear. In the general equilibrium model and thus for complete markets it is a well-known fact that any equilibrium is unique if all agents have utility functions which are quasi-linear in the same good.[33]
Similar results hold in the case of incomplete markets.

DEFINITION 6.13 (QUASI-LINEAR UTILITY FUNCTION)
*A utility function $U^i : \mathbb{R} \times \mathbb{R}_+^{S-1} \to \mathbb{R}$ is called quasi-linear (in the first good) if it has the form*

$$U^i(x) = x_1 + V^i(x_{-1})$$

[30] [Chipman, 1974, in particular Theorem 4]. The results apply to the Arrow-Debreu model where the positivity of prices is guaranteed. However, they can be carried over directly to our case.
[31] The utility functions $U^i$ of Theorem 6.8 and Theorem 6.2 may have different domains. However, since Assumption 1.1 is satisfied by the $V^i$, a direct application of Theorem 6.2 is possible.
[32] Without Assumption 1.1 uniqueness of the FM equilibria for economies can be derived from the (i). and (ii). part of the theorem, provided regularity is given. This follows from the fact that the representative agent's demand function always satisfies the weak axiom of revealed preferences.
[33] [Mas-Colell et al., 1995, Chapter 10.C and 10.G].

*with $V^i:\ \mathbb{R}_+^{S-1} \longrightarrow \mathbb{R}$ continuous on $\mathbb{R}_+^{S-1}$, twice continuously differentiable, strictly monotone and strictly concave on $\mathbb{R}_{++}^{S-1}$. Moreover, for all*

$$x_{-1} \in \mathbb{R}_{++}^{S-1} : \left\{ \tilde{x}_{-1} \in \mathbb{R}_+^{S-1} \middle| \quad V^i\left(\tilde{x}_{-1}\right) \geq V^i\left(x_{-1}\right) \right\} \subset \mathbb{R}_{++}^{S-1} \quad .$$

Note that, at the moment, we do not require consumption of the first good to be bounded from below.
We consider a special case of consumption in the first period, that is, the matrix $A \in \mathbb{R}^{S\times J}$ can be written as

$$A = \begin{pmatrix} 1 & 0 \\ 0 & \bar{A} \end{pmatrix} \quad ,$$

with $\bar{A} \in \mathbb{R}^{(S-1)\times(J-1)}$ with entries $\left(\bar{A}_s^j\right)_{\substack{s=2,\ldots,S \\ j=2,\ldots,J}}$.
For all $q \in Q$ $q_1 > 0$. Thus, after inserting the budget constraints, the agent's maximization problem can be written:

$$\max_{\theta_{-1}^i \in \mathbb{R}^{J-1}} \omega_1^i - \frac{1}{q_1} q_{-1}^T \theta_{-1}^i + V^i\left(\omega_{-1}^i + \bar{A}\,\theta_{-1}^i\right)$$

The conditions on $U^i$ ensure that for $\omega_{-1}^i \in \mathbb{R}_{++}^{S-1}$ the first-order condition is necessary and sufficient to solve this problem. It has the form:

$$-\frac{q_j}{q_1} + \sum_{s=2}^{S} \partial_{x_s} V^i\left(\omega_{-1}^i + \bar{A}\,\theta_{-1}^i\right) \bar{A}_s^j = 0,\ j = 2, \ldots, J$$

On multiplying by $q_1$:

$$-q_j + q_1 \sum_{s=2}^{S} \partial_{x_s} V^i\left(\omega_{-1}^i + \bar{A}\,\theta_{-1}^i\right) \bar{A}_s^j = 0,\ j = 2, \ldots, J \tag{6.9}$$

The total differential for $j = 2, \ldots, J$ is:

$$\begin{aligned} 0 \quad = \quad & -d\,q_j + \sum_{s=2}^{S} \partial_{x_s} V^i\left(\omega_{-1}^i + \bar{A}\,\theta_{-1}^i\right) \bar{A}_s^j \quad d\,q_1 \\ & + q_1 \sum_{k=2}^{J} \sum_{s=2}^{S} \sum_{t=2}^{S} \partial_{x_t} \partial_{x_s} V^i\left(\omega_{-1}^i + \bar{A}\,\theta_{-1}^i\right) \bar{A}_t^k\, \bar{A}_s^j \quad d\,\theta_k^i \end{aligned}$$

This is equivalent to:

$$0 = \begin{pmatrix} \sum_{s=2}^{S} \partial_{x_s} V^i \left(\omega_{-1}^i + \bar{A}\,\theta_{-1}^i\right) \bar{A}_s^2 & -1 & & 0 \\ \vdots & & \ddots & \\ \sum_{s=2}^{S} \partial_{x_s} V^i \left(\omega_{-1}^i + \bar{A}\,\theta_{-1}^i\right) \bar{A}_s^J & 0 & & -1 \end{pmatrix} dq$$
$$+q_1\, \bar{A}^T\, D^2_{x_{-1}\,x_{-1}} V^i \left(\omega_{-1}^i + \bar{A}\,\theta_{-1}^i\right) \bar{A} \quad d\theta_{-1}^i$$

The matrix $\bar{A}^T\, D^2_{x_{-1}\,x_{-1}}\, V^i\, (\omega_{-1}^i + \bar{A}\,\theta_{-1}^i)\, \bar{A}$ is invertible by reason of the conditions on $V^i$. [34] Since $q_1 > 0$ by virtue of the NA assumption, it follows by the implicit function theorem that[35]:

$$\begin{aligned} D_q\, g_{-1}^i\,(q) \;&=\; \frac{1}{q_1} \left[\bar{A}^T D^2_{x_{-1}x_{-1}} V^i \left(\omega_{-1}^i + \bar{A}\theta_{-1}^i\right) \bar{A}\right]^{-1} \\ &\quad\cdot \begin{pmatrix} -\sum_{s=2}^{S} \partial_{x_s} V^i \left(\omega_{-1}^i + \bar{A}\theta_{-1}^i\right) \bar{A}_s^2 & 1 & & 0 \\ \vdots & & \ddots & \\ -\sum_{s=2}^{S} \partial_{x_s} V^i \left(\omega_{-1}^i + \bar{A}\theta_{-1}^i\right) \bar{A}_s^J & 0 & & 1 \end{pmatrix} \end{aligned}$$

Therefore:

$$D_{q_{-1}} g_{-1}^i\,(q) = \frac{1}{q_1} \left[\bar{A}^T D^2_{x_{-1}x_{-1}} V^i \left(\omega_{-1}^i + \bar{A}\theta_{-1}^i\right) \bar{A}\right]^{-1}$$

By virtue of $q_1 > 0$ and the negative definiteness of $\bar{A}^T D^2_{x_{-1}x_{-1}} V^i \bar{A}$, this matrix is negative definite. Hence $D_q\theta^i$ satisfies the negative quasi-definiteness on $T_n$ for the normalizing vector $n = (1, 0, \ldots, 0)^T$ (Property 6.5 on page 109).[36]

However, in order to apply the Uniqueness Theorem 6.1 on page 110, consumption must have a lower bound for $s = 1$ as well. We therefore need to find a condition on the agents' initial endowments $\omega^i$ which always ensures $x_1^i \geq 0$ for the maximizer obtained from the first-order condition, which also explains why the solution is not affected by adding this constraint.

---

[34] The matrix even satisfies the property of negative definiteness. Suppose this were not given. Then there would exist a $v \in \mathbb{R}^{J-1} \setminus \{0\}$ with $v^T \bar{A}^T D^2_{x_{-1}x_{-1}} V^i \left(\omega_{-1}^i + \bar{A}\theta_{-1}^i\right) \bar{A} v \geq 0$. But this means: $\bar{v}^T D^2_{x_{-1}x_{-1}} V^i \left(\omega_{-1}^i + \bar{A}\theta_{-1}^i\right) \bar{v} \geq 0$ for $\bar{v} = \bar{A}v \neq 0$ (on the assumption that $rank \quad A = J$ we obtain $rank \quad \bar{A} = J - 1$). This contradicts the strict concavity of $V^i$, which is equivalent to the negative definiteness of the corresponding Hessian-Matrix.

[35] [Forster, 1991, Theorem 8.2 and Remark].

[36] $n^T q = e^1 q = q_1 > 0$ for all $q \in Q$.

From (6.9) we obtain the formula:

$$q_j = \sum_{s=2}^{S} \partial_{x_s} V^i \left(\omega_{-1}^i + \bar{A}\theta_{-1}^i\right) \bar{A}_s^j q_1, \quad j = 2, \ldots, J$$

With $q^T \theta^i = 0$ it follows that:

$$\begin{array}{rcl} q_1\theta_1^i & = & -\sum\limits_{j=2}^{J} \sum\limits_{s=2}^{S} \partial_{x_s} V^i \left(\omega_{-1}^i + \bar{A}\theta_{-1}^i\right) \bar{A}_s^j q_1 \theta_j^i \\ \Leftrightarrow \quad x_1^i & = & \omega_1^i - \sum\limits_{s=2}^{S} \partial_{x_s} V^i \left(x_{-1}^i\right) \left(x_s^i - \omega_s^i\right) \\ \Leftrightarrow \quad x_1^i & = & \omega_1^i + D_{x_{-1}} V^i \left(x_{-1}^i\right) \left(\omega_{-1}^i - x_{-1}^i\right) \end{array}$$

We only need to consider the maximizers that satisfy the feasibility constraint

$$\sum_{i=1}^{I} x^i \leq \sum_{i=1}^{I} \omega^i = \omega$$

because this is a precondition for an equilibrium. With $x_{-1}^i \geq 0$[37] we therefore get:

$$\omega_{-1} \geq x_{-1}^i \geq 0$$

The conditions on $V^i$ continue to ensure $D_{x_{-1}} V^i \left(x_{-1}^i\right) \in \mathbb{R}_{++}^{1 \times (S-1)}$ such that:

$$\begin{array}{rcl} x_1^i & \geq & \omega_1^i + D_{x_{-1}} V^i \left(x_{-1}^i\right) \left(\omega_{-1}^i - \omega_{-1}\right) \\ & = & \omega_1^i - D_{x_{-1}} V^i \left(x_{-1}^i\right) \sum\limits_{h \neq i} \omega_{-1}^h \end{array} \tag{6.10}$$

Let $I\left(\omega_{-1}^i\right)$ be the indifference curve of the utility function $U^i(x) = x_1 + V^i\left(x_{-1}^i\right)$ passing through the projection of the initial endowment $\tilde{\omega}^i = \begin{pmatrix} 0 \\ \omega_{-1}^i \end{pmatrix}$ on to the hyperplane $0 \times \mathbb{R}^{S-1}$.[38] We further define:

$$S\left(\omega_{-1}^i\right) := I\left(\omega_{-1}^i\right) \cap \left(0 \times \mathbb{R}_{+}^{S-1}\right)$$

By the conditions on $V^i$ and $\omega_{-1}^i \in \mathbb{R}_{++}^{S-1}$ the indifference curve does not cross the coordinate axes corresponding to $e^2, \ldots, e^S$. Thus:

$$S\left(\omega_{-1}^i\right) \subset \left(0 \times \mathbb{R}_{++}^{S-1}\right)$$

[37] Due to the properties of $V^i$, with $\omega_{-1}^i \gg 0$ for the maximizer even $x_{-1}^i \gg 0$, which has already been used earlier.

[38] The constraint $x - \omega^i \in \langle A \rangle$ is not applied here!

Now we consider the set:

$$H\left(\omega_{-1}^{i}\right) := \left\{ y \in \mathbb{R}_{++}^{S-1} \middle| \ \exists \quad z \in S\left(\omega_{-1}^{i}\right) \quad \text{mit} \quad z_{-1} \leq y \leq \omega_{-1} \right\}$$

Then $H\left(\omega_{-1}^{i}\right)$ is a compact subset of $R_{++}^{S-1}$. Consequently, $D_{x_{-1}}V^{i}$ is continuous on $H\left(\omega_{-1}^{i}\right)$ and assumes the maximum in a point $\bar{m} \in H\left(\omega_{-1}^{i}\right)$.[39] If

$$\omega_{1}^{i} \geq D_{x_{-1}} V^{i}(\bar{m}) \sum_{h \neq i} \omega_{-1}^{h} \quad ,$$

then $x_{1}^{i} \geq 0$.
Suppose $x_{1}^{i} < 0$. It then follows from the strict monotonicity of $U^{i}$ and by $\omega_{1}^{i} \geq 0$ that $x_{-1}^{i} \in H\left(\omega_{-1}^{i}\right)$, since the utility of the maximizer $x^{i}$ cannot be smaller than that of $\omega^{i}$. However, since $\bar{m}$ maximizes $D_{x_{-1}}V^{i}(\cdot)$ on $H\left(\omega_{-1}^{i}\right)$, it follows that:

$$D_{x_{-1}}V^{i}\left(x_{-1}^{i}\right) \leq D_{x_{-1}}V^{i}(\bar{m})$$

Because of (6.10):

$$\begin{aligned} x_{1}^{i} &\geq \omega_{1}^{i} - D_{x_{-1}}V^{i}\left(x_{-1}^{i}\right) \sum_{h \neq i} \omega_{-1}^{h} \\ &\geq \omega_{1}^{i} - D_{x_{-1}}V^{i}(\bar{m}) \sum_{h \neq i} \omega_{-1}^{h} \\ &\geq 0 \end{aligned}$$

This contradicts the above assumption.
Under (4.4)—that is, if the initial endowment in the first period ($s = 1$) is sufficiently large—consumption at that time can be bounded from below by 0 without invalidating the considerations on negative quasi-definiteness for attainable allocations. Regarding uniqueness the following can be said:

THEOREM 6.9 (UNIQUENESS)
*Let an economy $GEI = \left\{\mathbb{R}^{S}, \left(U^{i}, \omega^{i}\right)_{i \in I}, A\right\}$ satisfy the Differentiability Assumption 1.2 and have strictly positive endowments $\omega^{i} >> 0$, $i = 1, \ldots, I$. Let the utility functions be quasi-linear and let $A$ allow for consumption in the first period. Furthermore, let the $\omega^{i}$ satisfy condition (4.4) for all $i \in I$. Then: The FM equilibrium of the economy is unique (where non-negativity is required for consumption in both periods).*

[39] [Forster, 1991, Theorem 3.7].

PROOF 6.13
*The above considerations show that for all agents $i \in I$ the Jacobian-Matrix of the securities demand is negative quasi-definite with respect to the first unit vector if $x^i = \omega^i + A\, g^i(q)$ is feasible. The same applies to market demand so that the assertion is shown to be true by applying Theorem 6.1 on page 110.*[40]

*q. e. d.*

## 4.5 The Theorem of Mitjushin-Polterovich

### 4.5.1 The Case of Complete Markets

The theorem by Mitjushin-Polterovich establishes a connection between the curvature of the indifference curves and the monotonicity of the demand function. The curvature is measured by the so-called Mitjushin-Polterovich coefficient.

DEFINITION 6.14 (MITJUSHIN-POLTEROVICH COEFFICIENT)
*For a utility function $U^i: \mathbb{R}^S_+ \to \mathbb{R}$ the Differentiability Assumption 1.2, the Mitjushin-Polterovich coefficient is defined by*

$$MP_{U^i}(x) := -\frac{x^T D^2_{xx} U^i(x)\, x}{D_x U^i(x)\, x}$$

*for all $x \in \mathbb{R}^S_{++}$.*

If the examined utility function is a von-Neumann-Morgenstern function (Assumption 1.3), the Mitjushin-Polterovich coefficient measures the agent's relative risk aversion. On the one hand:

$$MP_{U^i}(x) := -\frac{x^T \begin{pmatrix} \rho^i_1 u^{i''}(x) & & 0 \\ & \ddots & \\ 0 & & \rho^i_S u^{i''}(x) \end{pmatrix} x}{\left(\rho^i_1 u^{i'}(x), \ \ldots \ , \rho^i_S u^{i'}(x)\right) x} = -\frac{\sum_{s=1}^{S} \rho^i_s u^{i''}(x)\, x_s^2}{\sum_{s=1}^{S} \rho^i_s u^{i'}(x)\, x_s}$$

On the other hand, it follows that

$$MP_{u^i}(x_s) := -\frac{x_s u^{i''}(x_s)\, x_s}{u^{i'}(x_s)\, x_s} = RRA^i(x_s)$$

From this one can show that for any given constant $K \in \mathbb{R}_{++}$:[41]

[40] The property of negative quasi-definiteness only needs to be satisfied in the equilibria, which is why it suffices when it is shown for all attainable allocations.
[41] [Hildenbrand, 1994, Appendix 4].

$$MP_{U^i}(x) < K \Leftrightarrow MP_{u^i}(x_s) < K \text{ for all } s \in S$$

Mitjushin/Polterovich proved the following theorem for the general equilibrium model:

THEOREM 6.10 (MITJUSHIN-POLTEROVICH) [42]
*Let the utility function $U^i: \mathbb{R}^S_+ \to \mathbb{R}$ satisfy Assumption 1.2, be concave and $MP_{U^i}(x) < 4$ for all $x \in \mathbb{R}^S_{++}$, $\omega^i \in \mathbb{R}^S_{++}$. Then the excess demand $z^i: \mathbb{R}^S_{++} \to \mathbb{R}^S$ is strictly monotone with respect to $\omega^i$, that is, for all $\pi$, $\tilde{\pi} \in \mathbb{R}^S_{++}$ with $(\pi - \tilde{\pi})^T \omega^i = 0$ and $z^i(\pi) \neq z^i(\tilde{\pi})$*

$$(\pi - \tilde{\pi})^T \left(z^i(\pi) - z^i(\tilde{\pi})\right) < 0$$

Proof: [Hildenbrand, 1994, Appendix 4].
According to Mas-Colell the Mitjushin-Polterovich coefficient depends on the utility function chosen for the corresponding preference relation. It therefore makes sense to examine the coefficient for the least concave utility function. As mentioned in Chapter 5, recently Quah [2002] has found a criterium to compute the MP-coefficient for the least concave utility by considering a single utility representation of the preference. If for all $x, x' \in \mathbb{R}^S_+$ $MP_u(x) - MP_{\bar{u}}(x') < 4$ then the preference relation that $u$ represents leads to a monotone demand function. Moreover, if the least concave utility function satisfies $MP_{U^i}(x) > 4$ for all $x \in \mathbb{R}^S_{++}$, excess demand is not monotone.[43]
By applying the theorem, we obtain the following corollary on uniqueness:

COROLLARY 6.1 (UNIQUENESS)
*Let a regular economy $GEI = \left\{\mathbb{R}^S, (U^i, \omega^i)_{i \in I}, A\right\}$ satisfy the following conditions:*

*(i) the securities markets are complete, that is, $A \in \mathbb{R}^{S \times S}$ with $rank\ A = S$,*

*(ii) Assumption 1.2 holds, the utility functions are concave and $MP_{U^i}(x) < 4$ for all $x \in \mathbb{R}^S_{++}$ and all $i \in I$,*

*(iii) $\omega^i \in \mathbb{R}^S_{++}$ and the initial endowments are collinear, that is, there exists a $\delta \in \mathbb{R}^S_{++}$ with $\sum_{i=1}^I \delta^i = 1$ and an $\omega \in \mathbb{R}^S_{++}$ with $\omega^i = \delta^i \omega$ for all $i \in I$.*

*Then the economy has a unique NA equilibrium.*

PROOF 6.14
*In accordance with Theorem 6.10 the individual excess demands $z^i(\pi)$ satisfy*

---

[42] [Mitjushin and Polterovich, 1978] (cited after Hildenbrand [1994, Appendix 4]).
[43] [Mas-Colell, 1991, p. 283].

*the property of monotonicity 5.5 with respect to $\omega^i$, and because of collinearity also with respect to $\omega$. Thus the same applies to $z(\pi) = \sum_{i=1}^{I} z^i(\pi)$ so that all we need to do is to apply Theorem 5.1 on page 82.*

*q. e. d.*

### 4.5.2 The Case of Incomplete Markets with Spanned Initial Endowments

First, we will examine an individual agent $i$ who is characterized by $(U^i, \omega^i)$. $U^i$ satisfies Assumption 1.2 and is concave. For $\omega^i \in \mathbb{R}^S_{++}$ there exists a $\bar{\theta}^i \in \mathbb{R}^J$ with $\omega^i = A\bar{\theta}^i$, that is, the initial endowment is in the span of the pay-off matrix.[44] [45]
Under the common assumptions the agent's maximization problem is given by:

$$\max_{\theta \in \mathbb{R}^J} U^i\left(\omega^i + A\,\theta\right) \quad \text{s.t.} \quad q^T\,\theta = 0 \quad \wedge \quad \omega^i + A\,\theta \geq 0 \tag{6.11}$$

Because $\omega^i = A\,\bar{\theta}^i$ this can be transformed into:

$$\max_{\hat{\theta} \in \mathbb{R}^J} \quad U^i\left(A\hat{\theta}\right) \quad \text{s.t.} \quad q^T\hat{\theta} = q^T\bar{\theta}^i \quad \wedge \quad A\,\hat{\theta} \geq 0 \tag{6.12}$$

By defining $W^i : \mathbb{R}^J_+ \to \mathbb{R}$ by $W^i(\theta) := U^i(A\theta)$ one can denote the Mitjushin-Polterovich coefficient $\hat{\theta} \in \mathbb{R}^J$ with $A\hat{\theta} \gg 0$ as:

$$MP_{W^i}(\hat{\theta}) = -\frac{\hat{\theta}^T D^2_{\theta\theta} W^i(\hat{\theta})\hat{\theta}}{D_\theta W^i(\hat{\theta})\hat{\theta}}$$

With respect to $U^i$, the following lemma is true:

LEMMA 6.2 (MITJUSHIN-POLTEROVICH COEFFICIENT)

$$MP_{W^i}(\hat{\theta}) = MP_{U^i}(x),$$

*with $x = A\hat{\theta} \in \mathbb{R}^S_{++}$.*

---

[44]This can be interpreted to mean that the agent receives his initial endowment in securities instead of goods, that is, exactly $\bar{\theta}^i$. The set of all spanned initial endowments is only a zero set (with respect of the Lebesgue measure) within the set of admissible initial endowments. [Magill and Quinzii, 1996, p. 176].
[45]In the case of positive initial endowments Assumption 1.5 is always satisfied.

PROOF 6.15 [46]

$$
\begin{aligned}
MP_{W^i}(\hat{\theta}) &= -\frac{\hat{\theta}^T D^2_{\theta\theta} W^i(\hat{\theta})\hat{\theta}}{D_\theta W^i(\hat{\theta})\hat{\theta}} = -\frac{\hat{\theta}^T A^T D^2_{xx} U^i(A\hat{\theta})A\hat{\theta}}{D_x U^i(A\hat{\theta})A\hat{\theta}} \\
&= -\frac{x^T D^2_{xx} U^i(x)x}{D_x U^i(x)x} = MP_{U^i}(x)
\end{aligned}
$$

*q. e. d.*

By defining $\hat{\theta}\,(q)$ as the function derived from (6.12), the property of monotonicity 6.5(iii) with respect to $\bar{\theta}^i$ can be shown to be true for that function by reason of the equivalence we have just examined on the condition that $MP_{U^i}\,(x) < 4$ for all $x \in \mathbb{R}^S_{++}$: [47] for all $q, \tilde{q} \in Q$ with $(q-\tilde{q})^T \bar{\theta}^i = 0$ and $\hat{g}^i\,(q) \neq \hat{g}^i\,(\tilde{q})$

$$(q-\tilde{q})^T \left(\hat{g}^i\,(q) - \hat{g}^i\,(\tilde{q})\right) < 0.$$

The proof is largely analogous to the proof of Mitjushin-Polterovich's theorem. However, we cannot apply the theorem directly to the function $W^i$ because the domain is different, strict monotonicity does not necessarily apply and the positivity of prices is no longer given.

THEOREM 6.11 (MONOTONICITY IN THE CASE OF SPANNED INITIAL ENDOWMENTS)
*Let an agent $i$ be given by*

*(i) a utility function $U^i: \mathbb{R}^S_+ \to \mathbb{R}$ which satisfies Assumption 1.2, is concave and for which $MP_{U^i}\,(x) < 4$ for all $x \in \mathbb{R}^S_{++}$,*

*(ii) $\omega^i \in \mathbb{R}^S_{++} \cap \langle A \rangle$ with $\mathrm{rank} A = J$.*

*Let $\hat{g}^i\,(q)$ be the solution of (6.12) on $Q$. Then $\hat{g}^i\,(q)$ satisfies the property of monotonicity 6.5 with $\bar{\theta}^i$ as normalizing vector ($\bar{\theta}^i$ spans $\omega^i$).*

PROOF 6.16 [48]
*$\hat{g}^i\,(q)$ is homogeneous of order 1 in $q$. Thus, instead of investigating monotonicity in the vectors $q, q \in Q$ which satisfy $q^T\bar{\theta}^i = q^T\bar{\theta}^i$ and $\hat{g}^i\,(q) \neq \hat{g}^i\,(q)$, we can confine our study to vectors which exhibit these properties and additionally satisfy $q^T\bar{\theta}^i = \tilde{q}^T\bar{\theta}^i = 1$.*
*A sufficient condition for the strict monotonicity of $\hat{g}^i\,(q)$ on this price set is the negative quasi-definiteness of the Jacobian-Matrix for all $q \in \{q \in Q \mid q^T\bar{\theta}^i = 1\}$, that is, for all $v \in \mathbb{R}^J \backslash \{0\}$ and corresponding $q$ $v^T D_q \hat{g}^i\,(q)\, v < 0.$* [49]

---

[46] [Hens, 1995, p. 168].
[47] For all $q \in Q$: $q^T\bar{\theta}^i = \pi^T A\bar{\theta}^i = \pi^T\omega^i > 0$.
[48] The proof follows Hildenbrand [1994, Appendix 4].
[49] Appendix 1 in Hildenbrand [1994] contains the proof for the incomplete case, which we can apply directly to our case.

*Now construct an auxiliary function $h^i$ which is the inverse function of $\hat{g}^i$ and satisfies the corresponding property of quasi-definiteness. This is sufficient because the Jacobian-Matrix of a function is negative quasi-definite if and only if this is true for the inverse function.*
*Let us begin with some preliminary remarks: Together with $\omega^i \gg 0$ Assumption 1.2 ensures that $A\hat{g}^i(q) \gg 0$ for all $q \in Q$. It then follows that*

$$\begin{aligned} &D_\theta W^i\left(\hat{g}^i(q)\right)\hat{g}^i(q) \\ &\qquad = D_x U^i\left(A\hat{g}^i(q)\right)A\hat{g}^i(q) > 0 \quad \text{for all} \quad q \in Q \quad . \end{aligned} \tag{6.13}$$

*We now examine the auxiliary function $h^i$, which is defined by*

$$h^i(\theta) := \frac{1}{D_\theta W^i(\theta)\theta}\left(D_\theta W^i(\theta)\right)^T ,$$

*where for all* $\theta \in \left\{\theta \in \mathbb{R}^J \,\middle|\, \exists q \in Q \quad \text{with} \quad q^T\bar{\theta}^i = 1 \quad \wedge \quad \theta = \hat{g}^i(q)\right\}$.
*Because of* (6.13), *this definition is admissible.*
*To show that $h^i$ is the inverse function of $\hat{g}^i$, we first have to examine the first-order conditions of* (6.12):

$$\partial_{\theta_j} W^i\left(\hat{g}^i(q)\right) - \lambda^i q_j = 0 \quad \text{for all} \quad j \in J \quad , \tag{6.14}$$

$$q^T\left(\hat{g}^i(q) - \bar{\theta}^i\right) = 0 \quad . \tag{6.15}$$

*For $q_j = 0$ we obtain from* (6.14) $\partial_{\theta_j} W^i\left(\hat{g}^i(q)\right) = 0$, *thus* $h^i_j\left(\hat{g}^i(q)\right) = 0$.
*For $q_j \neq 0$ it follows from* (6.14) *that* $\lambda^i = \frac{1}{q_j}\partial_{\theta_j} W^i\left(\hat{g}^i(q)\right)$. *On multiplying* (6.14) *with $\hat{g}^i_j(q)$ and summing over all $j \in J$, we get*

$$D_\theta W^i\left(\hat{g}^i(q)\right)\hat{g}^i(q) - \lambda^i q^T \hat{g}^i(q) = 0 \quad . \tag{6.16}$$

*Because of* (6.15) *and $q^T\bar{\theta}^i = 1$ it follows that $q^T\hat{g}^i(q) = 1$. When the latter together with $\lambda^i$ is inserted into* (6.16), *we get*

$$q_j = \frac{1}{D_\theta W^i\left(\hat{g}^i(q)\right)\hat{g}^i(q)}\partial_{\theta_j} W^i\left(\hat{g}^i(q)\right) = h^i_j\left(\hat{g}^i(q)\right) .$$

*All we need to do now is to show that the Jacobian-Matrix of $h^i$ is negative quasi-definite:*

$$
\begin{aligned}
\partial_{\theta_j} h_k^i(\theta) &= \partial_{\theta_j}\left[\frac{1}{D_\theta W^i(\theta)\,\theta}\partial_{\theta_k} W^i(\theta)\right] \\
&= \frac{1}{D_\theta W^i(\theta)\,\theta}\partial_{\theta_j}\partial_{\theta_k} W^i(\theta) - \frac{\partial_{\theta_k} W^i(\theta)\left[\sum_{l=1}^{J}\partial_{\theta_j}\partial\theta_l\, W^i(\theta)\,\theta_l + \partial_{\theta_j} W^i(\theta)\right]}{\left[D_\theta W^i(\theta)\,\theta\right]^2}
\end{aligned}
$$

*Thus*

$$
\begin{aligned}
D_\theta h^i(\theta) &= \frac{1}{D_\theta W^i(\theta)\,\theta} D^2_{\theta\theta} W^i(\theta) - \frac{1}{\left[D_\theta W^i(\theta)\,\theta\right]^2} \\
&\quad \cdot\left[\left(D_\theta W^i(\theta)\right)^T \left(D^2_{\theta\theta} W^i(\theta)\,\theta\right)^T + \left(D_\theta W^i(\theta)\right)^T D_\theta W^i(\theta)\right] \\
&= \alpha^i D^2_{\theta\theta} W^i(\theta) - \left(\alpha^i\right)^2 \\
&\quad \cdot\left[\left(D_\theta W^i(\theta)\right)^T \left(D^2_{\theta\theta} W^i(\theta)\,\theta\right)^T + \left(D_\theta W^i(\theta)\right)^T D_\theta W^i(\theta)\right],
\end{aligned}
$$

*with $\alpha^i = 1/\left(D_\theta W^i(\theta)\,\theta\right) > 0$ by reason of the domain of $h^i$ and (i).*
*Now we investigate $v \in \mathbb{R}^J \backslash \{0\}$ with $D_\theta W^i(\theta)\, v = 0$. Due to the strict quasi-concavity of $U^i$, it follows that*

$$
\begin{aligned}
v^T D_\theta h^i(\theta)\, v &= \alpha^i v^T D^2_{\theta\theta} W^i(\theta)\, v \\
&= \alpha^i v^T A^T D^2_{xx} U^i(A\,\theta)\, Av \\
&< 0.
\end{aligned}
$$

*For $v \in \mathbb{R}^J \backslash \{0\}$ with $D_\theta W^i(\theta)\, v \neq 0$ we can assume without loss of generality that $D_\theta W^i(\theta)\, v = 1/\alpha^i$ since*

$$
v^T D_\theta h^i(\theta)\, v < 0 \Leftrightarrow (rv)^T D_\theta h^i(\theta)\,(rv) < 0
$$

*is true for all $r \in \mathbb{R}_{++}$. It then follows that*

$$\begin{aligned}
& v^T D_\theta h^i(\theta) v \\
&= \alpha^i \left[ v^T D^2_{\theta\theta} W^i(\theta) v - \left( D^2_{\theta\theta} W^i(\theta) \theta \right)^T v \right] - 1 \\
&= \alpha^i \left( v - \frac{1}{2}\theta \right)^T D^2_{\theta\theta} W^i(\theta) \left( v - \frac{1}{2}\theta \right) - \frac{1}{4}\alpha^i \theta^T D^2_{\theta\theta} W^i(\theta)\theta - 1 \\
&= \underbrace{\alpha^i \left( v - \frac{1}{2}\theta \right)^T A^T D^2_{xx} U^i(A\theta) A \left( v - \frac{1}{2}\theta \right)}_{\leq\ 0, \quad since \quad U^i \quad is \quad concave} - \frac{1}{4}\alpha^i \theta^T D^2_{\theta\theta} W^i(\theta)\theta - 1 \\
&\leq -\frac{1}{4}\alpha^i \theta^T D^2_{\theta\theta} W^i(\theta)\theta - 1 \\
&= \frac{1}{4} \underbrace{\left( -\frac{\theta^T D^2_{\theta\theta} W^i(\theta)\theta}{D_\theta W^i(\theta)\theta} \right)}_{MP_{W^i}(\theta)} - 1 \\
&< 0 \quad \textit{because of Lemma 6.2.}
\end{aligned}$$

*q. e. d.*

Regarding uniqueness, we therefore conclude:

COROLLARY 6.2 (UNIQUENESS)
*Let a regular economy $GEI = \left\{ \mathbb{R}^S, (U^i, \omega^i)_{i \in I}, A \right\}$ satisfy the following conditions:*

*(i) the securities matrix has no redundant assets,*

*(ii) Assumption 1.2 holds, the utility functions are concave and $MP_{U^i}(x) < 4$ for all $x \in \mathbb{R}^S_{++}$ and all $i \in I$,*

*(iii) the initial endowments $\omega^i \in \mathbb{R}^S_{++}$ are in the span of $A$ and are collinear, that is, there exists a $\delta \in \mathbb{R}^S_{++}$ with $\sum_{i=1}^I \delta^i = 1$ and an $\omega \in \mathbb{R}^S_{++} \cap \langle A \rangle$ with $\omega^i = \delta^i \omega$ for all $i \in I$.*

*Then the economy has a unique FM equilibrium.*

PROOF 6.17
*Let $\bar{\theta} \in \mathbb{R}^J$ be such that $\omega = A\bar{\theta}$. It then follows that $\omega^i = A(\delta^i \bar{\theta})$. In accordance with the theorem $\hat{g}^i(q)$ therefore satisfies the property of monotonicity 6.5(iii) with respect to $\delta^i \bar{\theta}$, and thus also with respect to $\bar{\theta}$. The same is true for $g^i(q) = \hat{g}^i(q) - \bar{\theta}^i$. Consequently, market demand is also strictly monotone with respect to $\bar{\theta}$, so that the rest follows with Theorem 6.1 on page 110.*

*q. e. d.*

### 4.5.3 The Case of Incomplete Markets Given the Existence of Fundamental Sets

In this section we will study utility functions $U^i$ which satisfy Assumption 1.3 and whose relative risk aversion is smaller than 4. Bettzüge [50] transforms the agent's maximization problem in the $S + J$ variables $x_s$ and $\theta_j$ into a maximization problem in $J$ variables, allowing him to apply Mitjushin-Polterovich's theorem (Theorem 6.10 on page 145). He then shows an equivalence between the monotonicity properties of the solutions of both problems.
Let $A \in \mathbb{R}^{S\times J}$ be any pay-off matrix that has no redundant assets and that allows for desirable portfolios. Because of $rank\, A = J$, there is a subset $R \subseteq S$ with $\#R = J$ such that $A_R := (A_s)_{s\in R}$ is invertible. Accordingly, we define $A_{S\setminus R} := (A_s)_{s\in S\setminus R}$, $x_R := (x_s)_{s\in R}$ and $x_{S\setminus R} := (x_s)_{s\in S\setminus R}$.
By reason of Assumptions 1.3 and 1.5 the maximization problem has the form:

$$\max_{\substack{x\in\mathbb{R}^S_+ \\ \theta\in\mathbb{R}^J}} U^i(x) \quad \text{s.t.} \quad q^T\theta = 0 \quad \wedge \quad x = \omega^i + A\,\theta \tag{6.17}$$

From the second constraint it follows that

$$\theta = A_R^{-1}\left(x_R - \omega_R^i\right).$$

Thus, for all states $s \in S$

$$x_s = \omega_s^i + A_s A_R^{-1}\left(x_R - \omega_R^i\right).$$

The constraint $q^T\theta = 0$ is equivalent to

$$q^T A_R^{-1}\left(x_R - \omega_R^i\right) = 0.$$

Therefore, (6.17) is equivalent to

$$\max_{x_R\in\mathbb{R}^J_+} U^i\left(\omega^i + AA_R^{-1}\left(x_R - \omega_R^i\right)\right) \quad \text{s.t.} \quad q^T A_R^{-1}\left(x_R - \omega_R^i\right) = 0$$
$$\wedge \quad \omega^i + AA_R^{-1}\left(x_R - \omega_R^i\right) \geq 0 \tag{6.18}$$

We now examine so-called fundamental sets.

DEFINITION 6.15 (FUNDAMENTAL SET)
*A set $R \subseteq S$ is called a fundamental set of matrix $A$ if $\#R = J$, $A_R$ is invertible and $A_{S\setminus R}A_R^{-1} \geq 0$.*

---

[50] [Bettzüge, 1997, p. 55-64].

Additionally, the following assumption is being made:

ASSUMPTION 6.3
*There exists a fundamental set $R \subseteq S$ with*

$$\omega_s^i - A_s A_R^{-1} \omega_R^i \geq 0$$

*for all $s \in S \backslash R$.*

For in this case the second constraint in (6.18) is redundant. Without loss of generality let the fundamental set under consideration from now on always be $R = \{1, \ldots, J\}$. Then:

$$\omega^i + AA_R^{-1}\left(x_R - \omega_R^i\right) = \omega^i + \begin{pmatrix} I_R \\ A_{S\backslash R} A_R^{-1} \end{pmatrix}\left(x_R - \omega_R^i\right) \geq 0.$$

This is equivalent to

$$\begin{aligned} \omega_s^i + x_s - \omega_s^i = x_s \geq 0 \quad &\text{for} \quad s \in R, \\ \omega_s^i + A_s A_R^{-1}\left(x_R - \omega_R^i\right) \geq 0 \quad &\text{for} \quad s \in S \backslash R \quad . \end{aligned}$$

(4.5.3) is satisfied since maximization is achieved over $x_R \in \mathbb{R}_+^J$. (4.5.3) is redundant because

$$\omega_{S\backslash R}^i + \underbrace{A_{S\backslash R} A_R^{-1}}_{\geq 0} \underbrace{x_R}_{\geq 0} - A_{S\backslash R} A_R^{-1} \omega_R^i \geq \omega_{S\backslash R}^i - A_{S\backslash R} A_R^{-1} \omega_R^i \geq 0.$$

Now define a utility function $U_R^i : \mathbb{R}_+^J \to \mathbb{R}$ by

$$U_R^i(x_R) := U^i\left(x_R, \omega_{S\backslash R}^i + A_{S\backslash R} A_R^{-1}\left(x_R - \omega_R^i\right)\right)$$

and

$$p(R) := \left(A_R^{-1}\right)^T q,$$

then, by reason of Assumption 6.3, (6.18) is equivalent to

$$\max_{x_R \in \mathbb{R}_+^J} \quad U_R^i(x_R) \quad \text{s.t.} \quad p^T(R)\left(x_R - \omega_R^i\right) = 0 \quad . \tag{6.19}$$

Let $x_R^i(p(R))$ be the demand function resulting from this maximization problem. Define $g_R^i(q) := A_R^{-1}\left[x_R^i\left(\left(A_R^{-1}\right)^T q\right) - \omega_R^i\right]$. Since the maximization problems (6.17) and (6.19) are equivalent, it follows that

$$g^i(q) = g^i_R(q),$$

with $g^i(q)$ being the demand for securities resulting from (6.17).
By the following lemma Bettzüge establishes a relation between $g^i(q)$ and $x^i_R(p(R))$ regarding the property of monotonicity:

LEMMA 6.3 (EQUIVALENCE REGARDING MONOTONICITY)
*$x^i_R(p(R))$ is strictly monotone with respect to $n$ if and only if $g^i(q)$ is strictly monotone with respect to $A_R^{-1}n$, provided $n \in \mathbb{R}^J$ is chosen such that for all $q \in Q$ $q^T A_R^{-1} n > 0$.*

PROOF 6.18
*The strict monotonicity of $x^i_R$ with respect to an $n$ implies:*

*for $p^1(R), p^2(R) \in \mathbb{R}^J_{++}$[51] with $(p^1(R) - p^2(R))^T n = 0$ and $x^i_R(p^1(R)) \neq x^i_R(p^2(R))$:*

$$[p^1(R) - p^2(R)]^T [x^i_R(p^1(R)) - x^i_R(p^2(R))] < 0.$$

*By inserting the definitions of $\theta^i_R(q)$ and $p(R)$, the following equivalence becomes evident:*

*for $q^1, q^2 \in Q$ with $\left(q^{1T} A_R^{-1} - q^{2T} A_R^{-1}\right) n = 0$ and $A_R g^i_R(q^1) + \omega^i_R \neq A_R g^i_R(q^2) + \omega^i_R$:*

$$\left[q^{1T} A_R^{-1} - q^{2T} A_R^{-1}\right] \left[A_R g^i_R(q^1) + \omega^i_R - \left(A_R g^i_R(q^2) + \omega^i_R\right)\right] < 0.$$

*Since $g^i(q) = g^i_R(q)$ and rank $A_R = J$, this is equivalent to the strict monotonicity of $g^i$ with respect to $A_R^{-1}n$:*

*for $q^1, q^2 \in Q$ with $\left(q^{1T} - q^{2T}\right) A_R^{-1} n = 0$ and $g^i(q^1) \neq g^i(q^2)$:*

$$\left[q^{1T} - q^{2T}\right] \left[g^i(q^1) - g^i(q^2)\right] < 0.$$

*q. e. d.*

To demonstrate the strict monotonicity of $g^i(q)$ with respect to a normalizing vector $A_R^{-1}n$, it is therefore sufficient to prove that $x^i_R(p(R))$ is strictly monotone with regard to $n$. This can be done by applying Mitjushin-Polterovich's

[51] Because of $q \in Q$ there exists a $\pi \in \mathbb{R}^S_{++}$ with $q = A^T \pi$, thus

$$p(R) = \left(A_R^{-1}\right)^T A^T \pi = \left(A_R^T\right)^{-1} A^T \pi = (I_R, \underbrace{(A_R^T)^{-1} A^T_{S \setminus R}}_{\geq 0}) \pi \gg 0.$$

theorem. The following lemma shows that the function $U_R^i$ satisfies the conditions of this theorem together with $\omega_R^i$.

LEMMA 6.4 (MITJUSHIN-POLTEROVICH PROPERTY OF $U_R^i$)
*Let an agent $i$ be characterized by $(U^i, \omega^i)$, and*

*(i) the utility function $U^i: \mathbb{R}_+^S \to \mathbb{R}$ satisfy Assumption 1.3 and $MP_{u^i}(x) < 4$ for all $x \in \mathbb{R}_{++}$,*

*(ii) $\omega^i \in \mathbb{R}_{++}^S$,*

*(iii) $A$ satisfy Assumptions $rank A = J$ and 1.5,*

*(iv) $A$ together with $\omega^i$ satisfies Assumption 6.3.*

*Then $U_R^i$ and $\omega_R^i$ satisfy the conditions of Mitjushin-Polterovich's theorem for the fundamental set $R$.*

PROOF 6.19
*In addition to the above considerations, with $\omega^i \gg 0$ it follows from Assumption 6.3 that*

$$x_R \gg 0 \Rightarrow x_s = \omega_s^i + A_s A_R^{-1}\left(x_R - \omega_R^i\right) > 0 \; for \quad s \in S \backslash R$$

*(that is, the inequality applies strictly!). If $A_s A_R^{-1} = 0$[52], then $x_s > 0$ from $\omega_s^i > 0$. For $A_s A_R^{-1} > 0$ Assumption 6.3 applies.*
*By interpreting $U_R^i$ as the composite function of $U^i$ and the affine-linear mapping*

$$L_R^i(x_R) := \begin{pmatrix} 0 \\ \omega_{S\backslash R}^i - A_{S\backslash R} A_R^{-1} \omega_R^i \end{pmatrix} + \begin{pmatrix} I_R \\ A_{S\backslash R} A_R^{-1} \end{pmatrix} x_R \quad ,$$

*it becomes clear that all conditions of Mitjushin-Polterovich's theorem (Theorem 6.10 on page 145) are satisfied except $MP_{U_R^i}(x_R) < 4$ for all $x_R \in \mathbb{R}_{++}^J$, which we will show now.*
*The Mitjushin-Polterovich coefficient of $U_R^i$ is defined by*

$$MP_{U_R^i}(x_R) := -\frac{x_R^T D_{x_R x_R}^2 U_R^i(x_R)\, x_R}{D_{x_R} U_R^i(x_R)\, x_R}$$

*for all $x_R \in \mathbb{R}_{++}^J$. The condition $MP_{U_R^i}(x_R) < 4$ for all $x_R \gg 0$ is equivalent to*

[52] Because of $rank \quad A_R = J$ this is only possible if $A_s = 0$.

$$x_R^T D^2_{x_R x_R} U_R^i(x_R)\, x_R > -4 D_{x_R} U_R^i(x_R)\, x_R$$

*for all* $x_R \gg 0$. *Let* $\tilde{A} := A_{S\setminus R} A_R^{-1}$ *with the entries* $\tilde{A}_s^j$ *for* $s \in S\setminus R$ *and* $j \in R$. *Then* $U_R^i$ *can be written as*

$$U_R^i(x_R) = \sum_{s\in R} \rho_s^i u^i(x_s) + \sum_{s\in S\setminus R} \rho_s^i u^i\left(\omega_s^i + \tilde{A}_s\left(x_R - \omega_R^i\right)\right).$$

*The first partial derivatives for* $j \in R$ *are*

$$\partial_{x_j} U_R^i(x_R) = \rho_j^i u^{i\prime}(x_j) + \sum_{s\in S\setminus R} \rho_s^i u^{i\prime}\left(\omega_s^i + \tilde{A}_s\left(x_R - \omega_R^i\right)\right)\tilde{A}_s^j.$$

*For the second partial derivatives we get*

$$\partial^2_{x_j^2} U_R^i(x_R) = \rho_j^i u^{i\prime\prime}(x_j) + \sum_{s\in S\setminus R} \rho_s^i u^{i\prime\prime}\left(\omega_s^i + \tilde{A}_s\left(x_R - \omega_R^i\right)\right)\left(\tilde{A}_s^j\right)^2$$

*for* $j \in R$ *and*

$$\partial_{x_k}\partial_{x_j} U_R^i(x_R) = \sum_{s\in S\setminus R} \rho_s^i u^{i\prime\prime}\left(\omega_s^i + \tilde{A}_s\left(x_R - \omega_R^i\right)\right)\tilde{A}_s^j \tilde{A}_s^k$$

*for* $(j,k) \in R \times R$ *with* $j \neq k$. *It then follows that*

$$\begin{aligned}
&-4 D_{x_R} U_R^i(x_R)\, x_R \\
&\quad = \; -4\sum_{j\in R} \rho_j^i u^{i\prime}(x_j)\, x_j - 4\sum_{j\in R}\ \sum_{s\in S\setminus R} \rho_s^i u^{i\prime}(x_s)\, \tilde{A}_s^j x_j \\
&\quad < \; \sum_{j\in R} \rho_j^i u^{i\prime\prime}(x_j)\, x_j^2 + \sum_{j\in R}\ \sum_{s\in S\setminus R} \underbrace{\rho_s^i u^{i\prime\prime}(x_s)}_{<0}\ \underbrace{x_s}_{\substack{=\omega_s^i+\sum_{k=1}^J \tilde{A}_s^k\left(x_k-\omega_k^i\right) \\ \geq \sum_{k=1}^J \tilde{A}_s^k x_k}}\ \underbrace{\tilde{A}_s^j x_j}_{\geq 0} \\
&\quad \leq \; \sum_{j\in R} \rho_j^i u^{i\prime\prime}(x_j)\, x_j^2 + \sum_{j\in R}\ \sum_{s\in S\setminus R}\ \sum_{k\in R}\left[\rho_s^i u^{i\prime\prime}(x_s)\left(\tilde{A}_s^k x_k\right)\left(\tilde{A}_s^j x_j\right)\right] \\
&\quad = \; x_R^T D^2_{x_R x_R} U_R^i(x_R)\, x_R
\end{aligned}$$

*q. e. d.*

We therefore obtain the following variant of Mitjushin-Polterovich's theorem:

THEOREM 6.12 (MITJUSHIN-POLTEROVICH IN THE CASE OF FUNDAMENTAL SETS)

*Let an agent* $i$ *be characterized by* $(U^i, \omega^i)$ *where:*

(i) *the utility function* $U^i: \mathbb{R}_+^S \to \mathbb{R}$ *satisfies Assumption 1.3 and* $MP_{u^i}(x) < 4$ *for all* $x \in \mathbb{R}_{++}$,

(ii) $\omega^i \in \mathbb{R}_{++}^S$,

(iii) *A satisfies Assumptions* $rank A = J$ *and 1.5,*

(iv) *A together with* $\omega^i$ *satisfies Assumption 6.3.*

*Then* $g^i(q)$ *is strictly monotone with respect to* $A_R^{-1}\omega_R^i$ *(Property 6.5(iii)).*[53]

PROOF 6.20 *In accordance with Lemma 6.4* $U_R^i$ *and* $\omega_R^i$ *satisfy the condition of Mitjushin-Polterovich's theorem (Theorem 6.10 on page 145) so that* $x_R^i(p(R))$ *is strictly monotone with respect to* $\omega_R^i$. *Under Lemma 6.3* $g^i(q)$ *is strictly monotone with respect to* $A_R^{-1}\omega_R^i$.

*q. e. d.*

Regarding uniqueness it therefore follows:

COROLLARY 6.3 (UNIQUENESS)
*Let a regular economy* $GEI = \left\{\mathbb{R}^S, (U^i, \omega^i)_{i\in I}, A\right\}$ *satisfy the following conditions:*

(i) *the securities matrix A satisfies Assumption 1.5,*

(ii) *Assumption 1.3 holds and* $MP_{U^i}(x) < 4$ *for all* $x \in \mathbb{R}_{++}^S$ *and all* $i \in I$,

(iii) $\left((\omega^i)_{i\in I}, A\right)$ *satisfies the Assumptions* $rank A = J$, *1.5,* $\omega^i >> 0 \, \forall i$ *and 6.3 and the initial endowments are collinear, that is, there exists a* $\delta \in \mathbb{R}_{++}^S$ *with* $\sum_{i=1}^I \delta^i = 1$ *and an* $\omega \in \mathbb{R}_{++}^S$ *with* $\omega^i = \delta^i\omega$ *for all* $i \in I$.

*Then the economy has a unique FM equilibrium.*

PROOF 6.21 *Since the* $\omega^i$ *for all* $i \in I$ *and* $\omega$ *are collinear, this also holds true for the* $A_R^{-1}\omega_R^i$ *and* $A_R^{-1}\omega_R$. *Hence, the* $g^i(q)$ *are strictly monotone with respect to* $A_R^{-1}\omega_R$, *which carries over to* $g(q)$, *so that we only need to apply Theorem 6.1.(i) on page 110.*

*q. e. d.*

---

[53] $q^T A_R^{-1}\omega_R^i > 0$ for all $q \in Q$ since

$$q^T A_R^{-1}\omega_R^i = \pi^T A A_R^{-1}\omega_R^i = \underbrace{\underbrace{\pi^T}_{\gg 0}\begin{pmatrix} I \\ A_{S\setminus R}A_R^{-1}\end{pmatrix}}_{>0}\underbrace{\omega_R^i}_{\gg 0} > 0.$$

Finally, we would like to mention the following points:

- Bettzüge concludes from certain monotonicity properties of the securities demand that the FM equilibrium is unique in the case of not necessarily regular economies.[54] However, this is not possible because the proof requires the normalized equilibrium price set to be finite, which has been shown for regular economies only.

- Obviously, the collinearity of $\omega^i$ can be weakened into the collinearity of the $\omega^i_R$, where $R$ would again be the corresponding fundamental set.

- Bettzüge shows that Assumption 6.3 is obviously satisfied for complete markets. [55]

- For spanned initial endowments he shows that, for each fundamental set $R$, the part of Assumption 6.3 concerning initial endowments is always satisfied. Note that Corollary 6.2 on page 150 is more general since it neither requires the existence of a fundamental set[56] nor von-Neumann-Morgenstern utility functions.

- In general, the existence of a fundamental set does not imply that the condition on the initial endowment in Assumption 6.3 is satisfied. [57]

- Under the conditions $A \geq 0$ and $J = 2$ a fundamental set always exists. [58] The Assumption $A \geq 0$ is essential as the example $A = \begin{pmatrix} 1 & 0 \\ 0 & 1 \\ 0 & -1 \end{pmatrix}$ shows. The case $J = 2$ will be examined in greater detail in Chapter 4.7.

- Bettzüge also studies the special class of weakly separating matrices.[59] For these matrices we had defined: [60]

$$S^j_A := \left\{ s \in S \mid A^j_s \neq 0 \right\}.$$

  It is obvious that in the case $A \geq 0$ each subset $R \subseteq S$ with $R \cap S^j_A \neq \emptyset$ for all $j \in J$ is a fundamental set. By graph-theoretical reasoning Bettzüge demonstrates that the condition on the initial endowment is satisfied by Assumption 6.3 for at least one of these sets.

[54] [Bettzüge, 1997, Corollary 2.1].
[55] [Bettzüge, 1997, Example 2.5.1].
[56] [Bettzüge, 1997, Example 2.5.2].
[57] [Bettzüge, 1997, Example 2.5.5].
[58] [Aliprantis et al., 1996, p. 9].
[59] [Bettzüge, 1997, Example 2.5.4].
[60] Cf. Definition 6.9 on page 119.

The same results apply for weakly separating matrices which have the same sign per column, which means that each security has only non-negative or non-positive pay-offs.

## 4.6 Gross Substitution in the Case of Small Relative Risk Aversion

Before we consider the case of incomplete markets we briefly recast the simpler case of complete markets. In both cases we will assume the expected utility hypothesis in the strong for of Assumption 1.3. For complete markets the following relationship between low relative risk aversion and the property of strict gross substitution of market demand is well-known.

THEOREM 6.13 (GROSS SUBSTITUTION. [HENS AND LÖFFLER, 1995])

*For an economy* $GEI = \left\{\mathbb{R}^S, (U^i, \omega^i)_{i \in I}, A\right\}$ *let the following be true:*

*(i) the utility functions* $U^i$ *satisfy Assumption 1.3,*

*(ii)* $A \in \mathbb{R}^{S \times S}$ *satisfies Assumption* $rank A = J$*:* $rank\ A = S$*,*

*(iii)* $\omega^i \in \mathbb{R}^S_{+}$ *for all* $i \in I$*.*

*Moreover, if one of the following properties holds, the individual demand function and thus also market demand satisfy the property of strict gross substitution:*

*a)* $RRA^i(x) < 1$ *for all* $i \in I$ *and all* $x > 0$*,*

*b) for all* $i \in I$ *there exists a* $\bar{x}^i \in \mathbb{R}_+$ *such that* $RRA^i(x) \leq 1$ *for all* $x \geq \bar{x}^i, x \neq 0$ *and* $\omega^i_s > \bar{x}^i$ *for all* $s \in S$*.*

PROOF 6.22 *Cf. Hens and Löffler [1995].*

This immediately leads to:

COROLLARY 6.4 (UNIQUENESS)
*Let an economy* $GEI = \left\{\mathbb{R}^S, (U^i, \omega^i)_{i \in I}, A\right\}$ *satisfy Conditions (i)–(ii) and a) or b) of the above theorem. Then: If an NA equilibrium exists, it is unique.*

PROOF 6.23
*Theorem 6.13 and Theorem 6.3.*

In the following we exclusively examine weakly separating matrices[61] which are also non-negative. Thus, in each state only one security has a positive pay-off. Given low relative risk aversion, the property of strict gross substitution follows by the following theorem.

[61] Cf. Definition 6.9 on page 119.

THEOREM 6.14 (GROSS SUBSTITUTION)
*For an agent $(U^i, \omega^i)$ and a securities matrix $A$ let the following be true:*

*(i) the utility function $U^i$ satisfies Assumption 1.3 and $RRA^i(x) \leq 1$ for all $x > 0$,*

*(ii) $A \in \mathbb{R}_+^{S \times J}$ satisfies Assumption $rank A = J$, is weakly separating and has no zero row,*

*(iii) for all $j \in J$ there exists an $s \in S_A^j$ with $\omega_s^i > 0$,*

*(iv) $(\omega^i, A)$ satisfies Assumption 2.2.*

*Then the individual demand for securities $g^i(q)$ satisfies Gross Substitution 6.8.*

PROOF 6.24
*The strong cheaper point assumption (Assumption 6.1) follows from Conditions (ii) and (iv) together with Theorem 6.3 on page 105 so that, given a von-Neumann-Morgenstern utility function, the first-order condition is necessary and sufficient to solve the maximization problem. For the Jacobian-Matrix and the Lagrange multiplier ((6.3) on page 107) we therefore obtain:*

$$(J) \quad \begin{pmatrix} D_q g \\ D_q \lambda \end{pmatrix} = \begin{pmatrix} A^T D_{xx}^2 U(\omega + A\,\theta) A & -q \\ -q^T & 0 \end{pmatrix}^{-1} \begin{pmatrix} \lambda I_J \\ \theta^T \end{pmatrix}$$

*For the proof we neglect the index $i$. By virtue of Assumption 1.3 $D_{xx}^2 U(\omega + A\,\theta)$ is a diagonal matrix:*

$$D_{xx}^2 U(\omega + A\,\theta) = \begin{pmatrix} \rho_1 u''(\omega_1 + A_1\theta) & & 0 \\ & \ddots & \\ 0 & & \rho_S u''(\omega_S + A_S\theta) \end{pmatrix}.$$

*Hence, the entries of the Hessian-Matrix $H := A^T D_{xx}^2 U(\omega + A\,\theta) A$ are given by:*

$$\begin{aligned} H_j^j &= \sum_{s \in S_A^j} \rho_s u''(\omega_s + A_s\theta) \left(A_s^j\right)^2 < 0 \text{ for all } \quad j \in J \\ H_k^j &= 0 \text{ for all } \quad (j,k) \in J \times J \quad \text{with} \quad j \neq k \end{aligned}$$

*One can easily verify that the following applies to the bordered Hessian-Matrix:*

$$H_g^{-1} = -\frac{1}{\sum\limits_{l=1}^{J}\left(q_l^2 \prod\limits_{m\neq l} H_m^m\right)}$$

$$\begin{array}{c} \\ 1 \\ \vdots \\ j \\ \vdots \\ k \\ \vdots \\ J+1 \end{array}
\begin{array}{c} 1 \quad \ldots \quad k \quad \ldots \quad J+1 \\
\begin{pmatrix}
-\sum\limits_{l\neq 1}\left(q_l^2 \prod\limits_{m\neq 1,l} H_m^m\right) & \ldots & \ldots & \ldots & q_1 \prod\limits_{m\neq 1} H_m^m \\
\vdots & & & & \\
q_1 q_j \prod\limits_{m\neq 1,j} H_m^m & \ldots & q_k q_j \prod\limits_{m\neq j,k} H_m^m & \ldots & q_j \prod\limits_{m\neq j} H_m^m \\
\vdots & & & & \\
q_1 q_k \prod\limits_{m\neq 1,k} H_m^m & \ldots & -\sum\limits_{l\neq k}\left(q_l^2 \prod\limits_{m\neq k,l} H_m^m\right) & \ldots & q_k \prod\limits_{m\neq k} H_m^m \\
\vdots & & & & \\
q_1 \prod\limits_{m\neq 1} H_m^m & \ldots & q_k \prod\limits_{m\neq k} H_m^m & \ldots & \prod\limits_{m} H_m^m
\end{pmatrix}\end{array}$$

*Because $A \geq 0$ it follows from the NA condition that $Q \subseteq \mathbb{R}_{++}^J$. The homogeneity of $g(q)$ therefore means that, in proving the property of strict gross substitution, it is sufficient to show the positivity of the off-diagonal elements of the Jacobian-Matrix $D_q\, g(q)$, since for all $j \in J$ and for all $r \in \mathbb{R}_{++}$:*

$$g_j(q) = g_j(rq)$$

*By differentiation with respect to $r$ at $r = 1$ we obtain for all $j \in J$:*

$$0 = \sum_{k=1}^{J} \partial_{q_k}\, g_j(q)\, q_k$$

*Thus:*

$$\partial_{q_j}\, \theta_j(q) = -\sum_{k\neq j} \underbrace{\partial_{q_k} g_j(q)}_{>0} \underbrace{\frac{q_k}{q_j}}_{>0} < 0$$

*Given the above expression for the matrix $H_g^{-1}$, it follows from $(J)$ for $(j,k) \in J \times J$ with $j \neq k$ that*

$$\begin{aligned}
\partial_{q_k} g_j(q) &= -\frac{1}{\sum_{l=1}^{J}\left(q_l^2 \prod_{m\neq l} H_m^m\right)}\left[\lambda q_k q_j \prod_{m\neq j,k} H_m^m + \theta_k q_j \prod_{m\neq j} H_m^m\right] \\
&= -\frac{\overbrace{q_j \prod_{m\neq j,k} H_m^m}^{sign=(-1)^{J-2}}}{\underbrace{\sum_{l=1}^{J}\left(q_l^2 \prod_{m\neq l} H_m^m\right)}_{sign=(-1)^{J-1}}}\left[\lambda q_k + \theta_k H_k^k\right]
\end{aligned}$$

$\partial_{q_k} g_j(q) > 0,\ j \neq k$ *if and only if* $\lambda q_k + \theta_k H_k^k > 0$. *By inserting the first-order condition* ($D_x U(\omega + A\theta) A^k - \lambda q_k = 0$) *and* $H_k^k$ *we get:*

$$\begin{aligned}
\lambda q_k + \theta_k H_k^k &= \sum_{s\in S_A^k} \rho_s u'(x_s) A_s^k + \theta_k \sum_{s\in S_A^k} \rho_s u''(x_s)\left(A_s^k\right)^2 \\
RRA(x_s) \quad \{ &= \sum_{s\in S_A^k} \rho_s A_s^k \left[-\frac{u''(x_s)}{RRA(x_s)} x_s + u''(x_s)\theta_k A_s^k\right] \\
s \in S_A^k : x_s - \omega_s = A_s^k \theta_k \quad \{ &= \sum_{s\in S_A^k} \rho_s \underbrace{A_s^k}_{>0} \underbrace{u''(x_s)}_{<0} \left[\underbrace{\left(1 - \frac{1}{RRA(x_s)}\right) x_s}_{\leq 0} - \underbrace{\omega_s}_{\geq 0}\right] \\
&> 0
\end{aligned}$$

*because of Condition (iii).*

*q. e. d.*

Conditions (iii) and (iv) are satisfied if $\omega^i \gg 0$.
The theorem remains valid if the conditions are modified in one of the following ways:

a) Substitute Conditions (i) and (iii) by

(i)'. for all $i \in I$ the utility functions $U^i$ satisfy Assumption 1.3 and $RRA^i(x) < 1$ for all $x > 0$,

(iii)'. $\omega^i \in \mathbb{R}_+^S \setminus \{0\}$ for all $i \in I$.

b) Substitute Conditions (i), (iii) and (iv) by

(i)". for all $i \in I$ the utility functions $U^i$ satisfy Assumption 1.3 and there exists an $\bar{x}^i \in \mathbb{R}_+$ with $RRA^i(x) \leq 1$ for all $x \geq \bar{x}^i, x \neq 0$ and $\omega_s^i > \bar{x}^i$ for all $s \in S$.

Regarding uniqueness, we derive the following corollary.

COROLLARY 6.5 (UNIQUENESS)
*For an economy* $GEI = \left\{\mathbb{R}^S, (U^i, \omega^i)_{i\in I}, A\right\}$ *let the following be true:*

*(i) for all* $i \in I$ *the utility functions* $U^i$ *satisfy Assumption 1.3 and* $RRA^i(x) \leq 1$ *for all* $x > 0$,

*(ii)* $A \in \mathbb{R}_+^{S\times J}$ *satisfies Assumption* $rankA = J$, *is weakly separating and has no zero row,*

*(iii) for all* $i \in I$ *the* $\omega^i \in \mathbb{R}_+^S$ *is such that for all* $j \in J$ *there exists an* $s \in S_A^j$ *with* $\omega_s^i > 0$,

*(iv)* $\left((\omega^i)_{i\in I}, A\right)$ *satisfies Assumption 2.2 and for an* $i \in I$ $\omega^i \gg 0$.

*Then the economy has a unique FM equilibrium.*

PROOF 6.25
*The existence of an FM equilibrium follows from the main result of Chapter 2. Uniqueness is obtained by Theorem 6.5 on page 120 since the strict gross substitution of individual demand and thus also of market demand follow as a consequence of Theorem 6.14. Furthermore, by reason of the NA condition the no arbitrage price vectors are strictly positive, that is,* $Q \subseteq \mathbb{R}_{++}^J$ *since* $A \geq 0$.

*q. e. d.*

As in the corresponding theorem, the conditions may be modified.

### 4.6.1 Discussion of the Conditions Leading to Uniqueness

Condition (i) regarding the utility function makes sense because it leads to strict gross substitution in the case of complete markets (Cf. Theorem 6.13). However, the condition substantially limits the set of examined utility functions. The positivity of matrix $A$ is necessary in order to derive the uniqueness of the equilibrium from the property of strict gross substitution of the demand for securities.

States to which no income transfer is possible do not influence the agent's securities decision, which is why we need not consider any states in which no security pays off.

The requirement that $A$ is weakly separating is very strong, even if it can be weakened by the observations on spans (Theorem 6.1 on page 103). Even under the condition that $A \geq 0$ the property of strict gross substitution does not generally follow without this assumption (yet for $J = 2$ strict gross substitution does follow as Theorem 6.16 on page 171 shows).

EXAMPLE 6.5
*Let*

$$A = \begin{pmatrix} 1 & 0 & 0 \\ 0 & 1 & 0 \\ 0 & 1 & 1 \\ 0 & 1 & 1 \end{pmatrix}, \quad \omega^i = \begin{pmatrix} 1 \\ 1 \\ 1 \\ 1 \end{pmatrix}, \quad U^i(x) = \sum_{s=1}^{4} \frac{1}{4} \ln x_s.$$

*After strictly transforming the utility function $U^i$, i's maximization problem can be written as*

$$\max_{\theta \in \mathbb{R}^3} \sum_{s=1}^{4} \ln\left(\omega_s^i + A_s \theta\right) \text{ s.t. } q^T \theta = 0,$$

*thus*

$$\max_{\theta_1, \theta_2 \in \mathbb{R}} \ln(1 + \theta_1) + \ln(1 + \theta_2) + 2 \ln\left(1 - \frac{q_1}{q_3}\theta_1 + \left(1 - \frac{q_2}{q_3}\right)\theta_2\right).$$

*The corresponding first-order condition is*

$$(*) \quad \frac{1}{1 + \theta_1} - \frac{2q_1}{q_3 - q_1\theta_1 + (q_3 - q_2)\theta_2} = 0,$$

$$(**) \quad \frac{1}{1 + \theta_2} + \frac{2(q_3 - q_2)}{q_3 - q_1\theta_1 + (q_3 - q_2)\theta_2} = 0.$$

*Adding* $(*) \cdot \frac{1}{q_1}$ *and* $(**) \cdot \frac{1}{q_3 - q_2}$ *yields*

$$\frac{1}{q_1 + q_1\theta_1} + \frac{1}{q_3 - q_2 + (q_3 - q_2)\theta_2} = 0$$

*($q_1 \neq 0$ and $q_3 - q_2 \neq 0$ because of the NA condition), from which we obtain*

$$\theta_2 = -\frac{q_1(1 + \theta_1)}{q_3 - q_2} - 1.$$

*By inserting this into $(*)$ we get*

$$\frac{1}{1 + \theta_1} - \frac{2q_1}{q_3 - q_1\theta_1 - q_1 - q_1\theta_1 - q_3 + q_2} = 0$$

$$\Leftrightarrow \quad \frac{1}{1+\theta_1} + \frac{2q_1}{2q_1\theta_1 + q_1 - q_2} = 0.$$

*Obviously,* $\partial_{q_3} g_1(q) = 0$, *which contradicts the property of strict gross substitution.*

If this example were continued, one would obtain infinitely many no arbitrage prices for which parts of the Jacobian-Matrix of the strict gross substitution property have opposite signs.
However, from Theorem 6.1 on page 103 it is clear that a unique equilibrium nevertheless exists for an economy consisting of this securities matrix, this agent and properly defined other agents, because

$$\langle A \rangle \quad = \left\langle \begin{pmatrix} 1 & 0 & 0 \\ 0 & 1 & 0 \\ 0 & 0 & 1 \\ 0 & 0 & 1 \end{pmatrix} \right\rangle.$$

As for Condition (iii), a counter-example by Becker demonstrates the necessity of this condition: [62]

EXAMPLE 6.6
*Let*[63]

$$A = \begin{pmatrix} 1 & 0 \\ 0 & 1 \\ 0 & 1 \end{pmatrix}, \; \omega^i = \begin{pmatrix} 1 \\ 0 \\ 0 \end{pmatrix}, \; U^i(x) = \sum_{s=1}^{3} \frac{1}{3} \ln x_s.$$

*Once we have transformed the utility function, the maximization problem can be written as*

$$\max_{\theta \in \mathbb{R}^2} \sum_{s=1}^{3} \ln\left(\omega_s^i + A_s\theta\right) \;\; s.t. \quad q^T\theta = 0,$$

*thus*

$$\max_{\theta_1 \in \mathbb{R}} \ln(1+\theta_1) + 2\ln\left(-\frac{q_1\theta_1}{q_2}\right),$$

*from which we obtain the* $(FOC^i)$

$$\frac{1}{1+\theta_1^i} + \frac{2}{\theta_1^i} = 0.$$

---

[62] [Becker, 1995, p. 40].
[63] Assumption 2.2 is satisfied since $\omega^i + A\theta \geq 0$ and $q^T\theta < 0$ for $\theta^T = (\; -1, \quad 0 \;)$.

*It follows that*

$$\theta_1^i = -\frac{2}{3},\ \theta_2^i = \frac{2q_1}{3q_2}.$$

*As a result, the Jacobian-Matrix has the form*

$$D_q g^i = \begin{pmatrix} 0 & 0 \\ \frac{2}{3q_2} & -\frac{2q_1}{3q_2^2} \end{pmatrix}.$$

*This violates the strict gross substitution of the demand for securities.* [64]

In analogy to the above example, Becker examines a counter-example for three securities and four states with consumption in the first period. From his calculation of the Jacobian-Matrix of the excess demand for goods it is evident that the property of restricted gross substitution is not satisfied.[65]
As is clear from the proof and further supported by the examples, without Condition (iii) strict gross substitution exists in a weak form (that is, "$\leq$" or "$\geq$").
To maintain the strict strict gross substitution of total demand, it is sufficient if one agent has a strict gross substitutive demand function and all others a weak one. This means that we can weaken Condition (iii) of the corollary so as to require that $\omega^i \in \mathbb{R}_+^S \setminus \{0\}$. Because of Condition (iv) strict strict gross substitution applies for at least one $i \in I$.
The first part of Condition (iv) is necessary to ensure that the $(FOC^i)$ is sufficient to solve the maximization problem. In addition to uniqueness, the existence of an FM equilibrium follows from the second part of Condition (iv) ($\omega^i \gg 0$ for an $i \in I$).

### 4.6.2 Some Extensions

By applying Theorem 6.1 on page 103 it is possible to extend the propositions of Corollary 6.5 on page 162 regarding uniqueness. To do so, we investigate all matrices $\hat{A} \in \mathbb{R}^{S\times J}$ for which there exists a weakly separating matrix $A \in \mathbb{R}_+^{S\times J}$ with $\langle A \rangle = \left\langle \hat{A} \right\rangle$. To ensure Conditions (iii) and (iv), from now on let $\omega^i \in \mathbb{R}_{++}^S$.
Define the following sets:

---

[64]Recall Example 6.4 concerning the relationship between the strict gross substitution of the demand for securities and the restricted gross substitution of the demand for goods on page 118, where the agent is characterized in the same way as here and has the same options available to transfer his income, but in doing so must use different securities. In the Example 6.4 the strict gross substitution of the demand for securities is satisfied.

[65][Becker, 1995, p. 38-40].

$$M := \left\{ A \in \mathbb{R}^{S\times J} \quad | \quad rank \quad A = J \wedge \exists \quad \theta \in \mathbb{R}^J \quad \text{with} \quad A\theta > 0 \right\}$$

(the set of all admissible pay-off matrices)

$$M_{ss} := \{ A \in M \quad | \quad A_s > 0 \,\forall \quad s \in S \wedge A \quad \text{is weakly separating} \}$$

(the set of all matrices permitted under Corollary 6.5)

$$M_E := \left\{ \hat{A} \in M \quad | \quad \exists \quad A \in M_{ss} \quad \text{with} \quad \langle A \rangle \quad = \quad \left\langle \hat{A} \right\rangle \right\}$$

(the set of all matrices by which the corollary may be extended)
The following lemma describes the set $M_E$:

LEMMA 6.5

$$M_E = \{ \; \hat{A} \in \mathbb{R}^{S\times J} \quad | \quad \exists m_1, \ldots, m_J \in \mathbb{R}^J \quad with$$
$$(1) \quad \sum_{j=1}^{J} \alpha_j m_j = 0 \quad for \quad \alpha_j \in \mathbb{R} \Rightarrow \alpha_j = 0 \,\forall \quad j \in J$$
$$(2) \quad \forall \quad s \in S \quad \exists \quad \lambda_s \in \mathbb{R}_{++} \wedge \exists \quad j \in J \quad with \quad \hat{A}_s = \lambda_s m_j^T \; \}$$

PROOF 6.26
*"$\subseteq$": Let $\hat{A} \in M_E$. Then there exists an invertible matrix $S \in \mathbb{R}^{S\times J}$ and a matrix $A \in M_{ss}$ with $\hat{A} = AS$. From the property $A_s > 0$ for all $s \in S$ and the weak separability it follows that $S - J$ rows of the matrix $A$ are the positive multiples of one of the other $J$ linearly independent rows. Without loss of generality let $S^2 = \{J+1, \ldots, S\}$ and $S^1 = \{1, \ldots, J\}$ be the corresponding index sets. Let $A_s$ and $A_t$ ($s \in S^2, t \in S^1$) be two rows related in the above manner, that is, for a $\lambda_s \in \mathbb{R}_{++}$ $A_s = \lambda_s A_t$. Then also $\hat{A}_s = \lambda_s \hat{A}_t$ because $\hat{A}_t = A_t S$ and $\hat{A}_s = A_s S = \lambda_s A_t S = \lambda_s \hat{A}_t$. Since multiplication by $S$ is a linear mapping and $A_1, \ldots, A_J$ are linearly independent, it follows that $\hat{A}_1, \ldots, \hat{A}_J$ are also linearly independent.*
*Let "$\supseteq$": $\hat{A}$ satisfy the properties of the second set, that is, without loss of generality $\hat{A}$ has the form*

$$\hat{A} = \begin{pmatrix} m_1^T \\ \vdots \\ m_J^T \\ \lambda_1 m_{j_1}^T \\ \vdots \\ \lambda_{S-J} m_{j_{S-J}}^T \end{pmatrix}, where$$

*$m_1, \ldots, m_J$, are linearly independent and $\lambda_1, \ldots, \lambda_{S-J} \in \mathbb{R}_{++}$. Define the matrix*

$$S := \begin{pmatrix} m_1^T \\ \vdots \\ m_J^T \end{pmatrix},$$

*which can be inverted by virtue of the linear independence of the row vectors. With*

$$A = \begin{pmatrix} I_J \\ \lambda_1 e^{j_1 T} \\ \vdots \\ \lambda_{S-J} e^{j_{S-J} T} \end{pmatrix} \in M_{ss}$$

*the relation $\hat{A} = AS$ holds, which implies $\langle A \rangle = \left\langle \hat{A} \right\rangle$.*

*q. e. d.*

According to the above lemma each financial contract has either non-negative or non-positive pay-offs in each state. If two rows are the same except for the multiplication with a positive scalar, the pay-off ratio between the securities for both states is identical.
We can therefore substitute Conditions (ii) to (iv) of Corollary 6.5 by $\omega^i \in \mathbb{R}^S_{++}$ and by $A$ from the corresponding set of the lemma.

## 4.7 Two Securities and Small Relative Risk Aversion

### 4.7.1 Direct Proof

Investigating economies with two securities and von-Neumann-Morgenstern utility functions with low relative risk aversion always results in the uniqueness of the FM equilibrium.
Becker shows that uniqueness of the FM equilibrium follows in the case of Cobb-Douglas utility functions when only one security is traded in the context of the GEI model with consumption in the first period.[66] By considering any given von-Neumann-Morgenstern utility functions with a relative risk aversion $\leq 1$,[67] Bettzüge extends Becker's proposition to a model without consumption in the first period and two tradable securities, of which one has non-negative pay-offs. In the following we will show that the strict positivity of the initial

[66][Becker, 1995, p. 40-41].
[67][Bettzüge, 1997, Proposition 2.2].

endowments Bettzüge requires can be weakened. Furthermore, by applying Theorem 6.1 on page 103, we can extend his example to any two securities.

THEOREM 6.15 (UNIQUENESS)
*For an economy* $GEI = \left\{\mathbb{R}^S, (U^i, \omega^i)_{i\in I}, A\right\}$ *let the following hold:*

*(i) for all* $i \in I$ *the utility functions* $U^i$ *satisfy Assumption 1.3 and* $RRA^i(x) \leq 1$ *for all* $x > 0$*,*

*(ii) there exist* $J = 2$ *securities which are not redundant (that is,* $A \in \mathbb{R}^{S\times 2}$ *satisfies Assumption* $rank A = J$*) and for at least one* $j \in \{1,2\}$ $A^j \geq 0$*,*

*(iii)* $\left((\omega^i)_{i\in I}, A\right)$ *satisfies Assumption 6.1 and* $\omega^i \gg 0$ *for an* $i \in I$*.*

*Then the economy has a unique FM equilibrium.*

PROOF 6.27 [68]
*Without loss of generality Security 1 pays off non-negatively such that by Rank Assumption* $rank A = J$ $A^1 > 0$*. Thus there exists a* $\bar{\theta}$ *with* $A\bar{\theta} > 0$*. From our main result in Chapter 2 it follows from the other conditions that the economy has an FM equilibrium.*
*From the NA condition it follows that* $q_1 > 0$ *with the effect that price normalization by* $q_1 = 1$ *is possible. From the constraint* $q^T\theta^i = 0$ *it therefore follows that* $\theta_1^i = -q_2\theta_2^i$*.*
*Consequently, the maximization problem of an agent* $i$ *can be written as:*

$$\max_{\theta_2^i \in \mathbb{R}} \sum_{s=1}^{S} \rho_s^i u^i \left(\omega_s^i + \left(A_s^2 - q_2 A_s^1\right)\theta_2^i\right)$$

*Because of Condition (iii) there are no boundary solutions and it suffices to examine the first-order condition:*

$$F^i\left(q_2, \theta_2^i\right) := \sum_{s=1}^{S} \rho_s^i u^{i'} \left(\omega_s^i + \left(A_s^2 - q_2 A_s^1\right)\theta_2^i\right)\left(A_s^2 - q_2 A_s^1\right) = 0 \qquad (FOC^i)$$

68 [Bettzüge, 1997, Proposition 2.2].

*Now consider:*

$$\begin{aligned}
\partial_{q_2} F^i\left(q_2, \theta_2^i\right) &= \sum_{s=1}^{S} \rho_s^i u^{i''}\left(\omega_s^i + \left(A_s^2 - q_2 A_s^1\right)\theta_2^i\right)\left(-A_s^1\theta_2^i\right)\left(A_s^2 - q_2 A_s^1\right) \\
&\quad + \sum_{s=1}^{S} \rho_s^i u^{i'}\left(\omega_s^i + \left(A_s^2 - q_2 A_s^1\right)\theta_2^i\right)\left(-A_s^1\right) \\
&= \sum_{s=1}^{S} \rho_s^i \underbrace{A_s^1}_{\geq 0} \underbrace{u^{i''}\left(x_s^i\right)}_{<0} \left[\underbrace{\omega_s^i}_{\geq 0} + \underbrace{\left(\frac{1}{RRA^i\left(x_s^i\right)} - 1\right)}_{\geq 0} \underbrace{x_s^i}_{>0}\right] \\
&\leq 0
\end{aligned}$$

*Because of Condition (iii) we obtain* $\partial_{q_2} F^i\left(q_2, \theta_2^i\right) < 0$ *for an agent* $i$ *since* $A_s^1 > 0$ *for at least one* $s \in S$. *In addition:*

$$\partial_{q_2} F^i \left(q_2, \theta_2^i\right) = \sum_{s=1}^{S} \underbrace{\rho_s^i u^{i\prime\prime} \left(x_s^i\right)}_{<0} \quad \underbrace{\left(A_s^2 - q_2 A_s^1\right)^2}_{\substack{\geq 0 \text{ and for at least a} \\ s \in S > 0 \text{ since } \operatorname{rank} A = 2}} < 0$$

*By applying the implicit function theorem* [69] *we obtain from the* $(FOC^i)$:

$$\partial_{q_2} g_2^i = -\frac{\partial_{q_2} F^i}{\partial_{\theta_2^i} F^i} \leq 0 \quad , \tag{6.20}$$

*where the inequality holds strictly for at least one agent.*
*Suppose the economy has two FM equilibria with* $(1, \bar{q}_2) < (1, \overset{*}{q}_2)$ *as normalized price vectors. It then follows that* (6.20):

$$0 = \sum_{i=1}^{I} g_2^i \left(1, \bar{q}_2\right) > \sum_{i=1}^{I} g_2^i \left(1, \overset{*}{q}_2\right) = 0$$

*This is a contradiction.*

*q. e. d.*

In accordance with our considerations on Theorem 6.14 on page 159, the theorem continues to be valid if we modify the conditions in the following way: Substitute Conditions (i) and (iii) by

(i)'. the utility functions $U^i$ satisfy Assumption 1.3 and for all $i \in I$ there exists an $\bar{x}^i \in \mathbb{R}_+$ with $RRA^i(x) \leq 1$ for all $x \geq \bar{x}^i, x \neq 0$ and $\omega_s^i > \bar{x}^i$ for all $s \in S$.

In principle, the proof simply exploits the negative quasi-definiteness of the Jacobian-Matrix with respect to a normalizing vector. From $(*)$ this follows for $n = (\ 1, \ \ 0\ )^T$ because $A^1 > 0$ means that normalization with this vector is equivalent to normalizing $q_1 = 1$.[70] Since the same normalizing vector is required for all $i \in I$, the same holds for the market demand for securities. [71]

[69] [Forster, 1991, Theorem 8.2 and Remark].

[70] $n = (\ 1, \ \ 0\ )$ is an admissible normalizing vector since for all $q \in Q$ $q^T n > 0$, because

$$q^T \begin{pmatrix} 1 \\ 0 \end{pmatrix} = \pi^T A \begin{pmatrix} 1 \\ 0 \end{pmatrix} = \underbrace{\pi^T}_{\gg 0} \underbrace{A^1}_{> 0} > 0.$$

[71] Under the assumption $A \geq 0$ the property of monotonicity with respect to the other unit vector follows in the same way so that, in this case, the strict gross substitution of market demand follows by Theorem 6.6 on page 122. In the next section we provide a separate proof where the strict gross substitution of individual demand is shown under slightly stronger conditions on the initial endowment. When $A \geq 0$, strict gross substitution applies to market demand under the same conditions as monotonicity here.

Theorem 6.1 is not applied here because it presupposes Assumption $\omega^i >> 0\,\forall i$ and therefore makes stronger assumptions.
Furthermore, we obtain the following corollary:

COROLLARY 6.6 (UNIQUENESS)
*For an economy* $G\hat{E}I = \left\{\mathbb{R}^S, (U^i, \omega^i)_{i\in I}, \hat{A}\right\}$ *with* $J = 2$ *securities let the following be true:*

*(i) for all* $i \in I$ *the utility functions* $U^i$ *satisfy Assumption 1.3 and* $RRA^i(x) \leq 1$ *for all* $x > 0$,

*(ii)* $\hat{A} \in \mathbb{R}^{S\times 2}$ *satisfies Assumptions* $rank\ A = J$ *and 1.5,*

*(iii)* $\omega^i \gg 0$ *for all* $i \in I$ *(Assumption* $\omega^i >> 0\,\forall i$*).*

*Then the economy has a unique FM equilibrium.*

PROOF 6.28
*This follows by the considerations on Theorem 6.1 on page 103.*

Of course, the conditions of this corollary may be modified in accordance with (i)'.

### 4.7.2 Gross Substitution

Strict gross substitution is always given for the demand for securities (under certain conditions on the initial endowment) in the case of low relative risk aversion and a non-negative pay-off matrix, so that we can show the uniqueness of the FM equilibrium by this approach. Note, however, that the results of Theorem 6.15 and Corollary 6.6 have wider implications.

THEOREM 6.16 (GROSS SUBSTITUTION)
*For an agent* $(U^i, \omega^i)$ *and a securities matrix* $A$ *let the following be true:*

*(i) the utility function* $U^i$ *satisfies Assumption 1.3 and* $RRA^i(x) \leq 1$ *for all* $x > 0$,

*(ii) the matrix* $A$ *consists of two non-redundant securities with non-negative pay-offs (Assumption* $rank A = J$*) and of which at least one has a positive pay-off in each state,*

*(iii) for all* $j \in J$ *there is an* $s \in S$ *with* $\omega_s^i A_s^j > 0$,

*(iv)* $(\omega^i, A)$ *satisfies Assumption 2.2.*

*Then the demand for securities* $g^i(q)$ *satisfies the property of strict gross substitution 6.8.*

PROOF 6.29

*As a result of Condition (ii), it follows that Assumption 1.5 is also satisfied. There is even a $\bar{\theta}$ with $A\bar{\theta} \gg 0$. Therefore, Assumption 2.2 together with Theorem 6.3. 2 implies Assumption 6.1. To solve the maximization problem, it is therefore sufficient to examine the firsts-order condition obtained from the following Jacobian-Matrix (cf.* (6.3) *on page 107):*

$$(J) \quad \begin{pmatrix} D_q g \\ D_q \lambda \end{pmatrix} = \begin{pmatrix} \sum_{s=1}^{S} \rho_s u''(x_s) A_s^1 A_s^1 & \sum_{s=1}^{S} \rho_s u''(x_s) A_s^1 A_s^2 & -q_1 \\ \sum_{s=1}^{S} \rho_s u''(x_s) A_s^1 A_s^2 & \sum_{s=1}^{S} \rho_s u''(x_s) A_s^2 A_s^2 & -q_2 \\ -q_1 & -q_2 & 0 \end{pmatrix} \cdot \begin{pmatrix} \lambda & 0 \\ 0 & \lambda \\ \theta_1 & \theta_2 \end{pmatrix}$$

*For the proof we will neglect the index $i$. $\lambda$ is the corresponding Lagrange multiplier.Let $H = \left(H_k^j\right)_{(k,j)\in J^2}$ be the (non-bordered) Hessian-Matrix. For the bordered Hessian-Matrix verify that:*

$$H_g^{-1} = \frac{1}{-q_1^2 H_2^2 - q_2^2 H_1^1 + 2q_1 q_2 H_1^2} \cdot \begin{pmatrix} -q_2^2 & q_1 q_2 & -q_2 H_1^2 + q_1 H_2^2 \\ q_1 q_2 & -q_1^2 & -q_1 H_1^2 + q_2 H_1^1 \\ -q_2 H_1^2 + q_1 H_2^2 & -q_1 H_1^2 + q_2 H_1^1 & H_1^1 H_2^2 - \left(H_1^2\right)^2 \end{pmatrix}$$

*And*

$$\begin{aligned}\det H_g &= -q_1^2 H_2^2 - q_2^2 H_1^1 + 2q_1 q_2 H_1^2 \\ &= \sum_{s=1}^{S} \rho_s u"(x_s)\left[-q_1^2 A_s^2 A_s^2 - q_2^2 A_s^1 A_s^1 + 2q_1 q_2 A_s^1 A_s^2\right] \\ &= -\sum_{s=1}^{S} \rho_s u"(x_s) \underbrace{\left[q_1 A_s^2 - q_2 A_s^1\right]^2}_{\substack{\geq 0 \text{ forall } s\in S \text{ and} \\ >0 \text{ for at least one } s \in S, \text{ since } rank\, A=2}} \\ &> 0\end{aligned}$$

*Because of $q \gg 0$*[72] *and the homogeneity of $g(q)$, it is sufficient for the property of strict gross substitution to show that the off-diagonal elements of the Jacobian-Matrix are positive.*[73] *For $(j,k) \in \{(1,2),(2,1)\}$:*

$$\begin{aligned}\partial_{q_k} g_j &= \frac{1}{\det H_g}\left[\lambda q_j q_k - q_k H_j^k \theta_k + q_j H_k^k \theta_k\right] \\ &= \frac{1}{\det H_g}\left[q_j \sum_{s=1}^{S} \rho_s u'(x_s) A_s^k \right.\\ &\quad \left. - q_k \theta_k \sum_{s=1}^{S} \rho_s u"(x_s) A_s^j A_s^k + q_j \sum_{s=1}^{S} \rho_s u"(x_s) A_s^k A_s^k \theta_k\right] \\ &= \frac{1}{\det H_g}\sum_{s=1}^{S} \rho_s u"(x_s) A_s^k q_j \left[-\frac{x_s}{RRA(x_s)} - A_s^j \frac{q_k \theta_k}{q_j} + A_s^k \theta_k\right] \\ \theta_j = -\frac{q_k\theta_k}{q_j} \quad \{ \quad &= \underbrace{\frac{1}{\det H_g}}_{>0} \sum_{s=1}^{S} \underbrace{\rho_s}_{>0} \underbrace{u"(x_s)}_{<0} \underbrace{A_s^k}_{\geq 0} \underbrace{q_j}_{>0} \left[\underbrace{\left(1 - \frac{1}{RRA(x_s)}\right)}_{\leq 0} \underbrace{x_s}_{>0} - \underbrace{\omega_s}_{\geq 0}\right] \\ &> 0,\end{aligned}$$

*since at least one summand is strictly positive as a result of Condition (iii).*

*q. e. d.*

This theorem also yields the strict gross substitution of $z^i(\pi)$ because according to [Aliprantis et al., 1996, p. 9]. there exists a set $R \subseteq S$ with $\#R = 2$ such that $A_R = (A_s)_{s \in R}$ is invertible and $A_{S \setminus R} A_R^{-1} \geq 0$. Without loss of generality let $R = \{1, 2\}$. Then the relation $\langle A \rangle = \langle \hat{A} \rangle$ is true for

[72] This follows from $A \geq 0$, Rank Assumption $rankA = J$ and the NA condition.

[73] For the proof of Theorem 6.14, see page 159.

$$\hat{A} = A \cdot A_R^{-1} = \begin{pmatrix} I \\ A_{S\setminus R} A_R^{-1} \end{pmatrix} > 0$$

so that $z^i(\pi) = \hat{z}^i(\pi)$ for the individual excess demands. However, this also means that $D_\pi z^i(\pi) = D_\pi \hat{z}^i(\pi)$. It now follows that $\hat{z}^i(\pi)$ satisfies the property of restricted gross substitution if and only if $\hat{g}^i(q)$ satisfies strict gross substitution ($\hat{g}^i(q)$ is the individual demand for securities of the matrix $\hat{A}$). This follows from:

$$\begin{aligned}
\hat{z}^i(\pi) &= \hat{A}\hat{g}^i\left(\pi^T\hat{A}\right) \\
\Rightarrow \hat{z}^i_s(\pi) &= \hat{g}^i_s\left(\pi^T\hat{A}\right) \quad \text{for} \quad s = 1,2 \\
\Rightarrow \partial_{\pi_t}\hat{z}^i_s(\pi) &= \partial_{q_1}\hat{g}^i_s\left(\pi^T\hat{A}\right)\hat{A}^1_t + \partial_{q_2}\hat{g}^i_s\left(\pi^T\hat{A}\right)\hat{A}^2_t \\
&= \partial_{q_t}\hat{g}^i_s\left(\pi^T\hat{A}\right) \quad \text{for} \quad s = 1,2; t = 1,2
\end{aligned}$$

The agent $(U^i, \omega^i)$ and $\hat{A}$ satisfy the conditions of Theorem 6.16.[74] Thus, $\hat{g}^i(q)$ satisfies strict gross substitution, which implies that $\hat{z}^i(\pi)$ also satisfies the property of restricted gross substitution. Together with the above considerations, this then also applies to $z^i(\pi)$.

The conditions of Theorem 6.16 may be modified as in Theorem 6.14 on page 159.

If the aim is to obtain the strict gross substitution of the market demand for securities, it is sufficient if one agent satisfies Condition (iii).

Uniqueness follows in analogy to Corollary 6.5 on page 162.

## 4.8 Overview of Conditions for Uniqueness in the Finance GEI-Model

Figure 6.1 provides an overview of conditions which guarantee a unique FM- and therefore also NA-equilibrium in the GEI-model. It has to be read in the same way as the corresponding Figure 5.4 for complete markets (compare Section 5). Besides it is subjected to the same limitations.

Since complete markets constitute a special case for the GEI-model, actually Figure 5.4 would have to be contained in Figure 6.1 given here. However, we omitted those conditions which are only valid with complete markets to preserve clarity.

Besides we decided to assume $A_{.1}$ to be positive because otherwise it would become quite difficult to handle price normalization. In addition, the reader has

[74] Because of the invertibility of $A_R^{-1}$ and the associated linear independence of the rows, $A_s A_R^{-1} = 0$ for an $s \in S\setminus R$ is only possible with $A_s = 0$. But this contradicts the assumption that $A$ has no zero row.

to take care of the fact that it is sufficient if one of the representations of the asset span fits in the scheme (compare Proposition 6.1).

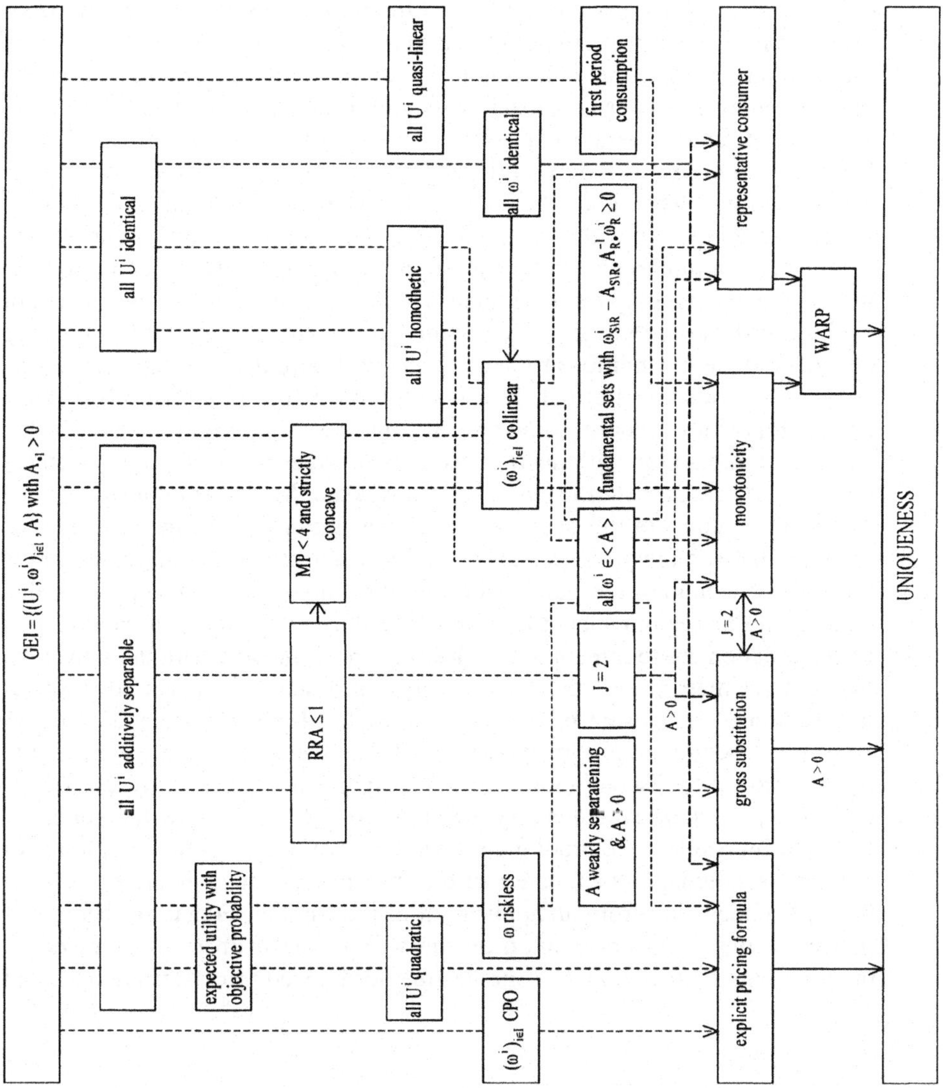


*Figure 6.1.* Conditions for uniqueness in the Finance GEI-model.

## 5. Robustness of the Number of Competitive Equilibria against Perturbations of the Asset Structure[76]

In the next section we give examples where although consumers' characteristics remain the same there might be a change from a unique to multiple equilibria when switching from complete to incomplete markets, i.e. when the dimension of the asset span changes. As well, for different incomplete asset structures of the same dimension the number of equilibria might vary. Section 7 proves by means of an example that changing from complete to (non-trivial) incomplete markets might also cause to switch from multiple to a unique equilibrium.

All these examples would not be very interesting if they were exceptional: but this section proves the examples to be robust against some changes of the asset structure. The general question is to what extent changes of the asset structure are possible without changing the number of equilibria. One reason why we attach importance to this question consists in the fact that it allows to get some understanding for the influence of the asset structure on the number of equilibria: the long-term aim is to use this understanding for establishing more general sufficient conditions for a unique equilibrium than given in the second section of this chapter, i.e. than those results known up to now in this topic; most of the propositions require some special structure for the asset matrix whether this is in combination with restrictions on endowments or not. The robustness result of this chapter clarifies that one can weaken these assumptions.

The main outcome of this section is the following one: starting with a regular Finance GEI-economy, one can allow that the asset structure is perturbed a little bit without changing the number of equilibria or—even stronger—such that equilibrium prices move continuously! The only restrictions on the direction of perturbation are to remain with a desirable portfolio and with the same rank of the asset matrix, i.e. the same number of assets. This fact corresponds to intuition if the closure of the set of normalized arbitrage-free asset prices constitutes a continuous correspondence of the asset matrix, but we prove it to be even true with discontinuous price-correspondences. Up to my knowledge even for the first case there is no general proof of this fact in the literature.

One interim result in the proof gives a kind of "continuous differentiability" of market asset demand as a function of the asset matrix and asset prices which is a simple conclusion from an application of the Implicit Function Theorem.[77] A second important observation on the way to the main result is given by the following fact: although arbitrage-free normalized price-sets are open and

[76] The results of this section are a very far-reaching extension of the ideas in Pilgrim [2002]

[77] One has to be careful: the range of definition of this function is neither open nor connected such that for some elements the derivatives have to be restricted in some directions and continuous differentiability in the common sense is obtained only on small open subsets.

sometimes unbounded, for equilibrium considerations it is possible to restrict attention to some compact subset which is even continuous in the asset structure. This section is organized as follows: in the next subsection we describe some extensions of notation for the underlying Finance GEI-model. Within this framework we thoroughly investigate the normalized arbitrage-free price set and its dependence on the asset structure. Afterwards we give a short proof of "continuous differentiability" of individual and market asset demand with respect to the asset matrix and asset prices. The third subsection uses this property to get continuity of equilibrium prices in "regular" asset structures because one can restrict attention to a compact subset of arbitrage-free asset prices which allows to apply uniform continuity.

## 5.1 Further Properties of the Set of Arbitrage-Free Prices

Recall the system of first order conditions given as necessary and sufficient conditions for consumers' maximization problems, i.e.

$$\nabla U^i \left(\omega^i + A\,\theta^i\right) A - \lambda^i\, q^T = 0 \tag{6.21}$$

$$q \cdot \theta^i = 0 \tag{6.22}$$

for all $i \in I$ where $\lambda^i > 0$ is the Lagrangian multiplier. Up to now, we considered a solution of this system $\left(g^i\left(q\right), \lambda^i\left(q\right)\right) \in \mathbb{R}^J \times \mathbb{R}_+$ as a function on $Q\left(A\right)$ and assumed $A$ to be fixed. However, since we want to clarify the dependence on the asset structure, from now on it is sometimes convenient to write $\left(g^i\left(q, A\right), \lambda^i\left(q, A\right)\right) \in \mathbb{R}^J \times \mathbb{R}_+$. We do not use different notations because the context clarifies whether the asset structure $A$ is fixed or not, i.e. whether $\left(g^i\left(q\right), \lambda^i\left(q\right)\right)$ or $\left(g^i\left(q, A\right), \lambda^i\left(q, A\right)\right)$ is the right notation.
If there is some $\bar{j} \in \{1, \ldots, J\}$ with $A_{\cdot\bar{j}} > 0$, a possible price normalization is given by $q_{\bar{j}} = 1$ such that asset $j$ is numeraire asset. Because of Proposition 6.1, under Assumption 1.5 it is no restriction to assume $A_{\cdot\bar{j}} > 0$ since for each $A$ satisfying this assumption one can find an asset matrix $\tilde{A}$ satisfying $rank\,\tilde{A} = J$ and $\tilde{A}_{\cdot\bar{j}} > 0$ with $\langle A\rangle = \langle\tilde{A}\rangle$. Therefore Assumption 1.5 can be substituted by

ASSUMPTION 6.4 (SOME ASSET WITH POSITIVE PAYOFF)
*$A \in \mathbb{R}^{S\times J}$ satisfies $A_{\cdot 1} > 0$.*

This means that the first asset is always desirable because its payoff is positive. Under this assumption one can restrict attention to the following projection of the normalized arbitrage-free asset price set:

$$\mathcal{Q}_{norm}\left(A\right) := \left\{\hat{q} \in \mathbb{R}^{J-1} \,\middle|\, \begin{pmatrix}1\\ \hat{q}\end{pmatrix} = A^T\,\pi \quad \text{for some} \quad \pi \in \mathbb{R}^S_{++}\right\} \quad .$$

$\mathcal{Q}_{norm}(A)$ is the projection of $\hat{\mathcal{Q}}(A)$ on $\mathbb{R}^{J-1}$.
Later on, it will become clear that—when investigating perturbations of the asset matrix—we have to distinguish three different classes of matrices:

(i) $A \in \mathbb{R}^{S\times J}$, satisfying Assumption 6.4 with $A_{\cdot 1} \gg 0$;

(ii) $A = \begin{pmatrix} 1 & 0 \\ 0 & \breve{A} \end{pmatrix} \in \mathbb{R}^{S\times J}$ where $\breve{A} \in \mathbb{R}^{(S-1)\times(J-1)}$ with $rank\, \breve{A} = J-1$, i.e. $A$ models first period consumption;[78]

(iii) $A \in \mathbb{R}^{S\times J}$, satisfying Assumption 6.4 with $A_{\cdot 1} > 0$, but not $A_{\cdot 1} \gg 0$.

Case (iii) includes case (ii). However, to remain within the framework of first period consumption later on we will have to define perturbations in case (ii) different from those in case (iii).
Define

$$\begin{aligned} \mathcal{S}^{+}(A_{\cdot 1}) &:= \{s \in \{1,\ldots,S\} \mid A_{s1} > 0\}, \\ \mathcal{S}^{0}(A_{\cdot 1}) &:= \{s \in \{1,\ldots,S\} \mid A_{s1} = 0\} \end{aligned}$$

such that $\mathcal{S}^{+}(A_{\cdot 1}) \cup \mathcal{S}^{0}(A_{\cdot 1}) = \{1,\ldots,S\}$.
With these definitions alternative representations of the normalized arbitrage-free asset price sets can be given which highlight the structure of these sets. Distinguish the classes of matrices:

(i)

$$\begin{aligned} &\mathcal{Q}_{norm}(A) \\ &= \left\{\hat{q} \in \mathbb{R}^{J-1} \,\middle|\, \begin{pmatrix} 1 \\ \hat{q} \end{pmatrix} = A^{T}\pi \quad \text{for some} \quad \pi \in \mathbb{R}^{S}_{++}\right\} \\ &= \left\{\hat{q} \in \mathbb{R}^{J-1} \,\middle|\, \hat{q} = A^{T}_{\cdot(-1)}\pi \wedge 1 = \sum_{s=1}^{S} \underbrace{A_{s1}\pi_s}_{=:\mu_s} \right. \\ &\qquad \left. \text{for some} \quad \pi \in \mathbb{R}^{S}_{++}\right\} \\ &= \left\{\hat{q} \in \mathbb{R}^{J-1} \,\middle|\, \hat{q} = \sum_{s=1}^{S} \frac{\mu_s}{A_{s1}} A^{T}_{s(-1)} \quad \text{for some} \quad \mu \in \hat{\mathcal{P}}_{1,1}\right\} \\ &= int\left(conv\left\{\frac{1}{A_{11}} A^{T}_{1(-1)}, \ldots, \frac{1}{A_{S1}} A^{T}_{S(-1)}\right\}\right) \end{aligned}$$

[78] For simplicity we numerate the rows of $\breve{A}$ by $2,\ldots,S$ and the columns by $2,\ldots,J$.

where $int$ defines the interior of a set[79] and $conv$ denotes the convex hull, i.e. the smallest convex set containing $\frac{1}{A_{11}} A^T_{1(-1)}, \ldots, \frac{1}{A_{S1}} A^T_{S(-1)}$. Obviously, $\mathcal{Q}_{norm}(A)$ is the interior of a convex polytop.

(ii)

$$\begin{aligned}
&\mathcal{Q}_{norm}(A) \\
&= \left\{ \hat{q} \in \mathbb{R}^{J-1} \middle| \begin{pmatrix} 1 \\ \hat{q} \end{pmatrix} = \begin{pmatrix} 1 & 0 \\ 0 & \check{A}^T \end{pmatrix} \pi \quad \text{for some} \quad \pi \in \mathbb{R}^S_{++} \right\} \\
&= \left\{ \hat{q} \in \mathbb{R}^{J-1} \middle| \hat{q} = \check{A}^T \tilde{\pi} \quad \text{for some} \quad \tilde{\pi} \in \mathbb{R}^{S-1}_{++} \right\} \\
&= \sum_{s=2}^{S} \left\{ \mu_s \check{A}^T_{s\cdot} \middle| \mu_s \in \mathbb{R}_{++} \right\},
\end{aligned}$$

i.e. $\mathcal{Q}_{norm}(A)$ is either the interior of a convex polyeder with $\hat{q} = 0$ being element of the boundary or the whole space $\mathbb{R}^{S-1}$.[80]

[79] In contrast $cl$ denotes the closure of a set.

[80] The sum of two sets $\mathcal{R}, \mathcal{W} \subseteq \mathbb{R}^N$ is defined as

$$\mathcal{R} + \mathcal{W} \quad := \quad \left\{ x \in \mathbb{R}^N \middle| \exists\, r \in \mathcal{R}, w \in \mathcal{W} \text{ with } x = r + w \right\} \quad .$$

(iii)

$$
\begin{aligned}
&\mathcal{Q}_{norm}(A) \\
&= \left\{ \hat{q} \in \mathbb{R}^{J-1} \middle| \begin{pmatrix} 1 \\ \hat{q} \end{pmatrix} = A^T \pi \quad \text{for some} \quad \pi \in \mathbb{R}^S_{++} \right\} \\
&= \left\{ \hat{q} \in \mathbb{R}^{J-1} \middle| \hat{q} = A^T_{\cdot(-1)} \pi \wedge 1 = \sum_{s \in \mathcal{S}^+(A_{\cdot 1})} A_{s1} \pi_s \right. \\
&\qquad \left. \text{for some} \quad \pi \in \mathbb{R}^S_{++} \right\} \\
&= \left\{ \hat{q} \in \mathbb{R}^{J-1} \middle| \hat{q} = \sum_{s \in \mathcal{S}^+(A_{\cdot 1})} \frac{\mu_s}{A_{s1}} A^T_{s(-1)} + \sum_{s \in \mathcal{S}^0(A_{\cdot 1})} \mu_s A^T_{s(-1)} \right. \\
&\qquad \left. \text{for some} \quad \mu \in \mathbb{R}^S_{++} \quad \text{with} \quad \sum_{s \in \mathcal{S}^+(A_{\cdot 1})} \mu_s = 1 \right\} \\
&= int \left( conv \left\{ \left( \frac{1}{A_{s1}} A^T_{s(-1)} \right)_{s \in \mathcal{S}^+(A_{\cdot 1})} \right\} \right) \\
&\qquad + \sum_{s \in \mathcal{S}^0(A_{\cdot 1})} \left\{ \mu_s A^T_{s(-1)} \middle| \mu_s \in \mathbb{R}_{++} \right\} \quad ,
\end{aligned}
$$

i.e. $\mathcal{Q}_{norm}(A)$ is either the interior of a convex polyeder where the extremal directions are contained in $\left\{ A^T_{s(-1)} \middle| s \in \mathcal{S}^0(A_{\cdot 1}) \right\}$, or it is the whole space $\mathbb{R}^{J-1}$.

Define

$$
\mathcal{E}_{norm}(A) := \left\{ \hat{q}^* \in \mathcal{Q}_{norm}(A) \middle| \exists \left(\theta^{*i}\right)_{i=1,\dots,I} \quad \text{with} \right. \\
\left. \left( \left(\theta^{*i}\right)_{i=1,\dots,I}, \begin{pmatrix} 1 \\ \hat{q}^* \end{pmatrix} \right) \quad \text{being an FM-equilibrium} \right\}
$$

as the set of normalized equilibrium price vectors. Remember that the GEI-economy exhibits a *unique* normalized financial markets equilibrium if $\sharp\mathcal{E}_{norm}(A) = 1$.

Note that the notation does not take into account the dependence on utility functions and endowments. This is because here we am only interested in the effect of changing the asset structure while consumers' characteristics remain fixed.

At first we have to specify the idea of perturbation of the asset matrix. Therefore, we define the maximum norm for a matrix $M \in \mathbb{R}^{N \times L}$ by

$$\|M\|_{\max} := \max\{|M_{nl}| \mid n \in \{1,\ldots,N\}, l \in \{1,\ldots,L\}\} \quad .$$

The same notation is used for all $N, L \in \mathbb{N}$. Besides, notice that for $L = 1$ or $N = 1$ one obtains a vector norm.
An *$\epsilon$-neighborhood* of some $\bar{M} \in \mathbb{R}^{N \times L}$ is defined as

$$\mathcal{V}_\epsilon(\bar{M}) := \left\{ M \in \mathbb{R}^{N \times L} \middle| \|\bar{M} - M\|_{\max} < \epsilon \right\} \quad .$$

Let $\bar{A} \in \mathbb{R}^{S \times J}$ and $\epsilon > 0$. An asset matrix $A \in \mathbb{R}^{S \times J}$ is an *$\epsilon$-perturbation* of $\bar{A}$ if and only if $\|\bar{A} - A\| < \epsilon$ or equivalently $A \in \mathcal{V}_\epsilon(\bar{A})$, i.e. $A$ differs in each entry by less than $\epsilon$ from the corresponding entry of $\bar{A}$. Therefore, the set of all $\epsilon$-perturbations of $\bar{A}$ is given by the $\epsilon$-neighborhood of $\bar{A}$.
Before we start with a detailed proof of the main theorem of this section (Theorem 6.18) let me give a brief outline.
To obtain robustness of the equilibrium price set against perturbations of the asset matrix, at first these perturbations are restricted such that the perturbed matrices display the same rank as the "original" one and their span remains to contain a desirable portfolio.[81] Then, the Implicit Function Theorem is applied to obtain an asset demand function on the—beforehand defined—reduced set of asset matrices and their no-arbitrage price systems which is continuously differentiable.[82] The same theorem is used a second time to get local uniqueness and lower hemi-continuity of equilibrium price sets under a further restriction of perturbations.[83] Besides, it is possible to reduce no-arbitrage price sets to a compact subset which has to contain all additional equilibrium price systems, but none of the "old" ones.[84] The compact price set allows to apply the Maximum Theorem on the function defined by the maximum norm of asset demand and restrict perturbations[85] such that this function is bounded away from zero and takes its minimum.
To summarize, the proof of Theorem 6.18 can be divided into three main steps:

(i) the proof of "continuous differentiability" of asset demand on some subset of its whole range;

(ii) the proof of lower hemi-continuity of the equilibrium price correspondence, i.e. perturbations of the asset matrix can be restricted such that for each

[81] This induces the definitions of $\epsilon_1$ and $\epsilon_2$ in the following proof.
[82] Within this context $\epsilon_4$ and $\epsilon_5$ will be defined.
[83] Compare $\epsilon_6$.
[84] Compare the definitions of $\epsilon_7$, $\epsilon_8$, $\epsilon_9$, and $\epsilon_{10}$ of which some are only used in the proofs presented in the appendix.
[85] Compare definition of $\epsilon_{11}$.

equilibrium price systems of the "original" matrix there is some "nearby" equilibrium price system of the "new" matrix;

(iii) the proof of upper hemi-continuity of the equilibrium price correspondence, i.e. perturbations can be restricted further such that in addition to the equilibrium price systems obtained by the second step no other equilibrium price systems arise.

One problem in the consideration of $\epsilon$-perturbations of some matrix $\bar{A}$ satisfying 1.5 respectively 6.4 consists in the fact that the set of all asset matrices satisfying these assumptions is not an open subset of $\mathbb{R}^{S \times J}$. Therefore, it might happen that for given $\bar{A}$ one cannot specify an $\epsilon > 0$ such that for all $A \in \mathcal{V}_\epsilon(\bar{A})$ Assumption 1.5 respectively 6.4 is satisfied.

EXAMPLE 6.7

*Take the asset matrix* $\bar{A} = \begin{pmatrix} 1 & 0 \\ 0 & 1 \\ 0 & 0 \end{pmatrix}$ *which satisfies Assumption 1.5 as well as Assumption 6.4. For all* $\epsilon > 0$ *one observes* $A = \begin{pmatrix} 1 & 0 \\ 0 & 1 \\ -\frac{\epsilon}{2} & -\frac{\epsilon}{2} \end{pmatrix} \in \mathcal{V}_\epsilon(\bar{A})$ *even though 1.5 respectively 6.4 are violated.*

Assume $\bar{A}$ satisfies Assumptions 1.6 and 6.4. Let me first start with the assumption of a maximal rank. If $rank\,\bar{A} = J$, there has to be some subset $G \subseteq \{1, \ldots, S\}$ with $\sharp G = J$ such that $rank\,\bar{A}_{G\cdot} = J$ or equivalently that the determinant of this matrix is unequal to zero. Therefore, one can define an $\epsilon_1$-neighborhood of $\bar{A}_{G\cdot}$ such that the determinant of all $J \times J$-dimensional matrices in this neighborhood is unequal to zero, i.e. the matrices satisfy $rank = J$. This implies for all $A \in \mathcal{V}_{\epsilon_1}(\bar{A})$ the property $rank\,A = J$.
Now consider Assumption 6.4, i.e. $A_{\cdot 1} > 0$. Here one has to distinguish the cases (i) to (iii) for $\bar{A}$.

(i) Choose $\epsilon_2 \in (0, \min\{\epsilon_1, \bar{A}_{11}, \ldots, \bar{A}_{S1}\ right\})$. Then all $A \in \mathcal{V}_{\epsilon_2}(\bar{A})$ satisfy Assumptions 1.6 and 6.4 and $\epsilon$-perturbations do not have to be restricted.

(ii) Modeling first period consumption only those $\epsilon$-perturbations of $\bar{A}$ seem to make sense which make it possible to stay within this framework, i.e. one only perturbs the matrix $\breve{A}$ and all the other entries of $\bar{A}$ remain fixed. Choose $\epsilon_2 > 0$ such that for all $\dot{A} \in \mathcal{V}_{\epsilon_2}\left(\breve{A}\right)$ it is $rank\,\dot{A} = J - 1$. The existence of such an $\epsilon_2 > 0$ follows from the explanations given above for Assumption 1.6.

Define the set of all restricted $\epsilon$-perturbations as

$$\left\{ A \in \mathbb{R}^{S \times J} \middle| A = \begin{pmatrix} 1 & 0 \\ 0 & \dot{A} \end{pmatrix} \quad \text{with} \quad \dot{A} \in \mathcal{V}_\epsilon \left( \check{A} \right) \right\} \quad .$$

Choosing $\epsilon = \epsilon_2$ all restricted $\epsilon$-perturbations of $\bar{A}$ model first period consumption and satisfy Assumptions 1.6 and 6.4.

(iii) Choose $\epsilon_2 \in 0, \min \left\{ \epsilon_1, \min \left\{ A_{s1} \left| s \in \mathcal{S}^+ \left( \bar{A}_{\cdot 1} \right) \right. \right\} \right\}$ and define the set of all restricted $\epsilon$-perturbations of $\bar{A}$ as

$$\left\{ A \in \mathbb{R}^{S \times J} \middle| A_{s1} = 0 \, \forall \, s \in \mathcal{S}^0 \left( \bar{A}_{\cdot 1} \right) \wedge \left\| \bar{A} - A \right\|_{\max} < \epsilon \right\} \quad .$$

With $\epsilon = \epsilon_2$ all restricted $\epsilon$-perturbations satisfy Assumptions 1.6 and 6.4.

In the general Finance GEI-model an asset matrix $\bar{A}$ does not satisfy Assumption 6.4, but only Assumption 1.5. Assume $\bar{A}\,\theta_{\bar{A}} > 0$ where without loss of generality $\theta_{\bar{A}1} \neq 0$. Then for

$$\tilde{A}\left(\bar{A}\right) := \bar{A}\left(\theta_{\bar{A}}, e^2, \ldots, e^J\right) \quad .$$

the Assumption 6.4 is satisfied and since $\langle \bar{A} \rangle = \left\langle \tilde{A}\left(\bar{A}\right) \right\rangle$ for the corresponding GEI-economies there is a one-to-one correspondence between the equilibria (compare Proposition 6.1 and Proposition 1.1). Therefore—since attention will be restricted to Assumption 6.4 and the above-defined (restricted) perturbations of matrices satisfying this assumption—the following point has to be clarified:

LEMMA 6.6
*Having defined a set of (restricted) $\tilde{\epsilon}$-perturbations of $\tilde{A}\left(\bar{A}\right)$, there is an $\epsilon$ and restricted $\epsilon$-perturbations of $\bar{A}$ such that the attainable matrices $A$ satisfy $\tilde{A}\left(A\right)$ to be (restricted) $\tilde{\epsilon}$-perturbations of $\tilde{A}\left(\bar{A}\right)$.*

Proof: The proof which requires distinction of the three types of matrices is deferred to Appendix 6.A.
Now assume a GEI-economy $\left\{ \mathbb{R}^S, \left(U^i, \omega^i\right)_{i=1,\ldots,I}, \bar{A} \right\}$ is given where $\bar{A}$ satisfies Assumption 6.4. The long-term aim is to investigate whether one is able to define some set of (restricted) $\epsilon$-perturbations of $\bar{A}$ such that all elements $A$ satisfy

$$\sharp\, GEI_{norm}\left(A\right) = \sharp\, GEI_{norm}\left(\bar{A}\right) \quad ,$$

i.e. the number of normalized equilibria for the perturbed asset structure is the same as for the original one.
To avoid the necessity of distinction of cases (i) to (iii) all the time, we define

$$\bar{C} := \begin{cases} \bar{A}, & \text{if } \bar{A} \text{ satisfies case (i);} \\ \breve{A}, & \text{if } \bar{A} \text{ satisfies case (ii);} \\ \left(\bar{A}_{sj}\right)_{(s,j)\in\{1,\ldots,S\}\times\{1,\ldots,J\}\setminus\left\{(s,1)|s\in\mathcal{S}^0\left(\bar{A}_{\cdot 1}\right)\right\}}, & \text{if } \bar{A} \text{ satisfies case (iii);} \end{cases}$$

and

$$\mathcal{R} := \begin{cases} \mathbb{R}^{S\times J}, & \text{if } \bar{A} \text{ satisfies case (i);} \\ \mathbb{R}^{(S-1)\times(J-1)}, & \text{if } \bar{A} \text{ satisfies case (ii);} \\ \mathbb{R}^{\sharp\mathcal{S}^+\left(\bar{A}_{\cdot 1}\right)} \times \mathbb{R}^{S\times(J-1)}, & \text{if } \bar{A} \text{ satisfies case (iii).} \end{cases}$$

Notice that for case (iii) $\bar{C}$ does not have the form of a matrix, but looks as follows:

$$\bar{C} = \left(\bar{C}_{\cdot 1}, \bar{C}_{\cdot(-1)}\right)$$

where $\bar{C}_{\cdot(-1)} = \bar{A}_{\cdot(-1)}$ is an $S \times (J-1)$ matrix and $\bar{C}_{\cdot 1} = \left(\bar{A}_{s1}\right)_{s\in\mathcal{S}^+\left(\bar{A}_{\cdot 1}\right)}$ is a column vector with $\sharp\mathcal{S}^+\left(\bar{A}_{\cdot 1}\right) < S$ entries. For simplification we transfer indexation from $A$ to $C$.
With this notation all (restricted) $\epsilon_2$-perturbations in the different cases can be summarized by

$$\mathcal{V}_{\epsilon_2}\left(\bar{C}\right) := \left\{C \in \mathcal{R} \,|\, \left\|\bar{C} - C\right\|_{\max} < \epsilon_2\right\}$$

where $\epsilon_2 > 0$ was specified before. Analogously, we define the reverse direction, i.e.

(i)

$$A_{sj}\left(C\right) := C_{sj} \quad \forall \left(s,j\right) \in \{1,\ldots,S\} \times \{1,\ldots,J\} \quad ;$$

(ii)

$$A_{sj}\left(C\right) := \begin{pmatrix} 1, & & \text{if} \quad (s,j) = (1,1)\,, \\ 0, & \text{if} & (s,j) \in (\{1\}\times\{2,\ldots,J\}) \cup (\{2,\ldots,S\}\times\{1\})\,, \\ C_{sj}, & & \text{else;} \end{pmatrix}$$

(iii)

$$A_{sj}\left(C\right) := \begin{pmatrix} C_{sj}, & \text{if} \quad (s,j) \in \{1,\ldots,S\} \times \{1,\ldots,J\} \setminus \left\{(s,1) |\, s \in \mathcal{S}^0\left(\bar{A}_{\cdot 1}\right.\right. \\ 0, & \text{else;} \end{pmatrix}$$

where $A\left(\bar{C}\right) = \bar{A}$ and $A\left(\mathcal{V}_{\epsilon_2}\left(\bar{C}\right)\right)$ is the set of all (restricted) $\epsilon_2$-perturbations of $\bar{A}$. From now on take asset demand as a function of $\hat{q}$ and $C$, i.e.

$$\tilde{g}(\hat{q}, C) := g(1, \hat{q}, A(C)) \quad .$$

Correspondingly, it is

$$\tilde{\mathcal{Q}}_{norm}(C) := \mathcal{Q}_{norm}(A(C))$$

such that $\tilde{\theta}$ is defined on $\mathcal{D}_{\epsilon_2}$ where

$$\mathcal{D}_{\epsilon_2} := \left\{ (\hat{q}, C) \in \mathbb{R}^{J-1} \times \mathcal{R} \middle| \|\bar{C} - C\|_{\max} < \epsilon_2 \wedge \hat{q} \in \tilde{\mathcal{Q}}_{norm}(C) \right\} \quad .$$

$\mathcal{D}_{\epsilon_2}$ is an open connected set in $\mathbb{R}^{J-1} \times \mathcal{R}$. This is a consequence of the following lemma because $\tilde{\mathcal{Q}}_{norm}(C)$ is an open convex set in $\mathbb{R}^{J-1}$ for all $C \in \mathcal{V}_{\epsilon_2}(\bar{C})$.

LEMMA 6.7
*Let $\mathcal{K} \subseteq \tilde{\mathcal{Q}}_{norm}(\bar{C})$ be a compact set. Then, there is an $\epsilon_3 \in (0, \epsilon_2)$ such that for all $C \in \mathcal{V}_{\epsilon_3}(\bar{C})$ it is $\mathcal{K} \subseteq \tilde{\mathcal{Q}}_{norm}(C)$.*

Proof: See Appendix 6.A.
Take, for example, case (ii) with $S = 4$ and $J = 3$ such that

$$\tilde{\mathcal{Q}}_{norm}(\bar{C}) = \left\{ \hat{q} \in \mathbb{R}^2 \middle| \hat{q} = \bar{C}^T \pi \quad \text{for some} \quad \pi \in \mathbb{R}^3_{++} \right\} \quad .$$

The intuition for the lemma is given by Figure 6.2 where

$$\bar{A} = \begin{pmatrix} 1 & 0 & 0 \\ 0 & 1 & 4 \\ 0 & 2 & 1 \\ 0 & 4 & 1 \end{pmatrix} \quad \text{or} \quad \bar{C}^T = \begin{pmatrix} 1 & 2 & 4 \\ 4 & 1 & 1 \end{pmatrix} \quad .$$

The shaded area defines $\tilde{\mathcal{Q}}_{norm}(\bar{C})$. It is obvious that small perturbations of $\bar{C}$ are possible such that $\mathcal{K}$ remains within the area defined by convex combinations of positive multiples of the row vectors of $C$.
Note that in case (ii) and (iii) the correspondence $cl\left(\tilde{\mathcal{Q}}_{norm}(C)\right)$ need not be continuous in $\bar{C}$.[86]

EXAMPLE 6.8
*Again take $\bar{A} = \begin{pmatrix} 1 & 0 \\ 0 & 1 \\ 0 & 0 \end{pmatrix}$. Therefore it is $\bar{C}_{case(ii)} = \begin{pmatrix} c1 \\ 0 \end{pmatrix}$ and $\bar{C}_{case(iii)} =$*

[86]For the concept of continuous correspondences we refer to Takayama [1974, p. 151].

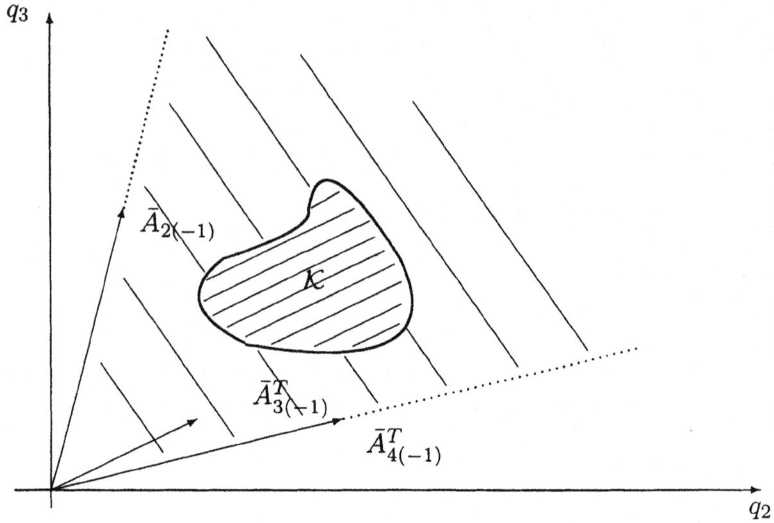


*Figure 6.2.* Example for Lemma 6.7.

$\left(1, \begin{pmatrix}0\\1\\0\end{pmatrix}\right)$. *Observe* $cl\left(\tilde{Q}_{norm}\left(\bar{C}_{case(ii)}\right)\right) = cl\left(\tilde{Q}_{norm}\left(\bar{C}_{case(iii)}\right)\right) = \mathbb{R}_+$. *On the other hand for* $C_{case(ii)} = \begin{pmatrix}1\\-\epsilon\end{pmatrix}$ *and* $C_{case(iii)} = \left(1, \begin{pmatrix}0\\1\\-\epsilon\end{pmatrix}\right)$ *it is* $cl\left(\tilde{Q}_{norm}\left(C_{case(ii)}\right)\right) = cl\left(\tilde{Q}_{norm}\left(C_{case(iii)}\right)\right) = \mathbb{R}$ *for* $\epsilon > 0$ *arbitrarily small.*

Note that in case (i) the correspondence $cl\left(\tilde{Q}_{norm}(C)\right)$ is continuous in $\bar{C}$ because the convex hull of a finite number of points is continuous in the coordinates of these points. For cases (ii) and (iii) one observes that even if one excludes such strange matrices with $\bar{A}_{s\cdot} = 0$ for some $s \in \{1, \ldots, S\}$ the correspondence $cl\left(\tilde{Q}_{norm}(C)\right)$ is not continuous in $\bar{C}$ because the set is unbounded and changing $\bar{C}$ to $C$ might change the extremal directions such that points on such an extremal ray are arbitrarily far away from $cl\left(\tilde{Q}_{norm}(\bar{C})\right)$ if their distance to the origin is sufficiently large.

## 5.2 Continuous Differentiability of Asset Demand

With respect to the first order conditions (6.21) and (6.22) define

$$F^i\left(\theta^i,\lambda^i,\hat{q},C\right) := \begin{pmatrix} \nabla U^i\left(\omega^i + A\left(C\right)\theta^i\right)A\left(C\right) - \lambda^i\binom{1}{\hat{q}} \\ \left(1,\hat{q}^T\right)\theta^i \end{pmatrix}$$

where one knows (compare, for example, Chapter 4 that for all $\left(\breve{q},\breve{C}\right) \in \mathcal{D}_{\epsilon_2}\left(\bar{C}\right)$ there is some $\breve{\theta}^i \in \mathbb{R}^J$ and $\breve{\lambda}^i \in \mathbb{R}_{++}$ solving

$$F^i\left(\theta^i,\lambda^i,\breve{q},\breve{C}\right) = 0 \quad .$$

Since $\mathcal{D}_{\epsilon_2}\left(\bar{C}\right)$ is an open set in $\mathbb{R}^{J-1} \times \mathcal{R}$, it is obvious that for all $\left(\breve{\theta}^i,\breve{\lambda}^i,\breve{q},\breve{C}\right)$ with $F^i\left(\breve{\theta}^i,\breve{\lambda}^i,\breve{q},\breve{C}\right) = 0$ there is an open neighborhood on which $F^i$ is continuously differentiable. Therefore, the Implicit Function Theorem can be applied: for all $\left(\breve{q},\breve{C}\right) \in \mathcal{D}_{\epsilon_2}\left(\bar{C}\right)$ there exist $\epsilon_4,\epsilon_5 > 0$ such that there is a continuously differentiable function

$$\left(\tilde{\theta}^i,\tilde{\lambda}^i\right) : \mathcal{V}_{\epsilon_4}\left(\breve{q},\breve{C}\right) \to \mathcal{V}_{\epsilon_5}\left(\breve{\theta}^i,\breve{\lambda}^i\right)$$

with

$$F^i\left(\tilde{\theta}^i\left(\hat{q},C\right),\tilde{\lambda}^i\left(\hat{q},C\right),\hat{q},C\right) = 0 \quad .$$

One only has to prove

$$\partial_{\theta^i,\lambda^i}F^i\left(\breve{\theta}^i,\breve{\lambda}^i,\breve{q},\breve{C}\right) := \begin{pmatrix} A^T\left(\breve{C}\right)D^2U^i\left(\omega^i + A\left(\breve{C}\right)\breve{\theta}^i\right)A\left(\breve{C}\right) & -\binom{1}{\breve{q}} \\ \left(1,\breve{q}^T\right) & 0 \end{pmatrix}$$

to be invertible which follows from strict quasi-concavity of $U^i$ and the assumption of non-redundant assets (Assumption 1.6).
Therefore, since $\mathcal{D}_{\epsilon_2}$ is connected, first order conditions (6.22) and (6.22) define a continuously differentiable function

$$\tilde{\theta}^i : \mathcal{D}_{\epsilon_2}\left(\bar{C}\right) \to \mathbb{R}^J \quad .$$

Continuous differentiability is an additive property such that $\tilde{G}\left(\hat{q},C\right) := \sum_{i=1}^I \tilde{g}^i\left(\hat{q},C\right)$ is also continuous differentiable on $\mathcal{D}_{\epsilon_2}\left(\bar{C}\right)$.

PROPOSITION 6.8 (CONTINUOUS DIFFERENTIABILITY OF ASSET DEMAND)

*For each GEI-economy* $\left\{\left(U^i,\omega^i\right)_{i=1,\ldots,I},\bar{A}\right\}$ *where* $\bar{A}$ *satisfies the Assumption 6.4, there is an* $\epsilon_2 > 0$ *such that market demand for assets*

$$\tilde{G} : \mathcal{D}_{\epsilon_2}(\bar{C}) \to \mathbb{R}^J$$

*is continuously differentiable.*

REMARK 6.2
*It would be nice to have the differentiability of asset demand $\theta(\hat{q}, A)$ on the whole set*

$$\mathcal{D} := \left\{ (\hat{q}, A) \in \mathbb{R}^{J-1} \times \mathbb{R}^{S \times J} \middle| \, rank\, A = J, A_{\cdot 1} > 0 \wedge \hat{q} \in \mathcal{Q}_{norm}(A) \right\} \quad .$$

*However, as already mentioned, this set is not open. Therefore, aiming at application of the Implicit Function Theorem it is at least necessary to restrict to the set*

$$\tilde{\mathcal{D}} := \left\{ (\hat{q}, A) \in \mathbb{R}^{J-1} \times \mathbb{R}^{S \times J} \middle| \, rank\, A = J, A_{\cdot 1} \gg 0 \wedge \hat{q} \in \mathcal{Q}_{norm}(A) \right\} \quad .$$

*Even this restriction is not sufficient to obtain a continuous function $G(\hat{q}, A)$ defined on $\tilde{\mathcal{D}}$ because*

$$\tilde{\mathcal{A}} := \left\{ A \in \mathbb{R}^{S \times J} \middle| \, rank\, A = J \wedge A_{\cdot 1} \gg 0 \right\}$$

*is not connected as can be proved with a simple example: assume $S = J$ and take two different matrices $\hat{A}, \check{A} \in \tilde{\mathcal{A}}$ with $\det\left(\hat{A}\right) > 0$ and $\det\left(\check{A}\right) < 0$. Since the determinant function is continuous in the entries of the matrix, for each continuous path connecting $\hat{A}$ and $\check{A}$ there has to be some element of the path with determinant value equal to zero. This contradicts the assumption on the rank.*

## 5.3 Robustness of the Number of Equilibria

Under the normalization used in this section regularity of asset demand requires

$$rank\, \partial_{\hat{q}} G_{-1}(1, \hat{q}, \bar{A}) = J - 1$$

for all $\hat{q} \in \mathcal{E}_{norm}(\bar{A})$. For given regularity the set of normalized equilibrium price systems is finite, i.e. $\mathcal{E}_{norm}(\bar{A}) = \left\{\hat{q}^{*1}, \ldots, \hat{q}^{*N}\right\}$ for some $N \in \mathbb{N}$. Because of Walras' Law, i.e. $\left(1, \hat{q}^T\right) \tilde{G}(\hat{q}, A(C)) = 0$, to investigate equilibrium properties of a price system it is sufficient to test for the clearing of $J - 1$ asset markets, i.e.

$$\tilde{F}(\hat{q}, C) := \tilde{G}_{-1}(\hat{q}, C) = 0 \quad . \tag{6.23}$$

This function $\tilde{F} : \mathcal{D}_{\epsilon_2} \rightarrow \mathbb{R}^{J-1}$ is continuously differentiable and satisfies $\tilde{F}\left(\hat{q}^{*1}, \bar{C}\right) = \ldots = \tilde{F}\left(\hat{q}^{*N}, \bar{C}\right) = 0$. Additionally—because of regularity—the matrices

$$\partial_{\hat{q}} \tilde{F}\left(\hat{q}^{*n}, \bar{C}\right) = \partial_{\hat{q}} \tilde{G}_{-1}\left(\hat{q}^{*n}, \bar{C}\right) = \partial_{\hat{q}} G_{-1}\left(1, \hat{q}^{*n}, \bar{A}\right), n = 1, \ldots, N,$$

are invertible which allows to apply the Implicit Function Theorem on equation (6.23) for $\bar{C}$ and all $\hat{q}^{*n}, n = 1, \ldots, N$: there exist $\delta^n > 0$ and $\epsilon^n \in (0, \epsilon_2)$ such that there are continuously differentiable equilibrium price functions

$$\hat{q}_*^n : \mathcal{V}_{\epsilon^n}\left(\bar{C}\right) \rightarrow \mathcal{V}_{\delta^n}\left(\hat{q}^{*n}\right)$$

with $\tilde{F}\left(\hat{q}_*^n\left(C\right), C\right) = \tilde{\theta}_{-1}\left(\hat{q}_*^n\left(C\right), C\right) = 0$ for all $C \in \mathcal{V}_{\epsilon^n}\left(\bar{C}\right)$ and for given $C \in \mathcal{V}_{\epsilon^n}\left(\bar{C}\right)$ the price system $\hat{q}_*^n\left(C\right)$ is the only element of $\mathcal{V}_{\delta^n}\left(\hat{q}^{*n}\right)$ which satisfies equation (6.23).
With $\epsilon_6 := \min\left\{\epsilon^n \middle| n = 1, \ldots, N\right\}$ this implies

$$\sharp\, \mathcal{E}_{norm}\left(\bar{A}\right) \leq \sharp\, \mathcal{E}_{norm}\left(A\left(C\right)\right)$$

for all $C \in \mathcal{V}_{\epsilon_6}\left(\bar{C}\right)$, i.e. for all (restricted) $\epsilon_6$-perturbations of $\bar{A}$ the corresponding GEI-economy is characterized by at least the same number of equilibria as the starting economy. Even stronger: there exist continuously differentiable equilibrium price paths!

THEOREM 6.17 (LOWER HEMI-CONTINUITY OF EQUILIBRIUM PRICES. [PILGRIM, 2001])[87]
*For all regular GEI-economies* $\left\{\left(U^i, \omega^i\right)_{i=1,\ldots,I}, \bar{A}\right\}$ *which satisfy Assumption 6.4 there exists some* $\epsilon > 0$ *such that all GEI-economies* $\left\{\left(U^i, \omega^i\right)_{i=1,\ldots,I}, A\right\}$ *with* $A$ *(restricted)* $\epsilon$*-perturbation of* $\bar{A}$ $\left(C \in \mathcal{V}_\epsilon\left(\bar{C}\right)\right)$ *satisfy*

$$\sharp\, \mathcal{E}_{norm}\left(\bar{A}\right) \leq \sharp\, \mathcal{E}_{norm}\left(A\right) \quad .$$

*If* $\mathcal{E}_{norm}\left(\bar{A}\right) = \left\{\hat{q}^{*1}, \ldots, \hat{q}^{*N}\right\}$, *there are continuously differentiable functions*

$$\hat{q}_*^n : \mathcal{V}_\epsilon\left(\bar{C}\right) \rightarrow \mathcal{V}_\delta\left(\hat{q}^{*n}\right), n = 1, \ldots, N,$$

*for some* $\delta > 0$ *with* $\left\{\hat{q}_*^1\left(C\right), \ldots, \hat{q}_*^N\left(C\right)\right\} \subseteq \mathcal{E}_{norm}\left(A\left(C\right)\right)$ *whenever* $C \in \mathcal{V}_\epsilon\left(\bar{C}\right)$.

---

[87]By application of Lemma 6.6 this theorem can be transferred for more general matrices satisfying Assumption 1.5.

In other words: the set $\mathcal{E}_{norm}(A(C))$ is a lower hemi-continuous correspondence in $\bar{C}$. At this point it seems to be interesting to know whether $\mathcal{E}_{norm}(A(C))$ is also upper hemi-continuous and therefore continuous in $\bar{C}$. It will be shown that this is even true for those market structures for which the set $cl\left(\tilde{\mathcal{Q}}_{norm}(C)\right)$ is not upper hemi-continuous.

LEMMA 6.8
*There is some $\epsilon_{10} \in (0, \epsilon_6)$ and a compact set $\mathcal{Q}^H \subset \mathbb{R}^{J-1}$ such that whenever $C \in cl(\mathcal{V}_{\epsilon_{10}}(\bar{C}))$*

- $\mathcal{Q}^H \subseteq \tilde{\mathcal{Q}}_{norm}(C) \cap \tilde{\mathcal{Q}}_{norm}(\bar{C})$,
- *for all equilibrium price systems $\hat{q}^*(C)$ with respect to $C$ which satisfy $\hat{q}^*(C) \notin \left\{\hat{q}^1_*(C), \ldots, \hat{q}^N_*(C)\right\}$ it is*

$$\hat{q}^*(C) \in \mathcal{Q}^H \quad ,$$

- *and $\tilde{\theta}_{-1}(\hat{q}, \bar{C}) \neq 0$ for all $\hat{q} \in \mathcal{Q}^H$.*

Proof: See Appendix 6.A.
Since $\tilde{\theta}_{-1} : \mathcal{D}_{\epsilon_2} \to \mathbb{R}^{J-1}$ is continuous, this is also true for $\left\|\tilde{\theta}_{-1}(.,.)\right\|_{\max}$ on $\mathcal{Q}^H \times cl(\mathcal{V}_{\epsilon_{10}}(\bar{C}))$ because $\mathcal{Q}^H \subseteq \tilde{\mathcal{Q}}_{norm}(C)$ when $C \in cl(\mathcal{V}_{\epsilon_{10}}(\bar{C}))$. Defining

$$m := \min_{\hat{q} \in \mathcal{Q}^H} \left\|\tilde{\theta}_{-1}(\hat{q}, \bar{C})\right\|_{\max}$$

it is $m > 0$ because $\left\|\tilde{\theta}_{-1}(\hat{q}, \bar{C})\right\|_{\max}$ is a continuous function on a compact set which takes its minimum, but is unequal to zero. Since $\left\|\tilde{\theta}_{-1}(.,.)\right\|_{\max}$ is a continuous function on a compact set, there is some $\epsilon_{11} > 0$ such that $C \in \mathcal{V}_{\epsilon_{11}}(\bar{C})$ implies

$$\left|\left\|\tilde{\theta}_{-1}(\hat{q}, C)\right\|_{\max} - \left\|\tilde{\theta}_{-1}(\hat{q}, \bar{C})\right\|_{\max}\right| < m$$

for all $\hat{q} \in \mathcal{Q}^H$ and therefore $\left\|\tilde{\theta}_{-1}(\hat{q}, C)\right\|_{\max} \neq 0$ for all $\hat{q} \in \mathcal{Q}^H$. Together with the last theorem one obtains:

THEOREM 6.18 (ROBUSTNESS OF THE NUMBER OF EQUILIBRIA) [88]
*For all regular GEI-economies $\left\{(U^i, \omega^i)_{i=1,\ldots,I}, \bar{A}\right\}$ satisfying Assumption 6.4*

[88] By application of Lemma 6.6 this theorem can be transferred for more general matrices satisfying Assumption 1.5.

*there exists some* $\epsilon > 0$ *such that all GEI-economies* $\left\{ (U^i, \omega^i)_{i=1,\ldots,I}, A \right\}$ *with* $A$ *(restricted)* $\epsilon$*-perturbation of* $\bar{A}$ $(C \in \mathcal{V}_\epsilon(\bar{C}))$ *satisfy*

$$\sharp\, \mathcal{E}_{norm}(\bar{A}) = \sharp\, \mathcal{E}_{norm}(A) \quad .$$

One could think about doing the proof of this theorem not in the way we do it, but via the so-called Grassmanian manifolds which are used in different proofs of existence of equilibria in GEI-models because they allow to circumvent the problem of a change in the rank of the matrix of income transfers.[89] we chose another approach for different reasons.

The first one is that the concept of Grassmanians takes into account changing rank of the matrix of income transfers, but not the existence of a desirable portfolio. This is why existence proofs using Grassmanians either assume first period consumption when a parameterization of the economy by consumers' characteristics is given or—when the economy is defined via a market demand function—assume Walras' Law which implicitly requires the existence of a desirable portfolio.

The second argument against the usage of Grassmanians is that for considerations of uniqueness of equilibria it is more appropriate to work with the concept of financial markets equilibrium instead of the no-arbitrage equilibrium. But application of the concept of Grassmanians requires the no-arbitrage equilibrium concept. This is especially because a no-arbitrage equilibrium is independent of the asset matrix itself, but only depends on the space of income transfers, and the considered Grassmanians are sets of spaces of income transfers with given dimension. In contrast, for financial markets equilibria asset demand and asset prices strongly depend on the representation of the space of income transfers.

It would be more interesting to examine the consequences of perturbations allowing changes of the dimension of the trading space than to investigate perturbations within the set of asset structures with constant dimension. The main problem within this context consists in defining a suitable concept of small perturbations: the examples in Sections 6 and 7 demonstrate that as soon as the market structure changes from $S-1$ assets to complete markets and vice versa the number of equilibria might change. It does not matter how large the entries of the additional asset are, the decisive point is the introduction of a *new* direction and it does not play any role which new (non-redundant) asset is introduced. This question leaves much scope for further research.[90]

---

[89] The Grassmanian manifold $\mathcal{G}_{K,N}$ is the set of all $N$-dimensional linear subspaces of $\mathbb{R}^K$.

[90] Cass and Citanna [1998] introduce a concept of "small" perturbations of the asset structure which allows changes in the rank of the matrix. They start with the introduction of either a redundant asset or one which is not traded and then vary the yield of this asset such that it becomes non-redundant respectively is traded. But Cass and Citanna's ([Cass and Citanna, 1998]) considerations strongly depend on a sufficient incompleteness

## 6. Limits of Transferability

When examining uniqueness of the equilibrium in incomplete markets models, one point is to check the limits of transferability from complete markets. In this section we refer to three different aspects.

The first one is quasi-linearity of utility. From Proposition 6.9 it is known that quasi-linearity is sufficient for a unique equilibrium whenever first period consumption is modeled. The example described here proves non-sufficiency of quasi-linearity for uniqueness of the equilibrium with incomplete markets in general. It stands out due to its simplicity because it is built on Kehoe's[91] well-established example on multiple Arrow-Debreu equilibria. Consumers' characteristics and the asset structure are explicitly given.

The second aspect of this section is to check what happens with Cobb-Douglas utility when markets are incomplete. We refer to an example given in Hens et al. [1999] where a computer algorithm is developed to compute "approximate" characteristics of an economy with multiple equilibria.

In the third part we demonstrate that even though all consumers satisfy the expected utility hypothesis with respect to an objective probability measure and there is no aggregate risk, there might exist multiple equilibria. The reason is that restricted trading hinders consumers from total risk sharing.

These examples examine restrictions on consumers' characteristics which are established to guarantee a unique Arrow-Debreu equilibrium. Since the only change is made for the asset structure while consumers' characteristics remain the same, the examples stress the decisive influence which the market structure has on uniqueness and multiplicity of equilibria. Regrettably, the results are quite destructive because they give the impression that it is much more difficult to obtain a unique equilibrium when markets are incomplete than when they are complete.

This section and the next one show that actual incompleteness of markets may generate effects that are in contrast to the well-established results in complete markets models: when transferring outcomes from complete to incomplete markets models—even under consideration of the simplest models—caution is advisible.

Due to Kehoe [1991] his example might be useful for testing the algorithms for computation of Arrow-Debreu equilibria. Similarly, the following examples could be used for computational algorithms developped for incomplete markets models. Since quite a lot of these new algorithms come from those ones originally developped for the Arrow-Debreu model, it seems reasonable to

---

of markets such that their concept also does not seem to be suitable for general situations, including the one with incompleteness of only one degree.

[91] [Kehoe, 1991, p. 2066]

check the changes by help of examples that emphazise the differences between the models.

## 6.1 Limits with Quasi-Linearity[92]

In this section we construct a GEI-economy with two consumers ($I = 2$) and three states ($S = 3$) which proves non-sufficiency of quasi-linearity for a unique equilibrium even though this follows in the Arrow-Debreu model.
Consumers are symmetrical to each other. Whereas utility is linear in state 1-consumption, for the other two states it is of CES-type, i.e.

$$U^i(x) = x_1 + \sum_{s=2}^{3} a_s^i \frac{\left(x_s^{b^i} - 1\right)}{b^i}$$

with $a_2^1 = a_3^2 = 1024$, $a_3^1 = a_2^2 = 1$, and $b^1 = b^2 = -4$. Consumers are endowed with

$$\omega^1 = (14, 12, 1)^T \quad \wedge \quad \omega^2 = (14, 1, 12)^T \quad .$$

When markets are complete, from Proposition 5.8 one knows the existence of a unique Arrow-Debreu equilibrium because in this case market demand is monotone.
The incomplete asset matrix is given by

$$\bar{A} = \begin{pmatrix} 0 & 0 \\ 1 & 0 \\ 0 & 1 \end{pmatrix} \quad .$$

When substituting tomorrow's budget constraint $x = \omega^i + A\,\theta$ and $\hat{\theta}_1 := \omega_2^i + \theta_1$ and $\hat{\theta}_2 := \omega_3^i + \theta_2$ the consumers' optimization problems become

$$\max_{\hat{\theta} \in \mathbb{R}_+^2} \omega_1^i + \left[\sum_{s=2}^{3} a_s^i \frac{\left(\hat{\theta}_{s-1}^{b^i} - 1\right)}{b^i}\right] \quad \text{s.t.} \quad q \cdot \hat{\theta} = q \cdot \begin{pmatrix} \omega_2^i \\ \omega_3^i \end{pmatrix} \quad .$$

This is equivalent to the consumers' maximization problems in Kehoe's[93] multiplicity-example. Moreover, market clearing conditions are equivalent as well. Therefore, the number of equilibria is also the same. According to Kehoe [1991, p. 2066] the equilibria are defined by

---

[92] Cf. Pilgrim [2002]

[93] [Kehoe, 1991, p. 2066]

$$\hat{\theta}^{a1} = \begin{pmatrix} 8.631 \\ 1.429 \end{pmatrix}, \quad \hat{\theta}^{a2} = \begin{pmatrix} 4.369 \\ 11.571 \end{pmatrix}, \quad q^a = \begin{pmatrix} 0.1129 \\ 0.8871 \end{pmatrix};$$
$$\hat{\theta}^{b1} = \begin{pmatrix} 10.4 \\ 2.6 \end{pmatrix}, \quad \hat{\theta}^{b2} = \begin{pmatrix} 2.6 \\ 10.4 \end{pmatrix}, \quad q^b = \begin{pmatrix} 0.5 \\ 0.5 \end{pmatrix};$$
$$\hat{\theta}^{c1} = \begin{pmatrix} 11.571 \\ 4.369 \end{pmatrix}, \quad \hat{\theta}^{c2} = \begin{pmatrix} 1.429 \\ 8.631 \end{pmatrix}, \quad q^c = \begin{pmatrix} 0.8871 \\ 0.1129 \end{pmatrix}.$$

Hence, an example has been found where the incompleteness of markets causes multiplicity of equilibria. However, the example would be very weak if multiplicity did hinge on the zero-row of the asset matrix for exactly that state for which utility functions are quasi-linear with respect to the corresponding consumption.

With reference to Section 5 the asset structure $\bar{A}$ is of type (iii) and allows only restricted perturbations. If the three known equilibria of the economy $GEI = \left\{\mathbb{R}^S, (U^i, \omega^i)_{i \in I}, \bar{A}\right\}$ are regular[94], Theorem 6.17[95] implies that the result is robust against restricted perturbations of $\bar{A}$, i.e. there is some $\epsilon > 0$ such that for all

$$A \in \left\{A \in \mathbb{R}^{S \times J} \middle| A_{11} = A_{31} = 0 \quad \wedge \quad \|A - \bar{A}\|_{\max} < \epsilon\right\}$$

the economy $GEI = \left\{\mathbb{R}^S, (U^i, \omega^i)_{i \in I}, A\right\}$ has multiple equilibria even though $GE = \left\{(U^i, \omega^i)_{i \in I}\right\}$ is characterized by a unique Arrow-Debreu equilibrium. Regularity of the three equilibria in $GEI = \left\{\mathbb{R}^S, (U^i, \omega^i)_{i \in I}, \bar{A}\right\}$ however follows directly from Kehoe's example[96] since he proves "his" second equilibrium to be regular and it is straightforward to show regularity of the other two equilibria.

REMARK 6.3

- *It can be shown that endowments $\omega_1^i = 14, i = 1, 2$, are sufficiently large to guarantee $x_1^i \gg 0, i = 1, 2$, in the relevant domain of feasible allocations for complete as well as for incomplete markets. Therefore, no problems arise because of corner solutions.*
- *Since it is not clarified whether $GEI = \left\{\mathbb{R}^S, (U^i, \omega^i)_{i \in I}, \bar{A}\right\}$ admits more than the three established equilibria and hence it is not known whether*

[94] Regularity of a single equilibrium price system is defined as the determinant of the Jacobian of market demand having maximal rank for this price system.

[95] To be more precise, this theorem has to be adapted in the following way: for a set of regular equilibria with respect to $\bar{A}$ an $\epsilon > 0$ can be defined such that for (restricted) $\epsilon$-perturbations of $\bar{A}$ the corresponding economies have at least the number of equilibria as are contained in the set.

[96] [Kehoe, 1991, p. 2066]

*further non-regular equilibria exist, Theorem 6.18 cannot be applied: the number of equilibria might change as a consequence of perturbing the asset structure. The only thing to be sure is the fact that there are at least three equilibria, i.e. multiplicity is guaranteed.*

- *The example is also robust against perturbations of consumers' characteristics* $a_s^i, b^i, i = 1, 2, s = 2, 3$.

The intuition behind the example is very simple: whereas individual asset demand functions are monotone with respect to the same normalizing vector when markets are complete, this property fails to hold for the considered incomplete asset structure.
To illuminate a little bit to what extent different asset structures effect the number of equilibria restrict attention to matrices of the form

$$A(\beta) := \begin{pmatrix} 0 & \beta \\ 1 & 0 \\ 0 & 1 \end{pmatrix}$$

with arbitrary $\beta \in \mathbb{R}$. For considerations of the number of equilibria this is equivalent to varying the second asset in

$$A = \left( \begin{pmatrix} 0 \\ 1 \\ 0 \end{pmatrix}, A_{\cdot 2} \right) \quad .$$

since the number of equilibria does not depend on the asset matrix itself, but on its span (Proposition 6.1). Because of symmetry of the example with respect to states 2 and 3 the same can be done for varying the first asset in

$$A - \left( A_{\cdot 1}, \begin{pmatrix} 0 \\ 0 \\ 1 \end{pmatrix} \right)$$

From the first considerations in this section one knows that for $\beta$ close or equal to zero there are multiple equilibria which excludes market asset demand to be monotone for any normalizing vectors. For $\beta \to \infty$ one observes collinearity between

$$\lim_{\beta \to \infty} A_{\cdot 2}(\beta) \quad \text{and} \quad \begin{pmatrix} 1 \\ 0 \\ 0 \end{pmatrix} \quad .$$

For the asset matrix

$$\bar{A}(\infty) := \begin{pmatrix} 0 & 1 \\ 1 & 0 \\ 0 & 0 \end{pmatrix}$$

however the function $\theta_1(q_1, 1, \bar{A}(\infty))$[97] is strictly decreasing in $q_1$ (eliminate state 3 from the maximization problem and then apply Proposition 6.9[98]) which implies uniqueness of the equilibrium. Since equilibria for $\bar{A}(\infty)$ are regular, because of Proposition 6.1 and Theorem 6.18 for large $\beta \in \mathbb{R}$ equilibria are unique. Besides the Implicit Function Theorem does not only assure continuity of the demand functions in prices and parameter $\beta \in \mathbb{R}$ for $\beta$ large, but also continuous differentiability. Therefore, demand for the first asset is strictly monotone in its own price for large $\beta \in \mathbb{R}$.[99]

Let us finish the considerations of the first example with some further remarks:

REMARK 6.4

- *Obviously, the monotonicity behavior of market demand for given $A(\beta)$ depends on the size of $\beta$.*
- *If the market demand function for given $A(\beta)$ is monotone with respect to some normalizing vector, then the market demand for other asset matrices with the same span is also monotone. Merely the normalizing vector changes (compare Proposition 6.4).*
- *For $\beta = -244/243$ the allocation $(\omega^1, \omega^2)$ is constrained Pareto-efficient with respect to $A(\beta)$ such that the equilibrium, namely the no-trade equilibrium, is unique (compare Proposition 6.5).*

The example given in this section is one of the easiest to imagine which proves the possibility of multiple equilibria for incomplete markets in spite of a unique Arrow-Debreu equilibrium. However, it would be interesting to know what happens under the expected utility hypothesis. Therefore, we refer to the following two subsections. Regrettably, examples given there violate Assumption 1.5 respectively are built on utility functions which are only implicitly defined by fixing some values of their first derivatives.

## 6.2 Limits with Cobb-Douglas Utility

One possibility to prove multiplicity of equilibria is to compute an equilibrium with a negative index because the Index Theorem 4.1 requires the existence of at

[97] Here, the price of the second asset is normalized to one.

[98] Note that the proposition is formulated for an economy with $\left(\bar{A}_{(-3)2}(\infty), \bar{A}_{(-3)1}(\infty)\right)$, but it is intuitive how to reformulate it to be appropriate at this point.

[99] One can apply the same reasoning for $\beta \to -\infty$, but another price normalization has to be chosen.

least one equilibrium with a positive index. However, standard computational methods are bound to compute equilibria with a positive index (compare Mas-Colell [1985]).

The example in Hens et al. [1999] is constructed by a new method to compute multiple equilibria. The main interest is to find out whether some class of economies, namely economies with Cobb-Douglas utility functions, admits multiple equilibria. The trick is to take the data of two prospective equilibria as given and use them to compute by means of a homotopy algorithm characteristics of an economy displaying these two equilibria. For a description of the algorithm compare Hens et al. [1999, Section 5]. The homotopy path is defined via transition from the first to the second equilibrium. Notice that Cobb-Douglas preferences allow to simplify the extended system which consists of the first order conditions and the market clearing condition (6.21), (6.22), and the market clearing condition. This system constitutes the basis for the algorithm. As pointed out in Section 4.1, when markets are complete an explicit pricing formula is given. Besides, market demand satisfies the property of strict gross substitution (Section 4.4). For incomplete markets this property fails and there does not exist an explicit pricing formula. As the following example (compare Hens et al. [1999, Example 4.2]) demonstrates, even the uniqueness of the equilibrium breaks down, i.e. all the merits of Cobb-Douglas preferences get lost when switching from complete to incomplete markets.

EXAMPLE 6.9 (HENS ET AL. [1999])
*Assume two agents are characterized by utility functions*

$$\begin{aligned} U^1\left(x^1\right) &= 0.1 \ln x_1^1 + 0.2 \ln x_2^1 + 0.3 \ln x_3^1 + 0.1 \ln x_4^1 + 0.3 \ln x_5^1\,, \\ U^2\left(x^1\right) &= 0.3 \ln x_1^2 + 0.2 \ln x_2^2 + 0.1 \ln x_3^2 + 0.3 \ln x_4^2 + 0.1 \ln x_5^2\,, \end{aligned}$$

*and endowments*

$$\omega^1 = \begin{pmatrix} 1.5042370526 \cdot 10^{-2} \\ 2.9374491276 \cdot 10^{-3} \\ 6.1116956313 \cdot 10^{-2} \\ 2.6125379370 \cdot 10^{-1} \\ 1.3112543254 \cdot 10^{-1} \end{pmatrix}, \omega^2 = \begin{pmatrix} 6.5484744962 \cdot 10^{-3} \\ 6.1159308802 \cdot 10^{-2} \\ 4.6047779430 \cdot 10^{-3} \\ 7.1874620630 \cdot 10^{-1} \\ 7.6887456746 \cdot 10^{-1} \end{pmatrix}.$$

*The asset structure is given by*

$$A = \begin{pmatrix} 1 & 0 & 0 \\ 0 & 1 & 0 \\ 0 & 0 & 1 \\ 1 & 5.7551080261 & -11.211070031 \\ -49.735960347 & -14.564562225 & 1.4276396811 \end{pmatrix}.$$

*This economy has at least the three equilibria:*

$$\left(\bar{x}^1,\bar{x}^2,\bar{\theta}^1,\bar{\theta}^2,\bar{q}\right) = \left( \begin{pmatrix} 3.1569068369\cdot 10^{-3} \\ 2.0847535004\cdot 10^{-2} \\ 5.6794692704\cdot 10^{-2} \\ 4.0\cdot 10^{-1} \\ 5.0\cdot 10^{-1} \end{pmatrix}, \begin{pmatrix} 1.9333947185\cdot 10^{-2} \\ 4.3249222926\cdot 10^{-2} \\ 8.9270415519\cdot 10^{-3} \\ 5.8\cdot 10^{-1} \\ 4.0\cdot 10^{-1} \end{pmatrix}, \begin{pmatrix} -1.2785472689\cdot 10^{-2} \\ 1.7910085876\cdot 10^{-2} \\ -4.3222636089\cdot 10^{-3} \end{pmatrix}, \begin{pmatrix} 1.2785472689\cdot 10^{-2} \\ -1.7910085876\cdot 10^{-2} \\ 4.3222636089\cdot 10^{-3} \end{pmatrix}, \begin{pmatrix} 1 \\ 1.1 \\ 1.6 \end{pmatrix} \right);$$

$$\left(\hat{x}^1,\hat{x}^2,\hat{\theta}^1,\hat{\theta}^2,\hat{q}\right) = \left( \begin{pmatrix} 3.2964558373\cdot 10^{-3} \\ 1.6548013477\cdot 10^{-2} \\ 5.2816066068\cdot 10^{-2} \\ 4.2\cdot 10^{-1} \\ 5.5\cdot 10^{-1} \end{pmatrix}, \begin{pmatrix} 1.9194398185\cdot 10^{-2} \\ 4.7548744453\cdot 10^{-2} \\ 1.2905668188\cdot 10^{-3} \\ 5.6\cdot 10^{-1} \\ 3.5\cdot 10^{-1} \end{pmatrix}, \begin{pmatrix} -1.2645923689\cdot 10^{-2} \\ 1.3610564349\cdot 10^{-2} \\ -8.3008902451\cdot 10^{-3} \end{pmatrix}, \begin{pmatrix} +1.2645923689\cdot 10^{-2} \\ -1.3610564349\cdot 10^{-2} \\ +8.3008902451\cdot 10^{-3} \end{pmatrix}, \begin{pmatrix} 1 \\ 1.6 \\ 1.1 \end{pmatrix} \right);$$

$$\left(\tilde{x}^1,\tilde{x}^2,\tilde{\theta}^1,\tilde{\theta}^2,\tilde{q}\right) = \left( \begin{pmatrix} 5.53593779\cdot 10^{-3} \\ 2.98288576\cdot 10^{-3} \\ 4.72273200\cdot 10^{-2} \\ 4.06826530\cdot 10^{-1} \\ 6.28208646\cdot 10^{-1} \end{pmatrix}, \begin{pmatrix} 1.69549162\cdot 10^{-2} \\ 6.11138722\cdot 10^{-2} \\ 1.84944143\cdot 10^{-2} \\ 5.73173470\cdot 10^{-1} \\ 2.71791354\cdot 10^{-1} \end{pmatrix}, \begin{pmatrix} -1.04064417\cdot 10^{-2} \\ 4.54366309\cdot 10^{-5} \\ -1.38896363\cdot 10^{-2} \end{pmatrix}, \begin{pmatrix} 1.04064417\cdot 10^{-2} \\ -4.54366309\cdot 10^{-5} \\ 1.38896363\cdot 10^{-2} \end{pmatrix}, \begin{pmatrix} -1 \\ 11.3031102 \\ 0.786198913 \end{pmatrix} \right).$$

Note that the asset matrix does not satisfy the assumption of a desirable portfolio, i.e. Assumption 1.5. However, this "defect" is innocuous since all consumers still satisfy their budget constraints with equality if at least one of the assets has a strictly positive price (compare Hens et al. [1999, Lemma 5.1]). This allows to work with the first order conditions (6.21) and (6.22). Otherwise one would have to apply the Kuhn-Tucker conditions (compare Mas-Colell et al. [1995, Theorem M.K.2]).

The Lagrangian multipliers are given by

$$\begin{aligned} \bar{\lambda}^1 &= 3.6, & \bar{\lambda}^2 &= 2.085, \\ \hat{\lambda}^1 &= 3.445, & \hat{\lambda}^2 &= 1.955, \\ \tilde{\lambda}^1 &= 5.4417381, & \tilde{\lambda}^2 &= 8.19317872 \cdot 10^{-2} \end{aligned}$$

Computation of the determinants of the Jacobians at the equilibria shows regularity and the first and third equilibrium to have a positive index while the second one has a negative index. Since neither Assumption 6.4 nor the weaker Assumption 1.5 is satisfied, it is by no means sure whether Theorem 6.17 can be applied to show robustness of this example against perturbations of the asset structure.

The characteristics of the economy here are only approximations: the iteration via the algorithm was used until a maximal error of $2.84 \cdot 10^{-14}$ for fulfillment of the extended system was obtained.

Up to now it could not be clarified what is the intuition for the failure of uniqueness with Cobb-Douglas utility when markets are incomplete. It was conspicuous that many starting-points for the algorithm (each consisting of two FM-equilibria) failed to deliver a Cobb-Douglas economy with multiple equilibria which gives a hint that the Propositions based on small risk aversion can be extended to more general cases.

## 6.3 Limited Risk Sharing

Since incomplete markets are much more realistic than complete markets, it seems reasonable to try to extend the idea of complete risk sharing from the Arrow-Debreu model to GEI-economies. However, as expected, a limitation of trading possibilities stops complete risk sharing when utility satisfies the expected utility hypothesis with respect to an objective probability measure and there is no aggregate risk. Even worse, the following example demonstrates that deviating from complete to incomplete markets might cause multiplicity of equilibria. This can be explained by the fact that with incomplete markets constrained Pareto-efficient allocations need not be co-monotone.[100]

[100] An allocation $(\bar{x}^i)_{i \in I} \in \mathbb{R}_+^{S \times I}$ is co-monotone if for each tuple $s, s' \in S$ whenever $\bar{x}_s^i \geq \bar{x}_{s'}^i$ for some consumer $i \in I$, then it is $\bar{x}_s^h \geq \bar{x}_{s'}^h$ for all $h \in I$. This implies $\omega_s \geq \omega_{s'}$ such that without aggregate risk it has to be $\bar{x}_s^h = \bar{x}_{s'}^h$ for all $s, s' \in S$. Since Pareto-efficient and hence Arrow-Debreu equilibrium allocations are co-monotone (cf. Borch [1962]), they have to be riskless and therefore first order conditions uniquely determine the equilibrium price system with complete markets.

Look at an economy with $I = 2$ consumers, $S = 3$ states, and $J = 2$ assets. Consumers are now characterized by endowments

$$\omega^1 = \frac{1}{4}\begin{pmatrix} 4 \\ 23 \\ 6 \end{pmatrix} \quad \text{and} \quad \omega^2 = \frac{1}{4}\begin{pmatrix} 36 \\ 17 \\ 34 \end{pmatrix} \quad .$$

such that aggregate endowment $\omega = (10, 10, 10)^T$ is riskless.[101]
The objective probability measure is given by

$$\bar{p} = \frac{1}{9}\begin{pmatrix} 1 \\ 6 \\ 2 \end{pmatrix}$$

and the von Neumann-Morgenstern utility functions satisfy the standard assumptions. Furthermore, fix the following values of the first derivatives (see Figures 6.3 and 6.4):

$$\begin{aligned} (u^1)'(3) &= 20, \quad (u^1)'\left(3\tfrac{1}{2}\right) = 4, \quad (u^1)'\left(3\tfrac{3}{4}\right) = 3\tfrac{2}{3}, \\ (u^1)'\left(4\tfrac{3}{4}\right) &= 3\tfrac{1}{3}, \quad (u^1)'(5) = 1, \quad (u^1)'\left(5\tfrac{1}{2}\right) = \tfrac{1}{2}. \end{aligned} \tag{6.24}$$

$$\begin{aligned} (u^2)'\left(4\tfrac{1}{2}\right) &= 3\tfrac{1}{4}, \quad (u^2)'(5) = 3, \quad (u^2)'\left(5\tfrac{1}{4}\right) = 2\tfrac{5}{6}, \\ (u^2)'\left(6\tfrac{1}{4}\right) &= 2\tfrac{1}{4}, \quad (u^2)'\left(6\tfrac{1}{2}\right) = 1\tfrac{1}{4}, \quad (u^2)'(7) = \tfrac{1}{2}. \end{aligned} \tag{6.25}$$

[101] $e$ is defined as $e = (1, \ldots, 1)^T$.

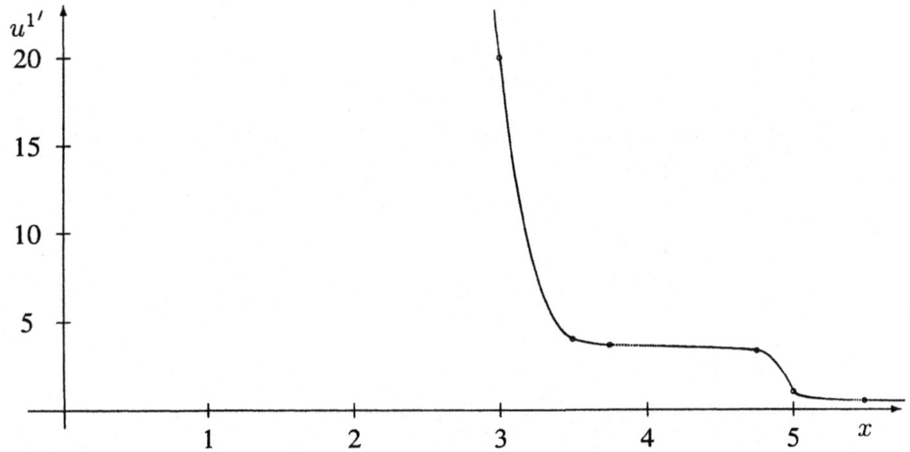


*Figure 6.3.* A possible form of $\left(u^1\right)'$.

Observe that these values are compatible with the standard assumptions on $u^i, i = 1, 2$. Again (compare Section 4.1) there is a change in the sign of the third derivative of $u^i$.

Trade in this economy is restricted by the asset structure

$$A = \begin{pmatrix} 3 & 2 \\ 0 & 1 \\ 0 & -2 \end{pmatrix} \quad ,$$

i.e. asset markets are incomplete.

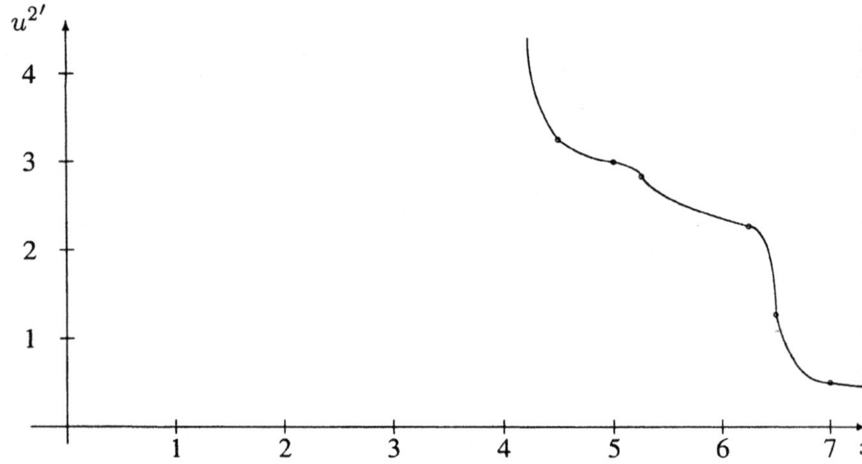


*Figure 6.4.* A possible form of $(u^2)'$.

If an economy is characterized by these data, there are at least the following two equilibria:

$$x^{*1} = \frac{1}{4}\begin{pmatrix}12\\15\\22\end{pmatrix}, \; x^{*2} = \frac{1}{4}\begin{pmatrix}28\\25\\18\end{pmatrix}, \; \theta^{*1} = -\theta^{*2} = \begin{pmatrix}2\\-2\end{pmatrix} \quad \text{and} \quad q^* = \begin{pmatrix}1\\1\end{pmatrix}, \tag{6.26}$$

$$\hat{x}^1 = \frac{1}{4}\begin{pmatrix}20\\19\\14\end{pmatrix}, \; \hat{x}^2 = \frac{1}{4}\begin{pmatrix}20\\21\\26\end{pmatrix}, \; \hat{\theta}^1 = -\hat{\theta}^2 = \begin{pmatrix}2\\-1\end{pmatrix} \quad \text{and} \quad \hat{q} = \begin{pmatrix}1\\2\end{pmatrix} \tag{6.27}$$

where the first asset price is normalized to one.
Market clearing properties are obvious and one easily computes $x^i = \omega^i + A\,\theta^i, i = 1, 2$, for the $^*$- and the $\hat{}$-equilibrium. To check the maximization condition substitute the values of (6.23)–(6.27) into the first order conditions (6.21) and (6.22) to obtain the following system of equations:
$i = 1$, $^*$-equilibrium:

$$\begin{aligned} 1 \cdot 20 \cdot 3 - \lambda^{*1} \cdot 1 &= 0\,, \\ 1 \cdot 20 \cdot 2 + 6 \cdot 3\frac{2}{3} \cdot 1 + 2 \cdot \frac{1}{2} \cdot (-2) - \lambda^{*1} \cdot 1 &= 0\,, \\ 1 \cdot 2 + 1 \cdot (-2) &= 0\,; \end{aligned}$$

$i = 1$, $\hat{}$-equilibrium:

$$\begin{aligned} 1 \cdot 1 \cdot 3 - \hat{\lambda}^1 \cdot 1 &= 0\,, \\ 1 \cdot 1 \cdot 2 + 6 \cdot 3\frac{1}{3} \cdot 1 + 2 \cdot 4 \cdot (-2) - \hat{\lambda}^1 \cdot 2 &= 0\,, \\ 1 \cdot 2 + 2 \cdot (-1) &= 0\,; \end{aligned}$$

$i = 2$, $^*$-equilibrium:

$$\begin{aligned} 1 \cdot \frac{1}{2} \cdot 3 - \lambda^{*2} \cdot 1 &= 0\,, \\ 1 \cdot \frac{1}{2} \cdot 2 + 6 \cdot 2\frac{1}{4} \cdot 1 + 2 \cdot 3\frac{1}{4} \cdot (-2) - \lambda^{*2} \cdot 1 &= 0\,, \\ 1 \cdot (-2) + 1 \cdot 2 &= 0\,; \end{aligned}$$

$i = 2$, $\hat{}$-equilibrium:

$$\begin{aligned} 1 \cdot 3 \cdot 3 - \hat{\lambda}^2 \cdot 1 &= 0, \\ 1 \cdot 3 \cdot 2 + 6 \cdot 2\frac{5}{6} \cdot 1 + 2 \cdot 1\frac{1}{4} \cdot (-2) - \hat{\lambda}^2 \cdot 2 &= 0\,, \\ 1 \cdot (-2) + 2 \cdot 1 &= 0\,. \end{aligned}$$

This system is solved for $\lambda^{*1} = 60$, $\hat{\lambda}^1 = 3$, $\lambda^{*2} = 1\frac{1}{2}$, and $\hat{\lambda}^2 = 9$. Therefore, the equilibrium properties are proved.
Note that nothing else than the derivatives (6.24) and (6.25) is fixed for von Neumann-Morgenstern utility functions. Therefore, it is not possible to compute the Jacobians of market demand and check their determinants for equilibrium price systems. Therefore, no statement about regularity is possible. However, since such a few restrictions are put on utility functions, it should be possible for each endowment allocation $(\omega^i)_{i \in I}$ to find a utility function exhibiting these derivative values such that the given two equilibria are regular. This allows to obtain robustness of the multiplicity against (restricted) perturbations of the asset structure (Theorem 6.17).

## 7. Uniqueness of Equilibria with Small Trading Volume

The first section on uniqueness of equilibria was based on the observation that when endowments are constrained Pareto efficient then there is a unique equilibrium with no trade. Using the technical results of section Section 5 we are now in a position to derive results similar to those of the first section however with a unique equilibrium having (small) positive trading volume. Section 6 contains negative results with respect to incomplete markets because it demonstrates that conditions on utility functions like quasi-linearity, Cobb-Douglas preferences, or the expected utility hypothesis under objectivity together with no aggregate risk alone are not sufficient for a unique FM-equilibrium. This section takes

the other way around: there exist economies such that the equilibrium with incomplete markets is unique though there are multiple Arrow-Debreu equilibria. This is obvious when the asset matrix contains none or only one asset because assets cannot be exchanged between consumers a priori. To avoid this trivial case, the following examples are based on more than one asset.
The idea is to exploit the power of constrained Pareto-efficiency (compare Chapter 1. We start with a leading example which again is built on Kehoe [1991, p. 2066] well-established example of multiple Arrow-Debreu equilibria (Subsection 7.1). This is generalized in Subsection 7.2.

## 7.1 A Leading Example

Consider an economy with $I = 2$ agents and $S = 3$ states. Consumers are characterized by CES-utility functions

$$U^i(x) = \sum_{s=1}^{3} a_s^i \frac{\left(x_s^{b^i} - 1\right)}{b^i}$$

with $a^1 = (1024, 1/2, 1/2), \omega^1 = (12, 1, 1)^T, b^1 = -4$ and $a^2 = (1, 512, 512)$, $\omega^2 = (1, 12, 12)^T$, $b^2 = -4$. In contrast to Kehoe [1991] there is a third good which for each consumer has the same value as the second one. The second and the third good sum up in weight to Kehoe's[102] second one.
Hence, for complete markets, one gets multiple equilibria in the same manner as in Kehoe [1991, p. 2066] since the second and the third state can be merged. The equilibria are the following ones:[103]

$$\hat{x}^1 = \begin{pmatrix} 8.631 \\ 1.429 \\ 1.429 \end{pmatrix}, \hat{x}^2 = \begin{pmatrix} 4.369 \\ 11.571 \\ 11.571 \end{pmatrix}, \hat{\pi} = \begin{pmatrix} 0.1129 \\ 0.44355 \\ 0.44355 \end{pmatrix} \quad ;$$

$$x^{*1} = \begin{pmatrix} 10.4 \\ 2.6 \\ 2.6 \end{pmatrix}, x^{*2} = \begin{pmatrix} 2.6 \\ 10.4 \\ 10.4 \end{pmatrix}, \pi^* = \begin{pmatrix} 0.5 \\ 0.25 \\ 0.25 \end{pmatrix} \quad ;$$

$$\bar{x}^1 = \begin{pmatrix} 11.571 \\ 4.369 \\ 4.369 \end{pmatrix}, \bar{x}^2 = \begin{pmatrix} 1.429 \\ 8.631 \\ 8.631 \end{pmatrix}, \bar{\pi} = \begin{pmatrix} 0.8871 \\ 0.05645 \\ 0.05645 \end{pmatrix} \quad .$$

From now on, consider incomplete markets. In the first step, focus on

[102] Kehoe [1991]
[103] Apply the price normalization $\pi_1 + \pi_2 + \pi_3 = 1$, i.e. $\pi \in \hat{\mathcal{P}}_{1,1}$.

$$\bar{A} = \begin{pmatrix} 1 & 1 \\ 1 & 0 \\ 0 & 1 \end{pmatrix}$$

which obviously shows also a kind of symmetry with respect to states 2 and 3. Hence, even though there are two different assets, the situation is the same as with a single asset because—as we will show—there is no trade. The reason for this is that both assets allow very similar trading opportunities. Therefore, after proving uniqueness of equilibria for $\bar{A}$, we apply Theorem 6.18 to consider perturbations of $\bar{A}$.

Assume the asset structure $\bar{A}$. The only possible equilibrium is the no-trade equilibrium $\theta^{*1} = \theta^{*2} = 0$ with $q_1^* = q_2^*$: symmetry of both consumers' utility functions and endowments according to states 2 and 3 and the particular asset structure $\bar{A}$ imply that for $q_1 > q_2$ both consumers demand for the second and supply the first one and vice versa for $q_2 > q_1$.

The intuition behind this example is very simple: the incomplete asset structure

$$\bar{A} = \begin{pmatrix} 1 & 1 \\ 1 & 0 \\ 0 & 1 \end{pmatrix}$$

is chosen such that the endowment distribution is constrained Pareto-efficient (but not Pareto-efficient!) which causes uniqueness of the equilibrium (compare Proposition 6.5). One easily computes that for all $\bar{\alpha} \in \mathbb{R}_+$ the asset structure

$$A = \begin{pmatrix} \bar{\alpha} & \bar{\alpha} \\ 1 & 0 \\ 0 & 1 \end{pmatrix}$$

causes the same effect.

$\bar{A}$ is an asset matrix which enables a portfolio with a strictly positive payoff. Therefore, instead of $\bar{A}$ one can consider the matrix

$$\tilde{A} = \begin{pmatrix} 2 & 1 \\ 1 & 0 \\ 1 & 1 \end{pmatrix} \quad .$$

Defining a set of $\epsilon$-perturbations of $\tilde{A}$, one can define a set of $\bar{\epsilon}$-perturbations of $\bar{A}$ of which the elements can be represented as $\epsilon$-perturbations of $\tilde{A}$ (compare Lemma 6.6).

Because of Proposition 6.1 not only $\bar{A}$, but also $\tilde{A}$ evokes the unique no-trade equilibrium. No-trade equilibria, however, are regular (compare Lemma 6.9 in the next section) such that Theorem 6.18 assures the existence of an $\epsilon > 0$ with all $\epsilon$-perturbations of $\tilde{A}$ and therefore all $\bar{\epsilon}$-perturbations of $\bar{A}$ being characterized by a unique equilibrium.

The example is robust against perturbations of the asset matrix even though the endowment distribution then stops to be constrained Pareto-efficient. The intuition for uniqueness of the equilibrium to remain is the fact that the allocation $(\omega^1, \omega^2)$ is very "close" to the set of constrained Pareto-efficient allocations which causes a "small" chance for the existence of multiple equilibria.

## 7.2 Generalization of the Leading Example

When generalizing the idea of the leading example, the number of consumers has to be less than the number of states which might give a hint that one has to put attention on this relation when looking for sufficient conditions for a unique equilibrium. We state that the no-trade equilibrium is always regular such that the results from Theorem 6.18 can be applied: for each fixed number of assets smaller than or equal to one plus the difference between number of states and consumers there exists a non-exceptional subset of all allowed asset matrices where the corresponding GEI-economy is described by a unique equilibrium. A remarkable point consists in the fact that—no matter which utility functions and endowments are assumed—for each strictly positive asset an asset matrix can be constructed containing this asset and generating a non-trivial GEI-economy with unique equilibrium.

For this subsection the fulfillment of Assumption 6.4 is required. Therefore, price normalization with respect to the first unit vector, i.e. restricting prices to be elements of $\hat{\mathcal{Q}}(A)$, is possible such that the first asset is numeraire asset.

Now, assume there is an Arrow-Debreu-economy $\left\{(U^i, \omega^i)_{i=1,\ldots,I}\right\}$ with multiple equilibria. According to Proposition 5.3 this implies that the no-trade allocation cannot be Pareto-efficient, i.e. there have to be two consumers $i, h \in \{1, \ldots, I\}$ with

$$\nabla U^i \left(\omega^i\right) \not\parallel \nabla U^h \left(\omega^h\right) \tag{6.28}$$

where without loss of generality $i = 1$. Now define $A_{\cdot 1}^T = (1, \ldots, 1) \gg 0$. Assume $\nabla U^i(\omega^i) A_{\cdot 1} = 1$ for all $i = 1, \ldots, I$ without loss of generality. Otherwise multiplication of $U^i$ with a positive constant is possible. A sufficient condition for $(\theta^i)_{i=1,\ldots,I}, \theta^i = 0$ for all $i = 1, \ldots, I$ to be constrained Pareto-efficient for some matrix $A = \left(A_{\cdot 1}, A_{\cdot(-1)}\right)$ is given by

$$\nabla U^1 \left(\omega^1\right) A_{\cdot(-1)} = \ldots = \nabla U^I \left(\omega^I\right) A_{\cdot(-1)} \tag{6.29}$$

or equivalently

$$\underbrace{\begin{bmatrix} \nabla U^1(\omega^1) - \nabla U^2(\omega^2) \\ \vdots \\ \nabla U^1(\omega^1) - \nabla U^I\left(\omega^I\right) \end{bmatrix}}_{:=H} A_{\cdot(-1)} = 0 \quad . \tag{6.30}$$

Together with Proposition 6.5 this implies a unique (no-trade) equilibrium for $GEI = \left\{\mathbb{R}^S, (U^i, \omega^i)_{i=1,\dots,I}, A\right\}$.

It has to be clarified under which conditions a solution $A_{\cdot(-1)} \in \mathbb{R}^{S\times(J-1)}$ for equation (6.30) exists. Obviously, each $A_{\cdot j}, j = 2, \dots, J$ has to be in the null space $\mathcal{C}$ of $H$: $\mathcal{C} := \left\{a \in \mathbb{R}^S \middle| \, H\,a = 0\right\}$. Therefore, considering that $A_{\cdot 1}$ is in $\mathcal{C}$, it is possible to find a solution for equation (6.30) with $rank\, A = J$ if and only if $dim\, \mathcal{C} \geq J$. Because of condition (6.28) $dim\ \mathcal{C} < S$. For $I = 2$ one observes $dim\, \mathcal{C} = S-1$, i.e. it would be possible to construct a counterexample for all $J < S$! In general it is

$$dim\, \mathcal{C} \geq \max\{1, S - (I-1)\} \quad , \tag{6.31}$$

i.e. if $S - (I-1) \geq 2$ or equivalently $S > I$, then one is able to construct a non-trivial counterexample for all $J \in \{2, \dots, S - I + 1\}$.[104]

Note that for $S \leq I$ any solution unequal to $A_{\cdot 1}$ only exists in the exceptional case where $I - S + 1$ consumers can be eliminated from equation (6.30) because they are characterized by the same marginal utility for their endowment as some other consumer.

The examples would not be very interesting if they only depend on constrained Pareto-efficiency of the endowment. However, from Theorem 6.18 it follows that as soon as one has found a GEI-economy $\left\{(U^i, \omega^i)_{i=1,\dots,I}, A\right\}$ with unique no-trade equilibrium, then $A$ can be disturbed a little bit without changing the uniqueness property, but leaving the no-trade equilibrium. Therefore, one needs the following lemma.

LEMMA 6.9 (REGULARITY OF NO-TRADE EQUILIBRIA)

*If* $GEI = \left\{\mathbb{R}^S, (U^i, \omega^i)_{i=1,\dots,I}, A\right\}$ *is characterized by the unique no-trade equilibrium, then this equilibrium is regular, i.e. the normalized Jacobian of market demand is regular.*

PROOF 6.30

*The Jacobian of an individual demand function can be split into two matrices for the substitution respectively income effect. Since there is no trade, the income effect is zero such that only the Slutzky-matrix remains which is negative definite*

[104] For $J = 1$ it is trivial because there cannot be any trade a priori.

*on the orthogonal space for q,* $q^{\perp} := \left\{ v \in \mathbb{R}^J \middle| q^T v = 0 \right\}$. *Adding up these individual Jacobians, one ends up with a negative definite Jacobian of market demand on* $q^{\perp}$.

*q. e. d.*

Now, application of Theorem 6.18 for regular GEI-economies with $A_{\cdot 1} \gg 0$ delivers:

PROPOSITION 6.9 (LIMITS OF TRANSFERABILITY) *[Pilgrim [2002]]* *Let* $\left\{ \mathbb{R}^S, (U^i, \omega^i)_{i=1,\dots,I} \right\}$ *be an Arrow-Debreu economy where* $S > I$[105] *and which displays multiple equilibria, then there exists a non-exceptional set of* $J$*-dimensional asset matrices,* $2 \le J \le S - I + 1$*, which enable a portfolio with strictly positive payoff and for which the GEI-economy* $\left\{ \mathbb{R}^S, (U^i, \omega^i)_{i=1,\dots,I}, A \right\}$ *displays a unique equilibrium.*

Non-exceptional means that small arbitrary changes in arbitrary entries of the asset matrix do not change the uniqueness property.[106]

Having a further look on the proof of this result, especially the construction method of the counter examples, one observes that instead of $A_{\cdot 1}^T = (1, \dots, 1)^T$ it is possible to take *any* other strictly positive vector[107], which means that each strictly positive asset can be part of a matrix generating a counterexample! This observation is quite important because it emphasizes that not the single assets are important, but their interaction. Having constructed a counterexample with a specified matrix $A \in \mathbb{R}^{S \times J}$ where $J < S$ it is always possible to define a vector $\tilde{A}_{\cdot 1} \notin \langle A \rangle$, but being strictly positive such that for an $\tilde{A}$ which is constructed by starting with $\tilde{A}_{\cdot 1}$ it is $\langle \tilde{A} \rangle \neq \langle A \rangle$.

# APPENDIX 6.A

## 1. Proof of Lemma 6.6

Distinguish the three types of matrices.

(i) Since multiplication by a matrix is a continuous function, Equation (5.1) makes clear that for each $\tilde{\epsilon}_2 > 0$ there is some $\epsilon_2 > 0$ such that $A \in \mathcal{V}_{\epsilon_2}(\bar{A})$ implies $\tilde{A}(A) \in \mathcal{V}_{\tilde{\epsilon}_2}(\tilde{A}(\bar{A}))$.

(ii) Modeling first period consumption, the matrix $\bar{A}$ always satisfies Assumption 6.4.

---

[105] This is a quite restrictive assumption, but it becomes weaker if one interprets $i = 1, \dots, I$ not as single consumers, but types of consumers.

[106] In other words: for a given Arrow-Debreu economy $\left\{ \mathbb{R}^S, (U^i, \omega^i)_{i=1,\dots,I} \right\}$ with multiple equilibria the set of $S \times J$ matrices generating corresponding GEI-economies with multiple equilibria is not generic in the set of all $S \times J$ matrices with $rank = J$ and the first asset being positive.

[107] If one does not want to admit disturbances in any direction, it is even sufficient to demand $A_{\cdot 1} > 0$.

(iii) For given $\tilde{\epsilon}_2$ define $\epsilon_2$ in analogy to case (i). Then those $\epsilon_2$-perturbations of $\bar{A}$ have to be considered which are elements of the set

$$\{A \in \mathcal{V}_{\epsilon_2}(\bar{A}) |\ A\theta_{\bar{A}} > 0\}.$$

This is a quite inconvenient restriction. A much stronger, but more convenient restriction is given by

$$\{A \in \mathcal{V}_{\dot{\epsilon}_2}(\bar{A}) |\ A_{sj} = \bar{A}_{sj} \text{ if } \bar{A}_{s\cdot}\theta_{\bar{A}} = 0\}.$$

where

$$\dot{\epsilon}_2 < \min\left\{\epsilon_2, \min\left\{\frac{\bar{A}_{s\cdot}\theta_{\bar{A}}}{\sum_{j=1}^{J}|\theta_{\bar{A}j}|} \mid s \in \dot{S}\right\}\right\}$$

with

$$\dot{S} = \{s \in S |\ \bar{A}_{s\cdot}\theta_{\bar{A}} > 0\} \quad .$$

q. e. d.

## 2. Proof of Lemma 6.7

Since $\mathcal{K}$ is compact, from the different representations of $\mathcal{Q}_{norm}(A)$ given on page 178 f. the existence of $l_s, u_s \in (0,1), s \in \mathcal{S}^+(\bar{A}_{\cdot 1})$, and $l_s, u_s \in (0,\infty), s \in \mathcal{S}^0(\bar{A}_{\cdot 1})$ is known, such that for all $\hat{q} \in \mathcal{K}$ there is some $\mu \in \prod_{s=1}^{S}[l_s, u_s]$ with

$$\begin{pmatrix} 1 \\ \hat{q} \end{pmatrix} = \sum_{s \in \mathcal{S}^+(\bar{A}_{\cdot 1})} \mu_s \begin{pmatrix} 1 \\ \frac{1}{\bar{A}_{s1}}\bar{A}^T_{s(-1)} \end{pmatrix} + \sum_{s \in \mathcal{S}^0(\bar{A}_{\cdot 1})} \mu_s \begin{pmatrix} 0 \\ \bar{A}^T_{s(-1)} \end{pmatrix} \quad .$$

Because of $rank\ \bar{A} = J$ there is some subset $G \subseteq \{1, \ldots, S\}$ with $\sharp G = J$ such that

$$\left( \begin{pmatrix} 1 \\ \frac{1}{A_{s1}(C)} A^T_{s(-1)}(C) \end{pmatrix}_{s \in G \cap \mathcal{S}^+(\bar{A}_{\cdot 1})}, \begin{pmatrix} 0 \\ A^T_{s(-1)}(C) \end{pmatrix}_{s \in G \cap \mathcal{S}^0(\bar{A}_{\cdot 1})} \right)$$

is invertible for all $C \in \mathcal{V}_{\epsilon_2}(\bar{C})$.[108] The inverse is called $I^{-1}(C)$. Define

$$\mu_G : \quad \mathcal{K} \times \prod_{s \in \{1,\ldots,S\} \setminus G} [l_s, u_s] \times cl(\mathcal{V}_{\frac{\epsilon_2}{2}}(\bar{C})) \quad \rightarrow \mathbb{R}^J$$

by

$$\mu_G(\hat{q}, (\mu_s)_{s \in \{1,\ldots,S\} \setminus G}, C) :=$$

$$I^{-1}(C) \left[ \begin{pmatrix} 1 \\ \hat{q} \end{pmatrix} - \sum_{s \in \mathcal{S}^+(\bar{A}_{\cdot 1}) \setminus G} \mu_s \begin{pmatrix} 1 \\ \frac{1}{A_{s1}(C)} A(C)^T_{s(-1)} \end{pmatrix} - \sum_{s \in \mathcal{S}^0(\bar{A}_{\cdot 1}) \setminus G} \mu_s \begin{pmatrix} 0 \\ A^T_{s(-1)}(C) \end{pmatrix} \right] .$$

---

[108] To be correct in notation assume without loss of generality that $s_1 \in \mathcal{S}^+(\bar{A}_{\cdot 1})$ and $s_2 \in \mathcal{S}^0(\bar{A}_{\cdot 1})$ implies $s_2 > s_1$. Otherwise renumerate the states.

This function is continuous and—because defined on a compact set—even uniformly continuous. Therefore, for some

$$\bar{\delta} \in (0, \min\{l_s |\ s \in G\})$$

there is an $\epsilon_3 > 0$ such that $\|C - \bar{C}\| < \epsilon_3$ implies

$$\|\mu_G(\hat{q}, (\mu_s)_{s\in\{1,\dots,S\}\setminus G}, C) - \mu_G(\hat{q}, (\mu_s)_{s\in\{1,\dots,S\}\setminus G}, \bar{C})\| < \bar{\delta}$$

for all $(\hat{q}, (\mu_s)_{s\in\{1,\dots,S\}\setminus G}) \in \mathcal{K} \times \prod_{s\in\{1,\dots,S\}\setminus G}[l_s, u_s]$. Hence, for all $\hat{q} \in \mathcal{K}$ one gets

$$\begin{aligned}
\begin{pmatrix} 1 \\ \hat{q} \end{pmatrix} &= \sum_{s\in G\cap \mathcal{S}^+(\bar{A}_{\cdot 1})} \underbrace{\mu_s(\hat{q}, (\mu_{s\in\{1,\dots,S\}\setminus G}, C)}_{\geq \mu_s(\hat{q}, (\mu_{s\in\{1,\dots,S\}\setminus G}, \bar{C}) - \bar{\delta} > 0} \begin{pmatrix} 1 \\ \frac{1}{A_{s1}(C)} A_{s(-1)}^T(C) \end{pmatrix} \\
&+ \sum_{s\in G\cap \mathcal{S}^0(\bar{A}_{\cdot 1})} \underbrace{\mu_s(\hat{q}, (\mu_{s\in\{1,\dots,S\}\setminus G}, C)}_{\geq \mu_s(\hat{q}, (\mu_{s\in\{1,\dots,S\}\setminus G}, \bar{C}) - \bar{\delta} > 0} \begin{pmatrix} 0 \\ A_{s(-1)}^T(C) \end{pmatrix} \\
&+ \sum_{s\in \mathcal{S}^+(\bar{A}_{\cdot 1})\setminus G} \underbrace{\mu_s}_{>0} \begin{pmatrix} 1 \\ \frac{1}{A_{s1}(C)} A_{s(-1)}^T(C) \end{pmatrix} \\
&+ \sum_{s\in \mathcal{S}^0(\bar{A}_{\cdot 1})\setminus G} \underbrace{\mu_s}_{>0} \begin{pmatrix} 0 \\ A_{s(-1)}^T(C) \end{pmatrix}
\end{aligned}$$

such that $\hat{q} \in \tilde{\mathcal{Q}}_{norm}(C)$ for all $C \in \mathcal{V}_{\epsilon_3}(\bar{C})$.

q. e. d.

## 3. Proof of Lemma 6.8

The set of attainable and individually rational consumption plans is defined as

$$\mathcal{C}^i(\omega^i, \omega) := \{x \in \mathbb{R}_+^S |\ U^i(x) \geq U^i(\omega^i) \ \wedge x \leq \omega\}$$

which obviously is a compact subset of $\mathbb{R}_+^S$.[109] Equilibrium portfolio allocations $(\theta^{*i})_{i=1,\dots,I}$ for asset structure $A$ have to satisfy $\omega^i + A\theta^{*i} \in \mathcal{C}^i(\omega^i, \omega)$ for all $i = 1, \dots, I$.
Let $\epsilon_7 \in (0, \epsilon_6)$. Define

$$\begin{aligned}
h^i : \quad \mathcal{C}^i(\omega^i, \omega) \times cl(\mathcal{V}_{\epsilon_7}(\bar{C})) &\to \mathbb{R}^{J-1} \\
(x, C) &\mapsto \left[\frac{1}{\nabla U^i(x) A_{\cdot 1}(C)} \nabla U^i(x) A_{\cdot(-1)}(C)\right]^T.
\end{aligned}$$

Because of $A_{\cdot 1}(C) > 0$ and $\nabla U^i(x) \gg 0$ this function is continuous and even uniformly continuous since it is defined on a compact set. Images of compact sets under continuous functions are compact such that

$$\mathcal{H}(C) := \bigcap_{i=1}^{I} h^i(\mathcal{C}^i(\omega^i, \omega), C)$$

[109] This is implied by the properties of $U^i$.

as finite intersection of compact sets is compact for $C \in cl(\mathcal{V}_{\epsilon_7}(\bar{C}))$. Since the first order conditions for asset demand have to be satisfied for all consumers $i = 1, \ldots, I$ one obtains

$$\mathcal{E}_{norm}(A(C)) \subseteq \mathcal{H}(C)$$

for all $C \in cl(\mathcal{V}_{\epsilon_7}(\bar{C}))$. There has to be some $\delta > 0$ with $\mathcal{H}(\bar{C}) + cl(\mathcal{V}_\delta(0)) \subseteq \tilde{\mathcal{Q}}_{norm}(\bar{C})$[110] because $\mathcal{H}(\bar{C}) \subseteq \tilde{\mathcal{Q}}_{norm}(\bar{C})$ is compact and $\tilde{\mathcal{Q}}_{norm}(\bar{C})$ is open. Application of Lemma 6.7 delivers the existence of some $\epsilon_8 \in (0, \epsilon_6]$ with

$$\mathcal{H}(\bar{C}) + cl(\mathcal{V}_\delta(0)) \subseteq \tilde{\mathcal{Q}}_{norm}(C)$$

for all $C \in \mathcal{V}_{\epsilon_8}(\bar{C})$. On the other hand there has to be some $\epsilon_9 > 0$ such that for all $C \in \mathcal{V}_{\epsilon_9}(\bar{C})$

$$\mathcal{H}(C) \subseteq \mathcal{H}(\bar{C}) + \mathcal{V}_\delta(0) \quad .$$

This follows from uniform continuity of $h^i$ because given $\delta > 0$ there is some $\check{\epsilon}^i > 0$ such that

$$\|(y, C) - (x, \tilde{C})\|_{\max} < \check{\epsilon}^i \Rightarrow \|h^i(y, C) - h^i(x, \tilde{C})\|_{\max} < \frac{\delta}{I}$$

for all $(y, C), (x, \tilde{C}) \in \mathcal{C}^i(\omega^i, \omega) \times cl(\mathcal{V}_{\epsilon_7}(\bar{C}))$ and therefore especially

$$C \in \mathcal{V}_{\check{\epsilon}^i}(\bar{C}) \Rightarrow \|h^i(x, C) - h^i(x, \bar{C})\|_{\max} < \frac{\delta}{I}$$

for all $x \in \mathcal{C}^i(\omega^i, \omega)$. Therefore for all $\hat{q} \in \mathcal{H}(C)$ there is some $\bar{\hat{q}} \in \mathcal{H}(\bar{C})$ with

$$\hat{q} \in \{\bar{\hat{q}}\} + \mathcal{V}_\delta(0)$$

when $\epsilon_9 := \min\{\check{\epsilon}^i \,|\, i = 1, \ldots, I\}$. If $\epsilon_{10} := \min\{\frac{1}{2}\epsilon_8, \frac{1}{2}\epsilon_9\}$, $C \in cl(\mathcal{V}_{\epsilon_{10}}(\bar{C}))$ implies

$$\mathcal{H}(C) \subseteq \mathcal{H}(\bar{C}) + cl(\mathcal{V}_\delta(0)) \subseteq \tilde{\mathcal{Q}}_{norm}(C) \cap \tilde{\mathcal{Q}}_{norm}(\bar{C}) \quad .$$

The set

$$\mathcal{Q}^H := \left[\mathcal{H}(\bar{C}) + cl(\mathcal{V}_\delta(0))\right] \setminus \bigcup_{n=1}^{N} \mathcal{V}_{\delta^n}(\hat{q}^{*n})$$

is a compact subset of $\mathbb{R}^{J-1}$. The construction of this set assures that as soon as $C \in cl(\mathcal{V}_{\epsilon_{10}}(\bar{C}))$ allows that additional equilibrium price systems unequal to $\hat{q}^1_*(C), \ldots, \hat{q}^N_*(C)$ exist, these systems have to be elements of $\mathcal{Q}^H$.

q. e. d.

[110] In other words: $\mathcal{H}(\bar{C})$ can be extended a little bit without leaving $\tilde{\mathcal{Q}}_{norm}(\bar{C})$.

II

# THE CAPITAL ASSET PRICING MODEL

# Chapter 7

# THE MODEL AND SOME FUNDAMENTALS

*Mean-variance analysis and the Sharpe-Lintner-Mossin CAPM are widely viewed as the major contributions of academic research in the post-war era.*

—Jagannathan and Wang [1996]

## 1. Introduction

One of the main issues in finance is to provide models which explain how agents make portfolio decisions. Moreover, by means of these models the equilibrium consequences in markets where every agent follows such decision rules can be analyzed. The Capital Asset Pricing Model (CAPM) is the most familiar of these models. It is a rich source of intuition but also the basis for many practical financial decisions. Being built around the means and covariances of the security payoffs, it has its roots in Markowitz [1952] description of the mean-variance portfolio selection problem. In its equilibrium form, the CAPM goes back to Sharpe [1964], Lintner [1965] and Mossin [1966]. The perhaps most important feature of the CAPM is that, given an assumption of "variance-aversion" on agents' preferences, it can be shown that, for every announced price system, all agents will be satisfied with holding shares of the same two funds, the riskless asset and a price dependent portfolio [Tobin, 1958]. The latter portfolio is usually called "pricing portfolio" [Duffie, 1988]. At equilibrium, the pricing portfolio can be replaced by the market portfolio, i.e. the collection of all assets available in the economy. Thus at a CAPM equilibrium all agents only hold shares in the riskless portfolio and the market portfolio. From this Mutual Fund Property a simple and linear pricing formula, which is expressed in terms of a proportionality factor—called beta coefficient—and rates of returns, can be deduced. This pricing relation says that the excess return of every asset is proportional to the excess return of the market portfolio, where the proportionality factor—the beta coefficient—is given by the covariance of the asset's payoff and the market portfolio's payoff per standard deviation of the market portfolio's payoff.

Recently new efforts have been devoted to the study of the CAPM as a general equilibrium model in which the natural questions of existence and uniqueness of an equilibrium play an important role. In the next section we show how the CAPM can be embedded into the GEI-model. There after we present a general existence proof of CAPM-equilibria, generalizing the seminal work of Nielsen [1990b] and Allingham [1991]. From the general equilibrium point of view the addtional difficulties to prove existence of equilibria in the CAPM stem from the fact that in the CAPM consumption sets are not bounded below and that satiation is possible. In Chapter 9 we show that parallel to the general equilibrium model (see Chapter 3) also the CAPM in general lacks any structure that is sufficient to have a well determined equilibrium! We show that given any choice of a finite number of normalized price systems and the respective demands satisfying Walras' Law and the Tobin Separation Property, there exist two variance-averse agents whose market demand coincides with the preassigned values. Our result shows that the Tobin Separation Property is *the* additional structure gained in the CAPM over and above the Arrow-Debreu model. As a corollary it is obtained that for any number $n$ there exists a CAPM economy which has at least $n$ equilibria. Across these equilibria relative prices of assets and asset allocations differ. Hence there are at least $n$ different beta-pricing formulas. Specific assumptions to derive a unique equilibrium have recently been given in Dana [1999] who applies the theorem of Mitjushin and Polterovich [1978]. Unfortunately, Dana's assumption implies increasing absolute risk aversion—a not too plausible property. In Chapter 10 we therefore give a joint restrictions on the agents' risk aversions and their endowments which are consistent with decreasing absolute risk aversion and imply uniqueness of equilibria.

## 2. Information Structure And Commodity Space

The model we consider is essentially a static two-period Capital Asset Pricing Model in a General Equilibrium framework, as it is presented in most modern Finance textbooks, see e.g. Duffie [1988]. There are two dates $t = 0, 1$. At date 1 several possible states, $s$, of the world can occur. The uncertainty about these states is common among all agents, and it is described by a probability space $(S, \mathcal{S}, \rho)$. We assume that $\mathcal{S}$ is countably generated. Consumption takes place only at date 1. Including date-zero-consumption would considerably change the features of the equilibrium. The simple mean-variance trade off would then have to be augmented by a third dimension: the trade off between first and second period consumption. In the CAPM, different to the standard general equilibrium model of Part I of this book, no non-negativity constraints on consumption are imposed. As for example Löffler [1996] has shown, requiring non-negativity

conflicts with the Tobin-Separation Property (see Proposition 7.1 below). The Tobin-Separation Property is *the* additional structure the CAPM-model has over and above the GEI-model, as we will demonstrate in Chapter 9.
A consumption bundle $x$ is a real-valued measurable function on $(S, \mathcal{S}, \rho)$. For technical reasons, the consumption set will be restricted to the set of measurable functions with finite variance:

$$L^2(\rho) = \left\{ x \middle| E\left(x^2\right) < \infty \right\}$$

where $E(x) := \int_S x(s)\, d\rho$ is the expected value of $x$. $L^2(\rho)$ is a Hilbert-space, when endowed with the scalar product $x \diamond y = E(x\, y) = \int_S x(s)\, y(s)\, d\rho$ and with the Norm $\|x\| = \sqrt{E(x^2)}$. The covariance-bilinearform $\text{cov}(x, y) = E(x\, y) - E(x)\, E(y)$ and the variance-operator $Var(x) = \text{cov}(x, x)$ and the standard deviation $\sigma(x) = \sqrt{Var(x)}$. are defined as usual.

## 3. The Agents' Decision Problem

Endowments of the agents are endowments of the consumption good in all states $s \in S$, and are thus functions in $L^2(\rho)$. In order to transfer consumption among states, the agents may trade assets at date zero, that is, before uncertainty has resolved. An asset is a contract that promises the delivery of some amount of the good in each state of the world at date one. This amount can be negative in some states, as it is for instance when the payoffs of the securities are normally distributed. It is modelled as well as a function in $L^2(\rho)$. The set of existing non-redundant assets is denoted by $A$. There can be potentially an infinite number of securities, but for notational convenience, we will always use the symbol '$\sum$', when summing over $A$. In any case $A$ is supposed to be closed. There are no short sales constraints, such that the agents may buy or sell any amount of these assets that they can afford. The set of possible trades of date-1-consumption is given by the linear combinations of securities in $A$, thus by $X = \langle A \rangle$, the space spanned by $A$.
An agent $i = 1, \ldots, I$ is described by his endowments $\omega^i$ and his utility function $U^i : L^2 \to \mathbb{R}$. Throughout this part of the book we assume that endowments are given in terms of claims to assets. Moreover we normalize the market portfolio to have unit expectation.

ASSUMPTION 7.1 (SPANNING)
*The endowments are 'spanned': for all i, $\omega^i \in \langle A \rangle$. Equivalently, there exist portfolios $\bar{\theta}^i \in \mathbb{R}^J$ such that $\omega^i = \sum_j \bar{\theta}^i_j A^j$. Furthermore, for the market portfolio $\omega = \sum_i \omega^i$, it is assumed that $E(\omega) = 1$ and $Var(\omega) > Var(\eta)$, where $\eta$ is defined as the solution to*

$$\min \{ Var(z) \, | E(z) = 1, z \in \langle A \rangle \} > 0 \quad .$$

The agent's decision problem is

$$\max_{x \in X, \ell \diamond x \leq \ell \diamond \omega^i} U^i(x) \tag{7.1}$$

Without loss of generality we can assume that $\ell \in X$ because any component of $\ell \in X^{\perp} = \{y \in L^2 | \, y \diamond x = 0 \quad \forall x \in X\}$ does not change the budget restriction. The essential assumption that makes the model a CAPM, is the

ASSUMPTION 7.2 (MEAN-VARIANCE PREFERENCES)
*Every agent $i = 1, \ldots, I$ has a mean-variance preference, i.e. there exist functions $v^i : \mathbb{R} \times \mathbb{R}_+ \to \mathbb{R}$, $(\mu, \sigma) \mapsto v^i(\mu, \sigma)$ increasing in $\mu$ and decreasing in $\sigma$ such that for all $x \in X$, $U^i(x) = v^i(\mu(x), \sigma(x))$, where $\mu(x) = E(x)$ and $\sigma(x) = \mathbb{E}(x^2) - \mathbb{E}^2(x)$.*

In addition, for demand to be a well defined function, we introduce the following assumption which goes back to Sharpe [1964].

ASSUMPTION 7.3 (STRICT QUASI-CONCAVITY)
*For every agent $i = 1, \ldots, I$ the utility function $v^i$ is continuous and strictly quasi-concave.*

DEFINITION 7.1
*A consumer satisfying Assumptions 7.2 and 7.3 is called a CAPM consumer.*

Under the assumptions made, the abstract decision problem (7.1) given above can be derived from an agent's portfolio choice problem by recognizing that asset prices must be arbitrage free and can, henceforth, be expressed in terms of the projection of the likelihood ratio process $\ell$ onto X. The method which allows to reduce a portfolio choice problem to a constraint Arrow-Debreu decision problem is commonly used in the incomplete markets' literature (cf. Chapter 1). Since the setting here is slightly different from the standard general equilibrium model with incomplete markets we briefly recast these arguments for the case of a finite number of assets.

Let $X$ be generated as the span of $(A^j)_{j=1,\ldots,J}$, a collection of securities in $L^2(\rho)$, one of which may be the riskless asset $\mathbb{1}$. The numbers $\theta^i_j$ denote the amount of security $j$ held by agent $i$, $q_j$ denotes the $j$-th securities price. Thus, when trading these securities, the agent can attain the consumption plan $x = \omega^i + \sum_{j=1}^J A^j \theta^i_j$ where $\theta^i$ is self-financing (i.e. $\sum_{j=1}^J q_j \theta^i_j = 0$). The portfolio choice problem is:

$$\max_{\substack{\theta \in \mathbb{R}^J : \sum_{j=1}^J q_j \theta_j = 0 \\ x = \omega^i + \sum_{j=1}^J A^j \theta_j}} U^i(x)$$

Using the notation $\omega = \sum_{j=1}^J A^j \bar{\theta}_j$ as in Chapter 1 the decision problem can be rewritten as:

$$\max_{\substack{\theta \in \mathbb{R}^J : \sum_{j=1}^J q_j \theta_j = \sum_{j=1}^J q_j \bar{\theta}_j \\ x = \sum_{j=1}^J A^j \theta_j}} U^i(x)$$

This problem only has a solution if the CAPM consumer cannot exploit an arbitrage opportunity. With mean-variance utility this means that the agent cannot find a portfolio that delivers positive mean and has zero variance. Asset prices are thus arbitrage free if the following equation holds:

$$\mathbb{R}_+ \mathbb{1} \cap \left\{ x \in L^2(\rho) \,\middle|\, x = \sum_{j=1}^J A^j \theta_j \quad \text{where} \quad \sum_{j=1}^J q_j \theta_j = 0 \right\} = \{0\} \quad .$$

A standard separation argument carried out explicitly in Chapter 1 shows the existence of a price vector $\pi \in L^2(\rho)$ with $\int_S \pi(s)\, d\rho > 0$ such that $q_j = \pi A^j$ for all $j = 1, \ldots, J$. Applying this linear pricing rule to the portfolio decision problem recognizing the spanning assumption then delivers the so called no-arbitrage decision problem $\max_{x \in X} U^i(x)$, $\pi x \leq \pi \omega^i$. When there are a finite number of states, i.e. $|S| < \infty$, the price of a security that pays off exactly one unit of the consumption good if and only if state $s \in S$ occurs is usually called the 'state price' of state $s$. In general let $\pi \in L^2(\rho)$ be the system of all such state prices. In terms of $\pi$, the price system $\ell$ is a 'probability adjusted state price system', more precisely, it is the Radon-Nikodym Derivative of $\pi$ with respect to $\rho$. Because of this representation of $\ell$, in Chapter 1 the price system $\ell$ has been called 'likelihood ratio process'. At an equilibrium the price system $\ell$ is also called 'ideal security' (cf. Magill and Quinzii [1996]) or 'pricing portfolio' (cf. Duffie [1988]). Note that the budget restriction written in terms of state prices is the inequality $\int_S \pi(s)\, x(s)\, d\rho \leq \int_S \pi(s)\, \omega^i(s)\, d\rho$. By the definition of the scalar product that we use in this paper, this inequality is indeed equal to $\ell \diamond x \leq \ell \diamond \omega^i$ and hence we have derived the abstract decision problem (7.1).

## 4. Mean-Variance Utility an Alternative to Expected Utility

How does the assumption agents maximize a mean-variance utility function relate to the expected utility hypothesis? In this section we will show that under some restrictive conditions a mean-variance utility is a special case of an expected utility. However in general an expected utility need not be a mean-variance utility nor the converse needs to hold.

EXAMPLE 7.1 (MEAN-VARIANCE BUT NOT EXPECTED UTILITY) *Consider three states* $s = 1, 2, 3$. *with fixed consumption* $x_1 = 2, x_2 = 4, x_3 = 6$. *Figure 7.1 displays the indifference curves of the most commonly used mean-variance utility function* $v(\mu, \sigma) = \mu - \sigma^2$. *As we have shown in Chapter 1, since the indifference curves are no parallel straight lines, the utility function is not compatible with the expected utility hypothesis.*

On the other hand, the Bernoulli utility function $u = \ln$ is a well known example for an expected utility function that is not a mean-variance function.
To find assumptions under which an expected utility leads to a mean-variance function one can go into two directions. Either one restricts the von Neumann Morgenstern utility $u$ or one restricts the set of possible asset pay offs. For any asset pay offs a quadratic von Neumann Morgenstern utility $u^i(x) = x - \frac{\phi^i x^2}{2}$ leads to a mean-variance utility because the second moment $\int_S x^2(s)\, d\rho$ is a function of the first moment and the variance. At the other extreme without any restrictions on the von Neumann Morgenstern utility an expected utility function is a mean-variance function if the return distribution of any portfolio can be modelled by the two parameters mean and variance. Since portfolios are any linear combination of assets this requires that the joint distribution is spherical a special case being the normal distribution. See Chamberlain [1983]. Going this way the most prominent case is that of normally distributed returns. Together with the assumption of an exponential von Neumann Morgenstern utility this leads to a mean-variance model that as in the case of quadratic utilities is also very tractable because int his case the mean-variance utility functions are linear in mean: $v^i(\mu, \sigma) = \mu - \frac{\phi^i \sigma^2}{2}$.
Unfortunately the assumptions under which an expected utility is a mean-variance function are very restrictive. Quadratic utility implies increasing absolute risk aversion and on the other hand returns are usually far from being

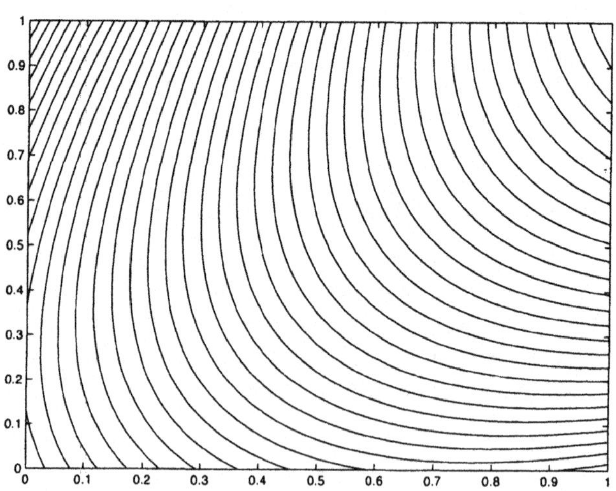


*Figure 7.1.* Mean-variance but not Expected Utility.

normally distributed. That is why we prefer to consider the mean-variance utility as an *alternative* to and not as a special case of the expected utility hypothesis.

## 5. Equilibria in the CAPM without a Riskless Asset

[1]

It may happen that there are no possibilities for complete hedging, that is, there is no riskless asset and no nontrivial combination of assets in $A$ is riskless:

$$\min \{Var(z) \,|E(z) = 1, z \in \langle A \rangle \} > 0 \quad .$$

The payoff of the portfolio that minimizes this expression is called the *quasi-bond*. It is denoted by $\eta$ (it exists, since $\langle A \rangle$ is closed). The following Lemma 7.1 summarizes two properties of $\eta$:

LEMMA 7.1 (PROPERTIES OF THE QUASI-BOND)

*(i) The vector $\eta$ is collinear to the orthogonal projection of the riskless asset $\mathbb{1}$ onto $\langle A \rangle$. This establishes the uniqueness of $\eta$.*

*(ii) For all $y$ in $\langle A \rangle$:* $\operatorname{cov}(\eta, y) = Var(\eta) \, E(y)$

PROOF 7.1

*(i) Let $\hat{\eta}$ be the projection of $\mathbb{1}$ onto $\langle A \rangle$.*

$$\begin{aligned}
\hat{\eta} &= \arg\min \left\{ \|z - \mathbb{1}\|^2 \Big| \, z \in \langle A \rangle \right\} \\
&= \arg\min \left\{ \left\| \mathbb{E}\left(z^2\right) - 2\mathbb{E}(z) + 1 \right\| \Big| \, z \in \langle A \rangle \right\} \\
&= \arg\min \left\{ \left\| (z) + \mathbb{E}(z)^2 - 2\mathbb{E}(z) + 1 \right\| \Big| \, z \in \langle A \rangle \right\} \\
&= \arg\min \left\{ V(z) + (\mathbb{E}(z) - 1)^2 \Big| \, z \in \langle A \rangle \right\} \quad .
\end{aligned}$$

*Since both $V(z) \geq 0$ and $(E(z) - 1)^2 \geq 0$ one can conclude*

$$\begin{aligned}
\hat{\eta} &= \arg\min \{V(z) \,|\, \mathbb{E}(z) = \mathbb{E}(\hat{\eta}), z \in \langle A \rangle \} \\
&= \mathbb{E}(\hat{\eta}) \, \eta \quad .
\end{aligned}$$

[1] We are grateful to Laitenberger [1999] who allow us to take this section from his Ph.D. Thesis.

*(ii) Consider the space spanned by $\eta$ and $y$. Clearly, since $y \in \langle A \rangle$,*

$$\eta = \arg\min \{ (z) \mid \mathbb{E}(z) = 1, z \in \langle \eta, y \rangle \} \quad .$$

*Any $z \in \langle \eta, y \rangle$ is of the form $z = \alpha_1 \eta + \alpha_2 y$ with some $\alpha \in \mathbb{R}^2$. The above minimization can be written as a Lagrange-problem of the following form:*

$$\min \alpha^T \Omega \alpha, \quad \textit{subject to} \quad \alpha \bar{y} = 1 \quad ,$$

*where $\Omega = \begin{pmatrix} V(\eta) & \operatorname{cov}(\eta, y) \\ \operatorname{cov}(\eta, y) & V(y) \end{pmatrix}$ and $\bar{y} = \begin{pmatrix} 1 \\ \mathbb{E}(y) \end{pmatrix}$ are the variance-covariance-matrix and the vector of expected returns, respectively. The solution of this problem computes as $\alpha = \lambda \Omega^{-1} \bar{y}$ with some Lagrange multiplier $\lambda > 0$. Since at the minimum $z = \eta$, it must be that $\alpha_2 = 0$. But this implies*

$$-\operatorname{cov}(\eta, y) + V(\eta)\, \mathbb{E}(y) = 0 \quad .$$

*q. e. d.*

The definition of an equilibrium of the asset market is standard:

DEFINITION 7.2 (CAPM EQUILIBRIUM)
*An equilibrium of the CAPM-economy is an allocation $x^{*,i} \in \langle A \rangle$ for every $i \in I$ and a price $\ell \in \langle A \rangle$, such that:*

*(i) $x^{*,i}$ maximizes (7.1) for all $i \in I$*

*(ii) $\sum_I x^{*,i} = \omega = \sum_I \omega^i$*

Given the properties of the quasi-bond we can now rewrite the abstract decision problem in $L^2$ to an equivalent decision problem in $\mathbb{R}^2$. This will allow us to give a very handy definition of CAPM-equilibria that is equivalent to the above definition. In order to do so, we first derive a fundamental property of individual demand in the CAPM.

PROPOSITION 7.1 (TOBIN SEPARATION PROPERTY)
*At any price vector $\ell \in X$ the following relations hold: for every agent $i$, there exist $\lambda^i \in \mathbb{R}$, $\xi^i \in \mathbb{R}_-$ such that*

$$x^{*,i} = \lambda^i \eta + \xi^i \ell \quad . \tag{7.2}$$

PROOF 7.2
*Let $x^i$ be the equilibrium choice of agent $i$ at the price $\ell$. Decompose $x^i =$*

*$y^i + z^i$, where $y^i \in \langle \eta, \ell \rangle$ and $z^i$ is orthogonal to $\langle \eta, \ell \rangle$. Since $z^i \diamond \ell = 0$, $\ell \diamond y^i = \ell \diamond x^i$ and $y^i$ lies in the budget frontier of agent $i$. Since $z^i \diamond \eta = 0$, $\eta \diamond x^i = \eta \diamond y^i$, but this implies*

$$\operatorname{cov}\left(\eta, x^i\right) + \mathbb{E}\left(x^i\right) = \operatorname{cov}\left(\eta, y^i\right) + \mathbb{E}\left(y^i\right)$$

*and with Lemma 7.1. This implies $\mathbb{E}\left(x^i\right) = \mathbb{E}\left(y^i\right)$.*
*Since $y^i$ and $z^i$ are orthogonal, $E\left(y^i z^i\right) = 0$, and with $E\left(z^i\right) = 0$, it immediately follows that $\operatorname{cov}\left(y^i, z^i\right) = 0$. This implies*

$$V\left(x^i\right) = V\left(y^i\right) + V\left(z^i\right) \geq V\left(y^i\right) \quad .$$

*Since $x^i$ is most preferred, it must be*

$$0 = V\left(z^i\right) = \mathbb{E}\left(\left(z^i\right)^2\right) - \left(\mathbb{E}\left(z^i\right)\right)^2 = \mathbb{E}\left(\left(z^i\right)^2\right) \quad ,$$

*This in turn implies $z^i = 0$.*
*Thus for all agents, there are real numbers $\lambda^i, \xi^i$, such that*

$$x^i = \lambda^i \eta + \xi^i \ell \quad .$$

*Let $x^i = \lambda^i \eta + \xi^i \omega$ be the choice of agent $i$, and assume $\xi^i > 0$. Take $y = \left(\lambda^i + \xi^i\right) \eta$. Clearly $\mathbb{E}\left(y\right) = \mathbb{E}\left(x^i\right)$ and $V\left(y\right) < V\left(x^i\right)$. Furthermore $\ell \diamond y = \left(\ell \diamond \eta\right)\left(\lambda^i + \xi^i\right) \leq \lambda^i \left(\ell \diamond \eta\right) + \xi^i \left(\ell \diamond \omega\right) = \ell \diamond x^i$. Thus $x^i$ cannot be maximizing agent $i$'s utility function. Therefore $\xi^i \leq 0$ for all $i$.*

*q. e. d.*

Now we derive the equilibrium consequences of the Tobin-Separation-Property. These are the Mutual-Fund Theorem and the property that in equilibrium the market portfolio cost less than the quasi-bond.

PROPOSITION 7.2 (MUTUAL FUND THEOREM)
*In an equilibrium, the following relations hold: for every agent $i$, there exist $\phi^i \in \mathbb{R}$, $\psi^i \in \mathbb{R}_-$ such that*

$$x^{*,i} = \phi^i \eta + \psi^i \omega \quad , \tag{7.3}$$

*and there are $\phi_0, \psi_0 \in \mathbb{R}$ such that:*

$$\ell = \phi_0 \eta + \psi_0 \omega \quad . \tag{7.4}$$

*Moreover in equilibrium, it must be that $\ell \diamond \omega < \ell \diamond \eta$.*

PROOF 7.3
*In equilibrium the agents consume their whole budget. This must be so, because in equilibrium markets clear and in the aggregate*

$$\sum_i \ell \diamond x^{*,i} = \sum_i \ell \diamond \omega^i \quad .$$

*If any agent had* $\ell \diamond x^{*,i} < \ell \diamond \omega^i$ *and all other agents respect their budget constraint* $\ell \diamond x^{*,j} \leq \ell \diamond \omega^j$*, then the market clearing condition could not hold.*

*(i) From the Tobin-Separation-Property, see Proposition 7.1, we know that for all agents, there are real numbers* $\xi^i > 0$*, and* $\lambda^i$*, such that*

$$x^i = \lambda^i \eta + \xi^i \ell \quad .$$

*(ii) In equilibrium* $\sum_i x^i = \sum_i \lambda^i \eta + \sum_i \xi^i \ell = \omega$*. Thus*

$$\ell = \frac{1}{\sum_i \xi^i} \omega - \frac{\sum_i \lambda^i}{\sum_i \xi^i} \eta \quad .$$

*Note that* $\sum_i \xi^i = 0$ *was excluded because* $\omega$ *and* $\eta$ *are not collinear.*

*Writing* $\ell$ *in the above form, one concludes:*

$$x^i = \left( \lambda^i - \frac{\xi^i}{\sum_i \xi_i} \sum_i \lambda^i \right) \eta + \frac{\xi^i}{\sum_i \xi^i} \omega \quad .$$

*(iii) Assume* $\ell \diamond \omega \geq \ell \diamond \eta$*. Let* $x^i = \phi^i \eta + \psi^i \omega$ *be the choice of agent* $i$*. As was shown in the proof of the Tobin-Separation Property* $\psi^i \leq 0$*. But then* $\sum_i \psi^i \leq 0$*, which is impossible, because at equilibrium* $\sum_i x^i = \omega$ *and therefore* $\sum_i \psi^i = 1$*. Thus it must be:* $\ell \diamond \omega < \ell \diamond \eta$*.*

*q. e. d.*

Algebraic manipulation of equation (7.4) implies the following linear pricing rule for payoff streams $y \in \langle A \rangle$:

$$\ell \cdot y = k\, E(y) + K \operatorname{cov}(\omega, y) \quad , \tag{7.5}$$

where $k = \phi_0 (1 - Var(\eta)) - \psi_0$ and $K = \psi_0$.
Let $R_y$ denote the return per unit of income on any payoff stream $y \in \langle A \rangle$ with non-zero market value, i.e. $R_y = \frac{y}{(\ell \cdot y)}$. Then, if one uses the portfolio $z = \eta - \frac{Var(\eta)}{Var(\omega)} \omega$ that has zero covariance with $\omega$ instead of writing equations (7.3) and (7.4) with $\eta$, the linear relationship of (7.5) can be written as:

$$E\left(R_y\right)-E\left(R_z\right)=\frac{\operatorname{cov}\left(R_y,R_\omega\right)}{Var\left(R_\omega\right)}\left(E\left(R_\omega\right)-E\left(R_z\right)\right) \quad ,$$

which is the famous 'zero-beta'-CAPM or 'two-factor'-CAPM.
Given the insights of the last proposition, information about the equilibrium can be gained by solving a simplified problem, namely one in which investors do not choose their portfolio among all securities in $A$, but only among $\eta$ and $\omega$. The investors' new problem then has the following shape:

$$\max U^i\left(\phi\,\eta+\psi\,\omega\right) \text{ subject to } \quad \ell\diamond\eta\,\phi+\ell\diamond\omega\,\psi\le\ell\diamond\eta\,\bar\phi^i+\ell\diamond\omega\,\bar\psi^i \quad ,$$

where $\bar\omega^i=\eta\,\bar\phi^i+\omega\,\bar\psi^i$ is the orthogonal projection of $\omega^i$ onto $\langle\eta,\omega\rangle$. $\bar\phi^i$ and $\bar\psi^i$ can be computed as:

$$\bar\psi^i=\frac{\operatorname{cov}\left(\eta,\omega^i\right)-\operatorname{cov}\left(\omega,\omega^i\right)}{V\left(\eta\right)-V\left(\omega\right)},\bar\phi^i=\mathbb{E}\left(\omega^i\right)-\bar\psi^i \quad .$$

It will turn out that it is more practical to use instead of the base elements $\eta$ and $\omega$, the equivalent base consisting of $\eta$ and $\omega-\eta$. The use of $(\omega-\eta)$ has several advantages. First, for the general perception of the facts, it is very intuitive to have one base element closely related to the entity "standard deviation". Secondly, since some computing will have to be done, it is obviously very helpful to have $\mathbb{E}\left(\omega-\eta\right)=\operatorname{cov}\left(\eta,\omega-\eta\right)=0$. Finally, the main reason for the use of $(\omega-\eta)$ as a base element is that due to the last line in the Mutual-Fund Theorem, in equilibrium its price has to be negative, so that we can use the price normalization $\ell\diamond(\omega-\eta)=-1$.
From now on we use the following notation. The space of allowed asset-trades is spanned by $\eta$ and $\hat\omega=\frac{1}{\|\omega-\eta\|^2}\left(\omega-\eta\right)$. Given the assumptions on $\omega$, one has:

$$\mathbb{E}\left(\hat\omega\right)-0, \quad V\left(\sigma\right)-1 \quad .$$

For a consumption vector $x=\alpha\,\eta+\beta\,\hat\sigma$, the following holds:

$$\mathbb{E}\left(x\right)=\alpha, \quad V\left(x\right)=V\left(\eta\right)\alpha^2+\beta^2 \quad .$$

The endowment of agent $i$ is given as

$$\bar\omega^i=\bar\alpha^i\,\eta+\bar\beta^i\,\hat\sigma \quad ,$$

with $\bar\alpha^i=\bar\phi^i+\bar\psi^i$ and $\bar\beta^i=\|\omega-\eta\|^2\,\bar\psi^i$.
Given that in equilibrium $\ell\diamond\hat\omega<0$, we normalize prices by setting $\ell\diamond\hat\omega=-1$. The price of $\eta$ will be denoted by $r$, which can be positive or negative. An equilibrium in these new notations is then defined as:

DEFINITION 7.3 (CAPM EQUILIBRIUM)
*An equilibrium of the $\mu - \sigma$-economy is an allocation $\alpha^{*,i}, \beta^{*,i} \in \mathbb{R}^2$ for every $i \in I$ and a price $r^* \in \mathbb{R}$, such that:*

*(i)* $\alpha^{*,i}, \beta^{*,i}$ *maximizes* $v^i\left(\alpha, \sqrt{Var(\eta)\,\alpha^2 + \beta^2}\right)$
*subject to* $r^*\,\alpha - \beta \leq r^*\,\bar{\alpha}^i - \bar{\beta}^i$,

*(ii)* $\sum_I \alpha^{*,i} = 1$, $\sum_I \beta^{*,i} = \|\omega - \eta\|^2$.

## 6. Equilibria in the CAPM with a Riskless Asset

In the standard CAPM the existence of a riskless asset is assumed. In this case the previous analysis simplifies considerably. In the Tobin-Separation-Property and the Mutual-Fund Theorem one can then replace the quasi-bond $\eta$ with the riskless asset $\mathbb{1}$. However, in the case of a riskless asset we prefer to work with a different price normalization. From the arbitrage argument given in Section 3 of this chapter we know that the price of the riskless asset has to be positive. Hence we normalize all prices such that $\ell \diamond \mathbb{1} = 1$. Note that a similar normalization in the case of the quasi-bond is not possible since it is not clear that the price of $\eta$ is positive. On denoting the price of $\sigma$ by $q$, going through the same reasoning as in the case of no riskless asset, with a riskless asset CAPM equilibria can then be defined as:

DEFINITION 7.4 (CAPM EQUILIBRIUM)
*An equilibrium of the $\mu$-$\sigma$-economy is an allocation $\mu^{*,i}, \sigma^{*,i} \in \mathbb{R}^2$ for every $i \in I$ and a price $q^* \in \mathbb{R}$, such that:*

*(i)* $\mu^{*,i}, \sigma^{*,i}$ *maximizes* $v^i(\mu, \sigma)$ *subject to* $\mu - q^*\,\sigma \leq \bar{\mu}^i - q^*\,\bar{\sigma}^i$,

*(ii)* $\sum_I \mu^{*,i} = 1$, $\sum_I \sigma^{*,i} = \sigma^2(\omega)$.

In this definition $\bar{\mu}^i = E(\omega^i)$ and $\bar{\sigma}^i = \frac{\text{cov}(\omega^i, \omega)}{\sigma^2(\omega)}$.

## 7. Risk Aversion in the CAPM

In this section we give a definition for risk aversion in the CAPM that parallels the demand for risk aversion in case of expected utility functions introduced in Chapter 1. There we had referred to Arrow and Pratt who defined the absolute risk aversion as the negative of the ratio of the second derivative of the von Neumann-Morgenstern utility function over its first derivative. How the absolute risk aversion changes with income determines how an investor changes his demand for risky assets when he is faced with an elementary situation of one risky and one riskless asset. In the case of mean-variance utility functions there need not be any von Neumann-Morgenstern utility function. Hence risk aversion cannot be defined in exactly the same way. The trick here is to define risk aversion for the CAPM by revealed preference. Referring back to Arrow and Pratt's result we *define* a mean-variance utility to have decreasing (increasing) absolute risk aversion if on the increase of wealth the demand for variance increases (decreases). In the GEI-model this comparative statics property referred to an elementary decision problem with one risky and one riskless asset. Therefore we define risk aversion in the CAPM with reference to the case in which there is a riskless asset. To this end, recall that the demand for variance is derived from the following maximization problem:

$$\max_{\sigma^i \in \mathbb{R}_+} v^i \left( \bar{\mu}^i + q(\sigma - \bar{\sigma}), \sigma^i \right)$$

where $\bar{\mu}^i = E(\omega^i)$ and $\bar{\sigma}^i = \frac{\text{cov}(\omega^i, \omega)}{\sigma^2(\omega)}$. The following figure shows a typical situation for this solution.
The definition of risk aversion will be in terms of the slope of the indifference curves in the $(\mu, \sigma)$- diagram,

$$S^i(\mu, \sigma) := -\frac{\partial_\sigma v^i(\mu, \sigma)}{\partial_\mu v^i(\mu, \sigma)} \quad .$$

DEFINITION 7.5
*A mean-variance utility function exhibits non- increasing (non-decreasing) risk aversion if for all $\sigma \geq 0$ the slope of its indifference curves are non increasing (non- decreasing) functions in mean. It exhibits constant absolute risk aversion if this slope is constant.*

The following proposition that goes back to Nielsen [1988] and Lajeri and Nielsen [2000]. It shows that the above definition is indeed the appropriate analogue of Arrow and Pratt' s definition:

PROPOSITION 7.3 (RISK AVERSION IN CAPM)
*For any investor $i = 1, \ldots, I$, and for all prices $q > 0$ we get:*

$$\partial_{\bar{\mu}} \sigma^i(q) \lesseqgtr 0 \quad \textit{iff} \quad \partial_\mu S^i\left(\mu^i(q), \sigma^i(q)\right) \gtreqless 0$$

PROOF 7.4 *To solve the maximization problem*

$$\max_{(\mu^i, \sigma^i) \in \mathbb{R} \times R_+} v^i\left(\mu^i, \sigma^i\right) \quad \textit{s.t.} \quad \mu^i - q\sigma^i \leq \bar{\mu}^i - q\bar{\sigma}^i$$

*note that since $v^i$ is increasing in $\mu$ the budget restriction must hold with equality. Thus supposing positivity of $\sigma^i$ the first order condition is*

$$\partial_{\mu^i} v^i\left(\bar{\mu}^i + q\left(\sigma^i - \bar{\sigma}^i\right), \sigma^i\right) q + \partial_{\sigma^i} v^i\left(\bar{\mu}^i + q\left(\sigma^i - \bar{\sigma}^i\right), \sigma^i\right) = 0. \quad (7.6)$$

*By strict quasi-concavity of $v^i\left(\mu^i, \sigma^i\right)$ the solution to the first order condition is necessary and sufficient for a solution of the mean-variance maximization problem.*
*Application of the implicit function theorem leads to.*

$$\partial_{\bar{\mu}} \sigma^i = \frac{\left(\partial^2_{\mu^i} v^i\right) q + \left(\partial_{\mu^i} \partial_{\sigma^i} v^i\right)}{-\left[\left(\left(\partial_{\sigma^i} \partial_{\mu^i} v^i\right) + \partial^2_{\mu^i} v^i q\right) q + \left(\partial_{\mu^i} \partial_{\sigma^i} v^i\right) q + \left(\partial^2_{\sigma^i} v^i\right)\right]} .$$

*For brevity of this expression we have omitted the arguments $\mu^i$ and $\sigma^i$ from the function $v^i$. Denoting the denominator by $-d^i$ and using the identity* $q = -\frac{\partial_{\sigma^i} v^i}{\partial_{\mu^i} v^i}$ *and the formula*

$$\partial_{\mu^i} S^i\left(\mu^i, \sigma^i\right) = -\frac{\left[\left(\partial_{\mu^i} \partial_{\sigma^i} v^i\right)\left(\partial_{\mu^i} v^i\right) - \left(\partial^2_{\mu^i} v^i\right)\left(\partial_{\sigma^i} v^i\right)\right]}{\left(\partial_{\mu^i} v^i\right)^2}$$

*proves our claim because:*

$$\partial_{\bar{\mu}} \sigma^i = \frac{\partial_{\mu^i} S^i\left(\mu^i, \sigma^i\right) \partial_{\mu^i} v^i}{-d^i} .$$

*Note that by strict quasi-concavity of $v^i$, $d^i$ is negative.*

*q. e. d.*

## 8. Monotonicity and Positive State Prices

One fundamental problem of the mean-variance model is that monotonicity of preferences is not guaranteed as the following example demonstrates:

EXAMPLE 7.2 (MEAN-VARIANCE-PARADOX)
*There are two states. An asset pays off $A = \binom{y}{0}$, where $y > 0$. The first state occurs with probability $\rho > 0$. Hence the expected pay off of the asset is $\mu(A) = \rho y > 0$. Moreover, the variance of the asset' pay off is $\sigma^2(A) = \mu(A)\, y + \mu^2(A)$. Now for any mean-variance utility function $v(\mu, \sigma)$ consider*

*the indifference curve through the origin* $(0,0)$. *The idea of this example is to construct a sequence of pay offs* $y\,(n)$ *and corresponding probabilities* $\rho(n)$ *so that eventually the mean-variance investor will not chose the asset over the point* $(0,0)$. *To do so, consider a sequence* $(y(n), \rho(n))_{n\in\mathbb{N}}$ *such that* $y(n)\,\rho(n) = \bar{\mu}$ *for all* $n \in \mathbb{N}$ *and for some* $\bar{\mu} > 0$. *Choose the sequence such that* $y(n) \to \infty$. *Then for some* $n$ *any mean-variance investor will eventually prefer the point* $(0,0)$ *over the asset A. See Figure 7.2 for an illustration:*

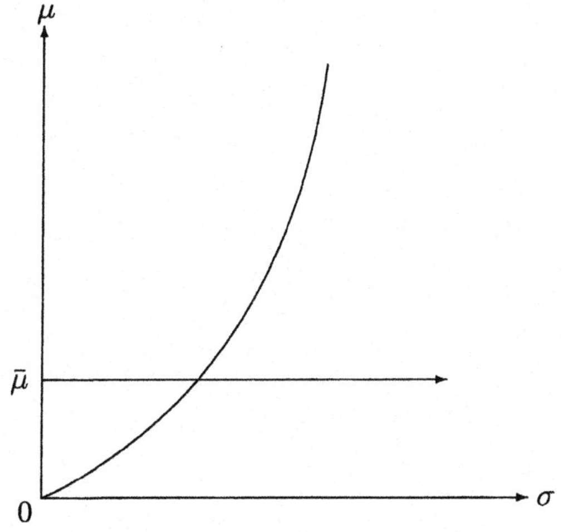


*Figure 7.2.* Mean-variance paradox

*Hence the mean-variance utility is not monotonic as defined in Chapter 1. In particular it does not satisfy first-order stochastic dominance.*

The lack of monotonicity of preferences can lead to negative state prices in equilibrium, as the following example, taken from Siwik [2001][chapter 2] shows:

EXAMPLE 7.3 (NEGATIVE STATE PRICES)
*Suppose the asset structure consists only of two assets: the riskless asset and the market portfolio* $\omega$. *The market portfolio shall be a non-negative random variable with positive variance. Furthermore, let the mean variance utility functions be linear in mean, so that* $v^i(\mu,\sigma) = \mu - \frac{\varphi^i\sigma^2}{2}$. *In this example one can easily compute the price of the market asset as:*

$$q(\omega) = \mu(\omega) + \frac{1}{\bar{r}}\sigma_\omega^2 \quad , \tag{7.7}$$

*where* $\bar{r} = -\sum_i \frac{1}{\varphi^i}$.

*For negative state prices one should have:*

$$q(\omega) < 0 \Leftrightarrow E(\omega^2) > \mu_\omega^2(1 - \bar{r}) \quad . \tag{7.8}$$

*To achieve this property, in some states of nature $\omega$ should have a very high pay-off with a very low probability so that the second moment outweighs the first moment. The inequality is fulfilled in the following economy:*

$$\begin{aligned} S &= \{s_1, s_2, s_3\}, \\ \rho(\{s_1\}, \{s_2\}, \{s_3\}) &= (0.01, 0.95, 0.04), \\ \omega &= (100, 1, 0), \\ (\varphi^1, \varphi^2) &= (1/18, 1/30), \\ \bar{r} &= -\left(\frac{1}{1/18} + \frac{1}{1/30}\right) = -48, \\ \mu(\omega) &= 1.95, \\ E(\omega^2) &= 100.95 \quad . \end{aligned}$$

*The pricing asset and the price of the market asset turn out to be:*

$$\begin{aligned} \ell &= \frac{1}{\bar{r}}[\omega - \mu(\omega)\mathbf{1}] + \mathbf{1} \\ &= -\frac{1}{48}[(100, 1, 0) - 1.95\,(1, 1, 1)] + (1, 1, 1) \\ &\approx (-1.0427, 1.0198, 1.0406) \text{ and} \\ q(\omega) &= E_Q(\omega) = E(\ell\omega) \\ &\approx -0.07389 < 0 \quad . \end{aligned}$$

In this example the non-negative market asset has positive pay-offs with positive probability. Nevertheless one would get money for buying this asset. A third asset, which would complete the market, does not change this result, since the bond and the market asset are already spanned. Imagine an additional Arrow-security, which pays only one unit in the first state of the world. Its price is negative, contradicting the no-arbitrage condition in GEI-models. The example raises a serious conceptual difficulty for the CAPM. One way of ruling out such an example is to make sure that some agent has a strictly monotonic utility function. To achieve this property one needs to assume that the agents' risk aversions are sufficiently small so that even the total endowments are not sufficient to induce satiation.

The most general result in this line of research was recently demonstrated by Siwik [2001][Chapter 2][Theorem 68]:

PROPOSITION 7.4 (POSITIVITY OF STATE PRICES. [SIWIK, 2001])
*Let* $\bar{r} = \sum_{i \in I} r^i$ *where* $r^i = r^i(\mu^i, \sigma^i) := \sigma^i \frac{\partial_\mu v^i(\mu^i,\sigma^i)}{\partial_\sigma v^i(\mu^i,\sigma^i)}$ *and* $(\mu^i, \sigma^i)$ *is the agents' equilibrium choice of mean and variance. Suppose that the market portfolio* $\omega$ *and the quasi-bond* $\eta$ *are not collinear, then in equilibrium state prices are strictly positive if*

$$(\bar{r} - \mathbb{E}(\omega))\,\eta + \mathbb{E}^2(\eta)\,\omega << 0. \tag{7.9}$$

PROOF 7.5 [2]
*Recall from 7.3 in the proof of the Mutual-Fund-Theorem that*[3]

$$l = \eta + \frac{1}{\xi}\left(\omega - \mathbb{E}(\omega)\,\eta\right). \tag{7.10}$$

*where* $\xi = \sum_{i=1}^{I} \xi^i$ *and every* $\xi^i$ *is determined from the Tobin-Separation Property, Proposition 7.1, in the following way:*
*According to the Tobin-Separation Property there exist* $\xi^i \in \mathbb{R}_-$ *and* $\mu^i \in \mathbb{R}$ *such that*

$$x^i = \mu^i \eta + \xi^i\,(l - \eta) \tag{7.11}$$

*The coefficients* $\mu^i, \xi^i$ *are determined by the solution of the agents' maximization problem:*

$$v^i\left(\mu^i, \sqrt{(\mu^i)^2\,V(\eta) + (\xi^i)^2\,V(l-\eta)}\right)$$

*subject to*

$$l \diamond \omega^i = l \diamond x^i = \mu^i\,\mathbb{E}^2(\eta) + \xi^i\,V(l-\eta).$$

*Since* $v^i$ *is strictly quasi-concave in* $(\mu^i, \sigma^i)$ *and therefore also in* $(\mu^i, \xi^i)$, *the first order conditions are sufficient to determine the unique optimum. With the Lagrangian multiplier for* $i$*'s budget constraint denoted by* $\gamma^i$ *these conditions are:*

$$\partial_\mu v^i + \frac{\partial_\sigma v^i}{\sigma^i}\mu^i V(\eta) - \gamma^i\,\mathbb{E}^2(\eta) = 0, \tag{7.12}$$

$$\left(\frac{\partial_\sigma v^i}{\sigma^i}\xi^i - \gamma^i\right) V(l-\eta) = 0. \tag{7.13}$$

*Solving* (7.12) *for* $\gamma^i$ *and inserting this into* (7.13) *yields:*

---

[2] We owe this proof to Thomas Siwik.

[3] Note that $\xi \neq 0$ because $\omega$ and $\eta$ are not collinear.

$$\xi^i = \frac{\frac{\partial_\mu v^i \sigma^i}{\partial_\sigma v^i} + \mu^i V(\eta)}{\mathbb{E}^2(\eta)} \tag{7.14}$$

*Using the definition* $r^i(\mu, \sigma) := \sigma^i \frac{\partial_\mu v^i(\mu,\sigma)}{\partial_\sigma v^i(\mu,\sigma)}$ *yields*

$$\xi^i = \frac{r^i + \mu^i V(\eta)}{\mathbb{E}^2(\eta)} \tag{7.15}$$

*Aggregating* (7.15) *over* $\xi^i$ *yields*

$$\xi = \sum_{i=1}^{I} \xi^i = \frac{\bar{r} + \mathbb{E}(\omega) V(\eta)}{\mathbb{E}^2(\eta)}, \tag{7.16}$$

*which, using* $V(\eta) = \mathbb{E}^2(\eta) - 1$ *yields:*

$$\xi = \frac{\bar{r} - \mathbb{E}(\omega)}{\mathbb{E}^2(\eta)} + \mathbb{E}(\omega). \tag{7.17}$$

*Inserting* (7.17) *into* (7.10) *yields the following expression for* $\ell$*:*

$$l = \eta + \frac{\mathbb{E}^2(\eta)}{\bar{r} - \mathbb{E}(\omega) + \mathbb{E}(\omega)\mathbb{E}^2(\eta)} \left(\omega - \mathbb{E}\left(\omega\right) \eta\right). \tag{7.18}$$

*Note that since* $\omega$ *and* $\eta$ *are not collinear,* $\xi$ *is strictly negative and hence* $\bar{r} - \mathbb{E}(\omega) + \mathbb{E}(\omega)\mathbb{E}^2(\eta) < 0$. *Thus* $\ell >> 0$ *iff the condition in the statement of the proposition holds.*
*Finally, note that the strictly positive projection of the likelihood ratio process* $\ell \in X$ *yields strictly positive state prices* $\pi$ *because the latter are derived from the former by addition of some component in* $X^\perp$.[4]

In the case of a riskless asset, for example, positivity of state prices follows from this theorem if in no state the market portfolio is too large as compared to the difference between the sum of the agents' risk aversion coefficients $\sum_{i \in I} r^i$ and the mean of the market portfolio. This general condition is considerable easier to interpret in the special cases considered so far in the literature. Suppose for example that the CAPM is derived from quadratic von Neumann Morgenstern utilities, $u^i(x) = x - \frac{\phi^i x^2}{2}$, then $r^i = \mu(x^i) - \frac{1}{\phi^i}$. and hence the Condition 7.9 becomes: $\sum_{i \in I} \frac{1}{\phi^i} > \omega(s)$ for all $s \in S$. Hence if in every state aggregate endowments are sufficiently small as compared to the harmonic mean of the risk aversion coefficients $\phi^i$ then positivity of state prices is obtained. A special case of this condition is the condition of Magill and Quinzii [1996] who have

[4]The converse is however not true. That is to say, in general, we need weaker conditions than (7.9) to obtain strictly positive state prices. For a thorough exposition see Siwik [2001].

shown that positivity of state prices results from $\frac{1}{\phi^i} > \omega(s)$ for all $s \in S$. Moreover, Pilgrim [1998] has shown that positivity of state prices results from $\frac{1}{\phi^i} > \omega^i(s)$ for all $s \in S$, which is also a special case of the condition found in Siwik [2001].

An alternative assumption leading positive state prices is the assumption that agents have expected utility functions and that the return distribution of any portfolio can be modelled by the two parameters mean and variance. Going this way monotonicity of preferences in the CAPM is inherited from the expected utility assumption.

# Chapter 8

# EXISTENCE OF EQUILIBRIA

We are grateful to Jörg Laitenberger who allow us to take this chapter from his Ph.D. Thesis, Laitenberger [1999].

## 1. Introduction

For a sound foundation of the CAPM based on the GEI-model the first issue is to prove the existence of competitive equilibria. The goal of this chapter is to give sufficient conditions for the existence of an equilibrium in the Capital Asset Pricing Model (CAPM) without a riskless asset, that are general enough to allow for any strictly quasi-concave and continuously differentiable mean-variance utilities. Moreover we allow for assets that can possibly have negative returns. Finally a riskless asset need not exist.

The CAPM with risky assets was first examined in 1972 by Black [1972]. He developed the formula, known as 'zero-beta'-CAPM or 'two-factor'-CAPM, that describes the pricing of financial assets in a capital market equilibrium. It was only in the late 1980's that the fundamental question of the existence of such an equilibrium was approached. Indeed, while the existence of an equilibrium in the CAPM with a riskless asset is always guaranteed, even though the methods required for its proof are different to the standard general equilibrium model, in the variant without a riskless bond it can happen that no equilibrium exists. This can even arise for very simple examples of utility functions and asset returns (cf. Nielsen [1990a], such that it is somehow amazing, why the results of the CAPM have remained unquestioned for so long. The nonexistence of a riskless security has to be taken as relevant, since, financial contracts being typically monetary contracts, the real purchasing power of a security that is riskless in nominal terms will be subject to inflationary risk.

Problems arise because mean-variance preferences may induce a preference ordering on the portfolios of asset demand that is not monotonic. Satiation in some assets is possible. When there is a riskless asset, this is not a problem, because investors always prefer more of the riskless asset. When there is no such riskless asset, satiation can lead to the impossibility of finding an equilibrium, in which investors invest their whole budget. This has been observed and analyzed by several authors. In the special case when the utility functions of the investors can be written as a linear function of the mean and the variance of the attainable portfolios, which implies constant risk aversion, equilibrium demand can be computed explicitly. In this case Nielsen [1990a]) has given necessary and sufficient conditions for an equilibrium to exist. In the same paper and in Nielsen [1990b] he partially extends these results to the general case. To derive sufficient conditions for existence, Nielsen relies on an abstract existence result for exchange economies with non-monotonic preferences. In short, satiation must not occur on the set of portfolios that are attainable and individually rational. These conditions ensure that this set, which is closely related to the core, is nonempty, and this is proved to be sufficient for existence. In contrast to Nielsen, Allingham [1991] gives sufficient conditions using demand correspondences and the market demand function. Unfortunately, Allingham considers demand for every security separately, which leads him to a high dimensional vector of conditions, one for every non redundant security. In this chapter, we follow Allingham's path, but, by virtue of the Tobin-Separation-Property, we reduce the economy to a two-asset-economy, where demand has to be considered only for two artificial securities, the 'minimum-variance-portfolio' and the 'market portfolio'. This allows us to find conditions that can be much more general than Allingham's.

Typically satiation occurs at some prices only. By their influence on the budget of the investors, conditions that ensure existence depend on the price system and on the initial endowments. Therefore a set of *necessary and sufficient* conditions can be formulated only when the aspired equilibrium price is known in advance. Except in the very special situation when utilities are linear in mean and in variance, this will not be the case, such that in general one has to content oneself with sufficient conditions that will guarantee non-satiation for a convex set of prices, that include the equilibrium price.

The analysis in Section 3 identifies 3 sets of conditions. Theorem 8.1, that holds for all possible endowments, is identical to Proposition 3 in Nielsen [1990b]. Still it is worthwhile to state it, since the proofs are fundamentally different. When stated as a joint condition on endowments and preference parameters, Theorem 8.2 and 8.3 give results that generalize Nielsen's and Allingham's results. The conditions identified in their papers give the impression that small risk aversion is one of the ingredients one cannot dispense with in order to ensure existence. This impression is falsified by Theorem 8.3 that holds only for investors having a degree of risk aversion *larger* than some lower bound.

## 2. Necessary Conditions for Existence

We consider the general case neither requiring spanning nor the existence of a riskless asset. Unlike in the case of the CAPM with a riskless asset, existence of an equilibrium is not guaranteed. It can happen, that there is no price at which all investors wish to consume all their income. A simple case where this can arise, is when at least one investor prefers nothing to any amount of $\eta$. This investor will never demand anything, since any portfolio, that is attainable by the existing market structure will be too risky. A more sophisticated example, where all investors exhaust their budget constraint at some prices, but these domains do not overlap, is given below and has been borrowed from Allingham [1991]:

EXAMPLE 8.1
*Let there be two assets $A^1$ and $A^2$ with $\mathbb{E}(A^1) = \mathbb{E}(A^2) = 18$, $Var(A^1) = Var(A^2) = 5$ and $\operatorname{cov}(A^1, A^2) = 4$. There are two investors with $u^1(x) = u^2(x) = \mu(x) - \frac{1}{2}\sigma(x)^2$ and with endowments $\omega^1 = A^1 + 4A^2$ and $\omega^2 = 4A^1 + A^2$ respectively. Note that in the space of mean and standard deviation, the endowments of the two agents are represented by the same point, although the covariance of the two endowments with the market portfolio is different. Denote by $r_i = \ell \diamond A^i$ the prices of the two assets. One computes now easily, that when $r_1/r_2 > 1/2$ agent 1 always demands the portfolio $z = 2(A^1 + A^2)\,(= 1/72\eta)$ although $\ell \diamond z = 2(r_1 + r_2) < r_1 + 4r_2 = \ell \diamond \omega^1$ and hence does not exhaust her budget, while agent 2 always demands $z$ when $r_1/r_2 < 2$. Therefore there is no price at which markets clear.*

The next lemma states a necessary condition for the budget identity to hold, in terms of the demand functions of the agents. Let $\alpha^i(r)$ and $\beta^i(r)$ denote agent $i$'s demand for $\eta$ and $\hat{\omega}$ at the price $r$, and

$$\hat{\beta}^i(r) = \arg\max_{\beta \in \mathbb{R}} v^i\left(\frac{r\bar{\alpha}^i - \bar{\beta}^i + \beta}{r}, \sqrt{Var(\eta)\left(\frac{r\bar{\alpha}^i - \bar{\beta}^i + \beta}{r}\right)^2 + \beta^2}\right), \tag{8.1}$$

be the solution to the maximization problem in Definition 7.3 when the investors are confined to consume their whole budget[1].

LEMMA 8.1
*When $\hat{\beta}^i(r) > 0$, then $\beta^i(r) = \hat{\beta}^i(r)$ and the budget identity holds: $r\alpha^i(r) - \beta^i(r) = r\bar{\alpha}^i - \bar{\beta}^i$.*

[1]Polemarchakis and Siconolfi [1993] have studied an equilibrium concept, the *weak competitive equilibrium*, with this restriction on consumers' choices.

PROOF 8.1

*Let* $x = \alpha^i(r)\eta + \beta^i(r)\hat{\omega}$ *and* $\hat{x} = \hat{\alpha}^i(r)\eta + \hat{\beta}^i(r)\hat{\omega}$ *with* $\hat{\beta}^i(r) > 0$ *denote the choice of agent* $i$ *in the two maximization problems respectively, and let* $b^i(r) = r\bar{\alpha}^i - \bar{\beta}^i$ *be the value of her endowment.*

*Assume* $x \neq \hat{x}$. *This is possible only when* $\beta^i(r) = 0$, *because if* $\beta^i(r) \neq 0$, *either* $r\alpha^i(r) < b^i(r)$ *or* $r\alpha^i(r) > b^i(r)$. *The first case implies that* $\alpha^i(r)\eta$ *is attainable, and since* $Var(\alpha^i(r)\eta) < Var(x)$, $x$ *cannot be the optimum. In the second case* $\beta^i(r) > r\alpha^i(r) - b^i(r)$. *But then* $\alpha^i(r)\eta + (r\alpha^i(r) - b^i(r))\hat{\omega}$ *is attainable and preferred to* $x$. *Thus* $x = \alpha^i(r)\eta$ *and* $r\alpha^i(r) < b^i(r)$.

$\hat{\beta}^i(r) > 0$ *together with the budget identity obviously imply* $r\hat{\alpha}^i(r) > b^i(r)$. *One concludes*

$$\frac{b^i(r)}{r} \in \left(\alpha^i(r), \hat{\alpha}^i(r)\right) \quad . \tag{8.2}$$

*Summing up,* $x \neq \hat{x}$ *implies that agent* $i$ *prefers* $\alpha^i(r)\eta$ *to* $\frac{b^i(r)}{r}\eta$ *and* $\hat{\alpha}^i(r)\eta$ *to* $\frac{b^i(r)}{r}\eta$. *But this is impossible, when preferences are strictly quasi-concave.*

*q. e. d.*

## 3. Sufficient Conditions for Existence

The sufficient conditions for the existence of an equilibrium will be formulated in terms of the slope of the indifference curves of the utility functions $v^i(\mu, \sigma)$. These are defined in the following way.

For each value $c$ in the image of $v^i$, there is a unique function $I_c^i$ of $\sigma$ such that the graph of $I_c^i$ is the indifference curve $v^i(\mu, \sigma) = c$:

$$\mu = I_c^i(\sigma) \Leftrightarrow v^i(\mu, \sigma) = c \quad \text{for all} \quad \left(I_c^i(\sigma), \sigma\right). \tag{8.3}$$

The slope of the indifference curve at a certain point $(\mu, \sigma)$ in the space of mean and standard deviation is denoted by

$$S^i(\mu, \sigma) := -\frac{\partial_\sigma v^i(\mu, \sigma)}{\partial_\mu v^i(\mu, \sigma)} = \partial_\sigma I_c^i(\sigma) \quad \text{with} \quad c = v^i(\mu, \sigma) \quad . \tag{8.4}$$

When there is no risk of confusion, we will sometimes write $S(x)$ instead of $S(\mu(x), \sigma(x))$ where $x \in \langle A \rangle$ is an attainable payoff-stream, and $S(\alpha, \beta)$ for $S\left(\alpha, \sqrt{\alpha^2 V(\eta) + \beta^2}\right)$.

Given Assumption 7.2, it is clear that $S^i(\mu, \sigma) > 0$ for all $(\mu, \sigma) \in \mathbb{R} \times \mathbb{R}_+$. As we have argued above, these slopes are a measure of the agents' risk aversion at the points in the $(\mu, \sigma)$-space. The conditions for the existence of an equilibrium are fundamentally different, depending on whether the equilibrium price $r^*$ is positive, zero or negative. Let $b^i(r) = r\bar{\alpha}^i - \bar{\beta}^i$ denote the value of investor $i$'s endowment at the price $r$. The following lemma summarizes some necessary conditions for the 3 cases to occur:

LEMMA 8.2
*Assume $r^*$ is an equilibrium price. Then for all agents*

*(i)* $r^* > 0$ *only if* $S\left(\frac{b^i(r^*)}{r^*}\eta\right) < \frac{1}{\sigma(\eta)}$ *when* $b^i(r^*) > 0$.

*(ii)* $r^* = 0$ *only if* $\bar{\beta}^i > 0$.

*(iii)* $r^* < 0$ *only if* $b^i(r^*) < 0$ *and* $S\left(\frac{b^i(r^*)}{r^*}\eta\right) > \frac{1}{\sigma(\eta)}$.

PROOF 8.2
*The proofs of all three cases always use the same type of arguments, such that we give a proof only for the case of a negative $r^*$.*
*With Lemma 8.2, a necessary condition for $r^*$ to be an equilibrium price is that $\beta^{i,*} = \sigma(\omega - \eta)\,\psi^{i,*} > 0$. In equilibrium $r^*\alpha^{i,*} - \beta^{i,*} = b^i(r^*)$. Assume $b^i(r^*) \geq 0$. Then $\alpha^{i,*} < 0$. But the origin is attainable and definitely preferred to negative mean and positive risk. Thus $b^i(r^*) < 0$.*
*The budget identity and $\beta^{i,*} > 0$ imply that $\alpha^{i,*} < \frac{b^i(r^*)}{r^*}$. Since the portfolio $\alpha^{i,*}\eta$ is preferred to the optimal choice, by transitivity it must be preferred to investing all wealth into $\eta$. But this is possible only if the condition on the indifference curve in the proposition holds.*

*q. e. d.*

Given the previous lemma, it is clear that the conditions that ensure the existence of an equilibrium, will influence the shape of this equilibrium. The conditions that lead to a negative or a positive $r$ cannot be of the same type. It has become clear as well, that the most general condition for existence will be a joint condition on the preference relation and the endowment of an investor[2]. A condition that ensures existence for all possible endowments, is the following, that is proved already in Nielsen [1990b]:

THEOREM 8.1 (EXISTENCE IN CAPM. [LAITENBERGER, 1999])
*If all investors have a preference relation, such that*

$$S(\lambda\eta) < \frac{1}{\sigma(\eta)}, \quad \textit{for all} \quad \lambda \geq 0 \quad , \tag{8.5}$$

[2]For the case of a utility function that is linear in mean and in variance, one can find an equation of some utility parameter and the endowment portfolio, that is a necessary and sufficient condition for existence, see Nielsen [1990b].

*then there exists an equilibrium with a positive $r^*$.*

PROOF 8.3
*Given (iii) of Lemma 8.2, it is clear, that only $r^* > 0$ is possible. Consider*

$$\hat{\beta}^i(r) = \arg\max v\left(\frac{r\bar{\alpha}^i - \bar{\beta}^i + \beta}{r}, \sqrt{Var(\eta)\left(\frac{r\bar{\alpha}^i - \bar{\beta}^i + \beta}{r}\right)^2 + \beta^2}\right). \tag{8.6}$$

*When $\hat{\beta}^i(r) > 0$, this corresponds to the demand for $\hat{\omega}$ of agent $i$ at the price $r$.*
*The assumptions on $v^i$ and the implicit function theorem make $\hat{\beta}^i(.)$ a continuous function of $r$.*
*Consider $S^i(\bar{\alpha}^i, \bar{\beta}^i)$ and the tangent to the budget frontier at the endowment point $t(r, \bar{\alpha}^i, \bar{\beta}^i)$. See Section 4 for a derivation of $t(.,.,.)$. Since the budget frontier is convex,*

$$\hat{\beta}^i(r) < (>)\,\bar{\beta}^i \quad \text{if} \quad S^i\left(\bar{\alpha}^i, \bar{\beta}^i\right) > (<)\,t\left(r, \bar{\alpha}^i, \bar{\beta}^i\right). \tag{8.7}$$

*Clearly, when $r$ goes to infinity, $t(r,.,.)$ goes to zero, such that the budget frontier approaches a horizontal half line starting to the right of $\bar{\alpha}^i\eta$. In this case investors wish only to minimize risk, such that $\hat{\beta}^i(r) \to 0$ for all $i \in I$.*
*On the other hand, at $r = 0$, either $t(0, \bar{\alpha}^i, \bar{\beta}^i) > \frac{1}{\sigma(\eta)}$ or $t(0, \bar{\alpha}^i, \bar{\beta}^i) < 0$. In both cases, the condition of the proposition implies $\hat{\beta}^i(0) > \bar{\beta}^i$.*
*Aggregate demand for $\hat{\omega}$ is given by $\sum_I \beta^i(r) = \sum_I \hat{\beta}^i(r)$. It is a continuous function, that exhibits $\sum_I \beta^i(0) > \sum_I \bar{\beta}^i$ and $\lim_{r\to\infty} \sum_I \beta^i(r) = 0$. The mean value theorem ensures the existence of a price $r^*$ such that $\sum_I \beta^i(r^*) = \sigma(\omega - \eta)$.*
*Finally $\hat{\beta}^i(r) > 0$ for all $i \in I$ and all $r > 0$ because $S(b^i(r)\eta) < \frac{1}{\sigma(\eta)} = t(r, b^i(r), 0)$ by assumption and this implies that $b^i(r)\eta$ is always preferred to any $(b^i(r) - \delta)\eta - r\delta\hat{\sigma}$ with $\delta > 0$ and $b^i(r) = r\bar{\alpha}^i - \bar{\beta}^i$ the value of agent $i$'s endowment at the price $r$. Therefore the budget identity holds for all $i$ and this implies that the market for $\eta$ clears as well.*

*q. e. d.*

The condition in the proposition is quite strict. In particular, it implies that risk aversion is uniformly bounded above for all values of mean and standard deviation. Nevertheless, it is necessary to ensure existence for all possible endowments. When the condition does not hold, one can easily distribute endowments such that at least one agent does not exhaust his budget.
When stated as a joint restriction on endowments and preferences one can considerably weaken the requirements of the last theorem. In fact, the key

requirement is that no agent is satiated at some relevant portfolios, which depend on $r^*$. Since $r^*$ is endogenous, it can be very difficult to find an appropriate range of parameters that describe these portfolios. Two cases will be analyzed. The first, where $r^* > 0$, summarizes and generalizes results for the existence, when agents tend to be not too risk averse.

THEOREM 8.2 (EXISTENCE IN CAPM. [LAITENBERGER, 1999])
*There exists an equilibrium with $r^* > 0$, when*

*(i)* $S^i\left(\bar{\alpha}^i\eta\right) < \frac{1}{\sigma(\eta)}$ *for all agents with* $\bar{\beta}^i \geq 0$*, and*

*(ii)* $S^i\left(\frac{b^i\left(r^{min}\right)}{r^{min}}\eta\right) < \frac{1}{\sigma(\eta)}$ *for those agents with* $\bar{\beta}^i < 0$*, where*

$$r^{min} = \min_I \left\{t^{-1}\left(.,\bar{\alpha}^i,\bar{\beta}^i\right)\left(S\left(\bar{\alpha}^i,\bar{\beta}^i\right)\right)\right\} \tag{8.8}$$

*is the price, at which all investors demand more $\hat{\sigma}$ than their initial endowment of $\hat{\sigma}$.*

PROOF 8.4
*The idea of the proof is almost identical to the proof of the previous theorem. The formulated conditions assure that $r^* \in (r^{min}, \infty)$ and, for this interval, one computes easily that $\hat{\beta}^i(r) > 0$ for all $i \in I$.*

*q. e. d.*

The figure depicts the case $\bar{\beta}^i \geq 0$. At $\bar{\alpha}^i\eta$ the slope of the indifference curve is smaller than $\frac{1}{\sigma(\eta)}$, which is the slope of the half-line $\{\lambda\eta | \lambda \geq 0\}$.
Observe that the condition is especially simple when all investors have nonnegative endowment of $\hat{\omega}$.
All results so far have been concerned with the existence problem in markets where investors exhibit 'small' risk aversion with respect to the minimum nondiversifiable risk of the economy. The only example known to us, where it has been pointed out, that small risk aversion is not an absolute "conditio sine qua non" is Nielsen [1990b]. For the special case of utilities that are linear in mean and in variance, he generates a result that allows for investors with large risk aversion. Our next theorem derives a result that extends this intuition to the case of general preferences.

THEOREM 8.3
*There exists an equilibrium with $r^* < 0$ if $\bar{\alpha}^i \geq 0$ and $\bar{\beta}^i \geq 0$ for all $i \in I$ and all investors exhibit:*

$$S^i\left(\bar{\alpha}^i\eta\right) > \frac{1}{\sigma(\eta)}. \tag{8.9}$$

PROOF 8.5

*The condition on the endowments ensures that $b^i(r) \leq 0$ for all $r < 0$. As in the proof of Theorem 8.1, one computes that aggregate demand for $\hat{\omega}$ is larger than $\sigma(\omega - \eta)$ when $r \to 0$ and approaches 0 when $r \to -\infty$, which gives the result.*

*q. e. d.*

REMARK 8.1

*Let us contrast the above results to the work of Allingham [1991]. The technique Allingham uses to prove his results are very similar to those in this chapter, since he considers the demand functions for the assets, as we do here. The difference is that he considers the demand for every asset separately, which gives rise to J conditions for existence, one for every asset in the market. This condition is similar to the condition of Theorem 8.1, but applied to every asset. More precisely, let there be the assets $A^1, \ldots, A^J \in Y$ with $\eta = \sum_{j \in J} \lambda_j A^j$ for some $\lambda_j \in \mathbb{R}$ and an endowment vector $\omega = \sum_{j \in J} \alpha_j A^j$. Then according to Allingham, a sufficient condition for an agent with this endowment to exhaust his budget is*

$$b(\mu, \sigma)\, \alpha_j < \lambda_j, \quad \textit{for all} \quad j \in J \quad , \tag{8.10}$$

*where $b(\mu, \sigma)$ is a measure of the agents risk aversion, related to $S(\mu, \sigma)$ and $b(\mu, \sigma) > 0$ for all $(\mu, \sigma)$. But when for instance it happens to be the case that $A^1 = \eta$, then $\lambda_j = 0$ for $j = 2, \ldots, J$. Nevertheless, it could very well be that some $\alpha_j < 0$. In such a case Allingham's condition never predicts the existence of an equilibrium, since $b$ cannot be non-positive.*

REMARK 8.2 *When consumption at date 0 is added to the model and when agents are non-satiated in date-0-consumption, then there is clearly no existence problem. In the above model the existence of an equilibrium could fail, because investors did not spend their whole budget at some prices. And this happened because satiation could occur at some allocations of portfolios. When there is a good (date-0-consumption) that is always desirable, then there will be no satiation point. Nevertheless, since an investor's preferences may still be non-monotonic in date-1-consumption, the standard existence theorems do not apply to the CAPM with date-0-consumption. A simple proof that applies to the present case is Bergstrom [1976].*

## 4. Efficient Frontier

The Efficient-Portfolio frontier is the set of those portfolios with the smallest variance at every level of expected return, for a given price $r$ and a wealth $b$ or an endowment $(\bar{\alpha}, \bar{\beta})$. In the setup of Definition 7.5, every portfolio that exhausts the budget is an efficient portfolio. For $x = \alpha\eta + \beta\hat{\omega}$, it is simply those $x$ with $r\alpha - \beta = r\bar{\alpha} - \bar{\beta}$. Expressed as functions of $\mu$ and $\sigma$:

$$\begin{aligned} Var(x) &= \alpha^2 Var(\eta) + \beta^2 \\ &= \alpha^2 Var(\eta) + (r(\alpha - \bar{\alpha}) + \bar{\beta})^2 \\ &= (\bar{\beta} - r\bar{\alpha})^2 + 2r(\bar{\beta} - r\bar{\alpha})\mathbb{E}(x) + \left(Var(\eta) + r^2\right) E(x)^2 . \end{aligned}$$

This is the equation of a parabola. In the space of mean and standard deviation, the curve is a hyperbola.
The slope of the tangent to this curve through a portfolio $\left(\hat{\alpha}, \hat{\beta}\right)$ computes as:

$$\begin{aligned} t\left(r, \hat{\alpha}, \hat{\beta}\right) &= \frac{\partial \mu}{\partial \sigma}\left(r, \hat{\alpha}, \hat{\beta}\right) = \frac{\partial \mu}{\partial Var}\frac{\partial Var}{\partial \sigma}\left(r, \hat{\alpha}, \hat{\beta}\right) \\ &= \frac{\sqrt{\hat{\alpha}^2 Var(\eta) + \hat{\beta}^2}}{r\hat{\beta} + Var(\eta)\hat{\alpha}} \end{aligned}$$

The following holds for $t\left(r, \hat{\alpha}, \hat{\beta}\right)$:

$$\lim_{r \to \pm\infty} t\left(r, \hat{\alpha}, \hat{\beta}\right) = 0, \tag{8.11}$$

$$\lim_{r \to \frac{Var(\eta)\hat{\alpha}}{\hat{\beta}}} t\left(r, \hat{\alpha}, \hat{\beta}\right) = \pm\infty, \tag{8.12}$$

$$t(r, \hat{\alpha}, 0) = \frac{|\hat{\alpha}|}{\hat{\alpha}} \frac{1}{\sigma(\eta)}, \quad \hat{\alpha} \neq 0 \quad . \tag{8.13}$$

Chapter 9

# MARKET DEMAND FUNCTIONS IN THE CAPM

## 1. Introduction

In this book we study the CAPM as a general equilibrium model in which the natural questions of existence and uniqueness of an equilibrium play an important role. Similar to Nielsen [1990b] and Allingham [1991] in the previous chapter we have given general proofs of existence within this framework where consumption sets are not bounded below and satiation is possible. As shown by an example with two equilibria constructed by Nielsen [1988], there is, however, no reason to expect uniqueness in general. We will continue along this line of research and will analyze the structure of market demand in the CAPM. We will show that given any choice of a finite number of normalized price systems and the respective demands satisfying Walras' Law and the Tobin Separation Property, there exist two variance-averse agents whose market demand coincides with the preassigned values. This result parallels the result proved in Chapter 3 which itself was a generalization of results known in the general equilibrium literature as the Sonnenschein-Mantel-Debreu result on the structure of market excess demand functions. The result proved in this chapter for the CAPM considers the market excess demand function on a finite set of prices which is then similar to the result of Andreu [1982].

Our main result will show that the Tobin Separation Property is *the* additional structure gained in the CAPM over and above the Arrow-Debreu general equilibrium model. As a corollary it is obtained that for any number $n$ there exists a CAPM economy which has at least $n$ equilibria. Across these equilibria relative prices of assets and asset allocations differ. Hence there are at least $n$ different beta-pricing formulas. Perturbing endowments in these economies cannot decrease the number of equilibria below $n$.

The Model is as outlined in Chapter 7. In this chapter we assume spanning and also the existence of a riskless asset. These assumptions simplify the exposition and they make our result stronger. Under these restrictive assumptions market demand still has no structure.

Let $\mathbb{1}$ be a riskless asset, in the sense that $\mathbb{1}(m) = 1$ for all $m$ in $M$. As mentioned above, we assume that $\mathbb{1} \in X$. This assumption is essential for our reasoning. It is not clear whether results similar to those of this paper hold without the presence of the riskless asset. It is convenient to decompose every $x \in L^2(\mu)$ as the sum of a riskless asset with the same mean as $x$ and a vector that has mean 0, $x \equiv \bar{x}\mathbb{1} + \tilde{x}$, where $\bar{x} = E(x)$ and $E(\tilde{x}) = \tilde{x} \diamond \mathbb{1} = 0$.

In this chapter we normalize prices such that $\bar{\ell} = 1$. Since $\bar{\ell} = E(x\ell) = \int_S \pi(s)d\rho > 0$ this normalization is always possible.

## 2. Structure of Market Demand

The Tobin-Separation Property, Proposition 7.1, in the case of spanned endowments and with a riskless asset reads:.

PROPOSITION 9.1 (TOBIN SEPARATION PROPERTY)
*For all $\ell \in X$ the demand of a CAPM consumer lies in the span of $\mathbb{1}$ and $\ell$.*

From the Tobin Separation Property the following additional properties of individual demand are obtained in the CAPM. The first property we consider is a special form of the weak axiom of revealed preference (WARP), (cf. Samuelson [1938]). We call this property the CAPM-WARP since it exactly translates the WARP to the $(\mu, \sigma)$-diagram, which is most commonly used in the CAPM.

LEMMA 9.1 (CAPM-WARP)
*A function $x(\ell)$ is a demand function of a CAPM consumer only if for all $\ell_1$ and $\ell_2$, $\ell_1 \neq \ell_2$, the following is true*

$$\bar{x}(\ell_1) \leq \ell_2 \diamond \omega + ||\tilde{\ell}_2|| \; ||\tilde{x}(\ell_1)|| \tag{9.1}$$

*implies*

$$\bar{x}(\ell_2) > \ell_1 \diamond \omega + ||\tilde{\ell}_1|| \; ||\tilde{x}(\ell_2)|| \quad or \quad x(\ell_1) = x(\ell_2) \quad . \tag{9.2}$$

PROOF 9.1 *Suppose* (9.1) *holds. Then consider the consumption bundle* $\bar{x}(\ell_2)\mathbb{1} + ||\tilde{x}(\ell_2)|| \frac{\tilde{\ell}_1}{||\tilde{\ell}_1||}$. (9.1) *implies that this portfolio is affordable with the price system $\ell_1$, hence by uniqueness of the optimal porfolio ($v^i$ is strictly quasi-concave) we have*

$$v\left(\bar{x}\left(\ell_2\right), \|\tilde{x}\left(\ell_2\right)\|\right) = u\left(\bar{x}\left(\ell_2\right) \mathbb{1} + \|\tilde{x}\left(\ell_2\right)\| \frac{\tilde{\ell}_1}{\|\tilde{\ell}_1\|}\right) < u\left(x\left(\ell_1\right)\right) = v\left(\bar{x}\left(\ell_1\right), \|\tilde{x}\left(\ell_1\right)\|\right) \quad . \tag{9.3}$$

*If (9.2) would not hold consider the bundle* $\bar{x}\left(\ell_1\right)+\|\tilde{x}\left(\ell_1\right)\| \frac{\tilde{p}_2}{\|\tilde{p}_2\|}$. *This portfolio is affordable with the price system* $\ell_2$, *hence by uniqueness of the optimal portfolio*

$$v\left(\bar{x}\left(\ell_2\right), \|\tilde{x}\left(\ell_2\right)\|\right) = u\left(x\left(\ell_2\right)\right) > u\left(\bar{x}\left(\ell_1\right) \|\tilde{x}\left(\ell_1\right)\| \frac{\tilde{\ell}_2}{\|\tilde{\ell}_2\|}\right) = v\left(\bar{x}\left(\ell_1\right), \|\tilde{x}\left(\ell_1\right)\|\right) \tag{9.4}$$

*which is a contradiction to the inequality from above.*

*q. e. d.*

The following proposition characterizes the demand of a CAPM consumer.

PROPOSITION 9.2 *For all* $p \in X$ *the demand of a CAPM consumer has the form*

$$x^i(p) = \begin{cases} \left(\ell \diamond \omega^i + \|\tilde{\ell}\|\phi^i\left(\tilde{\ell}\right)\right) \mathbb{1} - \phi^i\left(\tilde{\ell}\right) \frac{\tilde{\ell}}{\|\tilde{\ell}\|} & \text{for } \|\tilde{\ell}\| > 0 \\ \left(\ell \diamond \omega^i\right) \mathbb{1} & \text{for } \|\tilde{\ell}\| = 0 \end{cases} \tag{9.5}$$

*where* $\phi^i\left(\tilde{\ell}\right)$ *is a real valued non-negative function. The function* $\phi^i$ *depends only on* $\left(\ell \diamond \omega^i\right)$ *and* $\|\tilde{\ell}\|$ *and satisfies the following individual revealed preference constraint: For all* $\ell_1, \ell_2 \in X$, $\ell_1 \neq \ell_2$ $\left(\|\tilde{\ell}_2\| - \|\tilde{\ell}_1\|\right) \phi^i\left(\tilde{\ell}_2\right) \leq \left(\tilde{\ell}_1 - \tilde{\ell}_2\right) \diamond \omega^i$ *implies* $\left(\|\tilde{\ell}_1\| - \|\tilde{\ell}_2\|\right) \phi^i\left(\tilde{\ell}_1\right) < \left(\tilde{\ell}_2 - \tilde{\ell}_1\right) \diamond \omega^i$ *or* $\phi^i\left(\tilde{\ell}_1\right) = \phi^i\left(\tilde{\ell}_2\right)$. *Conversely, if on a finite set of prices* $\ell_1, \diamond, \ell_n \in X$, *a function* $\phi^i$ *has these properties and* $\phi^i\left(\tilde{\ell}_j\right) \neq \phi^i\left(\tilde{\ell}_k\right)$ *for* $\tilde{\ell}_j \neq \tilde{\ell}_k$, *then there exists a differentiable utility function satisfying Assumption 7.2 and 7.3 which rationalizes the corresponding demand* $x^i(p)$ *on* $\ell_1, \diamond, \ell_n$.

PROOF 9.2 *The argument in this proof refers to the same individual* $i$. *As before we will drop the superscript* $i$ *for the sake of a simpler notation. From*

*the Tobin Separation Property we know that* $x = \alpha \mathbb{1} - \phi \frac{\tilde{\ell}}{\|\tilde{\ell}\|}$ *for some scalars,* $\alpha, \phi$.
*Next we deduce* $\alpha = p \diamond \omega + \phi \|\tilde{\ell}\|$ *from the budget identity,* $\ell \diamond y = \ell \diamond \omega$.
*To show that* $\phi$ *is non-negative, note that* $E(x) = \ell \diamond \omega + \phi \|\tilde{\ell}\|$ *and* $Var(x) = \phi^2$. *Thus, since larger mean is preferred,* $\left(\ell \diamond \omega + \|\tilde{\ell}\| |\phi(\tilde{\ell})|\right) \mathbb{1} - |\phi(\tilde{\ell})| \frac{\tilde{\ell}}{\|\tilde{\ell}\|}$, *is preferred to* $\left(\ell \diamond \omega + \|\tilde{\ell}\| \left(-|\phi(\tilde{\ell})|\right)\right) \mathbb{1} - \left(-|\phi(\tilde{\ell})|\right) \frac{\tilde{\ell}}{\|\tilde{\ell}\|}$ *unless* $\phi = 0$, *where* $|\phi|$ *denotes the absolute value of* $\phi$. *This implies that* $\phi$ *is non-negative. Since, as we will show in the last part of this proof, the set of the attainable* $(\mu, \sigma)$ *combinations is convex, it follows that strict quasi-concavity implies the uniqueness of the optimal portfolio.*
*We now demonstrate that* $\phi$ *only depends on the two numbers* $p \diamond \omega$ *and* $\|\tilde{\ell}\|$. *For this conclusion, a closer analysis of the budget set is needed. Due to the Tobin separation property the solution to the individual optimization problem is the same as the solution of the problem*

$$\max_{x \in \mathbb{R}\mathbb{1} + \mathbb{R}\tilde{x} = E(x)\ell,\ \ell \diamond x = \ell \diamond \omega} u(x) \quad . \tag{9.6}$$

*Consequently, the budget set is a line in this space; it is given by the parametrization* $\phi \mapsto \left(p \diamond \omega + \left\|\tilde{\ell}\right\| \phi\right) \mathbb{1} - \phi \frac{\tilde{\ell}}{\|\tilde{\ell}\|}$. *We even know that an optimal consumption plan corresponds to some non-negative* $\phi$, *so that in the* $\mathbb{R}\mathbb{1} + \mathbb{R}\ell$ *plane, which admits an orthonormal basis* $\left(\mathbb{1}, -\frac{\tilde{\ell}}{\|\tilde{\ell}\|}\right)$, *the solution to the agent's problem is the same as the solution of*

$$\max_{\phi \geq 0} u\left((\ell \diamond \omega + \|\tilde{\ell}\| \phi) \mathbb{1} - \phi \frac{\tilde{\ell}}{\|\tilde{\ell}\|}\right) \quad . \tag{9.7}$$

*Figure 9.1 shows the plane generated by* $\mathbb{1}$ *and* $\tilde{\ell}$ *for a typical consumer.*
*The budget line in the* $(\mathbb{1}, \tilde{\ell})$ *plane has intercept* $\ell \diamond \omega$ *with the* $\mathbb{1}$*-axis and has slope* $\left\|\tilde{\ell}\right\|$. *It is important to note that, because of Assumption 7.2, the indifference curves of the agent are the same in every* $(\mathbb{1}, \tilde{\ell})$ *plane. Thus the demand function* $\phi$ *only depends on* $\ell \diamond \omega = \bar{\omega} + \tilde{\ell} \diamond \omega$ *and* $\left\|\tilde{\ell}\right\|$.
*Lemma 9.1 has demonstrated that the CAPM-WARP is a necessary condition which CAPM demand has to satisfy. Since in the CAPM (9.5) holds, we get* $\bar{x}(\ell) = \ell \diamond \omega + \phi(\tilde{\ell}) \|\tilde{\ell}\|$ *and* $\|\tilde{x}(\ell)\| = \phi(\tilde{\ell})$. *Hence the revealed preference constraint claimed to hold in Proposition 9.2 has been proved.*
*To see the converse, assume that* $x(\ell)$ *satisfies (9.5) where* $\phi$ *only depends on* $\ell \diamond \omega$ *and* $\|\tilde{\ell}\|$. *To rationalize* $x(\ell)$, *it is then sufficient to consider the agent's choice problem in terms of the two variables mean,* $\mu$, *and variance,* $\sigma^2$. *The budget set in the* $(\mu, \sigma)$ *plane is given by*

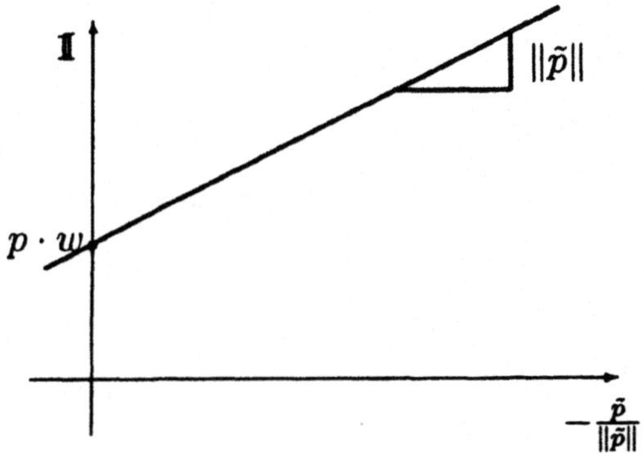


*Figure 9.1.* Tobin-Separation Property

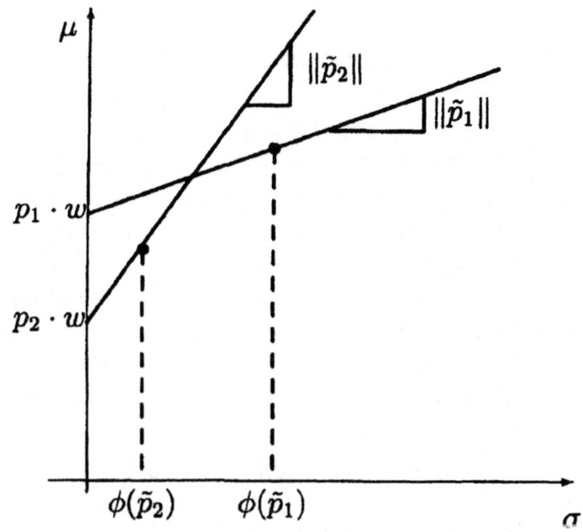


*Figure 9.2.* CAPM-WARP

$$B(\ell, \omega) = \{(\mu, \sigma) \in \mathbb{R} \times \mathbb{R}_+ \,|\, \mu \leq \ell \diamond \omega + \|\tilde{\ell}\|\sigma\} \quad . \tag{9.8}$$

*Note that the CAPM-WARP of Lemma 9.1 is exactly the WARP applied to the $(\mu, \sigma)$ budget sets $B(\ell, \omega)$. See Figure 9.2 for a situation in which the CAPM-WARP is not satisfied.*

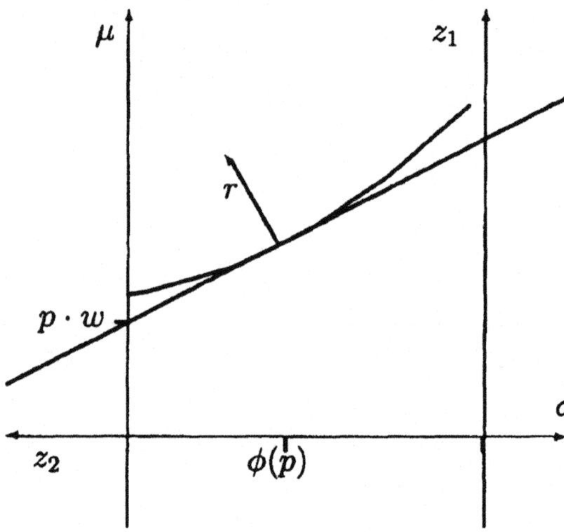


*Figure 9.3.* Transformation of CAPM-Demand

*Thus the second part of Proposition 9.2 follows from an extension of Afriat's theorem*[1] *given in Chiappori and Rochet [1987] and from the fact that once we have derived a mean variance utility function generating $\phi(\ell)$, by rotation of its indifference curves around $\mathbb{1}$, we get a consistent utility function $u$ generating $x(\ell)$. Note that since the $(\mu, \sigma)$ plane is two dimensional the weak axiom of revealed preference is equivalent of the strong axiom of revealed preference (cf. Rose [1958]). Afriat's theorem and its extensions hold in a framework where budget sets are compact and every commodity is desired. To put us in such a setting, a simple transformation of coordinates will do. Let $z_1 = \mu$, $z_2 = K - \sigma \geq 0$ for some sufficiently large $K$. The new price vector is $r = \binom{\|\tilde{\ell}\|}{1}$. Figure 9.3 shows the consumers' decision in the former $(\mu, \sigma)$ and the new $(z_1, z_2)$-diagram.*

*Hence, a continuously differentiable, strictly concave, monotonic utility function, $\hat{v}^i$, exists that rationalizes the demand $(z_1(\ell), z_2(\ell))$. The continuously differentiable and strictly convex mean-variance utility function is given by the function $v^i(\mu, \sigma) = \hat{v}^i(\mu, K - \sigma)$.*

*Therefore, a continuously differentiable and concave utility function $v^i(\mu, \sigma)$ exists so that for every $i = 1, 2$ and $l$,*

$$\left(\left(\ell_l \diamond \omega^i + \|\tilde{\ell}_l\| \phi^i(\tilde{\ell}_l)\right), \phi^i(\tilde{\ell}_l)\right) = arg \max_{(\mu,\sigma) \in B(\ell_l, \omega^i)} v^i(\mu, \sigma) . \qquad (9.9)$$

[1] [Afriat, 1967]

*Now, when considering the original good space*

$$\left(\ell_l \diamond \omega^i + \|\tilde{\ell}_l\| \phi^i(\tilde{\ell}_l)\right) \mathbb{1} - \left(\phi^i(\tilde{\ell}_l)\right) \frac{\tilde{\ell}_l}{\|\tilde{\ell}_l\|} = arg \max_{x \in X, \ell \diamond x \leq \ell \diamond \omega} U^i(x) \tag{9.10}$$

*where* $U^i(x) = v^i(\bar{x}, \|\tilde{x}\|)$.

*q. e. d.*

Market demand $x(\ell) = \sum_{i=1}^{I} x^i(\ell)$ inherits the Tobin Separation Property. Taking the market clearing condition $x(\ell) = \omega$ into account (where $\omega = \sum_{i=1}^{I} \omega^i$) establishes the Mutual Fund Property. This property says that at equilibrium every agent holds a certain fraction of just two funds: the market portfolio $\omega$ and the riskless asset $\mathbb{1}$.

The main result shows that the Tobin Separation Property is the chief additional structure a CAPM demand has in comparison to the classical Arrow-Debreu model.

THEOREM 9.1 (BOTTAZZI ET AL. [1998])

*For any market portfolio $\omega$ in the marketed subspace $X$ with positive mean and variance, and for any finite set of prices $P$ in $X$ with non-zero variance, any function $x(p)$ with $\|\tilde{x}(\ell)\| > 0$ and $\|\tilde{x}(\ell_1)\| \neq \|\tilde{x}(\ell_2)\|$ for all pairs of prices $\ell_1, \ell_2 \in P$ that satisfies Walras Law and the Tobin Separation Property is the aggregate demand on $P$ of two CAPM consumers.*

PROOF 9.3

*We prove that two CAPM consumers are enough to generate such functions $x(\ell)$. Recall from Proposition 7.1 that there are non-negative values $\phi(\tilde{\ell}_1), \diamond, \phi(\tilde{\ell}_n)$, so that for $\ell = \ell_1, \diamond, \ell_n$*

$$x(\ell) = \begin{cases} (\ell \diamond \omega + \|\tilde{\ell}\| \phi(\tilde{\ell}))\mathbb{1} - \phi(\tilde{\ell}) \frac{\tilde{\ell}}{\|\tilde{\ell}\|} & \|\tilde{\ell}\| > 0 \\ (\ell \diamond \omega)\mathbb{1} & \|\tilde{\ell}\| = 0 \end{cases} \tag{9.11}$$

*Furthermore, in the Tobin-Separation Property 7.1 we have shown that it suffices to generate the function $\phi(\ell)$ in the $(\mu, \sigma)$-plane. Thus, we have to find two agents described by endowments $\omega^i \in X, i = 1, 2$ with $\omega^1 + \omega^2 = \omega$ and two mean variance utility functions $v^i, i = 1, 2$ that satisfy Assumption 7.3, such that these utility functions rationalize some decomposition of $\phi(\ell)$ into two functions $\phi_1(\ell), \phi_2(\ell)$. As we already demonstrated in the second part of Proposition 1, in order to get these utility functions it is sufficient that the functions $\phi_1, \phi_2$ satisfy the WARP in the $(\mu, \sigma)$-plane.*

*The budget half-lines in $(\mu, \sigma)$ space $B(\ell, \omega^i) = \{(\mu, \sigma) \in R^2 | \mu = (p \diamond \omega^i + \|\tilde{\ell}\| \sigma), \sigma \geq 0\}$ may or may not intersect. We choose endowments and assign demands to the agents such that their demand is always to one side of all possible intersections.*

*Choose a vector $\hat{\omega} \in X$ such that for any pair of prices the value of $\hat{\omega}$ is different. Since there is a finite number of pairwise different prices such a $\hat{\omega}$ can indeed be found. Let $H_{kl}$ be the hyperplane $\{\omega \in X \mid (\ell_k - \ell_l) \diamond \omega = 0\}$ and consider the union of all such hyperplanes $H = \bigcup_{(k,l)} H_{kl}$. Since there is a finite number of pairs $(k, l)$ $H$ is a strict subset of $X$. Hence there exists $\hat{\omega} \in X \diamond H$ such that for any pair of prices the value of $\hat{\omega}$ is different.*
*We then endow agent one with $\frac{\bar{\omega}}{2}\mathbb{1} + \varepsilon\hat{\omega}$. Agent 2 is accordingly endowed with $\omega - (\frac{\bar{\omega}}{2}\mathbb{1} + \varepsilon\hat{\omega})$. Note by this choice the budget lines do not coincide for different $k$. The importance of this property is that otherwise it could happen that for a pair of prices market demand is different while the first agent's budget sets and hence his demand would have to be the same for both prices.*
*The $\sigma$ coordinate of all non empty intersections $B(\ell_k, \omega_1) \cap B(\ell_j, \omega_1)$ for $j \neq k$ can be made as small as required by letting $\varepsilon$ tend to zero.*
*Let $\phi^2(\tilde{\ell}_k) = 0$ and $\phi^1(\tilde{\ell}_k) = \|\tilde{x}(\ell_k)\|$, $k = 1, \ldots, n$.*
*One chooses $\varepsilon$ such that every $\sigma$ coordinate of the market demand that agent 1 has to pickup is larger than the $\sigma$ coordinates of all non empty intersections. Hence for both agents CAPM-WARP is fulfilled.*
*Figure 9.4 illustrates this decomposition. In this figure the $*$ symbol denotes the market demand that is decomposed into the first and the second agent's demand, denoted by ■ and •, respectively. Market demand, $*$, does not satisfy the weak axiom of revealed preference. The choice of the second agent, •, is to the left of any budget line intersection, and the budget lines of the first agent intersect to the left of his demands. Both agents satisfy the weak axiom of revealed preference.*
*Hence, by Proposition 9.2 for each agent there exists a continuously differentiable, concave utility function, $v^i$, rationalizing his demand behavior.*
*Hence for every $i = 1, 2$ and $l$,*

$$\left(\left(\ell_l \diamond \omega^i + \|\tilde{\ell}_l\| \phi^i(\tilde{\ell}_l)\right), \phi^i(\tilde{\ell}_l)\right) = \arg \max_{(\mu,\sigma) \in B(\ell_l, \omega^i)} v^i(\mu, \sigma) \,. \tag{9.12}$$

*Now when considering the two agents in the original good space*

$$\left(\ell_l \diamond \omega^i + \|\tilde{\ell}_l\| \phi^i(\tilde{\ell}_l)\right) \mathbb{1} - \left(\phi^i(\tilde{\ell}_l)\right) \frac{\tilde{\ell}_l}{\|\tilde{\ell}_l\|} = \arg\max_{x \in X, \ell \diamond x \leq \ell \diamond \omega} U^i(x) \tag{9.13}$$

*where $U^i(x) = v^i(\bar{x}, \|\tilde{x}\|)$.*
*Summing the demand $x^i(\ell)$ of the two agents concludes the proof of the theorem.*

*q. e. d.*

Theorem 9.1 parallels the Sonnenschein-Mantel-Debreu results which show that on a compact set of normalized prices any continuous function which satisfies Walras' Law can be generated as the market excess demand of an Arrow-Debreu exchange economy (cf. Chapter 3).

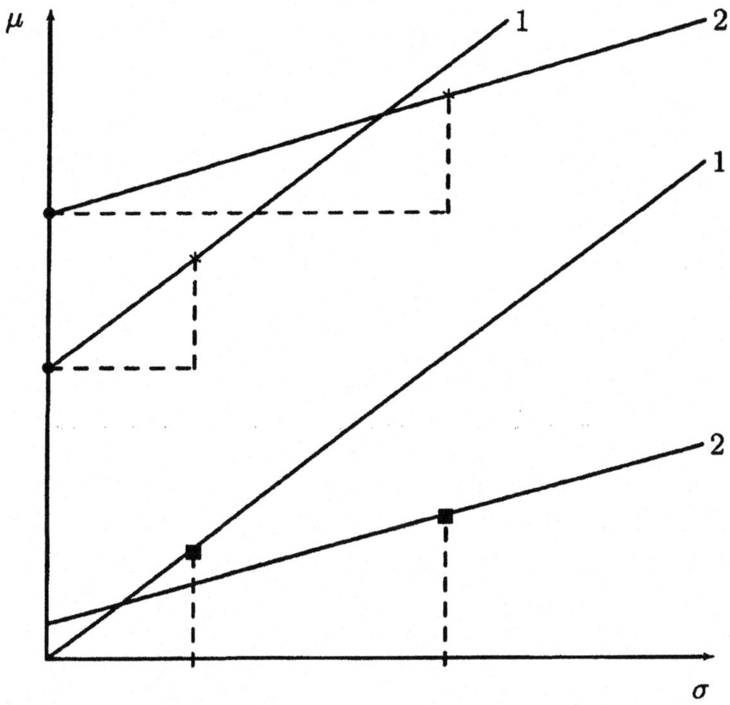


*Figure 9.4.* Decomposition of CAPM-Market Demand

An important aspect, however, in which the CAPM differs from the standard Arrow-Debreu model is that in the CAPM there are no non-negativity constraints on the set of attainable payoffs $X$. Introducing such constraints in the CAPM would rule out the important case of normally distributed returns, and moreover, would conflict with the Tobin separation property. See Löffler [1996] for an example where the Tobin separation property fails in the presence of non-negativity constraints. Without these constraints we are able to obtain a clean characterization of market demand functions, even though aggregate endowments are given at the outset. To understand the significance of this result recall that, due to the non-negativity constraints, which are naturally imposed in the Arrow-Debreu model, market demand functions do have some additional properties (cf. Sonnenschein [1973]). Moreover, with non-negativity constraints market excess demand functions have some additional properties when aggregate endowments are given at the outset (cf. McFadden et al. [1974].
In his Proposition 1 Debreu [1974] has shown that for the Sonnenschein-Mantel-Debreu results to be true one needs at least as many agents as the dimension of

the commodity space. In our result we only need two consumers to generate an infinite dimensional market demand. This is possible because, due to the mean-variance assumption, the "commodity space" we work with becomes effectively two-dimensional.

The most important difference is that our theorem holds on a finite set of prices only. One should think that, along the lines of Mas-Colell [1978] who generalizes Afriat's theorem to a compact set of prices, one should be able to extend our result to a compact set of prices as well. The problem that hinders this generalization does not occur in the rationalization step in which Afriat's theorem is applied, but actually originates in the decomposition step. In this first step the finiteness assumption is essential since not every function $\phi(\ell)$ can be decomposed as a (finite) sum of functions of $p \diamond \omega^i$ and $||\tilde{\ell}||$. Sums of the form $\sum_{i=1}^n \phi^i(\ell \diamond \omega^i, ||\tilde{\ell}||)$ cannot generate arbitrary cross derivatives of all orders.

Finally we would like to comment on Dana [1999]. Dana [1999] applies the Mitjushin-Polterovich criterion to the CAPM. She demonstrates that when for all agents the mean variance utility functions $v^i(\mu, \sigma)$ are additively separable, i.e. $v^i(\mu, \sigma) = g^i(v_1^i(\mu) + v_2^i(\sigma))\ \ \forall(\mu, \sigma) \in \mathbb{R} \times \mathbb{R}_+$ and when $-\frac{(v_1^i(\mu))''\mu}{(v_1^i(\mu))'} \leq 1$ for all $\mu > 0$, then CAPM equilibria are unique. This criterion cannot be given a simple interpretation in terms of risk aversion. It, however, has the disadvantage of implying, that the agents' risk aversion is non-decreasing in income (cf. Lajeri and Nielsen [1994]). Geometrically Dana's criterion essentially limits the curvature of the mean-standard deviation indifference curves. Yet Afriat's theorem and therefore our result relies on being able to bend the $(\mu, \sigma)$ indifference curves as much as we like. Our result stresses the importance of the condition exhibited in Dana [1999] since, as we demonstrate without such restrictions, anything can happen in the CAPM. And it would be interesting to know some criteria of this sort that have empirical support. An attempt in this direction is done in Section 10.

## 3. Number of CAPM-equilibria

In this section we show that for any number $n$ there exist CAPM economies with at least $n$ equilibria. The equilibria will differ in relative asset prices as well as in asset allocations. Hence there are at least $n$ different beta-pricing relations. Furthermore, endowment pertubations can only increase the number of equilibria above $n$.

COROLLARY 9.1 *For any number $n$ there exist CAPM-economies with at least $n$ equilibria. Furthermore, these economies can be chosen such that pertubations of the endowments cannot decrease the number of equilibria below $n$.*

PROOF 9.4 *Let the market portfolio be*

$$\omega = \bar{\omega}\mathbb{1} - \tilde{\omega}\ , \bar{\omega} > 0\ , \|\tilde{\omega}\| > 0\ . \tag{9.14}$$

*In terms of Proposition 7.2, a CAPM-equilibrium is a price system, $\ell$, such that*

$$\left(\ell \circ \omega + \|\tilde{\ell}\| \sum_i \phi^i(\tilde{\ell})\right)\mathbb{1} - \frac{\sum_i \phi^i(\tilde{\ell})}{\|\tilde{\ell}\|}\tilde{\ell} = \bar{\omega}\mathbb{1} - \tilde{\omega}\ . \tag{9.15}$$

*Hence equilibrium prices must be such that $\tilde{\ell}$ is collinear to $\tilde{\omega}$, say $\ell = \mathbb{1} + \beta\tilde{\omega}$ for some $\beta \geq 0$. Theorem 9.1 has shown that on finite domains the function $\phi(\tilde{\ell}) = \sum_i \phi^i(\tilde{\ell})$ does only need to satisfy the non-negativity condition $\phi(\tilde{\ell}) \geq 0$. Thus leaving the decomposition of $\phi(\tilde{\ell})$ to Theorem 9.1, pairs of non-negative scalars $(\beta, \gamma)$ describe a CAPM (price, demand)-situation. And the pair $(\beta, \gamma)$ is a CAPM equilibrium if $\gamma = \|\tilde{\omega}\|$. Indeed, then $\ell \circ \omega = (\mathbb{1} + \beta\tilde{\omega})(\bar{\omega}\mathbb{1} - \tilde{\omega}) = \bar{\omega} - \beta\|\tilde{\omega}\|^2$ and $\|\tilde{\ell}\| = \beta\|\tilde{\omega}\|$. Thus $\sum_i \phi^i(\tilde{\ell}) = \|\tilde{\omega}\|$ solves equation* (9.15).

$$(\bar{\omega} - \beta\|\tilde{\omega}\|^2 + \beta\|\tilde{\omega}\|\|\tilde{\omega}\|)\mathbb{1} - \frac{\|\tilde{\omega}\|\beta}{\beta\|\tilde{\omega}\|}\tilde{\omega} = \bar{\omega}\mathbb{1} - \tilde{\omega}\ . \tag{9.16}$$

*To prove the corollary consider the pairs of non-negative scalars $(\beta_k^+, \gamma_k^+)_{k=1,\ldots,n}$ and $(\beta_k^-, \gamma_k^-)_{k=1,\ldots,n}$ with*

$$\gamma_k^- < \|\tilde{\omega}\| < \gamma_k^+ \quad k = 1, \ldots, n\ . \tag{9.17}$$

*Applying Theorem 9.1 generates a CAPM economy with market demand $\phi(\mathbb{1} + \beta_k^+\tilde{\omega}) = \gamma_k^+$ and $\phi(\mathbb{1} + \beta_k^-\tilde{\omega}) = \gamma_k^-$ , $k = 1, \ldots, n$. Recalling the construction in the proof of Theorem 9.1, we see that the market demand function is given by the sum of the two agent's demand functions $\phi^1$, $\phi^2$ which, by the corollary in Chiappori and Rochet [1987], are continuous functions of income and (relative) prices, i.e. $\phi^1, \phi^2$ are continuous in its two arguments $\ell \circ \omega^i$ and $\|\tilde{\ell}\|$ and*

$$\phi(\mathbb{1} + \beta\tilde{\omega}) = \phi^1(0, \beta\|\tilde{\omega}\|) + \phi^2(\bar{\omega} - \beta\|\tilde{\omega}\|^2, \beta\|\tilde{\omega}\|)\ . \tag{9.18}$$

*Hence $\phi$ is a continuous function in $\beta$ and $\omega$. By the mean value theorem there then exist at least $2n - 1$ values $\beta_n$ such that $\phi(\mathbb{1} + \beta_n\tilde{\omega}) = \|\tilde{\omega}\|$, i.e. the economy has at least $n$ equilibria.*
*Furthermore due to the continuity of $\phi$ in $\omega$ there exists an open set of market portfolios $\hat{\omega}$, containing $\omega$, such that the Afriat inequalities still hold. Hence perturbing the market portfolio does not decrease the number of equilibria below $n$. See figure 9.5 for an illustration of our construction.*

*q. e. d.*

The equilibria which are constructed in Corollary 9.1 differ with respect to the size of the risk premium which is deducted from the expected value of an assets payoff. In the CAPM risk is measured by the covariance of an asset and the market portfolio. Recall that $\omega = \bar{\omega}\mathbb{1} - \tilde{\omega}$ and $\ell_k = \mathbb{1} + \beta_k\tilde{\omega}$.

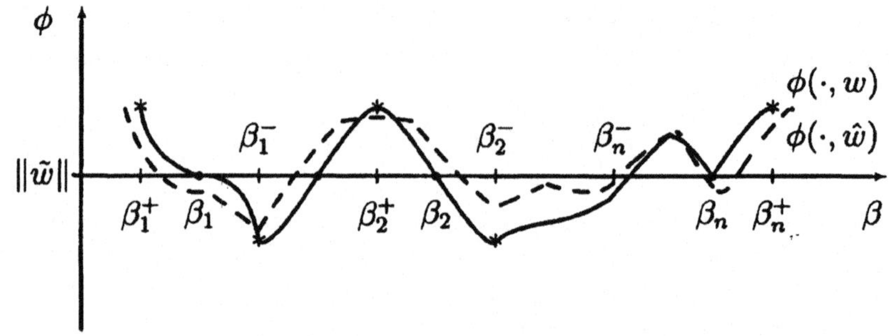


*Figure 9.5.* Construction of CAPM-Demand

Thus the value of an asset $x \in X$ is given by

$$\ell_k \diamond x = (1 + \beta_k \tilde{\omega}) \diamond x = \bar{x} + \beta_k \tilde{\omega} \diamond x \tag{9.19}$$

Note that $\tilde{\omega} \diamond x = cov(\tilde{\omega}, x) = -cov(\omega, x)$ thus

$$\ell_k \diamond x = \bar{x} - \beta_k cov(\omega, x) \tag{9.20}$$

Hence in every CAPM-equilibrium risk is measured in the same way. The risk premium however is indeterminate.
Figure 9.6 illustrates the equilibria constructed in Corollary 9.1 in an Edgeworth-Box diagram. Note that for the second agent's budget lines, higher intercepts correspond to lower slopes so that budget lines actually intersect. It is easily verified that all budget lines

$$B^2(\ell, \omega) := \{(\mu, \sigma) \in \mathbb{R}^2 | \mu = (\ell \diamond \omega + \|\tilde{\ell}\| \sigma \ , \ \ \sigma \geq 0\} \tag{9.21}$$

intersect at the point $(\bar{\omega}, \|\tilde{\omega}\|)$.

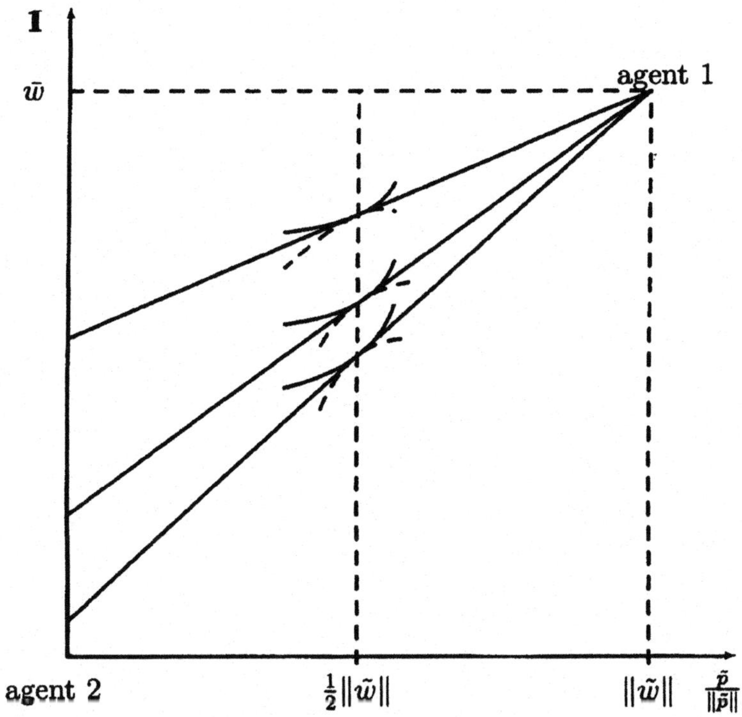


*Figure 9.6.* Multiplicity of Equilibria in the CAPM

# Chapter 10

# UNIQUENESS OF EQUILIBRIA IN THE CAPM

## 1. Introduction

Nowadays the classical two-period Capital Asset Pricing Model is one of the cornerstones of modern finance. Developed by Sharpe [1964], Lintner [1965], and Mossin [1966], it is widely used both by practitioners and theorists, since it gives us a manageable and attractive way of thinking about risk and required return on a risky investment. Given this successful theory one is forced to ask why the question of uniqueness of equilibria was not intensively investigated for a long time. It should be clear that without uniqueness the CAPM looses much of its relevance: if there are many equilibria, on which can investors base their investment decisions? And what is the "correct" risk premium for risky assets? In this chapter we give a condition for uniqueness of CAPM-equilibria which is based on the risk aversion and the endowments of the investors. Our condition is compatible with non-increasing absolute risk aversion.

It was Nielsen [1988] who showed that the static CAPM equilibrium (even in a very simplified example) need not to be unique. There may be several equilibria, all with identical expected total returns, covariances, utility functions, and initial distributions of cash flows. In every CAPM equilibrium, risk is measured in the same way (via the capital market line) but the risk premium is indeterminate. And even worse as it was shown in the previous chapter the situation described by Nielsen is by no means exceptional. For every risky market portfolio there are CAPM economies that have arbitrarily many equilibria. This result shows that one cannot expect a general theorem establishing uniqueness for a broad class of CAPM economies.

Up to now only special cases are known in which the static CAPM possesses a unique equilibrium: for example, if utility functions are quadratic or if investors have expected utility functions with constant absolute risk aversion and returns are jointly normally distributed. Nielsen [1988] considered the question of uniqueness but he did not give a result that relies on economic fundamentals, i.e. endowments or utility functions, alone. So far Dana [1999] seems to be the most general result on uniqueness. We got interested in studying this problem after having read the seminal paper of Dana [1999]. The sufficient condition for uniqueness given in Dana [1999] is based on the assumption of an additively separable mean-variance utility function. Furthermore, Dana [1999] assumes the mean-variance utility function to be concave. It can be shown that concavity of the mean-variance utility together with Dana's assumption implies non-decreasing absolute risk aversion.

Our purpose is to give a uniqueness result that relies on non-increasing absolute risk aversion. For this case we give a joint restriction on utility functions and endowments that implies uniqueness in the CAPM with a riskless asset. It is a common contention that non-increasing absolute risk aversion is a plausible property of utility functions of investors. For example, experiments (see Levy [1994]) as well as empirical studies (see Dalal and Arshanapalli [1993]) have shown that constant relative risk aversion is very plausible. This gives evidence for decreasing absolute risk aversion. In particular, our condition is satisfied if all investors exhibit constant absolute risk aversion.

Our uniqueness result relies heavily on the existence of a riskless asset. This assumption is far from being trivial. Indeed, we will show in Section 3 that even in the case when all investors exhibit constant absolute risk aversion, examples of economies with multiple equilibria can be constructed for the CAPM without a riskless asset. The only condition we know which guarantees uniqueness of equilibria even for the CAPM without a riskless asset has been given in Allingham [1991]. When the CAPM utility functions are derived from expected utility maximization and when asset returns are normally distributed, then agents do not only exhibit constant absolute risk aversion but represented in a mean-variance diagram indifference curves are parallel straight lines.

It should be noted why uniqueness of CAPM-equilibria cannot be derived as a corollary of the uniqueness results known in the standard general equilibrium model (cf. Arrow and Hahn [1971] or Mas-Colell et al. [1995]). After all the CAPM can be seen as a general equilibrium model with two goods: mean and variance. However, in some important aspects the CAPM differs from the standard general equilibrium model. One of the 'goods', the variance, is not desired and for the other good, the mean, there are no non-negativity constraints. In particular, there are no non-negativity constraints on the set of attainable payoffs. Introducing such constraints in the CAPM would rule out the important case of normally distributed returns, and moreover, would conflict with the Tobin separation property, a key property of the CAPM. Moreover, in contrast to the standard differentiable approach to general equilibrium theory

Mas-Colell [1985], indifference curves in the CAPM intersect with the boundary of the consumption set.

The model is the same as outlined in Chapter 7. In this chapter we assume that the endowments are 'spanned': for all $i$, $\omega^i \in \langle A \rangle$. Furthermore, for the market portfolio $\omega = \sum_i \omega^i$, it is assumed that $\mathbb{E}(\omega) = 1$, $Var(\omega) > 0$ and $Var(\omega) > Var(\eta)$. Where, as before, the portfolio $\eta$ is the portfolio which solves the minimization problem

$$\min\{Var(z) | \mathbb{E}(z) = 1, z \in \langle A \rangle\} > 0 \quad .$$

In our uniqueness result we assume that there is a riskless asset while in the last section we prove that there may be multiple equilibria without a riskless asset. As shown in Chapter 7, the equilibria of the CAPM can be described as equilibria of an economy with two artificial commodities, mean $\mu$ and standard deviation $\sigma$:

DEFINITION 10.1 *A CAPM-equilibrium is an equilibrium of the $\mu$–$\sigma$-economy, i.e. an allocation $\alpha^{*,i}, \beta^{*,i} \in \mathbb{R}^2$ for every $i \in I$ and a price $r^* \in \mathbb{R}$, such that:*

*(i) $\alpha^{*,i}, \beta^{*,i}$ maximizes*

$$v^i\left(\alpha, \sqrt{Var(\eta)\,\alpha^2 + \beta^2}\right)$$

$$\textit{subject to} \quad r^*\alpha - \beta \leq r^*\bar{\alpha}^i - \bar{\beta}^i,$$

*(ii)* $\sum_I \alpha^{*,i} = 1, \quad \sum_I \beta^{*,i} = \|\omega - \eta\|^2.$

In this definition, the endowment of agent $i$ is given as $\bar{\omega}^i = \bar{\alpha}^i\,\eta + \bar{\beta}^i(\omega - \eta)$, with $\bar{\alpha}^i = \bar{\phi}^i + \bar{\psi}^i$, $\bar{\beta}^i = \bar{\psi}^i$, where $\bar{\psi}^i = \frac{\mathrm{cov}(\eta,\omega^i) - \mathrm{cov}(\omega,\omega^i)}{Var(\eta) - Var(\omega)}$ and $\bar{\phi}^i = \mathbb{E}(\omega^i) - \bar{\psi}^i$.

Existence of equilibria has been proved in the CAPM with a riskless asset under assumptions weaker than those we stated above e.g. by Nielsen [1990b], Allingham [1991], and Hara [1998]. For the case without a riskless asset under some additional assumptions Hara [1998], Nielsen [1990b], Allingham [1991] and Laitenberger [1999] give existence results.

These remarks conclude the presentation of the model.

## 2. Uniqueness of equilibria in the CAPM with a riskless asset

In this section we assume that there is a riskless asset, i.e. $\mathbb{1} \in \langle A \rangle$. In this case $\eta = \mathbb{1}$ and the price of $\eta$ has to be positive as we have shown in Chapter 7. We can then normalize the price of $\eta$ to 1. Now the decision problem derived in the previous section can be simplified to

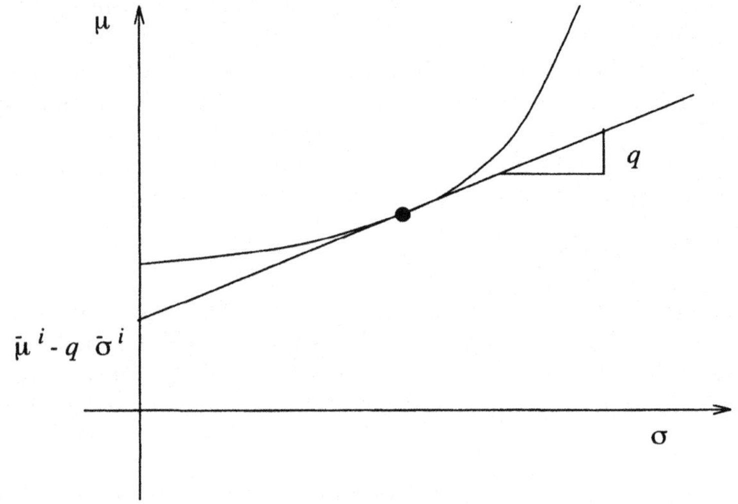


*Figure 10.1.* Mean-variance Optimization

$$\max_{\mu,\sigma\geq 0} \quad \in \quad \mathbb{R} \times \mathbb{R}_+ v^i(\mu,\sigma)\text{s.t.} \quad \mu \quad - \quad q\sigma \quad \leq \quad \bar{\mu}^i \quad - \quad q\bar{\sigma}^i$$

where $\bar{\mu}^i = \mathbb{E}\left(\omega^i\right)$ and $\bar{\sigma}^i = \frac{\mathrm{cov}\left(\omega^i,\omega\right)}{\sigma^2(\omega)}$.
In order for demand to be well defined, without loss of any equilibria, we can restrict $\sigma^i \leq 2\sigma(\omega)$. Since higher mean is preferred, the budget restriction will hold with equality and individual demand for $\sigma^i$ is derived from

$$\max_{2\sigma(\omega)\geq\sigma\geq 0} \quad v^i(\bar{\mu}^i - q\bar{\sigma}^i + q\sigma, \sigma).$$

Market demand is defined as $\sigma = \sum_I \sigma^i$. Since there are only two commodities and since Walras Law holds, an equilibrium is equivalently described by a price $q^*$ for standard deviation such that $\sigma(q^*) = 0$. The discussion of the various conditions for uniqueness will be in terms of the slope of the indifference curves in the $(\mu, \sigma)$-diagram,

$$S^i\left(\mu,\sigma\right) := -\frac{\partial_\sigma\, v^i\left(\mu,\sigma\right)}{\partial_\mu\, v^i\left(\mu,\sigma\right)}.$$

As we have argued in Chapter 7 this slope is a measure of the investor's risk aversion. Moreover, as we will show now, how $S^i(\mu,\sigma)$ changes with $\mu$ is the key determinant for the monotonicity of the agent's optimal choice $\sigma^i$ as a function of $q$.

The next Lemma shows how the slope of an agent's risk aversion $\partial_\mu S^i(\mu^i, \sigma^i)$ determines the slope of his demand for risk $\partial_q \sigma(q)$.

LEMMA 10.1 (CONTINUITY AND MONOTONICITY OF THE INDIVIDUAL DEMAND)

*Let*

$$\sigma^i(q) = \underset{2\,\sigma(\omega)\geq\sigma\geq 0}{\arg\max}\; v^i\left(\bar{\mu}^i - q\,\bar{\sigma}^i + q\,\sigma, \sigma\right) \quad .$$

*Then at $q \geq 0$, $\sigma^i$ is continuous and for $\bar{\sigma} > \sigma^i(q) > 0$, $\sigma^i$ is continuously differentiable. Moreover*

*(a)* $\partial_q\,\sigma^i\,(q) \gtreqless 0$ *iff* $\partial_\mu S^i\,(\mu^i\,(q)\,,\sigma^i\,(q))\,(\sigma^i\,(q) - \bar{\sigma}^i) \gtreqless 1$ *and*

*(b)* $\partial_q\,\sigma^i\,(q) > 0$ *if* $\partial_\mu\,S^i\,(\mu^i\,(q)\,,\sigma^i\,(q))\,(\mu^i\,(q) - \bar{\mu}^i\,(q)) \leq 0.$

PROOF 10.1
*Consider*

$$\max_{2\,\sigma(\omega)\geq\sigma\geq 0} v^i\left(\bar{\mu}^i - q\,\bar{\sigma}^i + q\,\sigma, \sigma\right) \quad .$$

*Since $\sigma$ lies in the compact set $[0, \bar{\sigma}]$ and since $v^i$ is continuous in $\sigma$ and $q$, by the maximum theorem of Berge [1959], see Appendix A, $\sigma^i\,(q)$ is upper-hemi-continuous for all $q \geq 0$. Moreover, since $v^i$ is strictly quasi concave $\sigma^i$ is continuous.*
*The first order condition for an interior optimal solution is*

$$\partial_\mu\,v^i\left(\bar{\mu}^i - q\,\bar{\sigma}^i + q\,\sigma, \sigma\right) q + \partial_\sigma\,v^i\left(\bar{\mu}^i - q\,\bar{\sigma}^i + q\,\sigma, \sigma\right) = 0 \quad . \qquad \text{(FOC)}$$

*Yielding*

$$\frac{d\,\sigma}{d\,q} = \frac{\left[(\partial_\mu\,v^i) + \left(\partial_\mu^2\,v^i\right) q\,(\sigma - \bar{\sigma}^i) + (\partial_\mu\,\partial_\sigma\,v^i)\,(\sigma - \bar{\sigma}^i)\right]}{-\left[\left((\partial_\sigma\,\partial_\mu\,v^i) + \partial_\mu^2\,v^i\,q\right) q + (\partial_\mu\,\partial_\sigma\,v^i)\,q + (\partial_\sigma^2\,v^i)\right]}$$

*Note that by strict quasi-concavity of $v^i$ the denominator in this expression is strictly positive, hence $\sigma^i$ is continuously differentiable at q. Furthermore, since $(\partial_\mu\,v^i) > 0$ it is obtained that*

$$\frac{d\,\sigma}{d\,q} > 0 \quad \textit{iff} \quad 1 + \frac{\left[\left(\partial_\mu^2\,v^i\right) q + (\partial_\mu\,\partial_\sigma\,v^i)\right](\sigma - \bar{\sigma}^i)}{(\partial_\mu\,v^i)} > 0 \quad .$$

*Substitution of $q = -\frac{\partial_\sigma\,v^i}{\partial_\mu\,v^i}$ from the (FOC) and using the identity $\partial_\mu\,S^i = -\frac{[(\partial_\mu\,\partial_\sigma\,v^i)(\partial_\mu\,v^i) - (\partial_\mu^2\,v^i)(\partial_\sigma\,v^i)]}{(\partial_\mu\,v^i)^2}$ proves our claim (a).*

*To see the second claim (b), substitute* $(\sigma - \bar{\sigma}^i) = \frac{(\mu - \bar{\mu}^i)}{q}$ *from the budget equation into claim (a), recognizing that, due to the monotonicity assumptions on* $v^i$, $q > 0$.

*q. e. d.*

From Lemma 10.1 we get the following condition for uniqueness of equilibria in the CAPM:

THEOREM 10.1 ([HENS ET AL., 2002])
*When there is a riskless asset, CAPM equilibria are unique if every agent has on the one hand non-decreasing (on the other hand non-increasing) absolute risk aversion for mean-variance combinations with mean smaller (resp. larger) than the expected value of her endowments and variance smaller (resp. larger) than the covariance of her endowments and the market portfolio.*

PROOF 10.2
*For each* $q \geq 0$, *every agent* $i = 1, \ldots, I$ *with positive demand* $\sigma^i$ *can be in one of the following situations:*

| | $\partial_\mu S^i$ | $\partial_q \sigma^i(q)$ | result follows |
|---|---|---|---|
| (1) $\sigma^i(q) < \bar{\sigma}^i, \mu^i(q) < \bar{\mu}^i$ | 0 | $> 0$ | from (a) |
| (2) $\sigma^i(q) < \bar{\sigma}^i, \mu^i(q) \geq \bar{\mu}^i$ | $\leq 0$ | $> 0$ | from (b) |
| (3) $\sigma^i(q) \geq \bar{\sigma}^i, \mu^i(q) < \bar{\mu}^i$ | $\leq 0$ | $> 0$ | from (a) |
| (4) $\sigma^i(q) \geq \bar{\sigma}^i, \mu^i(q) \geq \bar{\mu}^i$ | $\leq 0$ | $> 0$ | from (a) or from (b) |

*Furthermore, on increasing q, an investor with zero demand for* $\sigma$ *cannot decrease demand. Thus every individual demand function is monotone and for all q such that* $\sigma^i(q) > 0$ *at least one individual demand is strictly monotone and therefore on the set of potential equilibrium prices market demand* $\sum_{i=1}^{I} \sigma^i(q)$ *is strictly monotone. Moreover, market demand is continuous and therefore there is at most one equilibrium. The above mentioned existence results then demonstrate that there is a unique equilibrium.*

*q. e. d.*

Figure 10.2 shows a set of indifference curves satisfying the assumptions of Theorem 10.1. In the area (1), for all $\sigma$ the slope of the indifference curves are non-decreasing as a function of $\mu$. In areas (2), (3) and (4) for all $\sigma$ this slope is non-increasing in $\mu$.
The condition used in Theorem 10.1 is a joint restriction on individual's resources and their preferences. The following Corollary 10.1 demonstrates uniqueness of equilibria as being derived from an assumption on $v^i$ only.

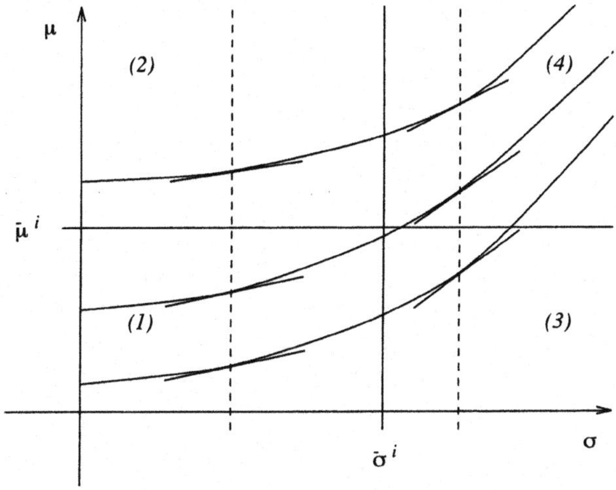


*Figure 10.2.* Non-increasing Absolute Risk Aversion

COROLLARY 10.1
*CAPM equilibria are unique if all agents have constant absolute risk aversion.*

PROOF 10.3
*In the case of constant absolute risk aversion, $\partial_\mu S^i = 0$ for all $i = 1, \ldots, I$. Hence condition (a) of Lemma 1 can be applied to obtain this result.*

*q. e. d.*

Corollary 10.1 establishes uniqueness in the CAPM for the case of constant absolute risk aversion without any distributional assumptions on the payoffs thus generalizing the well known uniqueness result for the case of exponential utility functions and normally distributed returns.
An interesting observation[1], is that constant absolute risk aversion holds if and only if the mean variance utility functions $v^i(\mu, \sigma)$ are quasi-linear, i.e. if they can be represented as $v^i(\mu, \sigma) = \mu - h_i(\sigma^2)$ for some convex function $h_i$. The "if" part of this claim follows directly from this functional form by applying it to the definition of constant absolute risk aversion, i.e. to $\partial_\mu S^i(\mu, \sigma) = 0$. To see the "only if" part note that constant absolute risk aversion implies that the mean-variance-preference ordering of any two points in $L^2$ or equivalently in the mean-variance diagram remains unchanged by addition of any scalar multiple of the riskless asset to both points. Hence for any two points $(\mu_1, \sigma_1)$,$(\mu_2, \sigma_2)$ such that $v^i(\mu_1, \sigma_1) = v^i(\mu_2, \sigma_2)$ we get that $v^i(0, \sigma_1) = v^i(\mu_2 - \mu_1, \sigma_2)$.

[1]This assertion was pointed out to us by one of the referees.

That is to say since the LHS is independent from $\mu$ the RHS must also be independent from $\mu$ thus there must exist some convex function $g_i$ such that $v^i(\mu, \sigma) = \mu - g_i(\sigma)$. Hence defining $h_i(\sigma^2) = g_i(\sigma)$ proves the claim.
This observation relates the uniqueness of CAPM-equilibria in this case nicely to the results on uniqueness found in the general equilibrium literature since quasi-linearity is a well known condition for uniqueness of general equilibria. However, without a riskless asset quasi-linearity does not need to follow from constant absolute risk aversion. And indeed in the next section we will demonstrate by means of an example that without a riskless asset CAPM-equilibria need not be unique even though all agents have constant absolute risk aversion. The following proposition provides a decomposition of the price induced change on demand for variance into the Slutsky-substitution effect, the Slutsky-income effect and the wealth effect.

PROPOSITION 10.1 (HENS [2001B])
*For any investor $i = 1, \ldots, I$, and for all prices $q > 0$ we get:*

$$\partial_q \sigma^i(q) = \frac{\partial_{\mu^i} v^i(\mu^i, \sigma^i)}{-d^i(\mu^i, \sigma^i)} + \frac{\partial_{\mu^i} R^i(\mu^i, \sigma^i) \partial_{\mu^i} v^i(\mu^i, \sigma^i)(\sigma^i - \bar{\sigma}^i)}{d^i(\mu^i, \sigma^i)}$$

*where*
$d^i(\mu^i, \sigma^i) = \partial^2_{\mu^i} v^i(\mu^i, \sigma^i) q^2 + 2\partial_{\mu^i}\partial_{\sigma^i} v^i(\mu^i, \sigma^i) q + \partial^2_{\sigma^i} v^i(\mu^i, \sigma^i) < 0.$
*At a no-trade allocation, i.e. at $\sigma^i = \bar{\sigma}^i$, the derivative of $\sigma^i$ with respect to $q$ is equal to the Slutsky-substitution effect, which then is*

$$\partial_q \sigma^i(q) = \frac{\partial_{\mu^i} v^i(\mu^i, \sigma^i)}{-d^i(\mu^i, \sigma^i)} > 0 \quad .$$

*Moreover, splitting the difference $(\sigma^i - \bar{\sigma}^i)$ into two parts results in the Slutsky-income effect*

$$\frac{\partial_{\mu^i} R^i(\mu^i, \sigma^i) \partial_{\mu^i} v^i(\mu^i, \sigma^i) \sigma^i}{d^i(\mu^i, \sigma^i)}$$

*and the wealth effect*

$$\frac{\partial_{\mu^i} R^i(\mu^i, \sigma^i) \partial_{\mu^i} v^i(\mu^i, \sigma^i) \bar{\sigma}^i}{-d^i(\mu^i, \sigma^i)} \quad .$$

PROOF 10.4

*To solve the maximization problem*

$$\max_{(\mu^i, \sigma^i) \in \mathbb{R} \times R_+} v^i\left(\mu^i, \sigma^i\right) \quad s.t. \quad \mu^i - q\sigma^i \leq \bar{\mu}^i - q\bar{\sigma}^i$$

*note that since $v^i$ is increasing in $\mu$ the budget restriction must hold with equality. Thus supposing positivity of $\sigma^i$ the first order condition is*

$$\partial_{\mu^i} v^i \left(\bar{\mu}^i + q\left(\sigma^i - \bar{\sigma}^i\right), \sigma^i\right) q + \partial_{\sigma^i} v^i \left(\bar{\mu}^i + q\left(\sigma^i - \bar{\sigma}^i\right), \sigma^i\right) = 0 \quad .$$

*By strict quasi-concavity of $v^i(\mu^i, \sigma^i)$ the solution to the first order condition is necessary and sufficient for a solution of the mean-variance maximization problem.*
*Application of the implicit function theorem leads to. For brevity of this expression we have omitted the arguments $\mu^i$ and $\sigma^i$ from the function $v^i$.*

$$\partial_q \sigma^i = \frac{\left[\left(\partial_{\mu^i} v^i\right) + \left(\partial^2_{\mu^i} v^i\right) q \left(\sigma^i - \bar{\sigma}^i\right) + \left(\partial_{\mu^i} \partial_{\sigma^i} v^i\right) \left(\sigma^i - \bar{\sigma}^i\right)\right]}{-\left[\left(\left(\partial_{\sigma^i} \partial_{\mu^i} v^i\right) + \partial^2_{\mu^i} v^i q\right) q + \left(\partial_{\mu^i} \partial_{\sigma^i} v^i\right) q + \left(\partial^2_{\sigma^i} v^i\right)\right]} \quad .$$

*Using the definition of $d^i$, the identity $q = -\frac{\partial_{\sigma^i} v^i}{\partial_{\mu^i} v^i}$ and the formula*

$$\partial_{\mu^i} R^i \left(\mu^i, \sigma^i\right) = -\frac{\left[\left(\partial_{\mu^i} \partial_{\sigma^i} v^i\right)\left(\partial_{\mu^i} v^i\right) - \left(\partial^2_{\mu^i} v^i\right)\left(\partial_{\sigma^i} v^i\right)\right]}{\left(\partial_{\mu^i} v^i\right)^2}$$

*proves our claim. Note that by strict quasi-concavity of $v^i$, $d^i$ is negative.*

*q. e. d.*

The Jacobian of market demand $S(q) := \sum_{i=1}^{n} \sigma^i(q)$ can most conveniently be written as a certain average of the individual investors' derivative terms. To this end, for all $i = 1, \ldots, I$, we define $\rho^i := \frac{\delta^i}{\sum_j \delta^j}$ where $\delta^i := \frac{\partial_{\mu^i} v^i(\mu^i, \sigma^i)}{-d^i(\mu^i, \sigma^i)} > 0$ and $\gamma^i := \frac{\delta^i \sigma^i}{\sum_j \delta^j \sigma^j}$. Using these definitions we get:

$$\partial_q S(q) = \left(\sum_{i=1}^{I} \delta^i\right) \sum_{i=1}^{I} \rho^i \left(1 + \partial_{\mu^i} R^i \left(\mu^i, \sigma^i\right) \bar{\sigma}^i\right) - \left(\sum_{i=1}^{I} \delta^i \sigma^i\right) \sum_{i=1}^{I} \gamma^i \partial_{\mu^i} R^i \left(\mu^i, \sigma^i\right)$$

where the first term is the average of the sum of investors' Slutsky-substitution and wealth effects and the second term is the average Slutsky-income effect. Note that $\rho := \left(\rho^1, \ldots, \rho^I\right)$ and $\gamma := \left(\gamma^1, \ldots, \gamma^I\right)$ are probability measures on the set of agents. Hence, the average Slutsky-income effect is non-negative iff the $\gamma$-average of the investors' absolute risk aversion is non-increasing. Following this decomposition of the derivative of market demand it is again easy to see that CAPM-equilibria are unique if all investors have constant absolute risk aversion. In this case the Slutsky-income effects are zero and market demand is monotone due to the substitution effect. Moreover, consider a CAPM-economy in which one set of investors is only endowed with riskless asset while the other set of investors has risky endowments. Assume that the latter ones are only interested in riskless consumption and hence inelastically supply all risky assets. Such an exchange economy is formally equivalent to the distribution economy mentioned in the introduction. Then for the second set of investors the derivative of their market demand with respect to q is zero while for the first set of investors, $\bar{\sigma}^i = 0$, and hence the derivative of market demand is positive provided that on average their absolute risk aversion is not increasing.

COROLLARY 10.2
*In distribution economies CAPM-equilibria are unique if the $\gamma$-average of investors' absolute risk aversion is non-increasing.*

Uniqueness of CAPM-equilibria can also be derived in economies where all investors have risky endowments provided that in addition to the just mentioned assumption on average the degree of reduction in an investors' absolute risk aversion $\partial_{\mu^i} R^i(\mu^i, \sigma^i)$, is bounded below by minus the reciprocal of the variance of his endowments. That is to say, provided that the first term in the above stated decomposition of the derivative of market demand is positive.

COROLLARY 10.3
*CAPM-equilibria are unique if the $\gamma$-average of investors' absolute risk aversion is non-increasing and if the $\rho$-average of the degree of reduction in their risk aversion is bounded by minus the reciprocal of the variance of their endowments.*

## 3. Multiplicity of equilibria in the CAPM without a riskless asset

The framework in this section is the same as in section 3, except that we assume now $\mathbb{1} \notin Y$.

In the following we will demonstrate that the condition given in Theorem 10.1 is not sufficient to guarantee a unique equilibrium in the CAPM with risky assets only. We give an example, taken from Hens et al. [2002], in which an economy si constructed with two assets and two constantly risk averse investors that exhibits (at least) two equilibria.

To make things easier we assume $Var(\eta) = 1$. Recall that every investor $i$ solves the maximization problem

$$\max\ v^i\left(\alpha, \sqrt{\alpha^2+\beta^2}\right) \qquad \text{s.t.} \quad r\alpha - \beta \leq r\bar{\alpha}^i - \bar{\beta}^i. \tag{10.1}$$

This formulation already reveals the intuition of our example. Although the utility function in $\mu$ and $\sigma$ is quasi-linear, the transformed problem in the $(\alpha, \beta)$

space will not be quasi-linear. Hence, multiple solutions might exist and it remains to show the details. To this end we choose the endowments of the investors as

$$\left(\bar{\alpha^1}, \bar{\beta^1}\right) = (0.1485, 0.0905), \qquad \left(\bar{\alpha^2}, \bar{\beta^2}\right) = (0.8515, 0.9095) \quad . \tag{10.2}$$

Notice that both endowments add to one which will be important later.
The utility functions exhibit constant absolute risk aversion, hence the utility $v^i$ are of the functional form

$$v^i\left(\mu, \sigma\right) = \mu - h_i\left(\sigma^2\right)$$

where $h_i$ is a strictly convex and strictly monotone function. For our example it will be enough to show that the first derivative is positive and monotone at two points since then $h_i$ can easily be extended accordingly on $\mathbb{R}_+$. In particular we assume that

$$\begin{array}{ll} h_1'(0.080) = 0.8 & h_1'(0.083) = 1.8 \\ h_2'(1.280) = 0.2 & h_2'(1.343) = 0.625 \end{array}$$

To derive the equilibria consider the first order conditions of (10.1) for an interior solution with binding budget constraint:

$$\begin{aligned} 1 - 2\alpha h_i'(\alpha^2 + \beta^2) - \lambda_i r &= 0 \\ -2\beta h_i'(\alpha^2 + \beta^2) + \lambda_i 1 &= 0. \end{aligned}$$

The budget constraint must be binding at equilibrium if $\lambda_i > 0$ which is implied by $1 - 2\alpha h_i'(\alpha^2 + \beta^2) > 0$. The first order conditions can therefore be simplified to

$$\frac{1 - 2\alpha h_i'(\alpha^2 + \beta^2)}{2\beta h_i'(\alpha^2 + \beta^2)} = r > 0$$

which will ensure non-satiation at equilibrium. If markets clear and since endowments add to one this condition can be written using the optimal portfolio $(\alpha^*, \beta^*)$ of investor one

$$\frac{1 - 2\alpha^* h_1'(\alpha^{*2} + \beta^{*2})}{2\beta^* h_1'(\alpha^{*2} + \beta^{*2})} = \frac{1 - 2(1-\alpha^*)h_2'((1-\alpha^*)^2 + (1-\beta^*)^2)}{2(1-\beta^*)h_2'((1-\alpha^*)^2 + (1-\beta^*)^2)} = r^* > 0. \tag{10.3}$$

Our example will be complete if we determine the optimal portfolio $(\alpha^*, \beta^*)$ of investor one and show that $(1 - \alpha^*, 1 - \beta^*)$ is optimal for investor two or, which is the same, satisfies (10.3). The following portfolios and prices will do

$$(\alpha^*_{(1)}, \beta^*_{(1)}) = (0.2, 0.2), \qquad (1 - \alpha^*_{(1)}, 1 - \beta^*_{(1)}) = (0.8, 0.8), \qquad r^*_{(1)} = 2.125,$$
$$(\alpha^*_{(2)}, \beta^*_{(2)}) = (0.27, 0.1), \qquad (1 - \alpha^*_{(2)}, 1 - \beta^*_{(2)}) = (0.73, 0.9), \qquad r^*_{(2)} = 0.0778$$

Using our assumption on the first derivative of $h_1$ and $h_2$ it is now straightforward to verify that both equilibria satisfy our condition (10.3). Moreover at these equilibria all budget constraints are indeed satisfied with equality. We therefore have constructed a CAPM with at least two equilibria.
Finally note that if the functions $h_i(\sigma^2)$ were of the functional form $c_i\sigma^2$ for some positive constant $c_i$, then our construction of multiple equilibria does not work because the single parameter $c_i$ is not sufficient to determine two values of $h'_i$. And indeed in this case, as Allingham [1991] has demonstrated, equilibria are unique even when there is no riskless asset.

# Appendix A
# Mathematics

THEOREM A.1 (ORTHOGONAL PROJECTION THEOREM)
*Let $C$ be a nonempty closed subset of $\mathbb{R}^n$. If $x \notin C$ then there exists a vector $y \in C$ which is closest to $x$*

$$\|x - y\| = \min \{ \|z - x\| \| z \in C\} \quad .$$

*If in addition $C$ is convex then the vector $y$ is unique.*

THEOREM A.2 (MINKOWSKI-FARKAS-SEPARATION THEOREM)
*If $K$ and $M$ are convex subsets of $\mathbb{R}^n$ with $K \neq \emptyset$ and $K \cap M = \emptyset$ then there exists $\pi \in \mathbb{R}^n$, $\pi \neq 0$, such that*

$$\sup_{x \in M} \pi \cdot x \leq \inf_{x' \in K} \pi \cdot x' \quad .$$

*If in addition $K$ is compact and $M$ is closed then*

$$\sup_{x \in M} \pi \cdot x < \inf_{x' \in K} \pi \cdot x' \quad .$$

For a proof compare Magill and Quinzii [1996, Theorem 9.1].

THEOREM A.3 (HILBERT SPACE PROJECTION THEOREM)
*Suppose $M$ is a closed vector subspace of a Hilbert space $H$ normed by $\|\cdot\|$, and let $x \in H$. Then there exists a unique $\hat{x} \in M$ such that $x - \hat{x} \in M^{\perp}$. Furthermore, $\hat{x}$ is the unique vector in $M$ satisfying $\|x - \hat{x}\| \leq \|x - m\|$ for all $m$ in $M$.*

CONTINUITY OF CORRESPONDENCES
Let $X, Y$ be open subsets of Euclidean spaces and let $\phi : X \to Y$ be a correspondence from $X$ to $Y$. Consider a $x \in X$, for which $\phi(x) \neq \emptyset$ and consider a sequence $(x^n)_{n \in \mathbb{N}}$ converging to $x$. Then $\phi$ is U.H.C. at $x$ if $y^n \in \phi(x^n)$ implies there exists a subsequence $y^n$ converging to $y$ and $y \in \phi(x)$. $\phi$ is **l.h.c.** at $x$ if for all $y \in \phi(x)$ there exists a sequence $y^n \in \phi(x^n)$, converging to $y$. Intuitively speaking hemi-continuity requires that a correspondence does not suddenly explode or implode.

See Figure A for an illustration.

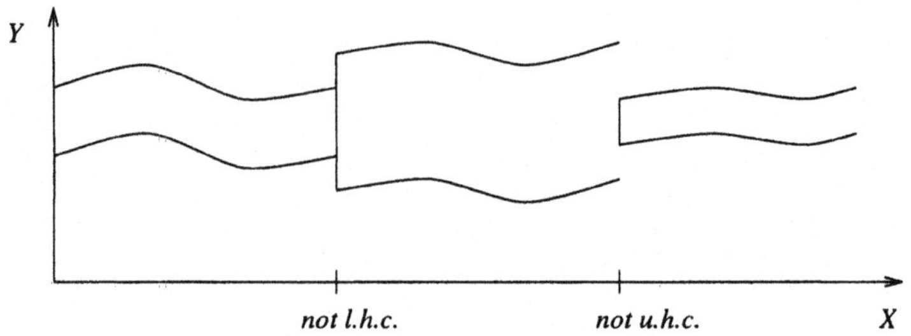


*Figure A.1.* Continuity of Correspondences Inward Pointing Vector Field

A correspondence $\phi : X \rightarrow Y$ where $X, Y$ are open sets of Euclidean spaces is CLOSED if for every sequence $(x^n, y^n)_{n \in \mathbb{N}} \in X \times Y$ which converges to $(x, y)$, $y^n \in \phi(x^n)$ implies $y \in \phi(x)$.

THEOREM A.4 (MAXIMUM THEOREM)
*Let $X, Z$ be open subsets of Euclidean spaces. Let $u(z, x)$ be a real valued continuous function in $Z \times X$, and $\phi(z)$ be a correspondence from $Z$ into $X$ such that $\phi(z) \neq \emptyset$ for all $z \in Z$ and $\phi$ is continuous in $Z$. Then $V(z) = \sup\{u(z, x) \mid x \in \phi(z)\}$ is continuous and $T(z) = \{x \mid u(z, x) = V(z)\}$ is u.h.c. in $Z$.*

VECTOR FIELDS
Let $S_+^{n-1} = \{x \in \mathbb{R}_+^n \mid \|x\| = 1\}$. Let $v : S_+^{n-1} \longrightarrow \mathbb{R}^n$ associate with every $x \in S_+^{n-1}$ a vector $y \in \mathbb{R}^n$. $v$ is called a vector field on $S^{n-1}$. $v$ is a tangent vector field on $S_+^{n-1}$ if $x \cdot v(x) = 0$. $v$ points inward on $S_+^{n-1}$ if $x_j = 0$ implies $v_j(x) > 0$, $j = 1, \ldots, n$.

THEOREM A.5 (INWARD POINTING VECTOR FIELD THEOREM)
*If $v : S_+^{n-1} \longrightarrow \mathbb{R}^n$ is a continuous inward pointing tangent vector field on the non-negative unit sphere $S_+^{n-1}$ then there exists $\bar{\pi} \in S_+^{n-1}$ such that $v(\bar{\pi}) = 0$.*
For an illustration in the case $n = 3$ see Figure A.1.

THEOREM A.6 (POINCARÉ AND HOPF)
*Let $\mathcal{N}$ be a compact n dimensional $C^1$ manifold with boundary and $f$ a continuous vector field on $\mathcal{N}$. Suppose that:*

*(i) $f$ points outward at $\partial \mathcal{N}$,*

*(ii) $f$ has a finite number of zeros.*

*Then the sum of the indices of $f$ at the different zeros equals the Euler characteristic of $\mathcal{N}$.*

THEOREM A.7 (IMPLICIT FUNCTION THEOREM (IFT)) *Let $f : U \times V \rightarrow \mathbb{R}^m$ be a continuously differentiable function on some open sets $U \subseteq \mathbb{R}^m, V \subseteq \mathbb{R}^k$. Suppose $rank\, \partial_x f(x, a) = m$ for some $(x, a)$ with $f(x, a) = 0$ then there exist neighbourhoods $N(x), N(a)$ and a continuously differentiable function $g : N(a) \rightarrow N(x)$ such that $f(g(a), a) = 0$ for all $a \in N(a)$.*

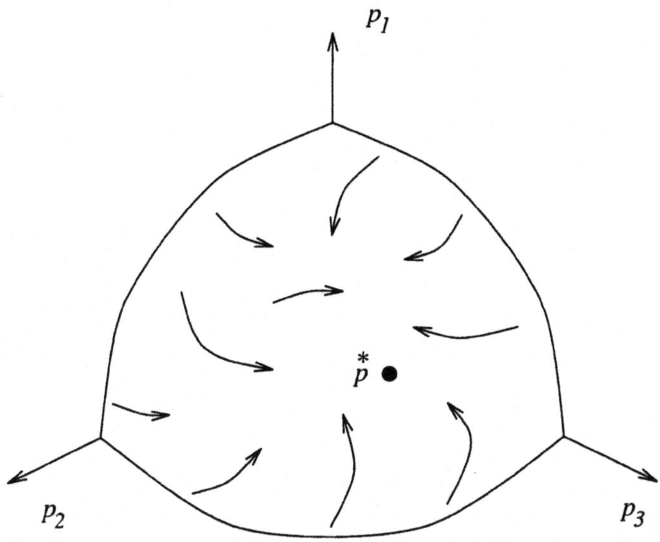


THEOREM A.8 (PARAMETRIC TRANSVERSALITY THEOREM (PTT)) *Consider two open subsets of full dimension $U \subseteq \mathbb{R}^n$, $V \subseteq \mathbb{R}^k$ and let $f : U \times V \to \mathbb{R}^m$ be a continuously differentiable function such that* $(*)$ $f(x,a) = 0$ *implies rank* $\partial_a f(x,a) = m$.
*Then, for all $a \in V$, except for a critical set $C$ of $k$-dimensional measure zero,* $f(x,a) = 0$ *implies* rank $\partial_x f(x,a) = m$. *Moreover, if the equilibrium correspondence $E : V \to U$ defined by $E(a) := \{x \in U |\ f(x,a) = 0\}$ is u.h.c., then $C$ can be taken to be closed.*

# Appendix B
# Assumptions

ASSUMPTION 1.1 (CONTINUITY ASSUMPTIONS)
*The agents' characteristics fulfill the following properties:*

*(i)* $X^i = \mathbb{R}^S_+$ *for all* $i \in I$*;*

*(ii)* $\omega^i \in \mathbb{R}^S_+$ *for all* $i \in I$*;*

*(iii)* $U^i : \mathbb{R}^S_+ \to \mathbb{R}$ *is continuous for all* $i \in I$*;*

*(iv)* $U^i : \mathbb{R}^S_+ \to \mathbb{R}$ *is strictly monotonic for all* $i \in I$*;*

*(v)* $U^i : \mathbb{R}^S_+ \to \mathbb{R}$ *is strictly quasi-concave for all* $i \in I$.

ASSUMPTION 1.2 (DIFFERENTIABILITY ASSUMPTIONS)
*The agents' characteristics fulfill the Continuity Assumptions 1.1 and additionally they satisfy:*

*(i)* $U^i : \mathbb{R}^S_+ \to \mathbb{R}$ *is infinitely often differentiable on* $\mathbb{R}^S_+$ *for all* $i \in I$*;*

*(ii)* $\nabla U^i(x) \in \mathbb{R}^S_{++}$ *for all* $x \in \mathbb{R}^S_+$ *and all* $i \in I$*;*

*(iii) for all* $i \in I$ *it is* $h\, D^2U^i(x)\, h < 0$ *for all* $x \in \mathbb{R}^S_+$ *and all* $h \in \mathbb{R}^S \setminus \{0\}$ *with* $\nabla U^i(x)\, h = 0$*;*

*(iv)* $\left\{x \in \mathbb{R}^S_+ \mid U^i(x) \geq U^i(\bar{x})\right\} \subset \mathbb{R}^S_{++}$ *for all* $\bar{x} \in \mathbb{R}^S_{++}$ *and all* $i \in I$

*(v)* $\omega^i \in \mathbb{R}^S_{++}$

ASSUMPTION 1.3 (DIFFERENTIABLE STRICTLY CONCAVE EXPECTED UTILITY)
$U^i : \mathbb{R}^S_+ \to \mathbb{R}$ *is a differentiable, strictly concave expected utility function if it has the representation* $U^i(x) = \sum_{s=1}^{S} \rho^i_s u^i(x_s)$*, where the beliefs satisfy:* $\rho^i \in \mathbb{R}^S_{++}$ *with* $\sum_{s=1}^{S} \rho^i_s = 1$ *and where the von Neumann Morgenstern utility function* $u^i : \mathbb{R}_+ \to \mathbb{R}$ *satisfies:*

1. $u^i$ *is continuous on* $\mathbb{R}_+$ *and twice continuously differentiable on* $\mathbb{R}_{++}$.
2. *For all* $x \in \mathbb{R}_{++}$ *we have* $u^{i\prime}(x) \in \mathbb{R}_{++}$.
3. *For all* $x \in \mathbb{R}_{++}$ *we have* $u^{i\prime\prime}(x) \in \mathbb{R}_{--}$.

*4. For all sequences* $(x_n)_{n\in\mathbb{N}} \in \mathbb{R}_{++}$ *with* $\lim_{n\to\infty} x_n = 0$ *it holds that* $\lim_{n\to\infty} u^{i'}(x_n) = \infty$.

ASSUMPTION 1.5 (EXISTENCE OF A DESIRABLE PORTFOLIO)
*There is a* $\bar{\theta} \in \mathbb{R}^J$ *such that* $A\bar{\theta} > 0$.

ASSUMPTION 1.6 (NO REDUNDANT ASSETS)
*There are no redundant assets, i.e.* $rank\ A = J$.

ASSUMPTION 2.1 (ENDOWMENTS)
*The collection of individual endwoments* $(\omega^i)_{i\in I}$ *satisfies:* $\omega^i \geq 0$ *for all* $i \in I$ *and* $\sum_{i\in I} \omega^i >> 0$.

ASSUMPTION 2.2 (CHEAPER POINT ASSUMPTION (C.P.A.))

$$\forall i \in I, \forall q \in Q, \mathring{\mathbb{B}}_0\left(q, \omega^i, A\right) = \left\{\theta \in \mathbb{R}^J \middle| q\theta < 0 \quad and \quad \omega^i + A\theta \geq 0\right\} \neq \emptyset$$

ASSUMPTION 2.3 (BOUNDARY BEHAVIOR ASSUMPTION (B.B.A.))

$$\forall q \in \bar{Q} \setminus \{0\}\, \exists i : \mathring{\mathbb{B}}_0\left(q, \omega^i, A\right) \neq \emptyset$$
$$where \quad \mathring{\mathbb{B}}_0\left(q, \omega^i, A\right) = \left\{\theta \in \mathbb{R}^J \middle| q\theta < 0 \quad and \quad \omega^i + A\theta \geq 0\right\}.$$

ASSUMPTION 2.4 (RESSOURCE RELATEDNESS ASSUMPTION (R.R.A.))
$\forall \{I_1, I_2\}, I_1 \cap I_2 = \emptyset, I_1 \cup I_2 = I, \forall \left(x^i\right)_{i\in I} \in \mathbb{R}_+^{SI}$, *such that:*

$$\sum_{i\in I} x^i = \sum_{i\in I} \omega^i \quad and \quad \left(x_s^i - \omega_s^i\right)_{s=1,\ldots,S} \in \langle A\rangle \quad \forall i \in I,$$

$\exists y \in \mathbb{R}^{SI}$ *such that:*

$$\sum_{i\in I} y^i = 0 \quad and \quad y_s^i, s = 1,\ldots,S \in \langle A\rangle, \omega^i + y^i \geq 0 \quad \forall i \in I_1$$

*and*

$$U^i\left(x^i + y^i\right) \geq U^i\left(x^i\right) \quad \forall i \in I_2 \quad ,$$

*the inequality being strict for some* $i \in I_2$.

ASSUMPTION 6.1 (STRONG CHEAPER POINT ASSUMPTION)
*For all* $i \in I$ *and for all* $q \in Q$ *there is some* $\theta \in \mathbb{R}^J$ *with* $q^T\theta \leq 0$ *and* $\omega^i + A\theta \gg 0$.

ASSUMPTION 6.2 (MONOTONICITY IN CAPM)
*Let* $\left(\left(\alpha^i\right)_{i\in I},\left(\omega^i\right)_{i\in I},A\right)\in\mathbb{R}^I_{++}\times\mathbb{R}^{S\times I}_{++}\times\mathbb{R}^{S\times J}$ *be such that:*

*(i) with* $\omega=\sum_{i=1}^I\omega^i$ *for all* $i\in I$ *and for all* $s\in S$: $1-\alpha^i\,\omega_s>0$,

*(ii) at least one security pays off only negatively, that is, there exists a* $j\in J$ *with* $A^j\geq 0$.

ASSUMPTION 6.3
*There exists a fundamental set* $R\subseteq S$ *with*

$$\omega^i_s-A_sA_R^{-1}\omega^i_R\geq 0$$

*for all* $s\in S\backslash R$.

ASSUMPTION 6.4 (SOME ASSET WITH POSITIVE PAYOFF)
$A\in\mathbb{R}^{S\times J}$ *satisfies* $A_{\cdot 1}>0$.

ASSUMPTION 7.1 (SPANNING)
*The endowments are 'spanned': for all i,* $\omega^i\in\langle A\rangle$. *Equivalently, there exist portfolios* $\bar{\theta}^i\in\mathbb{R}^J$ *such that* $\omega^i=\sum_j\bar{\theta}^i_j A^j$. *Furthermore, for the market portfolio* $\omega=\sum_i\omega^i$, *it is assumed that* $E(\omega)=1$ *and* $Var(\omega)>Var(\eta)$, *where* $\eta$ *is defined as the solution to*

$$\min\left\{Var(z)\,|E(z)=1,z\in\langle A\rangle\right\}>0\quad .$$

ASSUMPTION 7.2 (MEAN-VARIANCE PREFERENCES)
*Every agent* $i=1,\ldots,I$ *has a mean-variance preference, i.e. there exist functions* $v^i:\mathbb{R}\times\mathbb{R}_+\rightarrow\mathbb{R},(\mu,\sigma)\mapsto v^i(\mu,\sigma)$ *increasing in* $\mu$ *and decreasing in* $\sigma$ *such that for all* $x\in X$, $U^i(x)=v^i(\mu(x),\sigma(x))$, *where* $\mu(x)=E(x)$ *and* $\sigma(x)=\mathbb{E}(x^2)-\mathbb{E}^2(x)$.

ASSUMPTION 7.3 (STRICT QUASI-CONCAVITY)
*For every agent* $i=1,\ldots,I$ *the utility function* $v^i$ *is continuous and strictly quasi-concave.*

# Appendix C
# Main Results

THEOREM 1.1 (FUNDAMENTAL THEOREM OF ASSET PRICING. [MAGILL AND QUINZII, 1996])
*For a GEI-economy* $\left\{\mathbb{R}^S, \left(U^i, \omega^i\right)_{i \in I}, A\right\}$, *satisfying Assumptions 1.1 and 1.5, the following conditions are equivalent:*

*(i) The consumer's decision problem*

$$\max U^i(x) \quad s.t. \quad x \in \mathbb{B}\left(q, \omega^i, A\right)$$

*has a solution.*

*(ii) There are no arbitrage opportunities, i.e. NAC holds.*

*(iii) There is vector of state prices* $\pi$ *satisfying (Cone).*

*(iv) The consumer's budget set* $\mathbb{B}\left(q, \omega^i, A\right)$ *is compact.*

THEOREM 1.2 (FIRST WELFARE THEOREM)
*Let GEI =* $\left(\mathbb{R}^S, \left(U^i, \omega^i\right)_{i=1}^I, A\right)$ *with* $U^i$ *strictly monotone,* $i = 1, \ldots, I$. *If* $\left(\overset{*}{q}, \overset{*}{x}, \overset{*}{\theta}\right)$ *is a financial market equilibrium then its allocation* $\overset{*}{x}$ *is constrained Pareto-efficient.*

THEOREM 2.1 (EXISTENCE OF EQUILIBRIA. [GOTTARDI AND HENS, 1996])
*Let* $\left((U^i, \omega^i)_{i \in I}, A\right)$ *be a GEI model with*

*(i)* $rank A = J$ *and* $A\theta > 0$ *for some* $\theta \in \mathbb{R}^J$,

*(ii)* $(\omega^i, A)_{i \in I}$ *satisfies the cheaper point and the boundary behavior assumption,*

*(iii)* $(U^i)_{i \in I}$ *are strictly monotone, continuous and strictly quasi-concave,*

*Then there exists a GEI-equilibrium.*

THEOREM 3.2 (GEI-MANTEL. HENS [2001A])
*Let* $A \in \mathbb{R}^{S \times J}$ *be any asset structure with rank* $A = J$ *and* $A\theta > 0$ *for some* $\theta \in \mathbb{R}^J$. *Furthermore, let* $G : Q \to \mathbb{R}^J$ *be* $C^1$ *and* $C^2$ *on* $Q_\epsilon$ *and let G satisfy* $G(\lambda q) = G(q)$ *for all* $q \in Q, \lambda > 0$ *,and* $q \ldots G(q) = 0$ *for all* $q \in Q$. *Then for every* $\epsilon > 0$ *the following is true:*

*Let $\omega^i \in X, i = 1, \ldots, J$ be linearly independent vectors, then there exists a real $k > 0$, and $J$ consumers with continuous strictly quasi-concave, monotone, linearly homogeneous utility functions $U^i : X \to \mathbb{R}$ and initial endowments $k\,\omega^i$, whose asset excess demand functions add up to $G$ on $Q_\epsilon$.*

THEOREM 4.1 (GEI-INDEX THEOREM. [HENS, 1991])
*Let $\left(\mathbb{R}^S, \left(U^i, \omega^i\right)_{i \in I}, A\right)$ be a GEI model with*

(i) $rank\, A = J$ *and* $A\,\theta > 0$ *for some* $\theta \in \mathbb{R}^J$,

(ii) $U^i$ *differentiable, strictly concave* $i = 1, \ldots, I$,

(iii) $\omega^i \gg 0, \quad i = 1, \ldots, I$

*then for all* $\bar{\theta}^1 \in \left\{\theta \in \mathbb{R}^J \middle| e^1 + A\,\theta \gg 0\right\}$, *except for a closed set of measure zero, the set* $E(\bar{\theta}^1) := \left\{q \in Q \middle| G\left(q, \bar{\theta}^1\right) = 0\right\}$ *is finite and* $\sum_{q^* \in E} index\,(q^*) = +1$, *where* $index\,(q^*) := sign\left|-\partial\,\hat{G}\,(q^*)\right|$; $\partial\,\hat{G}\,(q^*)$ *is obtained from* $\partial\,G\,(q^*)$ *by deleting the last row and column.*

THEOREM 6.13 (GROSS SUBSTITUTION. [HENS AND LÖFFLER, 1995])
*For an economy* $GEI = \left\{\mathbb{R}^S, \left(U^i, \omega^i\right)_{i \in I}, A\right\}$ *let the following be true:*

(i) *the utility functions* $U^i$ *satisfy Assumption 1.3,*

(ii) $A \in \mathbb{R}^{S \times S}$ *satisfies Assumption* $rank A = J$: $rank\, A = S$,

(iii) $\omega^i \in \mathbb{R}^S_+$ *for all* $i \in I$.

*Moreover, if one of the following properties holds, the individual demand function and thus also market demand satisfy the property of strict gross substitution:*

a) $RRA^i\,(x) < 1$ *for all* $i \in I$ *and all* $x > 0$,

b) *for all* $i \in I$ *there exists a* $\bar{x}^i \in \mathbb{R}_+$ *such that* $RRA^i\,(x) \leq 1$ *for all* $x \geq \bar{x}^i, x \neq 0$ *and* $\omega^i_s > \bar{x}^i$ *for all* $s \in S$.

THEOREM 6.8 (REPRESENTATIVE AGENT. [DETEMPLE AND GOTTARDI, 1998])
*Let an economy* $\varepsilon = \left\{\left(U^i, \omega^i\right)_{i \in I}, A\right\}$ *satisfy Assumptions 1.2. Furthermore, let the utility functions* $U^i$ *be quasi-homothetic, the functions* $V^i$ *continuous on* $\mathbb{R}^S_+$ *and strictly monotone and strictly quasi-concave on* $\mathbb{R}^S_{++}$, *and for the initial endowments the inequality* $\alpha^i + \omega^i \gg 0$ *holds. Then:*

(i) *A representative agent exists where the utility functions* $U^i$ *are such that* $V^i = V$ *for all* $i \in I$ *and for all* $i \in I$ *there exists a* $\bar{\theta}^i \in \mathbb{R}^J$ *with* $\alpha^i + \omega^i = A\,\theta^i$.

(ii) *A representative agent exists where the utility functions* $U^i$ *are such that* $V^i = V$ *for all* $i \in I$ *and there exists* $\delta \in \mathbb{R}^I_{++}$ *with* $\sum_{i=1}^I \delta^i = 1$, *an* $\alpha \in \mathbb{R}^S$ *and an* $\omega \in \mathbb{R}^S_{++} - \{\alpha\}$ *with* $\alpha^i + \omega^i = \delta^i\,(\alpha + \omega)$.

(iii) *The economy has a representative agent if the* $V^i$ *satisfy Assumption 1.1, there exists a* $\delta \in \mathbb{R}^I_{++}$ *with* $\sum_{i=1}^I \delta^i = 1$, *an* $\alpha \in \mathbb{R}^S$ *and an* $\omega \in \mathbb{R}^S_{++} - \{\alpha\}$ *with* $\alpha^i + \omega^i = \delta^i\,(\alpha + \omega)$ *and for all* $i \in I$ *there exists a* $\bar{\theta}^i$ *with* $\alpha^i + \omega^i = A\,\bar{\theta}^i$.

THEOREM 6.17 (LOWER HEMI-CONTINUITY OF EQUILIBRIUM PRICES. [PILGRIM, 2002])[1]

*For all regular GEI-economies* $\left\{ \left(U^i, \omega^i\right)_{i=1,\dots,I}, \bar{A} \right\}$ *which satisfy Assumption 6.4 there exists some* $\epsilon > 0$ *such that all GEI-economies* $\left\{ \left(U^i, \omega^i\right)_{i=1,\dots,I}, A \right\}$ *with A (restricted)* $\epsilon$*-perturbation of* $\bar{A}$ $\left(C \in \mathcal{V}_\epsilon\left(\bar{C}\right)\right)$ *satisfy*

$$\sharp\, \mathcal{E}_{norm}\left(\bar{A}\right) \leq \sharp\, \mathcal{E}_{norm}\left(A\right) \quad .$$

*If* $\mathcal{E}_{norm}\left(\bar{A}\right) = \left\{\hat{q}^{*1}, \dots, \hat{q}^{*N}\right\}$, *there are continuously differentiable functions*

$$\hat{q}^n_* : \mathcal{V}_\epsilon\left(\bar{C}\right) \to \mathcal{V}_\delta\left(\hat{q}^{*n}\right), n = 1, \dots, N,$$

*for some* $\delta > 0$ *with* $\left\{\hat{q}^1_*\left(C\right), \dots, \hat{q}^N_*\left(C\right)\right\} \subseteq \mathcal{E}_{norm}\left(A\left(C\right)\right)$ *whenever* $C \in \mathcal{V}_\epsilon\left(\bar{C}\right)$.

PROPOSITION 6.9 (LIMITS OF TRANSFERABILITY. [PILGRIM, 2002])

*Let* $\left\{ \left(U^i, \omega^i\right)_{i=1,\dots,I} \right\}$ *be an Arrow-Debreu economy where* $S > I^2$ *and which displays multiple equilibria, then there exists a non-exceptional set of J-dimensional asset matrices,* $2 \leq J \leq S - I + 1$, *which enable a portfolio with strictly positive payoff and for which the GEI-economy* $\left\{ \left(U^i, \omega^i\right)_{i=1,\dots,I}, A \right\}$ *displays a unique equilibrium.*

PROPOSITION 7.4 (POSITIVITY OF STATE PRICES. [SIWIK, 2001])

*Let* $\bar{r} = \sum_{i \in I} r^i$ *where* $r^i = r^i(\mu^i, \sigma^i) := \sigma^i \frac{\partial_\mu v^i(\mu^i, \sigma^i)}{\partial_\sigma v^i(\mu^i, \sigma^i)}$ *and* $(\mu^i, \sigma^i)$ *is the agents' equilibrium choice of mean and variance. Suppose that the market portfolio* $\omega$ *and the quasi-bond* $\eta$ *are not collinear, then in equilibrium state prices are strictly positive if*

$$7.9\left(\bar{r} - \mathbb{E}(\omega)\right) \eta + \mathbb{E}^2(\eta)\, \omega << 0. \tag{C.1}$$

THEOREM 8.1 (EXISTENCE OF CAPM-EQUILIBRIA. [LAITENBERGER, 1999])

*If all investors have a preference relation, such that*

$$S\left(\lambda \eta\right) < \frac{1}{\sigma\left(\eta\right)}, \quad \text{for all} \quad \lambda \geq 0 \quad , \tag{C.2}$$

*then there exists an equilibrium with a positive* $r^*$.

THEOREM 8.2 (EXISTENCE OF CAPM-EQUILIBRIA. [LAITENBERGER, 1999])

*There exists an equilibrium with* $r^* > 0$, *when*

1. $S^i\left(\bar{\alpha}^i \eta\right) < \frac{1}{\sigma(\eta)}$ *for all agents with* $\bar{\beta}^i \geq 0$, *and*
2. $S^i\left(\frac{b^i\left(r^{min}\right)}{r^{min}} \eta\right) < \frac{1}{\sigma(\eta)}$ *for those agents with* $\bar{\beta}^i < 0$, *where*

---

[1] By application of Lemma 6.6 this theorem can be transferred for more general matrices satisfying Assumption 1.5.

[2] This is a quite restrictive assumption, but it becomes weaker if one interprets $i = 1, \dots, I$ not as single consumers, but types of consumers.

$$r^{min} = \min_{I} \left\{ t^{-1} \left( ., \bar{\alpha}^i, \bar{\beta}^i \right) \left( S \left( \bar{\alpha}^i, \bar{\beta}^i \right) \right) \right\} \tag{C.3}$$

*is the price, at which all investors demand more $\hat{\sigma}$ than their initial endowment of $\hat{\sigma}$.*

THEOREM 9.1 (BOTTAZZI ET AL. [1998])
*For any market portfolio $\omega$ in the marketed subspace $X$ with positive mean and variance, and for any finite set of prices $P$ in $X$ with non-zero variance, any function $x(p)$ with $\|\tilde{x}(\ell)\| > 0$ and $\|\tilde{x}(\ell_1)\| \neq \|\tilde{x}(\ell_2)\|$ for all pairs of prices $\ell_1, \ell_2 \in P$ that satisfies Walras Law and the Tobin Separation Property is the aggregate demand on $P$ of two CAPM consumers.*

THEOREM 10.1 (HENS ET AL. [2002])
*When there is a riskless asset, CAPM equilibria are unique if every agent has on the one hand non-decreasing (on the other hand non-increasing) absolute risk aversion for mean-variance combinations with mean smaller (resp. larger) than the expected value of her endowments and variance smaller (resp. larger) than the covariance of her endowments and the market portfolio.*

# GLOSSARY

$x \geq y$ for $x, y \in \mathbb{R}^n$ means $x_i \geq y_i$, $i = 1, \ldots, n$

$x > y$ for $x, y \in \mathbb{R}^n$ means $x \geq y$ and $x \neq y$

$x >> y$ for $x, y \in \mathbb{R}^n$ means $x_i > y_i$, $i = 1, \ldots, n$

$\mathbb{R}^n_+$ means $\{x \in \mathbb{R}^n |\ x \geq 0\}$

$\mathbb{R}^n_{++}$ means $\{x \in \mathbb{R}^n |\ x >> 0\}$

$\mathbb{1} \in \mathbb{R}^n$ means $(1, \ldots, 1)^T \in \mathbb{R}^n$

$e_i \in \mathbb{R}^n$ means $i$-th unit vector in $\mathbb{R}^n$

$x^\perp$ for $x \in \mathbb{R}^n$ means $\{y \in \mathbb{R}^n |\ y \cdot x = 0\}$

$M^\perp$ for a set $M \subset \mathbb{R}^n$ means $\{y \in \mathbb{R}^n |\ y \cdot m = 0 \quad \text{for all} \quad n \in M\}$

$\langle A \rangle$ for $A \in \mathbb{R}^{n \times m}$ means $\{y \in \mathbb{R}^n |\ y = Ax \quad \text{for some} \quad x \in \mathbb{R}^m\}$

$I_J$ means identity matrix in $\mathbb{R}^{J \times J}$

$I_m^{\setminus n}$ means the identity matrix in $\mathbb{R}^{m \times m}$ without its $n$-th column

$\hat{x}$ for a vector in $\mathbb{R}^n$ means the vector $(x_1, \ldots, x_{n-1})$

$\hat{A}$ for a matrix in $\mathbb{R}^{n \times n}$ means the $(n-1) \times (n-1)$ upper left submatrix of $A$

$\Lambda(x)$ for a vector in $\mathbb{R}^n$ is the diagonal matrix with the vector $x$ on its main diagonal

$|A|$ means determinant of the matrix $A \in \mathbb{R}^{n \times n}$

$|x|$ for $x \in \mathbb{R}$ means absolute value of $x$

$|x|$ for $x \in \mathbb{R}^n$ means the vector with components $(|x_1|, \ldots, |x_n|)^T \in \mathbb{R}^n$

$\operatorname{tr} A$ means the trace of the matrix $A \in \mathbb{R}^{n \times m}$

$\|x\|$ for $x$ in $X$, being endowed with scalar product $\cdot$, means $\sqrt{x \cdot x}$

$X \times Y$ for two sets means the Cartesian product

$X \setminus Y$ for two sets means $\{x \in X |\ x \notin Y\}$

$\operatorname{int} X$, $\mathring{X}$ means the interior of the set $X$

$\operatorname{cl} X$, $\bar{X}$ means the closure of the set $X$

$\partial X$ means boundary of the set $X$, i.e. $\operatorname{cl} X \setminus \operatorname{int} X$

$C^r$ means the set of $r$-times continuously differentiable functions

$\partial f(x)$ for $f \in C^1$ means the derivative of $f$ (Jacobian matrix)

$\nabla f(x)$ for $f \in C^1$ means $\partial f(x)$

$D f(x)$ for $f \in C^1$ means $\partial f(x)$

$\partial_x f(x, y)$ for $f \in C^1$ means the derivative of $f$ with respect to $x$

$f'(x)$ for $f \in C^1$ means $\partial f(x)$ in the case that $x$ is a real number

$D^2 f(x)$ for $f \in C^2$ means matrix of second derivatives of $f$ (Hessian matrix)

$f''(x)$ for $f \in C^2$ means $D^2 f(x)$ in the case that $x$ is a real number

$(S, \mathcal{S}, \rho)$ $(S, \mathcal{S}, \rho)$probability space

$L^2(\rho)$ $\{x \,|E(x^2) < \infty\}$

$E(x)$ $:= \int_S x(s)\, d\rho$

$x \diamond y$ $= E(xy) = \int_S x(s)\, y(s)\, d\rho$

$\|x\|$ $\sqrt{E(x^2)}$

$\operatorname{cov}(x, y)$ $E(xy) - E(x)\, E(y)$

$Var(x)$ $\operatorname{cov}(x, x)$

$\sigma(x)$ $\sqrt{Var(x)}$

$x \,\square\, y$ For two vectors $x, y \in \mathbb{R}^{LS}$ being partitioned as $(x_1, \ldots, x_S)$, $(y_1, \ldots, y_S)$ where $x_s = (x_{s1}, \ldots, x_{sL})$, $y_s = (y_{s1} \ldots, y_{sL})$, $s = 1, \ldots, S$, denotes the vector of scalar products $(x_1 \cdot y_1, \ldots, x_S \cdot y_S) \in \mathbb{R}^S$

**Some common abuse of notation:**

$S = \{1, \ldots, S\}$ a set is denoted by its last element.
Thus is particular $\sum_{s=1}^{S}$ and $\sum_{s \in S}$ are equivalent.
For a function $f : \mathbb{R}^n \times \mathbb{R} \longrightarrow \mathbb{R}^n$, $(p, b) \mapsto h(p, b)$ we denote by $\partial h(p, p \cdot w)$ the derivative w.r.t. second variable $b$, evaluated at $b = p \cdot w$ and by

$\partial_p h(p, p \cdot w)$ the derivative w.r.t. first variable, taking $b = p \cdot w$ as fixed.
For instance, let $f(p) := h(p, p \cdot w)$, then
$\partial_p f(p) = \partial_p h(p, p \cdot w) + \partial_b h(p, p \cdot w)\, w^T$.

# Bibliography

S. Afriat. The construction of a utility function from expenditure data. *International Economic Review*, 8:67–77, 1967.

Charalambos D. Aliprantis, Donald J. Brown, and Jan Werner. Hedging with derivatives in incomplete markets. Mimeo. Cowles Foundation Discussion Paper, 1996.

Michael Allingham. Existence theorems in the CAPM. *Econometrica*, 59: 1169–1174, 1991.

J. Andreu. Rationalization of market demand on finite domains. *Journal of Economic Theory*, 28:201–204, 1982.

Giovanni B. Antonelli. *Sulla Teoria Matematica della Economia Politica*. Nella Tipografia del Folchetto, Pisa, 1886. English translation by John S. Chipman, and Alan P. Kirman, edited and annotated by John S. Chipman, with revisions supplied by William Jaffé, in *Preferences, Utility, and Demand: A Minnesota Symposium*, ed. by John S. Chipman, et al., pp. 333–364. Hartcourt Brace Jovanovich, New York, et al.

Kenneth J. Arrow. Le rôle des valeurs boursières pour la répartition la meilleure des risques. *Econométrie, Colloques Internationaux Du Centre National De La Recherche Scientifique*, 40:41–47, 1953. English Version: The role of securities in the optimal allocation of risk bearing. *Review Of Economic Studies*, 31:91–96, 1963.

Kenneth J. Arrow. *Essays In The Theory Of Risk-Bearing*. North Holland, Amsterdam et al., 1970.

Kenneth J. Arrow and Gerard Debreu. Existence of an equilibrium for a competitive economy. *Econometrica*, 22:265–290, 1954.

Kenneth J. Arrow and Frank Hahn. *General Competitive Analysis*, volume 6 of *Mathematical Economic Texts*. Holden Day, San Francisco, 1971.

Yves Balasko and David Cass. The structure of financial equilibrium with exogenous yields: The case of incomplete markets. *Econometrica*, 57:135–162, 1989.

Ralf Becker. Zur Eindeutigkeit von Marktgleichgewichten. Diploma thesis, 1995. University of Bonn.

Claude Berge. *Espaces Topologiques: Fonctions Multivoques*. Collection Universitaire de Mathématiques. Dunod, Paris, 1959.

T.C. Bergstrom. How to discard 'free disposability' – at no cost. *Journal of Mathematical Economics*, 3:131–134, 1976.

Marc Oliver Bettzüge. *Financial Innovation from a General Equilibrium Perspective*. PhD thesis, University of Bonn, 1997.

Alberto Bisin and Piero Gottardi. When are asymmetric information economies walrasian? a survey. MIT and University of Venice, 1996.

Alberto Bisin and Piero Gottardi. Competitive equilibria with asymmetric information. *Journal of Economic Theory*, 87(1):1–48, 1999.

Fischer Black. Capital market equilibrium with restricted borrowing. *Journal of Business*, 45:444–455, 1972.

Fischer Black and Myron S. Scholes. The valuation of options contracts and a test of market efficiency. *Journal of Finance*, 27(2), May 1972.

Fischer Black and Myron S. Scholes. The pricing of options and corporate liabilities. *Journal Of Political Economy*, 81(3):637–654, 1973.

Karl H. Borch. Equilibrium in a reinsurance market. *Econometrica*, 30:424–444, 1962.

Kim C. Border. *Fixed point theorems with applications to economics and game theory*. Cambridge University Press, Cambridge, 1985.

Jean-Marc Bottazzi and Thorsten Hens. Excess demand functions and incomplete markets. *Journal of Economic Theory*, 68:49–63, 1996.

Jean-Marc Bottazzi, Thorsten Hens, and Andras Löffler. Market demand functions in the CAPM. *Journal of Economic Theory*, 79:192–206, 1998.

Donald J. Brown, Peter DeMarzo, and Curtis Eaves. Computing equilibria when asset markets are incomplete. *Econometrica*, 64(1):1–27, 1996.

John Y. Campbell. Asset pricing at the millenium. *Journal of Finance*, 55: 1515–1567, 2000.

David Cass and Alessandro Citanna. Pareto improving financial innovation in incomplete market. *Economic Theory*, 11:467–494, 1998.

David Cass and Karl Shell. Do sunspots matter? *Journal of Political Economy*, 91:193–227, 1983.

G. Chamberlain. Funds, factors, and diversification in arbitrage pricing models. *Econometrica*, 51(1):1305–23, 1983.

Pierre-André Chiappori and Ivar Ekeland. Individual excess demands. Mimeo. University of Chicago, 2002.

Pierre-André Chiappori and Roger Guesnerie. Sunspot equilibria in sequential markets models. In Werner Hildenbrand and Hugo F. Sonnenschein, editors, *Handbook of Mathematical Economics*, volume IV, chapter 32. North-Holland, Amsterdam, et al., 1991.

Pierre-André Chiappori and J.C. Rochet. Revealed preferences and differentiable demand. *Econometrica*, 55:687–691, 1987.

John S. Chipman. Homothetic preferences and aggregation. *Journal of Economic Theory*, 8:26–38, 1974.

John S. Chipman and J. Moore. On the representation and aggregation of homothetic preferences. Manuscript, 1976. cited from Shafer and Sonnenschein 1982.

Thomas E. Copeland and J. Fred Weston. *Financial Theory and Corporate Policy*. Addison Wesley, third edition, 1998.

Hervé Crès and Isabelle Rossi. Symmetry breakings in malinvaud's model with individual risks. *Journal of Mathematical Economics*, 33:239–269, 2000.

A. Dalal and B. Arshanapalli. Estimating the demand for risky assets via the indirect utility function. *Journal of Risk and Uncertainty*, 6:277–288, 1993.

Rose-Anne Dana. Existence, uniqueness and determinacy of equilibrium in the c.a.p.m. with a riskless asset. *Journal of Mathematical Economics*, 32: 167–175, 1999.

Werner De Bondt. A portrait of the individual investor. *European Economic Review*, 42:831–844, 1999.

Gerard Debreu. Market equilibrium. In *Proceedings of the National Academy of Sciences*, volume 42, pages 876–878, 1956.

Gerard Debreu. *Theory of Value*. Wiley, New York, 1959.

Gerard Debreu. Smooth preferences. *Econometrica*, 40(4):603–615, 1972.

Gerard Debreu. Excess demand functions. *Journal Of Mathematical Economics*, 1:15–21, 1974.

Gerard Debreu. Existence of competitive equilibrium. In Kenneth Arrow and M. Intriligator, editors, *Handbook of Mathematical Economics*, chapter 15. North-Holland, Amsterdam, 1982.

Jérôme B. Detemple and Piero Gottardi. Aggregation, efficiency and mutual fund separation in incomplete markets. *Economic Theory*, 11:443–455, 1998.

Egbert Dierker. Two remarks on the number of equilibria of an economy. *Econometrica*, 40:951–953, 1972.

P. Dubey, John D. Geanakoplos, and M. Shubik. Default and efficiency in a general equilibrium model with incomplete markets. Cowles Foundation, Yale University, 1996.

Darrell Duffie. *Security Markets: Stochastic Model*. Academic Press, San Diego, 1988.

John Eatwell, Murray Milgate, and Peter Newman. *The New Palgrave Finance: A Dictionary Of Economics*. Macmillan Press Limited, London and New York, 1989.

Jürgen Eichberger and Ian R. Harper. *Financial Economics*. Oxford University Press, 1997.

B. Eisenberg. Aggregation of utility functions. *Management Science*, 7:337–350, 1961.

Helmut Elsinger and Martin Summer. Arbitrage and optimal portfolio choice with constraints. Research paper University of Vienna, http://finance2.bwl.univie.ac.at/members/elsinger/papers/constraint.pdf, 2000.

Irving Fisher. *The Rate of Interest*. Macmillan, New York, 1907.

Hans Föllmer and D. Sondermann. Hedging of non-redundant contingent claims. In Werner Hildenbrand and Andreu Mas-Colell, editors, *Contributions to Mathematical Economics in Honour of Gerard Debreu*, pages 205–223. North-Holland, Amsterdam, et al., 1986.

Otto Forster. *Analysis 2: Differentialrechnung im* $\mathbb{R}^n$*, Differentialgleichungen*. Vieweg, Braunschweig, 5th edition, 1991.

G. Franke, R. Stapleton, and M. Subrahmanyam. Idiosyncratic risk, sharing rules and the theory of risk bearing. INSEAD Working Papers 92/34/FIN, INSEAD, 1992.

John D. Geanakoplos. An introduction to general equilibrium with incomplete asset markets. *Journal Of Mathematical Economics*, 19:1–38, 1990.

John D. Geanakoplos and Andreu Mas-Colell. Real indeterminacy with financial assets. *Journal of Economic Theory*, 47:22–38, 1989.

Christian Gollier and J.W. Pratt. Risk vulnerability and the tempering effect of background risk. *Econometrica*, 64:1109–1123, 1996.

W.M. Gorman. Community preference fields. *Econometrica*, 21:63–80, 1953.

Piero Gottardi and Thorsten Hens. The survival assumption and existence of competitive equilibria when asset markets are incomplete. *Journal of Economic Theory*, 71:313–323, 1996.

Jean-Michel Grandmont. Temporary equilibrium theory. *Econometrica*, 45: 535–572, 1977.

Nils H. Hakansson. The fantastic world of finance: Progress and the free lunch. *Journal of Financial and Quantitative Analysis*, 14:717–734, November 1979.

Chiaki Hara. Prices of the market portfolio in the CAPM with incomplete markets. Mimeo. Cambridge University, 1998.

J. Michael Harrison and David M. Kreps. Martingales and arbitrage in multiperiod securities markets. *Journal of Economic Theory*, 20:381–408, 1978.

J. Heaton and D. Lucas. Evaluating the effects of incomplete markets on risk sharing and asset pricing. *Journal of Political Economy*, 104:443–487, 1996.

Thorsten Hens. *Structure of General Equilibrium Models with Incomplete Markets*. PhD thesis, University of Bonn, 1991.

Thorsten Hens. A note on Savage's theorem with a finite number of states. *Journal Of Risk And Uncertainty*, 5:63–71, 1992.

Thorsten Hens. General equilibrium foundations of finance. Habilitation thesis, 1995. University of Bonn.

Thorsten Hens. Incomplete markets. In Alan P. Kirman, editor, *Elements of General Equilibrium Theory, Festschrift in Honour of Gerard Debreu*, chapter 5. Blackwell, Oxford, 1998.

Thorsten Hens. An extension of Mantel (1976) to incomplete markets. *Journal of Mathematical Economics*, 36:141–149, 2001a.

Thorsten Hens. A theoretical analysis of the mean Slutsky-income effect in the CAPM. In Gerard Debreu, Wilhelm Neuefeind, and Walter Trockel, editors, *Economics Essays*, pages 213–212. Springer, Heidelberg, 2001b. A Festschrift in Honor of Werner Hildenbrand.

Thorsten Hens and Andras Löffler. Gross substitution in financial markets. *Economics Letters*, 49:39–43, 1995.

Thorsten Hens, Andras Löffler, and Jean-Marc Bottazzi. Two remarks on the uniqueness of equilibria in the CAPM. *Journal of Mathematical Economics*, 37:123–132, 2002.

Thorsten Hens, Karl Schmedders, and B. Voß. On multiplicity of competitive equilibria when financial markets are incomplete. In P.J.J. Herings, G. van der Laan, and A.J.J. Talman, editors, *The Theory of Markets*, pages 165–191. North-Holland, Amsterdam, et al., 1999.

John R. Hicks. *A Revision of Demand Theory*. Oxford University Press, London, 1956.

Werner Hildenbrand. Equilibrium analysis of large economies. Discussion Paper A 72, SFB 303, University of Bonn, 1986.

Werner Hildenbrand. *Market Demand: Theory and Empirical Evidence*. Princeton University Press, Princeton, 1994.

Werner Hildenbrand and M. Jerison. The demand theory of the weak axiom of revealed preference. *Economic Letters*, 29:209–213, 1989.

Werner Hildenbrand and Alan P. Kirman. *Equilibrium Analysis: Variations on Themes by Edgeworth and Walras*, volume 28 of *Advanced Textbooks in Economics*. North-Holland, Amsterdam, et al, 1988.

David Hirshleifer. Investor psychology and asset pricing. *Journal of Finance*, 56(4):1533–97, 2001.

Chi-Fu Huang and Robert H. Litzenberger. *Foundations for Financial Economics*. Prentice Hall, 1998.

Leon Hurwicz and H. Uzawa. On the integrability of demand functions. In John S. Chipman, L. Hurwicz, M. K. Richter, and Hugo F. Sonnenschein, editors, *Preferences, utility, and demand*, chapter 6, pages 114–148. Harcourt Brace Jovanovich, New York, 1971.

Ravi Jagannathan and Zhenyu Wang. The conditional CAPM and the cross-section of expected returns. *Journal of Finance*, 51(1):3–53, 1996.

Kenneth L. Judd, Felix Kübler, and Karl Schmedders. The impact of portfolio constraints in infinite-horizon incomplete-markts models. In P.J.J. Herings, G. van der Laan, and A.J.J. Talman, editors, *The Theory of Markets*. North-Holland, Amsterdam, 1999.

Timothy J. Kehoe. Multiplicity of equilibria and comparative statics. *The Quaterly Journal of Economics*, 100:119–147, 1985.

Timothy J. Kehoe. Computation and multiplicity of equilibria. In Werner Hildenbrand and Hugo F. Sonnenschein, editors, *Handbook of Mathematical Economics*, volume 4, chapter 38. North-Holland, Amsterdam, et al., 1991.

Timothy J. Kehoe and Andreu Mas-Colell. An observation on gross substitutability and the weak axiom of revealed preference. *Economics Letters*, 15:241–243, 1982.

M. Kimball. Precautionary saving in the small and in the large. *Econometrica*, 58:53–73, 1990.

Alan P. Kirman. The intrinsic limits of modern economic theory: The emperor has no clothes. *The Economic Journal*, 99:126–139, 1989. Conference 1989.

Alan P. Kirman and K. Koch. Market excess demand functions in exchange economies with identical preferences and collinear eondowments. *Review of Economic Studies*, 53:457–463, 1986.

Jörg Laitenberger. *Demand Theory in Models of Financial Markets*. PhD thesis, University of Bonn, Bonn, 1999.

Fatma Lajeri and Lars T. Nielsen. *Risk Aversion and Prudence: The Case of Mean-Variance Preferences*. ?, 1994.

Fatma Lajeri and Lars T. Nielsen. Parametric characterization of risk aversion and prudence. *Economic Theory*, 15:469–476, 2000.

Yvan Lengwiler. Endogenous endowments and equilibrium starvation in a walrasian economy. *Journal of Mathematical Economics*, 30:37–58, 1998.

Stephen LeRoy and Jan Werner. *Principles of Financial Economics*. Cambridge University Press, Cambridge, UK, 2001.

David Levine and William Zame. Risk sharing and market incompleteness. In P.J.J. Herings, G. van der Laan, and A.J.J. Talman, editors, *The Theory of Markets*, pages 217–227. North-Holland, Amsterdam, et al., 1999.

H. Levy. Absolute and relative risk aversion: An experimental study. *Journal of Risk and Uncertainty*, 8:289–307, 1994.

J. Lintner. The valuation of risky assets and the selection of risky investments in stock portfolios and capital budgets. *Review of Economics and Statistics*, 47:13–37, 1965.

Andras Löffler. *Capital Asset Pricing Model mit Konsumtion*. Deutscher Universitätsverlag, Wiesbaden: Gabler, 1996.

Michael Magill and Martine Quinzii. *The Theory Of Incomplete Markets*, volume 1. MIT-Press, London, 1996.

Michael Magill and Wayne Shafer. Incomplete markets. In Werner Hildenbrand and Hugo F. Sonnenschein, editors, *Handbook of Mathematical Economics*, volume 4, chapter 30. North-Holland, Amsterdam, et al., 1991.

Edmond Malinvaud. The allocation of individual risk in large markets. *Journal of Economic Theory*, 4:312–328, 1972.

Edmond Malinvaud. Markets for an exchange economy with individual risks. *Econometrica*, 41:383–410, 1973.

Rolf R. Mantel. On the characterization of excess demand. *Journal of Economic Theory*, 7:348–353, 1974.

Rolf R. Mantel. Homothetic preferences and community excess demand functions. *Journal of Economic Theory*, 12, 1976.

Harry M. Markowitz. Portfolio selection. *Journal of Finance*, 7:77–91, 1952.

Andreu Mas-Colell. On revealed preference analysis. *Review of Economic Studies*, 45(1):121–131, 1978.

Andreu Mas-Colell. *The Theory of General Economic Equilibrium: A Differential Approach*. Econometric Society Monographs. Cambridge University Press, Cambridge, 1985.

Andreu Mas-Colell. On uniqueness of equilibrium once again. In W.A. Barnett et al., editors, *Equilibrium Theory and Its Applications: Proceedings of the Sixth International Symposium in Economic Theory and Econometrics*, chapter 12. Cambridge University Press, Cambridge, 1991.

Andreu Mas-Colell, M.D. Whinston, and J.R. Green. *Microeconomic Theory*. Oxford University Press, Oxford, 1995.

Daniel McFadden, Andreu Mas-Colell, R. Mantel, and K. Richter. A characterization of community excess demand functions. *Journal of Economic Theory*, 9:361–374, 1974.

Lionel W. McKenzie. On the existence of general equilibrium for a competitive market. *Econometrica*, 27:54–71, 1959.

McMullen and Shepherd. *Convex Polytopics and the Upper Bound Conjecture*. Cambridge University Press, Cambridge, 1971.

Frank Milne. Consumer preferences, linear demand functions and aggregation in competitive asset markets. *Review of Economic Studies*, 46:407–417, 1979.

L.G. Mitjushin and W.M. Polterovich. Criteria for monotonicity of demand functions. *Ekonomika i Matematicheskie Metody*, 14:122–128, 1978. cited from Hildenbrand 1994.

Takeshi Momi. Excess demand functions with incomplete markets: A global result. Working Paper No. 96, IEW-Zurich, 2002.

Jan Mossin. Equilibrium in a capital asset market. *Econometrica*, 34:768–783, 1966.

Y. Murata. *Mathematics for Stability and Optimization of Economic Systems*. Acadamic Press, New York, et al., 1977.

A. Nataf. Sur des questionnes d'aggrégation en économétrie. Technical Report 2, L'Institute de Statistique, Université de Paris, 1953. cited from Shafer, and Sonnenschein 1982.

Wilhelm Neuefeind. Notes on the existence of equilibrium proofs and boundary behaviour of supply. *Econometrica*, 48(7):1831–1837, 1980.

Lars T. Nielsen. Uniqueness of equilibrium in the classical capital asset pricing model. *Journal of Financial and Quantitative Analysis*, 23:329–336, 1988.

Lars T. Nielsen. Equilibrium in CAPM without a riskless asset. *Review of Economic Studies*, 57:329–336, 1990a.

Lars T. Nielsen. Existence of equilibrium in CAPM. *Journal of Economic Theory*, 52:223–231, 1990b.

G. Oh. Some results in the CAPM with non-traded endowments. Research paper series, Financial Markets Institute, University of Iowa, 1994.

Beate Pilgrim. *Understanding Financial Markets from a General Equilibrium Perspective: Uniqueness of Competitive Equilibria*. PhD thesis, University of Bielefeld, 2001.

Beate Pilgrim. Non-equivalence of uniqueness of equilibria in complete and in incomplete market models. *Research in Economics*, 2002.

Jan Pilgrim. Eine numerische Analyse evolutionärer Finanzmärkte. Master's thesis, University of Bielefeld, Bielefeld, 1998.

Herakles M. Polemarchakis and Paolo Siconolfi. The existence of a competitive equilibrium when the asset market is incomplete: Short proofs and further results. *Journal of Mathematical Economics*, 1991. to appear.

Herakles M. Polemarchakis and Paolo Siconolfi. Competitive equilibria without free disposal or nonsatiation. *Journal of Mathematical Economics*, 22:85–99, 1993.

R.A. Pollak. Additive utility functions and linear engel curves. *Review of Economic Studies*, 38:401–414, 1971.

J. Pratt. Risk aversion in the small and in the large. *Econometrica*, 32:122–136, 1964.

Edward C. Prescott and Robert M. Townsend. Pareto optima and competitive equilibria with adverse selection and moral hazard. *Econometrica*, 52:21–45, 1984.

John Quah. The law of demand and risk aversion. Working Paper 2002-W3, Nutfield College, Oxford, 2002.

Roy Radner. Existence of equilibrium of plans, prices and price expectations in a sequence of markets. *Econometrica*, 40:289–303, 1972.

Roy Radner. Rational expectations equilibrium: Generic existence and the information revealed by prices. *Econometrica*, 40:655–678, 1979.

H. Rose. Consistency of preference: the two-commodity case. *Review of Economic Studies*, 35:223–231, 1958.

Steve A. Ross. Some stronger measures of risk aversion in the small and in the large with applications. *Econometrica*, 49:621–638, 1981.

Steve A. Ross. Finance. In John Eatwell, Murray Milgate, and Peter Newman, editors, *The New Palgrave Finance: A Dictionary of Economics*. Macmillan, London, and New York, 1989.

Mark Rubinstein. An aggregation theorem for securities markets. *Journal of Financial Economics*, pages 225–244, 1974.

Paul A. Samuelson. A note on the pure theory of consumer behavior. *Economica*, 5:61–71, 1938.

Leon Savage. *The Foundations of Statistics*. Wiley, New York, 1954.

Karl Schmedders. Damped asset trading in the general equilibrium model with incomplete asset markets. IMSSS-Technical Report 96-11, Stanford University, 1996.

Joseph Schumpeter. *History of Economic Analysis*. George Allen and Unwin, London, London, 1954.

Wayne Shafer. Revealed preference and aggregation. *Econometrica*, 45:1173–1182, 1977.

Wayne Shafer and Hugo F. Sonnenschein. Market demand and excess demand functions. In Kenneth J. Arrow and M.D. Intrilligator, editors, *Handbook of Mathematical Economics*, volume II, chapter 14. North-Holland, Amsterdam, et al., 1982.

William Sharpe. Capital asset prices: A theory of market equilibrium under conditions of risk. *Journal of Finance*, 19:425–442, 1964.

J.B. Shoven and J. Whalley. *Applying General Equilibrium*. Cambridge University Press, 1992.

Thomas Siwik. *Two Essays on General Equilibrium Foundations of Finance*. PhD thesis, University of Bielefeld, 2001.

Adam Smith. *An Inquiry Into The Nature And Causes Of The Wealth Of Nations*. W. Strahan and T. Candell, London, 1776.

Hugo F. Sonnenschein. Market excess demand functions. *Econometrica*, 40: 549–563, 1972.

Hugo F. Sonnenschein. Do Walras identitiy and continuity characterize excess demand functions? *Journal of Economic Theory*, 6:345–354, 1973.

Larry Summers. On economics and finance. *Journal of Finance*, 40, 1985.

Akira Takayama. *Mathematical Economics*. Dryden, Hinsdale (Ill.), 1974.

Akira Takayama. *Mathematical Economics*. Cambridge University Press, Cambridge, second edition, 1985.

Linda L. Tesar. International risk sharing and non-traded goods. *Journal of International Economics*, 35:69–89, 1993.

James Tobin. Liquidity preferences as behavior towards risk. *Review of Economic Studies*, 25:65–86, 1958.

Robert M. Townsend. Financial systems in northern thai villages. *Quaterly Journal of Economics*, 110:1011–1046, 1995.

Peter Wakker. *Additive Representations of Preferences: A New Foundation of Decision Analysis*. Kluwer, Dordrecht, 1989.

Léon Walras. *Eléments d'Economie Pure*. Corbaz, Lausanne, 1874. English Translation: *Elements Of Pure Economics*, Homeswood, Il.: Irwin, R.D., 1954.

Paul Weil. Equilibrium asset prices with undiversifiable labor income risk. *Journal of Economic Dynamics and Control*, 16:769–790, 1992.

Jan Werner. Equilibrium in economies with incomplete financial markets. *Journal of Economic Theory*, 36:110–119, 1985.

Herman Wold. *Demand Analysis: A Study in Econometrics*. Wiley, New York, et al., 1953.

Jean-Pierre Zigrand. Arbitrage and endogenous market integration. FMG Discussion Papers dp0319, Financial Markets Group and ESRC, London, 2002.

# Index

Printed by Printforce, the Netherlands